Software Requirements and Design:
The Work of Michael Jackson

Edited by Bashar Nuseibeh and Pamela Zave

GOOD FRIENDS PUBLISHING COMPANY
CHATHAM, NEW JERSEY

ISBN: 978-0-557-44467-0

Cover and book design: Yolanda V. Fundora / www.urban-amish.com
Back cover photograph of Michael Jackson: © Daniel N. Jackson, 2009.

Good Friends Publishing Company. Chatham, NJ.

TABLE OF CONTENTS

Contributors

Anthony Hall
22 Hayward Road, Oxford, UK
anthony@anthonyhall.org

Tony Hoare
Microsoft Research, Cambridge, UK
thoare@microsoft.com

Daniel Jackson
Computer Science and Artificial Intelligence Lab,
Massachusetts Institute of Technology, Cambridge, Massachusetts, USA
dnj@mit.edu

Michael Jackson
The Open University, Milton Keynes, UK
jacksonma@acm.org

Cliff B. Jones
School of Computing Science, Newcastle University, Newcastle-upon-Tyne, UK
cliff.jones@ncl.ac.uk

Eunsuk Kang
Computer Science and Artificial Intelligence Lab,
Massachusetts Institute of Technology, Cambridge, Massachusetts, USA
eskang@mit.edu

Bashar Nuseibeh
Lero—The Irish Software Engineering Research Centre, Limerick, Ireland
The Open University, Milton Keynes, UK
b.nuseibeh@open.ac.uk

Axel van Lamsweerde
Département d'Ingénierie Informatique, Université catholique de Louvain
Louvain-la-Neuve, Belgium
avl@info.ucl.ac.be

Pamela Zave
AT&T Laboratories—Research, Florham Park, New Jersey, USA
pamela@research.att.com

Introduction

Pamela Zave

If you have ever met Michael Jackson or read even a little of his writing, you know you are going to enjoy this book. Half the chapters are an anthology of some of his best articles from the past. The other half of the chapters are new. Michael gives his latest perspective on a few of his favorite topics, and the other contributors write about Michael's influence on their research—and the results of that influence.

This book originated with an event at the 2009 International Conference on Software Engineering in Vancouver, chaired by Steve Fickas. It was a workshop at which Bashar Nuseibeh and I, along with Michael's other colleagues and friends John Cameron, Anthony Hall, Tony Hoare, Daniel Jackson, Cliff Jones, and Axel van Lamsweerde, paid tribute to Michael's career in computing. It was a great day: the meeting room was full in the morning, and packed to overflowing by mid-afternoon.

Although many people have observed that software development should be more of an engineering discipline, few have drawn from the wider engineering literature more deeply or usefully than Michael. Part One consists of two of his essays on this subject, one old and one new. They are fine introductory examples of the clarity, elegance, and wisdom for which his writing is so well known.

After earning a degree in classics from Oxford, where he first met Tony Hoare, and a degree in mathematics from Cambridge, Michael began his career in computing at the John Hoskyns & Co. consultancy. Soon after, Michael and his wife Judy had their first son, Daniel. Meanwhile Michael's thoughts were beginning to coalesce into the program-design method JSP.

From 1970 to 1990 Michael headed his own company, Michael Jackson Systems Ltd., to provide tools, consultancy, and other support for his methods. The company had immediate success: in 1974 the UK government adopted JSP as its standard method for programming design. In 1975 the JSP book *Principles of Program Design* was published.

During these years came the origins of the system-development method JSD.

After John Cameron joined the company in 1977, he assisted with this project. Michael's book *System Development* and John's IEEE tutorial book on JSP and JSD were both published in 1983.

Part Two of this book covers JSP and JSD. It begins with "Getting It Wrong," an amusing story that Michael used to deliver in his program-design courses, then eventually wrote down. Part Two contains two retrospective articles by Michael. Also, Daniel Jackson resurrected an unpublished report on JSP by Tony Hoare, and edited it for this book. Daniel's introduction explains some of the reasons why JSP and JSD are still interesting today, despite changes in technology that have made them appear outdated. As Daniel says, "JSP is unusually rigorous, not only amongst the approaches known as 'methods' at the time of its invention, but even by comparison with programming methods today."

In 1990 Michael left his company and became an independent consultant, also commencing many productive years as a writer and researcher. He had been thinking about requirements, and published the book *Software Requirements & Specifications* in 1995.

In 1990 Michael also took a part-time position at AT&T Laboratories—Research that he occupied for thirteen years. There I joined him in his work on requirements and specifications. Part Three of the book covers the work that is the best-known result of our early collaboration. Chapter 7 is a reprint of the 1995 paper that received the Most Influential Paper award from the International Conference on Software Engineering in 2005. (An earlier paper on this subject had received the Most Influential Paper award from the International Symposium on Requirements Engineering in 2003.) Based on this work, Anthony Hall and others developed the requirements-engineering process REVEAL. Anthony's experiences and personal reflections can be found in Chapter 8.

Research on requirements and specifications naturally entails a great deal of attention to description techniques. Part Four is a tribute to Michael's work in this area. It has reprints of two papers on descriptions in general, and a new contribution by Daniel Jackson and Eunsuk Kang on a notation for characterizing dependence in software architectures.

During his long association with AT&T, Michael and I worked together on software for telecommunication services. Chapter 11 is a reprint of our original paper on the Distributed Feature Composition architecture. Chapter 12 is my new retrospective on DFC, focusing in particular on its highly successful approach to feature modularity.

The original patent on DFC won AT&T's Strategic Patent Award in 2004. So far DFC has been used to build and deploy two large telecommunication systems, and has become part of an important standard.

Michael received the Stevens Award in 1997, the Lovelace Medal of the British Computer Society in 1998, the IEE Achievement Medal in 1998, and the ACM SIGSOFT Outstanding Research Award in 2001. While Axel van Lamsweerde was editor-in-chief of *ACM Transactions on Software Engineering and Methodology*, Michael was an associate editor. In 2000 he joined the University of Newcastle as a visiting professor, working with Cliff Jones. In the same year he also joined The Open University as a visiting professor, working with Bashar Nuseibeh. He is a long-time member of IFIP Working Group 2.3 on Programming Methodology, and a charter member of IFIP Working Group 2.9 on Requirements Engineering.

Michael's most recent major contribution to software engineering is the concept of problem frames, which is covered in Part Five of this book. Michael's book *Problem Frames* came out in 2001. Part Five contains a new summary of the ideas by Michael, and also new papers by his collaborators Cliff and Bashar.

Throughout his life's work Michael has lavished attention on the almost-universally-misunderstood boundary between the "machine" driven by software and the real outside "world" it is supposed to serve. Our cover design is based on the necessary primacy of the world over the machine. So it is fitting that the book closes with Part Six on "The World and the Machine," containing a reprint of Michael's keynote address at the 1995 International Conference on Software Engineering, and a new paper on the subject by Axel van Lamsweerde.

Because computing as a field of research is harnessed to technology that is changing so rapidly, there is a strong tendency to forget the past—even though our past goes back only a few decades. We hope that this book, which mixes old with new and shows how much the two have to say to each other, will serve as a reminder that there was some very good software engineering from the 1960s onward, and that Michael Jackson was and is one of its most important contributors.

PART I
SOFTWARE
ENGINEERING
IN GENERAL

Chapter 1

Software Development as an Engineering Problem

Michael Jackson

Abstract: It is hoped that software development can become a branch of engineering, but there are important differences. Software is intangible, complex, and capable of being transformed by a computer. Much effort has been devoted to overcoming the difficulties due to intangibility and complexity, but too little has been devoted to exploiting the third characteristic. A process-oriented view of software may lead to substantial improvements in this and other respects.

The phrase 'software engineering' was chosen as the title of the NATO conference which took place in Garmisch in October 1968 [1]. The phrase was "... deliberately chosen as being provocative, in implying the need for software manufacture to be based on the types of theoretical foundations and practical disciplines that are traditional in the established branches of engineering," Fourteen years after that conference, it is still hard to resist that implication. We still need a wide range of practical disciplines, and practical disciplines need theoretical foundations. We still look wistfully at the established branches of engineering, hoping to model our own activities after the pattern that has served them so well.

But it is not clear that there is any single pattern. There are many branches of engineering, differing greatly one from another. The automobile engineer, designing a new automobile model, is doing something very different from a civil engineer designing a dam; an electronic engineer has little in common with a chemical engineer, an aeronautical engineer with a mining engineer. We should not necessarily expect that a software engineer will be like all of them, when they are so unlike each other. There is no one discipline of physical engineering; instead, there are many disciplines, each broadly characterised by the products which its practitioners are competent to design. Should software engineering model itself on one of these disciplines? If so, which one? Or should software engineering be more eclectic, taking what it can from each of the established branches of engineering to form a new synthesis? Perhaps the idea of a single discipline of software engineering is itself mistaken. Perhaps we need to recognise distinct branches of software engineering, formalising the specialisations that are already apparent: certainly there are specialists in compiler construction, in operating system design, in various aspects of artificial intelligence, in computer graphics, and in several other fields. It may be that no single discipline of software engineering can apply to all of these fields without being so general that it is useless for practical application: theory can be general, but practice must be specific. Even so, at the present early stage in the development of software engineering we can reasonably direct our attention to those characteristics which are common to all or most software, drawing the appropriate contrasts or analogies with branches of physical engineering, and hoping to increase our understanding of present practice and future possibilities. The most obvious characteristic of software is its intangible, immaterial, nature, distinguishing it sharply from the products of physical engineering. A software product is no more a reel of tape or a floppy disk than a piece of music is the paper on which its score is written. From this intangible nature many consequences flow, some beneficial and some potentially harmful. Another, related, characteristic is that the software product is itself capable of being reproduced, analysed, and transformed by computer; it seems that we have not yet taken full advantage of this capability, especially the capability of transformation. A third characteristic is a high level of complexity: most software is very complex, and a central purpose of software development methods is to master this complexity, to allow us to build software that is complex but highly reliable.

These characteristics, and some of their consequences and implications are discussed in the sections that follow. A concluding section draws together the threads of the discussion, and suggests some possible directions for future development.

1. The intangible product

The engineer whose product is a physical object works under severe constraints. He must take account of the physical limitations of the materials he uses, choosing appropriate material for each purpose from a relatively small set of available materials. A load-bearing wall must be built of a material with a high compressive strength; the chains or cables of a suspension bridge must have high tensile strength: a window must be transparent; an automobile tyre must be resilient. Both the chosen material and the shape into which it is formed must be adequate to the purpose. The engineer must also consider how the materials will behave over the lifetime of the product. Some materials corrode; some cannot withstand high or low temperatures without long-term degradation; the junction between two dissimilar metals may suffer electrolytic action; a building material may be vulnerable to wind erosion.

The software engineer, whose product is intangible, is almost entirely free from such constraints. The ultimate constituents of the product are the statements of the programming language, and these constituents are, in effect, infinitely strong and entirely free from degradation over time. The addition operator works just as well on large numbers as on small numbers; it does not become worn out after a million additions; it works equally well whether the adjacent operator is a multiplication or an assignment This freedom from constraint is at once an advantage and a difficulty. The advantage is that quite a small set of statements can be used to program any computable function; the difficulty is that there are infinitely many ways of constructing any program, and too few criteria for choosing one way. More constraint is needed.

The need for more constraint has been recognised from the early days of computing. M. V. Wilkes, writing about his experiences [2] in machine-language programming on the EDSAC in 1950, gives a nice illustration:

> "... the integration was terminated when the integrand became negligible. This condition was detected in the auxiliary subroutine and the temptation to use a global jump back to the main program was resisted; instead an orderly return was organised via the integration subroutine. At the time I felt somewhat shy about this feature of the program since I felt that I might be accused of undue purism, but now I can look back on it with pride."

Essentially, the recognition was that a program must be constructed of larger constituent parts than the elementary programming language statements, and that these larger parts must themselves be fitted together in an orderly fashion.

An immediate question arises: what should these larger parts be? The implicit answer for Wilkes in 1950 was that the parts should be subroutines; Wilkes is credited with the invention of the subroutine. This answer was widely accepted for many years, and still has much validity. Fortran, Algol 60, COBOL and PL/I all offer a subroutine construct as the primary part type for program structuring; modular programming and some simpler versions of structured programming rely heavily on it also.

Subroutines, or procedures, can be seen as enlarging the repertoire of machine operations. A machine without a hardware multiplier can be equipped with a multiplication subroutine; a machine without matrix arithmetic can be equipped with a set of subroutines providing the necessary matrix operations; a machine without a 'calendar date' data type can be equipped with subroutines to compare, increment and decrement dates. This is a powerful idea, but much less than a complete solution to the difficulty. With subroutines we can build a sequential process, but there is a need for concurrency also. The essence of concurrency is that during execution of a program two of its parts can both be in non-initial states, although neither is a subroutine of the other. A crude form of concurrency in this sense can be obtained by using 'own variables' in procedures: but this is an uncomfortable technique and leads to obscure and difficult programs. A far better solution is provided by coroutines, which allow a program to be constructed from parts which are themselves sequential processes, communicating by passing control from one to another [3].

The availability of the sequential process as a part type frees the software developer from the unwelcome need to view every problem and every program as a hierarchy. Procedures must be organised into hierarchies, but processes are naturally organised as networks: increasingly, as we tackle more ambitious development tasks, we find problems that can not be readily fitted into the hierarchical mould. Communication among sequential processes need not be by direct control flow, as in coroutines. Processes may communicate by shared variables [14], with suitable provision for synchronisation and mutual exclusion; they may communicate by sending and receiving streams of messages [5]; either buffered or unbuffered; they may communicate by shared events which require the participation of two or more processes [6]. All of these forms of communication allow a 'true concurrency': any process may proceed at any time if it is not held up by communication with another process and if a processor is free.

A different line of development leads to the idea of program parts which are instances of abstract data types [7]. The part is a data object, packaged with the operations which can be performed on that object; the definition of an abstract data type hides information about the representation of the object and the implementation of its operations.

We have here been considering procedures, processes, and abstract data types as general constituent parts from which programs may be constructed; their value, from this point of view, is that they offer the possibility of development in terms of a smaller number of larger parts rather than a larger number of the very small parts which are the statements of the programming language. There is an entirely different question which we will consider later: given a set of part types, and a specific problem, which parts of which types are needed to solve the problem, and how should they be connected together?

2. Designing and building

In the established branches of engineering there is a clear distinction between designing a product and building it. The design work is an intellectual activity, using intellectual tools and techniques on intellectual material. The building work is a physical activity, creating physical products from physical material. This distinction between the intellectual and the physical has important consequences.

One consequence is that the activities are naturally separated, and performed by different people. The engineer who designs a bridge does not build it with his own hands; he passes his design to a separate construction organisation. The automobile engineer who designs a car does not work in the factory that produces it. Because of this separation of people and responsibilities, and because of the need to deal correctly with the characteristics of the physical materials used, the design must be fully detailed. The automobile engineer does not leave the factory manager the freedom to decide the shape of the engine's combustion chamber or the size of the wheels; the civil engineer does not allow the builder to choose the quality of steel or the formulation of the concrete. The interface between design and building is, within the limits of human fallibility, exact.

Another consequence is that costs can be allocated between the two, and that the costs of physical construction are almost always much greater than the costs of design. Building a bridge costs much more than designing it. Where a product is made in large numbers, as are automobiles, aeroplanes, computers and washing machines, the cost of the complete production run is what matters here, not the marginal cost of one additional unit. Because the physical production cost is so high, the design cost is a relatively small part of the total cost. It is therefore perfectly reasonable to carry out the whole design work more than once before embarking on production. Many automobile designs reach the stage of completed prototypes and are then abandoned without a single production model being built.

A third consequence is that the engineer's work can be examined both in its intellectual and in its physical manifestations. A colleague can look at the design documents critically, checking the design before it is committed to production. Customers and competitors can, and do, look at the finished physical product, discerning its internal structure and design as well as its behaviour in use. Most physical engineering products make their design public property in his sense, and the engineer could not hide the design even if he wished to. The automobile engineer cannot conceal from his customers and competitors the fact that he has decided to place the engine transversely, or that he has used independent rear suspension, or that the engine has six cylinders.

The situation is very different in software engineering. The internal structure of a software product can be largely concealed, especially if the product is delivered in directly executable machine language form. Many of the designer's choices are therefore largely hidden from the world, and, in particular, from his customers and competitors.

The production costs of software are relatively small. Where a software package is produced and sold to many customers, the marginal cost of producing each copy is entirely insignificant. Within the development process itself, we may consider there to be a distinction between designing and building; but however we draw that distinction we will find that the cost of building does not dominate the cost of designing as it does for the established branches of physical engineering.

Nor is it clear that the distinction between designing and building exists at all for software. Both the design and the product itself are intellectual and intangible, and no convincing separation can be made. There is no point at which the development team puts away the drawing board and begins to use the lathe, or to pour concrete. Some efforts have been made to separate design from programming, sometimes by defining a design language which is distinct from the programming language. For example, the designer might produce a hierarchical diagram showing that the program is to consist of certain procedures connected in a certain way; or a network showing processes and their connections [8]. But such a design is grossly incomplete; it is like a design for a bridge which states only that the bridge is to be a suspension bridge with two piers 50 metres high and a span of 250 metres. The separation that has been made is not a separation of design from programming; it is rather a separation of preliminary design from detailed design. Other design languages have been proposed which are essentially forms of 'pseudocode': the design is itself a program, but a program written in a language for which no compiler is available [9]. If the design is complete, it is appropriate to obtain or create a compiler for the design language, thus automating the building activity. If it is incomplete, then again the separation is merely between preliminary and detailed design. In software, the design is the product.

3. Specifying and implementing

Abandoning the attempt to distinguish design from building, we will use the term 'implementing' to replace both of them. It seems fruitful then to draw a different distinction, between specifying and implementing.

A specification states the criteria by which the product will be judged. For example, an audio amplifier may be specified by stating the required gain, harmonic distortion, noise level, output power, and so on. A bridge may be specified by stating traffic patterns, height above the channel which it crosses, the roadways to be connected, and so on. A procedure to compute the sin function may be specified by stating the range and format of the argument and the precision required in the result. An inventory control system may be specified by stating the required reduction in inventory holding costs and the required service level for a given pattern of customer demands. It is then the task of the engineer to find and implement a satisfactory solution to the stated problem. But these are all implicit specifications, and are not typical of the specifications found in software engineering, which are most often explicit rather than implicit. C. B. Jones defines [10] the difference:

> "The explicit [specification] is analogous to a program. ... The essence of an implicit specification is to state the relationship required between arguments and results without having to write an explicit rule for computing the latter from the former."

We could not, for example, give a implicit specification of a payroll program or system; we must specify exactly the rules for computing the gross pay and the tax and other deductions under all the circumstances that can arise. We cannot give an implicit specification for a syntax checker: we must specify all the acceptable syntactic combinations, usually by giving the grammar of the language to be checked.

This need for explicit specifications has caused a difficulty in separating out the specification task from the rest of the development activity, much like the difficulty of separating design from programming. This has been especially evident in data processing, where specifications have often been written which are essentially natural language programs, leaving the customer dissatisfied with a specification he cannot understand, and the design or programmer dissatisfied with the narrowing of his task to that of mere translation. It has seemed that, just as the design is the product, so the specification is the design.

4. Processes and procedures

But the specification is not the design—or it should not be. We can certainly distinguish between the exact specification of a set of connected sequential processes and the arrangement of those processes so that they can run efficiently on the machine. This will be a natural way of viewing the development of software systems whose subject matter is sequentially ordered in time. Specification captures the time ordering of the real world events; implementation rearranges the ordering, within the freedom given by the specification, to fit the machine. Consider, for example, a payroll system, whose subject matter is the behaviour of the employees to be paid: their working hours, perhaps their production achievements, their holidays and periods of sickness, their promotions, their eventual retirement. It is natural to specify such a system by stating the time-ordering of the events affecting one employee, and the entitlement to pay based on those ordered events. The resulting specification is a sequential process, whose execution models or simulates the behaviour of the employee over the whole period of employment. For an organisation with 10,000 employees, there would be 10,000 instances of this process to be executed. No existing operating system is capable of running these 10,000 processes directly with acceptable efficiency; it becomes the task of the implementer to rearrange these processes into a form allowing efficient execution. Typically, this form will be a set of 10,000 'employee database segments' together with an updating procedure which is executed on a database segment whenever an event occurs for the associated employee in the real world.

We can regard this rearrangement essentially as a scheduling, at implementation time, of the set of processes. The most important aspects of the rearrangement will be:

+ conversion of the sequential processes into procedures, so that the behaviour of a process when a relevant event occurs can be treated as an execution of an invoked procedure;
+ choosing a representation of the process activation records in terms of a suitable database system;
+ choosing a scheduling of the processes so that response to each event is fast enough and the whole system runs efficiently.

Conversion of the processes into procedures can be mechanised; choice of the database representation will depend on the particular database system to be used; the chosen scheduling of the processes must be expressed in an explicit scheduling algorithm to be devised by the implementer.

5. Development methods

In software engineering we pay much attention to the subject of development methods, certainly much more than is paid in the established branches of engineering. Indeed, it sometimes seems as if there is little in software engineering other than development methods. Where other engineers seem to talk about the products of their activities, and the characteristics of those products, software engineers talk about their activities directly, and about the characteristics of those activities. In part, this is due to the intangible nature of the software product and to the lack of a physical manifestation that can be readily examined and critically evaluated. In part, it is due to the comparative youthfulness of the field, and to the lack of self-confidence in its practitioners: social scientists too spend a lot of time discussing their methods. In part, it is due to the combination in software of great complexity with a stringent requirement for correctness.

Ideally, we would like to have a fully algorithmic method of software development, in which each step is predetermined and each decision can be reliably deduced from what has gone before. This can be achieved for certain problems that are very well understood. The designer of a small transformer, given a statement of the power and of the input and output voltages, can deduce the number and form of the necessary iron laminations for the core and the gauge and number of turns in the primary and secondary windings. The designer of a syntax analysis phase of a compiler can construct the parsing program directly from the specification of the grammar. The designer of a conventional batch program to update a serial master file from a serial transaction file can deduce the algorithm for matching the file records from a specification of the files themselves.

But these are very simple problems. Their solution can be—and has been—automated, and it then ceases to form a significant part of the development activity. Our interest centres on those development decisions which are not apparently amenable to automation, both decisions in the specification and decisions in the implementation activities.

We may regard a development method as a structuring of the development decisions. Here we mean 'decision' in a wide sense, covering the explicit consideration and recording of any relevant fact or choice. It would, in this sense, be a decision in the specification stage of a program to generate prime numbers that the product of two primes cannot itself be a prime; it would be a decision in developing a data processing system for insurance that each policy must be renewed annually; it would equally be a decision that there should be a subsystem for claims and another for premiums, or that a particular subroutine should have certain parameters and should call certain common subroutines, or that the policy master records should be held in an index sequential file.

Different decisions will have different characteristics. Some can be easily taken and carry little risk of error, especially where they record facts which are known a priori. Some will be error-prone, but have very limited impact on later decisions. Some, such as a decision to decompose a system into two subsystems, will have a very wide impact. Obviously, there are some general methodological principles which should govern the arrangement of development decisions into a development method. Decisions which record facts known *a priori* should be taken early, before decisions which record choices within the developer's discretion. High risk decisions should be postponed as long as possible, because it will be easier to make them correctly in a later than in an earlier stage of development. Decisions which have a wide impact should not, ideally, be highly error-prone. Error-prone decisions should be followed as soon as possible by consideration of anything which may invalidate them. Decisions about implementation should be taken after decisions about specification.

From this point of view, it seems clear that 'top-down' and 'stepwise refinement' methods are to be studiously avoided. Using such a method, the developer begins by deciding the top-level structure of the system, decomposing it into its largest constituent parts. Undoubtedly, this is the worst possible decision to place at the beginning of development. It is a decision about the system itself, which, ex hypothesi, is not yet well-known: it is therefore highly error-prone. It has the widest impact of all those decisions within the developer's discretion, because it sets the context for all later structural decisions: if the top-level structure is wrong, it will not be easy to salvage much of the work done on lower levels. And, finally, if this first decision is wrong, it may not be invalidated until late in the development,

We may suspect that developers who claim to be using top-down or stepwise refinements methods are, in fact, doing something quite different. The real work of development is done, informally and invisibly, in the developer's head, where something approximating to an outline of the complete system is visualised. This outline is then documented in a top-down fashion, and enough details filled in to complete the work. A brilliant, or even highly competent, developer may be able to work quite effectively in this manner, but its limitations are obvious [11].

6. Maintenance and complexity

Many kinds of software system—perhaps most kinds—must be readily adaptable to changes in their specifications. We call this adaptation 'maintenance', a usage which is unique to software engineering. In other branches of engineering, the word 'maintenance' usually means the activity of guarding against or repairing the physical degradation which afflicts the product. Bridges must be painted to avoid corrosion; resistors must be examined and replaced if their value has strayed outside the specified tolerance; the oil in the engine sump must be drained and replaced; the potholes in the road must be filled in. Analogous activity is needed in software systems of some kinds: a database system may need periodic examination to detect and repair errors in chaining between records; an index sequential file may need reloading when too many insertions have reduced the access speed or filled the overflow area; a partitioned data set may need to be reorganised to make dead space available for new members. But we do not usually mean such things by 'maintenance': we mean the activity of changing the system to satisfy changed specifications, much as the design of an aeroplane may be changed to give a 'stretched' version, or a bridge may be widened to carry a greater load of traffic.

It is well known that maintenance in this sense accounts for a large part of the expenditure on data processing systems. This need not be a cause for dismay or concern: we might congratulate ourselves because our products are so adaptable that our customers' needs can be satisfied at the lower cost of maintenance rather than the higher cost of complete redevelopment. But few software engineers, and even fewer customers, would join in the congratulations. The cost of maintenance is generally considered to be too high, in the sense that comparatively small changes in specification often require very difficult and expensive changes to the system. We might also consider the cost of the maintenance that is not carried out because it is too difficult or expensive for the customer to accept it at the offered price. We rarely get the opportunity to measure the cost of non-maintenance.

The source of excessive maintenance cost is disparity between the structure of the specification and the structure of the system. The change to the specification may be small, simple, and local; if the consequent change to the system is large, complex, and diffuse, that must mean that the structure of the system is different from the structure of the specification. Often, the system will also be excessively complex in itself, making any change difficult and even dangerous.

Our chief tool for mastering and avoiding complexity is the ability to view a system as a relatively small number of relatively large parts, connected in a clear and simple way. If the cost of maintenance is to be low, then the parts and connections in the system must correspond closely to the parts and connections in the specification. At the same time, the parts and connections in the specification must correspond closely to the parts and connections in the customer's view of the problem domain. A fundamental difficulty in achieving this goal is the inevitable difference between the structure of a good specification and the structure of an efficient implementation. To return to the earlier example of the payroll system, the specification should be structured so that one of its distinct parts is a statement of what happens to one employee during the whole period of his employment; but an efficient implementation may require to contain a distinct part which is a weekly batch program dealing with the events that have affected all current employees during the past week. We cannot avoid the problem of mediating between these two different structures; the mechanised conversion from process to procedure form is a significant component in a solution to this problem. To the greatest possible extent, we should aim to take advantage of this tractability of the software medium, of the ability to transform one piece of software into another of related but different structure [12].

7. Standard products and parts

Most engineering products are highly standardised, and their designers work within narrowly defined bounds. Each product falls into a well-known type, and has a readily recognisable structure; the engineer is not expected to produce a revolutionary design, but rather a carefully crafted set of choices within the accepted parameters. The introduction of a significantly different structure for a product is a revolution, and regarded as potentially dangerous. After countless suspension and cantilever bridges has been designed and built, it was a daring engineer who conceived the box girder bridge. After sixty years of reciprocating internal combustion engines, it was a daring innovation to produce a car powered by a rotary engine.

There are many reasons for this high degree of standardisation. One important reason is the visibility of the physical product, which we have referred to previously. The automobile manufacturer who first abandoned the separate chassis and body and adopted the integral design could hardly hope to keep the advance a secret from his competitors. Another reason is the widespread use which most physical engineering products receive. Huge numbers of people use automobiles of a particular design, or cross a particular bridge on their way to work, or ride in elevators of a particular design. And they use other automobiles and bridge and elevators, too. So there is a strong tendency towards uniformity in customer's expectations of a particular class of products. This tendency is much less marked in software, where many products are created for customers who have no experience of other similar products to guide their evaluation. Where usage of a class of product is widespread, as of Fortran compilers, there is a stronger tendency toward uniformity of expectation and hence of product.

Yet another reason for standardisation of products is the use of standard parts. The manufacturer of a physical product is usually forced to buy many or even all of the parts he uses; these parts are bought from component companies who supply identical parts to the other manufacturers. In software, the developer always has the option—even if it is not necessarily the best option—of building everything in-house. At the 1968 NATO conference, M. D. McIlroy, advocating the creation of a software components industry, complained: [13]

> "When we undertake to write a compiler, we begin by saying 'what table mechanism shall we build?' Not 'what mechanism shall we use?', but 'what mechanism shall we build?' I claim we have done enough of this to start taking such things off the shelf."

A dramatic illustration of the way standardisation comes about is provided by the microcomputer industry. Where discussion about standard machine architecture had limped along for ten years in the mainframe and minicomputer industry, the microcomputer industry has standardised itself immediately, simply because very cheap standard CPU chips are available which the manufacturer can not produce in-house.

This has scarcely happened in the software industry. There are a few examples of standard components or packages, such as libraries of mathematical routines, that were already visible in 1968. But remarkably little else. We may perhaps attribute the lack of standard components to both economic and technical factors. If a putative standard component is small, the cost of building it in-house may be no greater than the cost of identifying and obtaining the required item from the supplier. If it is larger, its specification is likely to be larger, and there is correspondingly less likelihood of finding what is needed in a supplier's catalogue. The technical factors are associated with the interface specification. Traditionally, the general-purpose software components contributed to an installation's program library by hopeful authors have been cast in the form of procedures. The procedure interface is very satisfactory for mathematical functions, but not for much else. The interface specified for the library routine always looks to the potential user to be arbitrary, difficult to understand, and impossible to reconcile with his existing design; so he writes his own version to his own interface specifications. We may note that one environment where general purpose software does seem to be widely used is the UNIX environment. Not surprisingly, a typical UNIX component is a sequential process communicating by message streams (pipes) with other processes; the message stream interface, for a wide class of application, is both convenient and well-suited to the definition of standard software components.

8. Some conclusions and suggestions

The use of the term software engineering expresses an aspiration, not a fact. The established branches of engineering are old; we are young. Their work is organised into well-defined specialisations; ours is still largely ill bounded and undifferentiated. Their products are standardised wherever possible; ours are most often built *ad hoc*. They examine and evaluate their products; we spend more time contemplating our navels. They have components industries; we do not. Their disastrous mistakes make headlines in the newspapers; ours are too commonplace to merit remark.

Many of these differences, and many of our difficulties, flow from the intangible nature of the software product. It is hard for us to draw boundaries between different development stages and activities; it is hard to constrain the engineer's choices enough to make his work manageable without preventing him from building an efficient product. But this intangible nature of the product is our greatest advantage, and we have derived too little benefit from it. We can manipulate, rearrange, reconfigure, and transform a software product at a very low cost, by using the computer itself; we have not done so as we should.

The crux of the matter is the relationship among three structures: the structure of the problem in the problem domain; the structure of the written specification; and the structure of the implementation. For a large class of problems, including many in data processing, process control, message switching, and embedded applications, the problem domain is sequentially ordered in time: the natural specification structure to capture the essence of the problem in its context is that of a set of communicating sequential processes. Where the number of these processes, their elapsed execution times in the real world, and the densities of their activities are well-fitted to the available machine, operating system, and programming language, the development of the system can proceed reasonably smoothly. The ideal development here is one in which the specification processes are programmed directly in a process-orientated programming language, and the resulting program can be executed directly on the machine.

But often, especially in data processing applications, the configuration and dimensions of the specification process set are ill-fitted—even to the point of incompatibility—to the programming language and to the machine and its operating system. Present operating systems are conceived for the execution of procedures (whose execution is, conceptually, instantaneous), or of small sets of processes with short execution times and dense demands for machine cycles. A specification with 10,000 processes, each taking 50 years to execute, and demanding only 100 seconds of machine time over the 50 years, simply does not fit the machine. Traditionally, the incompatibility has been resolved by choosing between Scylla and Charybdis. Either the specification is cast in a problem orientated form which the customer can hope to understand, whereupon the structure of the design will bear no visible relation to the structure of the specification: or the specification is cast in design-orientated form, whereupon the structure of the specification will bear no visible relation to the structure of the problem in its domain.

We should cast the specification in the problem-orientated form (of course!), and we should derive the design structure (that is, the implementation structure) by systematic transformation. The explicit, process-structured, specification is itself a fully detailed executable text. But it needs to be rearranged and transformed before it can be executed efficiently. The computer should be the essential tool in this activity. The transformations should be carried out mechanically, so that the correctness of the specification is preserved; but they should be chosen by the engineer, interacting with the transformation system. Some transformations of the appropriate kinds have been studied and described; some have already been mechanised [14, 15]. But there is a long way to go before use of such transformations becomes widespread and well-supported.

One benefit that might accrue from this approach to software development is a separation of languages. Our present languages are disgracefully complicated, as they must inevitably be, serving simultaneously the incompatible purposes of specification and implementation. In place of a programming language, we might have a pair of related languages: a specification language, ruthlessly purged of implementation features; and a language for directing the transformation of specifications into efficient implementations. Each language of the pair could be much simpler than today's programming languages. Along with this separation of languages would come a separation of development activity along more rational and intelligible lines. It would be easier to determine a boundary between the specification engineer and the implementation engineer, and fruitful specialisation might develop both within an organisation and between one organisation and another. Perhaps specialisation is both the precondition and the hallmark of a mature discipline of engineering.

References

1. Software Engineering: Report on a conference sponsored by the NATO Science Committee; ed P. Naur and B. Randell; 1969.

2. The Preparation of Programs for an Electronic Digital Computer; M. V. Wilkes, D. J. Wheeler and S. Gill; AddisonWesley, 1951. Quoted in *A History of Computing in the Twentieth Century*; ed N. Metropolis, J. Howlett and G-C. Rota; Academic Press, 1980.

3. Hierarchical Program Structures; O-J. Dahl and C. A. R. Hoare; in *Structured Programming*; O-J. Dahl, E. W. Dijkstra and C. A. R. Hoare; Academic Press, 1972. See also Design of a Separable Transition-diagram Compiler; M. E. Conway, *Comm ACM* July 1963.

4. Cooperating Sequential Processes; E. W. Dijkstra; in *Programming Languages*; ed F. Genuys; Academic Press, 1968.

5. Message Passing Between Sequential Processes: the Reply Primitive and the Administrator Concept; W. M. Gentleman; *Software Practice and Experience*, May 1981.

6. Communicating Sequential Processes; C. A. R. Hoare; *Comm ACM*, August 1978.

7. The Design of Data Type Specifications; J. V. Guttag, E. Horowitz and D. R. Musser; in *Current Trends in Programming Methodology, IV*; ed R. T. Yeh; Prentice-Hall, 1978.

8. *Structured Design*; E. Yourdon and L. L. Constantine; Prentice-Hall, 1979.

9. *Structured Programming*; R. C. Linger, H. D. Mills and B. L Witt; Addison-Wesley, 1979.

10. *Software Development: A Rigorous Approach*; C. B. Jones; Prentice-Hall, 1980.

11. Programming as a Cognitive Activity; T. R. Green; in *Human Interaction with Computers*; ed H. T. Smith and T. R. Green; Academic Press, 1980.

12. Information Systems: Modelling, Sequencing and Transformations; M. A. Jackson; *Proc 3rd international Conference on Software Engineering*, 1978.

13. Op cit [1].

14. Some Transformations for Developing Recursive Programs; R. M. Burstall and J. Darlington; *Proc International Conference on Reliable Software*, 1975.

15. A System for Developing Programs by Transformation; M. S. Feather; PhD Thesis, University of Edingburgh, 1978.

Chapter 2

Engineering and Software

Michael Jackson

Abstract: Software development has long aspired to merit the status of a professional engineering discipline like those of the established engineering branches. This paper discusses this aspiration with particular reference to software-intensive or computer-based systems. Some opportunities are pointed out for learning important lessons from the established branches. These lessons stem above all from the highly specialised nature of traditional engineering practice. They centre on the crucial distinction between radical and normal design, the content of normal design practice, and the social and cultural infrastructures that make effective specialisation possible.

1. Introduction

In the earliest years of software development some notable successes were achieved. Perhaps the most remarkable was the development of business data processing systems for J Lyons, an English company that blended its own teas and baked its own breads and cakes for sale in its restaurants and teashops. As early as 1947, the company understood the potential benefit of computerised data processing at a time when few people imagined that workable computers would eventually become commercial products available for purchase and use. The company contributed to the funding of the EDSAC computer being built at Cambridge University, and on the basis of the EDSAC design they developed and manufactured their own electronic computer, LEO 1. The name LEO was an acronym—Lyons Electronic Office—and the computer was intended to run business data processing applications that Lyons own staff would design and program. The first application, bakery valuation, computed the money value of the cakes, pies and pastries produced by the company's bakeries and distributed to their teashops, restaurants and other sales channels: it ran successfully on 16th November 1951 and every week thereafter for many years. In 1954 the J Lyons payroll application began weekly operation, and from December 1955 the payroll of the Ford Motor Company's Dagenham plant ran on LEO as a service outsourced by Ford to J Lyons. By the end of 1956 [Caminer97], "LEO was processing a representative load of office applications—payroll, distribution, sales invoicing, accounting and stock control—and, at the same time, expediting the physical operations of Lyons and providing timely information for remedial managerial action."

A remarkable system of a very different kind was SAGE, the Semi-Automatic Ground Environment system designed to defend North America against bombing attack by aircraft fleets of potentially hostile powers. Based on an earlier prototype system, and using AN/FSQ-7 and AN/FSQ-8 computers specially developed by IBM, SAGE collected and processed radar inputs for display to operators, and helped the operators to react appropriately and to communicate indirectly with interceptor aircraft. The system first became operational in 1959 and ceased operation nearly twenty five years later in 1983. The system was never put to the test by a real hostile attack, and became obsolete quite early in its life when the perceived threat from long-range missiles superseded that from bombers; but its development was judged to have been very successful, and was certainly extremely ambitious for its time. Herbert D Benington was one of the leaders of the software development for SAGE, and described the work in a 1956 paper [Benington56]. When his 1956 paper was republished [Everett83] in 1983, Benington added a foreword in which he reflected on his experiences. He was in no doubt about the foundation of the project's success:

"It is easy for me to single out the one factor that I think led to our relative success: we were all engineers and had been trained to organize our efforts along engineering lines. We had a need to rationalize the job; to define a system of documentation so that others would know what was being done; to define interfaces and police them carefully; to recognize that things would not work well the first, second, or third time, and therefore that much independent testing was needed in successive phases; to create development tools that would help build products and test tools and to make sure they worked; to keep a record of everything that really went wrong and to see whether it really got fixed; and, most important, to have a chief engineer who was cognizant of these activities and responsible for orchestrating their interplay. In other words, as engineers, anything other than structured programming or a top-down approach would have been foreign to us."

In the later 1950s, and in the first half of the 1960s, there were still successes, but now there were very many failures too. As machines became more affordable there was a need for many more programmers, and inevitably few, if any, of the new recruits were trained engineers like Herbert Benington or deeply experienced business analysts like David Caminer. Jules Schwartz [Buxton70] colourfully described the later recruitment to the SAGE project:

"People were recruited and trained from a variety of walks of life. Street-car conductors, undertakers (with at least one year of training in calculus), school teachers, curtain cleaners and others were hastily assembled, trained in programming for some number of weeks and assigned parts in a very complex organization."

Whatever the reasons, by the early 1960s there was widespread talk of a 'software crisis'. It was commonly said that software was full of errors; that software systems did not deliver the functionality that was needed; and that software projects too often grossly exceeded their budgets and schedules—many very expensive software projects even failing to deliver anything usable at all. Something had to be done.

In 1967 the NATO Science Committee established a Study Group on Computer Science. The Study Group recommended the holding of a working conference on 'Software Engineering', and two NATO conferences were held: one in Garmisch in 1968 and one in Rome the following year. The introduction to the report of the first conference [Naur69] states the motivation clearly:

"The phrase 'Software Engineering' was deliberately chosen as being provocative, in implying the need for software manufacture to be based on the types of theoretical foundations and practical disciplines, that are traditional in the established branches of engineering."

The perception was clear: software developers should learn from engineers. What exactly they should learn was less clear. For some people, 'Software Engineering' meant simply an improved and more careful approach to the programming task: programmers should be more meticulous; they should pay more attention to design, and should check their programs before executing, or even before compiling, them; they should abandon the 'code-and-fix' approach that had caused so much trouble. For others, there were more specific lessons to be learned.

Some saw software development as an essentially industrial production process that could, and should, be subjected to fine-grain industrial disciplines of the kind that Frederick Taylor had devised and promoted in the early 20th century under the title 'scientific management'. Unsurprisingly, some programmers, like factory workers, were inclined to resist the imposition of this kind of managerial rule, seeing it as an assault on their dignity. In a book [Kraft77] published in 1977, the sociologist Philip Kraft argued that the introduction of structured programming was essentially an attempt by managers to control their workers by imposing a form of Taylorism on them:

"Until human programmers were eliminated altogether, their work would be made as machine-like—that is, as simple and limited and routine—as possible. Briefly, programmers using structured programming would be limited to a handful of logical procedures which they could use—no others were permitted. They could call only for certain kinds of information ... They could not, for example, call for information not contained in the original data set assigned to them. ..."

"Structured programming, in short, has become the software manager's answer to the assembly line, minus the conveyor belt but with all the other essential features of a mass-production workplace: a standardized product made in a standardized way by people who do the same limited tasks over and over without knowing how they fit into a larger undertaking."

Kraft had misunderstood the nature both of software development and of the disciplines of structured programming. Twenty years later, Watts Humphrey [Humphrey00] softened the harsh wind of Taylorism by inviting programmers to be their own managers, but his view of their work was consciously based on a comparison with Taylor's principles for achieving efficiency:

"The principal difference between manual and intellectual work is that the knowledge worker is essentially autonomous. That is, in addition to deciding how to do tasks, he or she must also decide what tasks to do and the order in which to do them. The manual worker commonly follows a relatively fixed task order, essentially prescribed by the production line. So studying and improving the performance of intellectual work must not only address the most efficient way to do each task but also consider how to select and order these tasks. This is essentially the role of a defined process and a detailed plan. The process defines the tasks, task order, and task measures, while the plan sizes the tasks and defines the task schedule for the job being done."

Less harshly yet, some people saw the software problem as an interplay of technical and managerial aspects, but still with a strong emphasis on the definition and management of the development process.

There was general agreement that software development should become like engineering, but little agreement about what that would mean. The present author has suggested (in Chapter 1 of this book) that specialisation is a basic characteristic of successful engineering, but that suggestion was not related in any detailed way to the practices of the established engineering branches. The present paper aims to repair that omission to some extent.

In an insightful paper [Shaw90] published in 1990, Mary Shaw described the evolution of the established branches of engineering from their beginnings in crafts and cottage industries. Chemical engineering—which she took as her primary example—evolved in three stages. An industrial process emerged in the late 18th century, under the commercial pressure for more efficient production of the alkali needed for the manufacture of glass, soap and textiles. Early in the 19th century Dalton's atomic theory provided a scientific foundation by explaining the underlying chemistry. In the mid-19th century G E Davis recognised that chemical manufacturing depended on a core set of basic operations, later called unit operations, of which every manufacturing process in use was composed.

Shaw also points out the distinction between routine and innovative design, and the crucial value of a handbook in which known good designs and their applicable parameters are recorded and codified. Finally, among her recommendations for the steps necessary for software development to become a true engineering discipline, she includes the development of specialisation: internal specialisation in the technical content of program design "as the core of software grows deeper"; and external specialisation in "applications that require both substantive application knowledge and substantive computing knowledge."

The intent of this paper is to build on some of these insights, especially Shaw's, and to draw some further lessons from a consideration of the practice of the established engineering branches. The central role of specialisation, and its essential preconditions, are discussed, and a particular dimension of specialisation—specialisation by artifact—is identified that has played a vital role in achieving dependably successful engineering products.

2. Software-intensive systems

We can learn the deepest lessons from the traditional branches of engineering, and can gain most from learning them, for software development of the very broad class of system that are often called *computer-based* or *software-intensive* systems. In such systems the computer's role is to interact with other systems and with the physical world—that is, with the natural world of the universe, the physical products of electronic, electrical and mechanical engineering, and with human beings themselves in activities of many kinds. These systems include embedded systems, control systems, medical systems, and business and administrative systems of all types. The central purpose of the software is not to compute symbolic values from symbolic inputs. Rather, it is to evoke a continuing behaviour of the computer by which it can play its role as a physical *machine* in its *problem world*—the relevant parts of the physical world—functioning as one part among several, monitoring and controlling the behaviours of the other parts and establishing and maintaining the required relations among them. In this paper, then, we will be concerned with systems of this kind.

For an avionics system the earth's atmosphere is a part of its problem world, along with the aircraft itself, the pilot, the airport runways, the passengers, the air traffic control system, and so on. For a heart pacemaker system the problem world contains the human patient, regarded from both behavioural and physiological points of view, the external devices by which the pacemaker's behaviour can be monitored and adjusted, and the operators of those devices. For a theatre booking system the problem world contains the theatres, the potential audiences, credit cards, the physical tickets to be issued, and so on. For a medical radiation therapy system the problem world includes the patients, the radiation equipment, the equipment operators, the medical staff, and the movable bed on which patients lie and are precisely positioned for treatment. For a system to control the lifts in an office building the problem world contains the electrical and mechanical lift equipment, the arrangement of the building's floors, the behaviour of individual users, and their group behaviour evidenced in patterns of traffic between the building's floors.

These parts, or *domains*, of the physical world are heterogeneous, varying greatly in the inherent properties and behaviours they exhibit, both in general and in their participation in different systems. The relevant capabilities and propensities of an airline pilot flying an aircraft are different from those of the same person engaged in booking a theatre seat. The properties of the earth's atmosphere that are important in an avionics system are different from those that matter in a system to control fuel injection in a motor car. For each system the developers must investigate and analyse the properties of the problem world domains and of their interactions with each other and with the machine to be built: they must devise a machine whose interactions with the domains to which it is directly connected will ensure that the system requirements—the purposes of the system—are satisfied. If they misunderstand the requirements, or misunderstand the behaviours and properties of the problem world domains, they will fail as surely as if they produce erroneous programs. This possibility of failure is not confined to control systems: an information system, too, will fail if its developers have misunderstood how the phenomena about which information is to be produced are related by the domain properties to the phenomena directly accessible to the machine.

The success or failure of the developed software, then, is not to be judged by its satisfaction of a formal specification of machine behaviour, but by its observable effects in the problem world. The theatre booking system is successful if people can book seats conveniently, if duplicate tickets for the same seat at the same performance are never issued, if better seats at each price are sold first, if credit cards are correctly charged, and so on. The radiation therapy system is successful if the patients receive their doses of radiation exactly as prescribed, if the equipment is efficiently utilised, and if safe operation of the equipment is ensured.

This character of the development is shared by the work of the established branches of engineering. G F C Rogers defined [Rogers83] engineering as

"the practice of organising the design and construction of any artifice which transforms the physical world around us to meet some recognised need."

The artifice, or artifact, constructed by software developers is the *machine*— the computer executing the software; the physical world around us is the *problem world*; and the system *requirements* are the recognised need. In this fundamental sense, software development of a system is indeed engineering, and should be able to profit from what engineers have learned over their long history.

3. Specialisation by artifact

An obvious aspiration has been to enrol software engineering as one new member of the established college: automotive engineers develop motor cars, and naval engineers develop ships: clearly, people who develop software should be enrolled as software engineers. This aspiration is based on the identification of the software itself, considered in its narrow confines within the computer, as the artifact produced by software development: the product of software development is identified with the program text.

Certainly, from a pure programming point of view this aspiration to a single engineering discipline seems to make good sense: the software of practically all systems has much in common. The program text describes the computer's internal behaviour and states by which it can be brought to exhibit the desired behaviour at its interface with the problem world. From a pure programming point of view, this internal behaviour, and the technical challenge of designing it and describing it in a program text, are of direct and intense interest. The programmer must take proper account of the relevant algorithms and data structures, the practicalities of the operating system and programming language, the allocation of the computer's resources, the possible failures of the hardware and software infrastructure on which the program is to be executed, and many other matters that engage the attention of software engineers.

Nonetheless, in the case of software-intensive systems, and perhaps of some other software systems too, this identification of the product with the program text is misplaced: software engineering is not one aspiring engineering discipline, but many. The real artifact produced by the software developers is the combined behaviour of the machine and of the physical problem world: not only at the interface where they meet and interact, but also in their respective hinterlands remote from that interface. The pure programming point of view does not capture the essential purpose of the work: the internal computations signify nothing except as an instrumental means to achieve the machine's external behaviour; and the external behaviour signifies nothing except as an instrumental means to achieve the purposes of the system in its problem world. The meaningful artifact is the whole system, considered with a primary focus on the problem world. The huge variety in the physical problem worlds, together with the variety of their required functions in those worlds, is then seen to constitute a huge variety in the artifacts of software development. From this point of view, the most conspicuous practical characteristic of the established branches is their very plurality. There is not just one established branch of physical engineering. We should not expect, then, that there should be just one branch of software development. We should expect a broad structure of specialisation according to the different classes of system—or subsystem—to be developed.

Certainly, there are common intellectual principles shared by all engineers, and both the 'hard' science of physics and chemistry and the 'soft' behavioural sciences are of shared relevance because of engineers' intense concern with the physical and human world. However, most of this common ground lies far below the working practice of engineering, which is concerned with particular outcomes in particular situations. As more scientific knowledge becomes available it informs the possibilities of innovation; but engineering practice is concerned with the design and analysis of particular artifacts. At the level of particularities, the artifacts and the associated problem worlds of the different engineering branches are very different. This is why they specialise. Civil engineers do not design chemical plants, and automobile engineers do not design ships or networks for the distribution of electrical power. If we hope to emulate their successes, and achieve the levels of quality and dependability that we have come to expect in their products, we must study and emulate their degree and manner of specialisation.

Specialisation in the established branches has many dimensions, and software development can legitimately claim to exhibit parallel or analogous specialisations in some of those dimensions. They have specialisations by theory, such as control and structural engineering, and fluid dynamics; software has concurrency, type theory and complexity theory. They have specialisations by technology, such as micro-electronics and welding; software has functional and object-oriented programming. They have specialisations by materials, such as pre-stressed concrete and electrically conducting plastics; software has Java and PHP and SQL. All of these specialisations are important, and all feed into the overall success of the established branches, and into the successes of software developers.

Where software development falls short in specialisation is in the most fundamental dimension of all: specialisation by artifact. The other dimensions are important, but the crucial dimension is specialisation by artifact. Only the specialist in a particular class of artifact—motor cars, or dams, or electric motors, or disk drives—can bring together and understand all the particular factors that determine the quality of the artifact and its value for its designed purpose, and make judicious choices about the interactions of those factors. The extent to which engineering rests chiefly on a foundation of science is debatable; but science alone is quite certainly not enough, even when expanded into its own branching specialisations. The full effects of applicable scientific laws on a particular artifact in the particular situations it will encounter are in principle incalculable: the phenomena that might affect the outcomes cannot be exhaustively enumerated; nor can their effects be quantified with enough precision for the engineer to know with certainty which laws will have the largest effects and will thus combine to dominate the outcome. This is why one must not expect a group of physicists, however brilliant and however perfect their understanding of the laws of physics, to be able to design and build a good motor car or aeroplane or bridge. In this difficulty, only the engineer specialised by artifact can address the totality of what the 'end-user' of the artifact (who may, of course, be another engineer for whose artifact the first engineer's artifact is one of several components) can expect to experience.

Software development does show some specialisations by artifact, but too few of them are found in the development of systems that interact with the physical world. For example, one very successful specialisation is in SAT solvers, which solve the completely abstract problem of finding an assignment of values to variables that satisfies a given predicate; another is in model checking, which is again an entirely abstract problem. Others are in compilers, file systems, relational database systems, and networking, in all of which the problem world is approximately bounded by the world of other software systems and of hardware devices—for example, disk drives—specifically designed for high reliability and for interacting conveniently with software. Certainly there is clear evidence of specialisation in some kinds of computer-controlled system or subsystem that work very well and very reliably: these probably include modern lift-control systems provided by the major manufacturers, ATMs, credit-card charging software used by major e-commerce websites, ABS braking systems in cars, and others. However, artifact specialisation is more than the production of successful examples: it is essentially the product of an evolved culture.

4. The growth of specialisations

Specialisation is fundamental to intellectual progress. In the earliest stages outstandingly able people can master all the existing knowledge of a field. As knowledge increases, acquired from experience or from a deepening understanding of an underlying science, the sum of available knowledge in the field becomes more than any one person, however able, can master. Eventually, each able individual must choose between becoming a generalist, who knows less and less about more and more, or a specialist, who knows more and more about less and less. In the first half of the 19th century, the great engineer Isambard Kingdom Brunel pursued a masterful career as an engineer of railways, bridges and tunnels, large ocean liners, artillery pieces, and modular, transportable, military hospitals. Today, with the exception of bridges and tunnels, both of which fall within the competence of some practising civil engineers, knowledge in each one of these artifact categories has developed to a point at which only a specialist can be fully competent: Brunel himself would be unable to master them all.

The pressure to specialise is not felt only by individuals. In fact, is it only in the earliest stages that specialisation is the possession of individuals. The touchstone of this kind of specialisation is that the artifact knowledge becomes the valued possession of a community rather than of individual people. Individual people pursue specialised careers; companies specialise their products; there are research journals and educational curricula; there are careful descriptions, models, and sometimes even repositories or museums of notable exemplars— all of these focused on the design on the specialised artifact classes in question. The community works to increase its knowledge and improve the quality of its products, often under pressure of competition among individuals or companies within the community.

For the most part, specialisations emerge in response to commercial opportunities, technical opportunities and challenges, and sometimes legal and social pressure arising from a high incidence of failures in a particular class of artifacts. The specialisation in compilers arose in response to a commercial opportunity of the early 1960s when computer hardware architecture was still hugely varied. Some computers used a machine order code in which each instruction specified one address; some used two; some used three addresses. Word length could be 12, 16, 24, 36, 48 or almost any other even number of bits. There were different schemes for structuring and addressing primary and secondary storage; some machines had a built-in hardware stack. The manufacturers needed to be able to supply a free Fortran compiler to each customer who bought or rented one of their very expensive machines. Companies like Digitek and Computer Sciences Corporation saw the commercial opportunity and rushed to exploit it. Over the next twenty years or more, compiler construction became a notable specialisation. Applied theory of grammars, parsing, code generation and optimisation developed along with a recognition of the accepted decomposition of a compiler: lexical analyser, symbol table, syntax analyser, semantic routines to be associated with nodes of the syntax tree, global and peephole optimiser. The field has continued to develop: faster machines allow just-in-time compilation and compilation to a bytecode for interpretation by a virtual machine; integrated development environments integrate compilation into program design, editing, and debugging, along with the use of comprehensive module libraries. The result was that compilers eventually exhibited high quality and reliability, and were easily capable of compiling programs in languages that in earlier years would have been thought impossibly difficult to compile.

5. The benefits of artifact specialisation

In engineering, the primary benefit of artifact specialisation is the emergence, adoption and evolution of *normal design* for the artifacts. Following Constant [Constant80], Vincenti describes [Vincenti93] normal design:

"[Normal design is] the improvement of the accepted tradition, or its application under new or more stringent conditions. ... The engineer engaged in such design knows at the outset how the device in question works, what are its customary features, and that, if properly designed along such lines, it has a good likelihood of accomplishing the desired task."

"A designer of a normal aircraft engine prior to the turbojet, for example, took it for granted that the engine should be piston-driven by a gasoline-fueled, four-stroke, internal-combustion cycle. The arrangement of cylinders for a high-powered engine would also be taken as given (radial if air-cooled and in linear banks if liquid-cooled). So also would other, less obvious, features (eg, tappet as against, say, sleeve valves). The designer was familiar with engines of this sort and knew they had a long tradition of success. The design problem— often highly demanding within its limits—was one of improvement in the direction of decreased weight and fuel consumption or increased power output or both."

Normal design in this sense is conspicuous in modern cars, in large passenger aircraft, in mobile phones, in television sets, and in many other well designed and reliable artifacts with which we are familiar. Certainly, there are differences between one manufacturer's products and another's, and between this year's models and last year's. There are also differences between subclasses within one class—in cars, for example, between people carriers and five-door hatchbacks. But these differences are less significant than the similarities, which have emerged from the gradual evolution of normal design and its adoption by the specialised engineering communities.

Vincenti contrasts normal design with *radical design*:

"In radical design, how the device should be arranged or even how it works is largely unknown. The designer has never seen such a device before and has no presumption of success. The problem is to design something that will function well enough to warrant further development."

A clear example of radical design is Karl Benz's Patent Motorwagen of 1886, arguably the first successful motor car. (A very careful replica of the car has been built, and a good selection of photographs is available at [Benz86]). The car was completely open to the elements; there were three wire-spoked wheels with solid tyres, and an unsprung single front wheel; the driver sat in the centre and steered with a small tiller. The engine was started by manually turning the large horizontally mounted flywheel; it was lubricated by a drip feed; the single crank was unenclosed; the drive to the rear wheels was by belt and pulley, and there was no gearbox to vary the ratio of engine speed to road speed. It was a remarkable achievement by Benz's wife, Berta, to drive this car 65 miles from Mannheim to Pforzheim in the course of a single day. Benz had succeeded in solving the radical design problem exactly as Vincenti characterised it: he had "designed something that functioned well enough to warrant further development."

In the following years, the growing community of specialised automobile engineers developed their products to the point at which by about 1920 they could be said to embody a normal design: an electric starter for the engine; four sprung wheels, all with pneumatic tyres and brakes; a closed cab with the driver sitting on the offside and controlling front-wheel Ackerman steering geometry by a raked steering wheel; a standard layout of the drive train, including a friction clutch, three-speed or four-speed gearbox, longitudinal propeller shaft, and a rear axle casing enclosing a differential driving the rear wheels through half-shafts.

The successful evolution of a normal design does not mark the end of innovation. On the contrary: it provides a stable and dependable foundation on which further innovations can be developed. In automobile engineering the last eighty or ninety years have seen continual incremental innovation within the established but still evolving normal design. The overall vehicle structure has been improved: for example, the separate body and chassis frame have been replaced by a unitary pressed steel body that combines the functions of both, and the front beam axle has been replaced by independent front suspension. Individual components and subsystems have been improved by the introduction of tubeless tyres, automatic gearbox, fuel injection and many other new features.

6. The content of normal design

'Design', of course, is both a noun and a verb. The phrase 'normal design' denotes both the standard configuration and component structure of the designed artifact in its particular class, and also the practical disciplines that its designers are expected to follow in developing each new instance of the class. These practical disciplines do conform to some very general notions of engineers' responsibilities that are common to all or most engineering branches, and they rest on a common basis of scientific knowledge of the physical world; but their most significant practical content is special to each product class and is largely focused on its component structure at all levels.

This is what makes possible the reliable division of a design project among a group of several designers. Vincenti outlines parts of the typical project structure in aeroplane design as "Major-component design—division of project into wing design, fuselage design, landing-gear design, electrical-system design, etc" and "Subdivision of areas of component design ... according to engineering discipline required (eg aerodynamic wing design, structural wing design, mechanical wing design)." This project structuring is, of course, closely tied to the normal product structure. While some details of the decomposition into work assignments may be open to doubt, the general shape is clearly mandated by the normal design.

The central point here, which deserves repetition, is this: the decomposition of artifact functionality in a normal design is not *ad hoc*. Parnas rightly identified [Parnas78] the importance of "the decomposition of programming projects into work assignments (modules)." In a normal design discipline this decomposition is already broadly known, and the assignment of the components to individuals or groups is likely to be determined by their known specialisations at the component level. Any significant departure from the established decomposition into components arranged in the standard configuration, is to be recognised as an innovation, and as the introduction of an element of radical design that inevitably brings with it an increased risk of failure.

The development work within each part of the project is quite tightly constrained by the standard, normal, design. In extreme cases the designer is choosing from a small set of design options and fixing parameters from a well-defined range. The chosen design must be validated, eventually by testing, but in the earlier design stages by analysing the properties of each successively proposed design version to determine whether the choices it embodies would enable the design to satisfy its requirements. This analysis is typically mathematical, and rests on two foundations: one is scientific knowledge of the physical phenomena involved; the other is a set of known procedures for sufficiently accurate analysis of significant properties of versions that fall within the bounds of the established normal design. Without the scientific knowledge, reliable analysis is impossible; it may also be impossible if the design to be analysed is unprecedented and arbitrarily chosen. Theoretical scientific knowledge is concerned with physical phenomena such as mechanical forces and chemical processes acting in isolation. Engineering requires a good enough understanding of specific situations and artifacts in which, inescapably, many different forces and processes are at work. This good enough understanding can be achieved only by analytical models which are simultaneously good enough approximations to the enormously complex reality and also tractable by the available mathematics and science. It is a crucial characteristic of normal designs that they are susceptible of adequate standard analysis in this way.

7. Component structure

In developing, understanding, or analysing a system, it is necessary to consider the *machine*—the computer or computers executing the developed software— not alone, but in conjunction with the *problem world domains*—the other parts of the whole system. The end product of the software development is not the software alone: it is the machine and the problem world, and the behaviour that is the product of their interactions. From the point of view of the whole system, the machine makes sense only in its role of monitoring and controlling the problem world. Without knowledge of the problem world and the requirement, the machine must appear as an entirely arbitrary device, imposing an inexplicably obscure and complex regime on the electrical and magnetic phenomena at its ports.

The same perspective is necessary when we consider the decomposition of a system into its constituent components. A component of a system is not a software module, a fragment of the machine in the system: it is an assemblage whose parts are a fragment of the machine, a fragment of the problem world, and a fragment of the system requirement. Conceptually, each component has its own machine, interacting with some subset of the problem domains in the physical world and responsible for satisfying some part of the requirement of the whole system. The problem domains of the components are not, in general, disjoint: each domain can play different roles in different components, each of the components depending on different properties of all or part of the same domain. (This multiplicity of roles of a problem world domains is no different in a car. Different properties of the earth's atmosphere play their parts in the functioning of the tyres, the engine cooling system, the air conditioning, the fuel injection and combustion, and the aerodynamic performance of the body.)

Nor are the component machines themselves likely to remain disjoint in the software as it is finally implemented: in addition to communicating by shared problem domains, they will need to communicate within the machine, and they will certainly contend for shared computer resources such as RAM and disk access. Furthermore, software is intangible and malleable, and component machines can be dismembered, recombined and reconstituted almost at will. The system requirement, also, is decomposed into requirements of the individual components. This decomposition, too, is not disjoint: the component requirements can interfere with each other in many ways, including cooperation, but not excluding outright conflict.

The general conception of such components can be illustrated, superficially, in the context of a system to control the lifts in an office building. The overall purpose of the system is to provide convenient, efficient and safe lift service in response to users' requests. The requirement of convenience and efficiency can be separated from the requirement of safety. The lift_service component operates the electrical and mechanical equipment to provide service in response to users' requests. The lift_safety component continually monitors the behaviour of the equipment, including its reactions to the commands issued by lift_service, to detect any evidence that the equipment has developed a fault, whereupon the lift_safety component ensures user safety, for example, by applying the emergency brake to lock the lift in the shaft to prevent it from falling freely. Another component, lobby_display, may be responsible for maintaining the display in the ground floor lobby that shows the current positions of the lifts.

We may also suppose that for convenience and efficiency it is necessary to apply different priorities at different times—for example, distinguishing the traffic demand patterns of weekends from weekdays, and weekday morning, evening and lunchtime rush hours from other times. The priorities must be specified by the building manager, changed when necessary, and appropriately applied by the machine in scheduling responses to competing requests. In a decomposition of our original *lift_service* component, we may now recognise two components: *edit_ priority*, which is the specification and editing of priority schemes by the manager, and *priority_lift_service*, which is the provision of lift service in accordance with the currently chosen scheme. These two components share a newly introduced domain: the data structure *schemes*, whose values represent the edited priority schemes.

For the whole system, the *schemes* data structure is a local variable of the undecomposed machine; but for each of the two components, it is a part of the component's problem world. The problem domains for *edit_priority* are *manager* and *schemes*; for *priority_lift_service* they are *schemes* together with the electrical and mechanical lift equipment, the request buttons, the floors and the users. Introducing the *schemes* data structure has allowed the *priority_lift_service* function to be decoupled from the *edit_priority* function. The introduction of the data structure exploits the characteristic power of computers to store and manipulate data. Its introduction is analogous to the introduction of the propeller shaft in a car with front engine and rear wheel drive. The propeller shaft both connects and decouples the engine and rear axle components. It separates the function of converting fuel energy into rotary motion from the function of applying rotary motion to the wheels; it also forms a common subcomponent, conveying the rotary motion from one to the other.

This briefly sketched decomposition also illustrates how the same problem domain plays different roles in different components, the components relying on different—and even mutually contradictory—domain properties. For example, for the *priority_lift_service* component the lift equipment must be assumed to be functioning correctly: when the machine sets the direction *up* and turns the motor *on*, the lift rises in the shaft; when the lift car reaches a floor the corresponding floor sensor is set *on*; and so on. These are the properties necessary for provision of the service to users. For the *lift_safety* component, however, the lift equipment may possibly be faulty, and its various failure modes are associated with phenomena that the machine can monitor: if the motor is not functioning, the lift car does not rise when expected, and the floor sensor at the departure floor remains set *on*; if the hoist cable has broken the lift moves downwards at increasing speed; and so on. The *lift_safety* component is concerned with the whole range of equipment faults, all of which the *priority_lift_service* component properly ignores. The decomposition allows the different properties of each problem domain to be considered in the design of the component to which they are relevant.

This approach to system decomposition is the central theme of the problem frames technique [Jackson00]. It is radical in two ways. First, it is radical because it aims to address, explicitly, questions that lie at the root of the system and its requirement. What is the system's purpose? How can this purpose be structured for clearer understanding? How can different purposes be composed and, if necessary, reconciled? What monitoring and control behaviour must the machine exhibit for each individual purpose? How can these behaviours be composed into a coherent overall behaviour? The approach aims to allow the developer to address these questions without premature concern for the eventual programming and implementation of the component machines.

Second, it is radical because it is geared to the needs of radical, rather than normal, design. That is, its primary use is as a tool for the developer who does not already know how to solve the problem. If the problem is already the object of a normal, accepted, artifact design, the questions asked by the problem frames approach should already been addressed, and satisfactory answers embodied, by the normal design: they should not be asked again for the design task in hand. The developer of a system embodying a subproblem that perfectly fits the assumptions of the normal Model-View-Controller pattern should not reconsider the design from first principles: a satisfactory design is already available. The designers of the earliest motor cars tried many different positions for the driver: sitting sideways; sitting on the near side; sitting in the centre; even perched high at the back of the car, like the driver of a horse-drawn hansom cab. A designer today who considers anything other than the standard position—in the front on the off-side, facing forwards—would be engaging in gratuitously radical design, 'rethinking the motor car', or designing a 'concept car', aiming to question the established standard design rather than to accept and exploit it. The consequences of such an innovation cannot be dependably predicted.

The radical character of the approach does not disqualify it completely, even if the design task is substantially normal. As Vincenti says [Vincenti93] of aircraft design:

"Whether design at a given location in the [component] hierarchy is normal or radical is a separate matter—normal design can (and usually does) prevail throughout, though radical design can be encountered at any level."

One place in software development where radical design tasks are commonplace is in the composition of components. Even if the components themselves are objects of normal design, their composition may pose an entirely new problem.

8. Composition of the components

Karl Benz's radical design of 1886 was a remarkable achievement. He had solved many difficult problems in the development of the components, especially in refining the design of the petrol engine that drove the car, with its inlet and exhaust valves, carburettor and high-voltage ignition, and of the differential gear by which power was distributed to the two driven wheels. He was also remarkably successful in arranging all the components together in the space behind the bench seat, finding room for the large horizontal flywheel in a position that allowed the driver to grip the rim and pull it round to start the engine. The result of his work [Benz86] conveys a striking sense of improvisation; but it is brilliantly inventive and successful improvisation.

Designing the composition is not, of course, independent of the design of the individual components to be combined, but it can be considered a distinct, though related, problem; in a more complex component hierarchy, it is not one but several design problems. An important question for any design procedure is: Which of the two tasks—component and composition design—should be carried out first? Or should they proceed wholly or partly in parallel?

In a fully evolved normal design the standardised content of the design embraces both the individual components and their compositions. Further, the interfaces that implement the composition designs have been integrated into the design of the components to be composed. In a modern car, for example, almost every interface between two directly interacting components consists of a unique design in two mating parts, one on each of the interacting components: for example, the exhaust and inlet manifolds fit exactly to the corresponding locations on the engine block, sharing a flat surface, and the engine crankshaft is connected to the transmission by matching internal and external splines. In the evolution of the normal design the components have evolved, not only to fulfil their individual functions, but also to fit more efficiently and exactly with each other. The designer working on a car of normal design has no more need to ponder how the exhaust manifold should be connected to the engine than to consider whether five wheels might be better than four.

In radical design, by contrast, the individual components are not well understood at the outset, and the problems that will be posed by the design of their composition cannot be reliably anticipated. It makes sense, therefore, to postpone consideration of the compositions until more is known about the components themselves. The danger that some rework of components design will be needed in the light of the composition design may be judged less than the danger that a top-down design approach will set inappropriate or even impossible contexts for the component designs. Richard Feynman [Ferguson92] contrasted top-down with bottom-up design:

> "In bottom-up design, the components of a system are designed, tested, and if necessary modified before the design of the entire system has been set in concrete. In the top-down mode (invented by the military), the whole system is designed at once, but without resolving the many questions and conflicts that are normally ironed out in a bottom-up design. The whole system is then built before there is time for testing of components. The deficient and incompatible components must then be located (often a difficult problem in itself), redesigned, and rebuilt—an expensive and uncertain procedure."

Premature composition may carry another, larger, penalty than the danger that it will distort the design of the components. The chosen nature of the composition itself may be heavily dependent on the exact functions of the components. In the lift control system, for example, it is necessary to compose the *edit_priority* and the *priority_lift_service* components. Either on explicit command of the building manager, or at a point specified by the new priority *scheme* itself, lift service must switch from the current scheme to the new one. The design of this switching composition will depend on the nature of the permissible schemes. For example, we may consider two possible forms of priority scheme.

The first scheme specifies relative weights to be assigned to each request as a function of the request time, the direction and the floor at which it was issued. Switching between two schemes of this form is relatively straightforward: the old weights already assigned to unsatisfied requests are retained; new assignments will use the new weights. The chief composition concern is then to respect the necessary mutual exclusion between reading the old and writing the new scheme into the local store of the *priority_lift_service* machine. It will be relatively easy to show that the new priorities will take effect incrementally as the outstanding requests carrying the old weights are satisfied.

The second scheme specifies what is in effect an iterative algorithm of the scheduling procedure. Each lift or bank of lifts is assigned to a subset of the floors—for example, to provide express service for heavily used upper floors. Switching between two schemes of this second form is probably more complex. The composition must not only respect the necessary mutual exclusion; it must also such concerns as the treatment of a case in which a lift is currently serving a floor under the old schedule to which it is not assigned under the new schedule. There is much more here than mutual exclusion. If the switchover is not properly designed, there may be such troublesome results as ignored requests issued at a floor, failure to deliver a passenger already in the lift to the floor requested, or even, conceivably, deadlock of the scheduling system when the scheduling system encounters a state in which its behaviour is unspecified. Essentially, the switchover must take place at a point in the execution of the old scheme at which the invariant of the new scheme is also satisfied.

It is also necessary to design the composition of the *priority_lift_service* with the *lift_safety* component. Here there is a clear conflict between the two components' requirements. When a fault is detected while there are outstanding requests, *priority_lift_service* is required to service the requests, but *lift_safety* may be required to lock the lift car in the shaft, preventing further movement, or to take some other, less dramatic, action such as forcing the return of the car to the next floor, opening the doors, and preventing further movement after that. When *lift_safety* detects a fault requiring action, the function of *priority_lift_service* is no longer required, and it is necessary to consider how the system can switch from service mode to safety-action mode.

In summary, the design of a composition will often be most effective in the light of a substantial degree of understanding of the components in their initial, uncomposed, forms.

9. Learning from failure

The capacity to learn from failures is a hallmark of the established engineering branches. As Henry Petroski writes [Petroski94]:

"Engineering advances by proactive and reactive failure analysis, and at the heart of the engineering method is an understanding of failure in all its real and imagined manifestations."

Since failures in the products of the established engineering branches are usually extremely expensive, and often involve actual or potential loss of life, they are frequently examined with the greatest care, and major efforts made to identify the lessons to be learned. Well known examples of such disasters include the 1940 collapse of the Tacoma Narrows Bridge [Holloway99], the mid-air break-up of several Comet 1 aircraft in the early 1950s [Levy92, RAE54], the failure of the Ariane-5 launch in 1996 [Lions96], and the severe injury or death of several patients treated with the Therac-25 radiation therapy system [Leveson93].

The lessons that can be learned from engineering failures are most effective when they are highly specific: lessons that can be associated with a specific design fault in a normally designed artifact are arguably the most effective of all. At first sight, it may seem that more general lessons, being more widely applicable, can spread their benefit more widely. However, generality carries a serious disadvantage. A lesson that applies to everything applies to nothing: even when explicitly articulated in a disaster enquiry report it is likely to add only a grain of additional emphasis to what was already known to be good general practice. If the lesson is "documentation should not be an afterthought," few software developers (except perhaps adherents of some of the various schools of agility) would deny its truth; but a lesson like this is blunted by endless repetition until it ceases to be heard at all.

The lessons from the Tacoma Narrows and Comet disasters, by contrast, were very specific and affected engineering design quite specifically. The Tacoma Narrows Bridge collapsed because a moderate wind, of about 40mph, provoked vertical oscillation in the bridge's very slender roadway. The oscillations built up quickly, and in a very short time destroyed the bridge completely. The lesson learned was specifically about suspension bridge roadways and the aerodynamic effects to which they are subject: the roadway was not stiff enough to resist the wind-induced oscillation. The associated lesson about the normal design procedure was clear: the designer, Leon Moisseiff, had made the mistake of taking account of horizontal, but not of vertical, oscillation. After the disaster, its lessons were taken to heart. Steps were taken to strengthen other bridges whose roadways were thought to be too slender or too shallow. The normal design discipline for suspension bridges changed: designers were subsequently expected to check explicitly for vertical roadway oscillation.

In the case of the Comet 1, the aircraft broke up because of metal fatigue. In an enormously expensive investigation, pieces of one of the destroyed aircraft were recovered from the sea bed and reassembled in a hangar in a research establishment. The tentative results of that part of the investigation were then confirmed by destructive tests on another sample of the same design. The investigation showed that the cause was metal fatigue in the fuselage, and that the fatigue cracks had started at the corners of the square passenger windows. Again, the normal design, in this case, of pressurised jet aircraft, was specifically modified: no such aircraft today has square corners in the passenger windows or cargo apertures. The normal design discipline, too, was affected.

It was recognised that fuselage tests for torsional rigidity and for resistance to pressurisation and depressurisation must be carried out in combination: separate testing had been proved insufficient.

The Tacoma and Comet investigations were concerned with failures of the physical fabric of the engineered products. When the failure is attributable to software, it is harder for the investigation to reach very specific conclusions and to offer very specific lessons. Partly, this is because software failures, unlike physical failures, often leave no trace in the resulting wreckage. As Donald MacKenzie writes [MacKenzie94]:

"A more particular problem concerns what this data set suggests are the two most important 'technical' causes of computer-related accidental death: electromagnetic interference and software error. A broken part will often survive even a catastrophic accident, such as an air crash, sufficiently well for investigators to be able to determine its causal role in the sequence of events. Typically, neither electromagnetic interference nor software error leave physical traces of this kind. Their role can often only be inferred from experiments seeking to reproduce the conditions leading to an accident."

Of equal, or perhaps greater, importance, is the fact that in most cases the software under investigation was not the object of normal design. The investigators, even when they can identify defects in the software as a contributory cause of failure, cannot express their conclusions in sufficiently specific terms to be confident of affecting either the usual design practices or an identifiable, currently accepted, standard design that has proved dangerous. Instead, they must content themselves with generalities that, if the truth is told, are unlikely to have a substantial effect. The case of the Ariane-5 launch, whose failure was entirely attributed to software error, is to some extent an exception. The investigation conclusions contained some general recommendations such as "Include external participants in reviews" and "Pay the same attention to justification documents as to code;" but they also included some quite specific recommendations for designers of software of the Ariane-5 class:

"✦ Failing sensors should not cease to transmit, but should send best-effort data.
  ✦ Alignment functions should be switched off immediately after lift-off.
  ✦ Design of the switchover between on-board computers needed more care.
  ✦ More data should be sent to telemetry on any component failure.
  ✦ Trajectory data should be included in specifications and in test requirements."

These specific recommendations are possible only because the terms used—'failing sensors', 'alignment functions', 'computer switchover', 'data sent to telemetry', and 'trajectory data'—have specific meanings, referring to specific parts of their designs, that designers working on this class of software will certainly understand.

The Therac-25 disasters also were essentially attributable to software failures. In their excellent unofficial investigation [Leveson93] of these failures, Nancy Leveson and Clark Turner identified specific software errors that had certainly played a major, or even decisive, role in the failures. Yet, in the absence of even a vestigial normal design for software to control radiation therapy equipment, they were compelled to content themselves with identifying 'basic software engineering principles that apparently were violated with the Therac-25':

"◆ Documentation should not be an afterthought.
 ◆ Software quality assurances practices and standards should be established.
 ◆ Designs should be kept simple.
 ◆ Ways to get information about errors—for example, software audit trails—should be designed into the software from the beginning.
 ◆ The software should be subjected to extensive testing and formal analysis at the module and software level: system testing alone is not adequate."

A reiterated general principle has value, especially when its application is in the hands of managers who can mandate improvements in development practice; but its effect for a practising design engineer is dissipated by its very generality. It calls for a degree of culture change across the whole range—or, at least, across an unspecified segment—of software development, and a quality change across the whole range of designed software. For a practising engineer, a lesson directly associated with a specific design artifact has a more restricted, but far stronger and more certain effect. That can be seen today by every airline passenger, in the frustrating rounded shape of the window that obscures the view of the terrain over which they are flying. Unlike too many software design mistakes, the design mistake of square corners for aeroplane windows has not been repeated.

10. Harder and softer systems

What may be called the 'softer' systems are concerned with business and administration—which are primarily human activities—rather than with lift equipment and radiotherapy devices and chemical plants. For these systems the emphasis on the physical world, as the basis for suggesting analogies with the established branches of engineering, may seem misplaced.

Not so. It is true that such systems are rarely safety-critical; and in most cases some part of the required functionality may be very loosely textured and imprecise, admitting wide variations in quality and exactness without causing failure or even significant difficulty. For example, some of the functionality in an e-commerce system may be of this kind. If the collaborative filtering doesn't work well, or the purchase recommendations offered to regular customers are poorly calculated, the company will make less profit than it could, but otherwise no great harm is done. But this kind of looseness is exceptional. Some softer systems are definitely safety-critical: for example, a system to maintain criminal records and make them available to the appropriate authorities in the appropriate circumstances; or a system to manage the prescription and delivery of patients' drugs in a large hospital. The core of the functionality in a softer system is no less demanding for the software developer than the core functionality in a 'harder' system: the system that the hospital pharmacist finds difficult, inconvenient and confusing to use is exhibiting exactly the same kind of defect as the avionics system that is ill-adapted to the needs of the pilot.

The characteristic difficulty in the design of any system arises because the problem world—whether a hospital pharmacy or an aeroplane—is not a formal system. This, above all, distinguishes a software-intensive system from a program whose function is to compute about a formal abstraction, untainted by a real semantics in the non-formal, physical and human world. An innovative program to factorise very large integers, for example, is not concerned with the purpose of the factorisation, or with what the integers may denote. It is concerned with pure mathematics, in the sense explained [Weyl40] by Hermann Weyl:

> "We now come to the decisive step of mathematical abstraction: we forget about what the symbols stand for. [The mathematician] need not be idle; there are many operations he may carry out with these symbols, without ever having to look at the things they stand for."

In dealing with the integers, which are a mathematical domain, we can state exact theorems to which there are no exceptions. For example: "If the sum of the digits of an integer's decimal expression is evenly divisible by 3, then the integer itself is evenly divisible by 3." There is no approximation here, and no exceptions. By contrast, if we try to state a theorem about the behaviour of the lift equipment we will find that it must always be hedged around with caveats: the power supply may be interrupted; a sensor may stick on; the drive gears may be worn; the hoist cable may break. The same is true, for example, of the problem world of a system to administer social benefits: a recipient may change gender; a benefit payment sent by post may be delayed or lost; an immigrant recipient may have no birth certificate and be unable to state their date of birth; there may be family relationships between recipients that do not conform to the assumptions on which the entitlement regulations were framed. It is never possible to exhaust the problem world's capacity to produce new counterexamples to the assumptions on which the system design is based.

Dealing adequately with the problem world of any system, then, is not a matter of discovering and proving formal theorems. Rather, it is a practical matter of constructing descriptions that are formal enough to allow tentative formal reasoning and analysis, and close enough to the problem world reality to accommodate all eventualities except those that have a tolerable combination of low occurrence probability and limited consequential damage. This practical necessity is close—though not identical—to the necessity that bears on engineers in the established branches. In both softer and harder systems, the development of artifact specialisation, with the evolving normal design that each artifact specialisation supports, must play the central role in addressing this practical engineering necessity. As a normal artifact design evolves, it comes to accommodate more and more of the important eventualities in its problem world as lessons are learned from failures.

11. A concluding personal remark

In this paper much has been said about the practice of engineering in the traditional branches. The reader should not infer that the author has either the education or the practical experience of an engineer. What is asserted here about engineering is drawn, often very directly, from the statements of those engineers who have written about their profession for a non-professional readership. Foremost among them is Walter Vincenti. His deep and brilliant book, *What Engineers Know and How They Know It*, should be required reading for all thoughtful software engineers. Its lessons, drawn from aeronautical engineering in the period from the earliest years to the arrival of the turbojet revolution in the later 1940s, are not exhausted after many readings. I remain very grateful to Tom Maibaum for introducing me several years ago to this wonderful book.

Acknowledgements

Daniel Jackson, Mary Shaw and Pamela Zave kindly read an earlier draft of this paper and made several very helpful suggestions for improvements.

References

[Benington56]   H D Benington; Production of Large Computer Programs; in *Proc ONR Symposium on Advanced Program Methods for Digital Computers*, June 1956, pages 15-27. Reprinted with additional comment in *IEEE Annals of the History of Computing*, Volume 5 Number 4, October 1983, pages 299-310.

[Benz86]   http://www.conceptcarz.com/vehicle/z10986/Benz-Motorwagen-Replica.aspx (accessed 23 October 2008).

[Buxton70]   J N Buxton and B Randell eds; Software Engineering Techniques; *Report on a conference sponsored by the NATO Science Committee*, Rome, Italy, 27th to 31st October 1969; NATO, April 1970.

[Caminer97]   David Tresman Caminer OBE; LEO and its Applications: The Beginning of Business Computing; *Computer Journal* Volume 40 Number 10, pages 585-597, 1997.

[Constant80]   Edward W Constant; *The Origins of the Turbojet Revolution*; The Johns Hopkins University Press, Baltimore 1980.

[Everett83]   Robert R Everett, Charles A Zraket, Herbert D Benington; SAGE—A Data Processing System for Air Defense; *IEEE Annals of the History of Computing*, Volume 5 Number 4, pages 330-339, Oct-Dec, 1983.

[Ferguson92]   Eugene S Ferguson; *Engineering and the Mind's Eye*; MIT Press, 1992.

[Holloway99]   C Michael Holloway; From Bridges and Rockets, Lessons for Software Systems; *Proceedings of the 17th International System Safety Conference*, Orlando, Florida, pages 598-607, August 1999.

[Humphrey00]   W S Humphrey; The Personal Software Process: Status and Trends; *IEEE Software* Volume 17 Number 6, November/December 2000, page72.

[Jackson00]   Michael Jackson; *Problem Frames: Analysing and Structuring Software Development Problems*; Addison-Wesley, 2001.

[Kraft77]   Philip Kraft; Programmers and Managers: The Routinization of Computer Programming in the United States; Springer-Verlag, 1977, pages 57-58.

[Leveson93]   Nancy G Leveson and Clark S Turner; An Investigation of the Therac-25 Accidents; *IEEE Computer* Volume 26 Number 7, pages 18-41, July 1993.

[Levy92]   Matthys Levy and Mario Salvadori; *Why Buildings Fall Down: How Structures Fail*; W W Norton and Co, 1992.

[Lions96]   ARIANE 5 Flight 501 Failure; Report by the Inquiry Board; The Chairman of the Board: Prof. J L Lions; Paris 19 July 1996; available at: http://sunnyday.mit.edu/accidents/Ariane5accidentreport.html (accessed 23 October 2008).

[MacKenzie94]   Donald MacKenzie; Computer-Related Accidental Death: An Empirical Exploration; *Science and Public Policy* Volume 21 Number 4, pages 233-248, 1994.

[Naur69]   Peter Naur and Brian Randell eds; Software Engineering: Report on a conference sponsored by the NATO Science Committee, Garmisch, Germany, 7th to 11th October 1968; NATO, January 1969.

[Parnas78]   D L Parnas; Some Software Engineering Principles; in *Structured Analysis and Design*, Infotech, 1978.

[Petroski94]   Henry Petroski; *Design Paradigms: Case Histories of Error and Judgment in Engineering*; Cambridge University Press, 1994.

[RAE54]   Royal Aircraft Establishment; Report on Comet Accident Investigation; Ministry of Supply, 1954.

[Rogers83]   G F C Rogers; *The Nature of Engineering: A Philosophy of Technology*; Palgrave Macmillan, 1983; (ISBN: 0333347412).

[Shaw90]   Mary Shaw;. Prospects for an Engineering Discipline of Software; *IEEE Software*, November 1990, pages 15-24.

[Vincenti93]   Walter G Vincenti; *What Engineers Know and How They Know It: Analytical Studies from Aeronautical History*; The Johns Hopkins University Press, Baltimore, paperback edition, 1993.

[Weyl40]   Herman Weyl; The Mathematical Way of Thinking; address given at the Bicentennial Conference at the University of Pennsylvania, 1940.

Part 2
JSP and JSD

Chapter 3

Getting It Wrong
—A Cautionary Tale*

Michael Jackson

There is a very simple kind of programming problem that appears everywhere in business data processing—you have a serial file of transactions, sorted into ascending order by some group identifier, and you have to print a summary showing the total for each group. It's the kind of problem everyone knows about—at least everyone who has been around in business programming for more than a month or two. Well, this story is about a programmer named Fred, who was such a novice that he hadn't seen the problem before. So when it came his way he just did a nice simple piece of top-down design, and arrived at the following structured pseudocode:

```
PA:   open INFILE; display 'SUMMARY'; read INFILE;
      do while not eof-INFILE
            if new group
                  end old group;
                  start new group with record data
            else add record data to group
            endif;
            read INFILE
      enddo;
      display 'END SUMMARY';
      close INFILE
end PA;
```

Now you, my readers, can probably see at once that something here is not quite right; but Fred was only a novice. So he went right ahead and coded his

---

*This is an edited version of a cautionary tale used in Michael Jackson Systems Ltd program design courses from about 1973 and reproduced in: John Cameron; *JSP & JSD: The Jackson Approach to Software Development*; IEEE CS Press, 1989.

solution in COBOL, and compiled it, linked it, and ran it on some test data. What came out was a little surprising (to our hero, though not to us, who are more experienced):

```
SUMMARY
..V/* V..K$/K
A172632 +15
A195923 -60
A198564 0
...
Z749321 +8755
END SUMMARY
```

What, he wondered, could that curious second line be? In quite a short time he understood. It was, of course, the effect of ending the old group before the first group—only there was no old group before the first group. But how to make it disappear? Luckily, he knew his COBOL quite well. The first part of the curious line was of course, the group identifier, and could be removed by setting a *VALUE* clause in the *WORKING-STORAGE* item

```
02 PREVIOUS-RECORD-ID PIC X(7) VALUE SPACES.
```

The right-hand part of the line was the total, and required slightly more subtle treatment:

```
02 GROUP-TOTAL PIC S9(6)
      VALUE ZERO
      BLANK WHEN ZERO.
```

After a recompilation he reran the test, and was delighted to see:

```
SUMMARY

A172632 +15
A195923 -60
A198564
...
A200135 -157
Z749321 +8755
END SUMMARY
```

He was poring happily over this printout, when his manager happened to come by. "What's this?" asked the manager, pointing to the total for group A198564, "why is the total blank?" "That's zero," said the programmer. "No it isn't," said the manager, "it's blank, and I want it to print a zero, not a blank." Fred, although a novice, was very quick to learn the tricks of the programmer's trade, and immediately replied "well, there are technical reasons why it has to print as blank." This was a testing moment for the manager. He might have made the catastrophic mistake of asking "what technical reasons?" But he was cleverer than that; so he just said, "technical reasons or no technical reasons, it must print as zero."

So it was back to the drawing board for Fred. Luckily, he happened to overhear one of his colleagues at lunch talking about something called a "first-time switch." He had never heard of such a thing before, but, being very intelligent, he saw at once what the name implied and how such a device could help him. That afternoon he added one to his program:

```
PA:    open INFILE; display 'SUMMARY'; read INFILE;
       move 0 to switch1;
       do while not eof-INFILE
            if new group
                 if switch1 = 1
                      end old group
                 else move 1 to switch1
                 endif;
                 start new group with record data
            else add record data to group
            endif;
            read INFILE
       enddo;
       display 'END SUMMARY';
       close INFILE
end PA;
```

When he ran it again, the output looked really fine, and the program went into production running. It ran happily for six months, and then one day a clerk from the user department came to see our hero. "Look," said the clerk, pointing to the end of that week's report, "there's no total for the last group." Well, I expect that all of you readers knew all along that this was going to happen: after all, the end-group and start-group operations had originally been paired, and the introduction of switch1 removed one of the end-groups; so there must have been a group that was being started but not ended. And indeed there was, and it was the last group in the file.

Of course, the error had been there on every one of the twenty-five reports produced since the program had been put into production, but no one had noticed it before. There's a lot of computer printout that nobody reads in most installations. Fred, of course, didn't like to say anything about this to the clerk, so he just said "OK, I'll fix it." Why had he not noticed the error in testing? Really, because he was too conscientious. He had decided to test the program thoroughly, by using the whole of last year's actual data as test data. This is a special kind of testing, called "volume testing" or "soak testing". It's a special kind of testing because you run the program on the input, but you don't look at the output. After all, who could look through a pile of paper five inches high? What you do when you get five inches of output is this: you throw away the front two sheets, because they're JCL, which no ordinary mortal understands (experts sometimes look to see that the system completion code is zero, but not everyone's an expert);

you check to see that there is no core dump; you look at the first and last lines; you spot-check a few of the totals; then you riffle through the whole five inches by raising the edge of the pile and letting the sheets peel off against your thumb, to make sure that if there is anything really nasty, like forty consecutive pages on which every line is printed with zeros all across the page, it will force itself on your attention. And that's all. So the error had remained undetected.

But it was very easily fixed. Near the end of the program the programmer inserted the statements to end the last group:

```
      ...
            read INFILE
      enddo;
      end last group;
      display 'END SUMMARY';
      close INFILE
end PA;
```

All went well for the next 17 months. And then the program showed that it was sensitive to something you wouldn't have expected a program to be sensitive to: the US Bicentennial celebrations. What happened was that the company gave everyone a week's vacation; the next Monday morning they came back to work and ran the program, just like they ran it every Monday morning. What came out was:

```
SUMMARY
$$..V/*  ..D>>K./
END SUMMARY
```

It was immediately obvious that something was wrong. There had been no transactions the previous week, so there were no groups, and the mystery line was, of course, the result of ending the last group—only there wasn't a last group. But again the problem was easily solved.

Fred, more experienced now, was tempted to do something clever with switch1, but he resisted the temptation. He had heard about "defensive programming." Defensive programming is a theory based on the idea that when you are programming you don't have the faintest idea whether what you are doing is right or not, so you ought to do something that won't cause too much harm. In accordance with this admirable theory—whose applicablity in his own case he was beginning to recognise—he resisted the temptation to do something with switch1 and instead introduced switch2:

```
PA;   open INFILE; display 'SUMMARY'; read INFILE;
      move 0 to switch1; move 0 to switch2;
      do while not eof-INFILE
            if new group
                  if switch1 = 1
                        end old group
                  else move 1 to switch1
```

```
                    endif;
                    start new group with record data
              else add record data to group;
                    move 1 to switch2
              endif;
              read INFILE
        enddo;
        if switch2 = 1
              end last group
        endif;
        display 'END SUMMARY';
        close INFILE
end PA;
```

After recompiling, he ran the program again on the empty file and produced the hoped-for result:

```
SUMMARY
END SUMMARY
```

Clearly, his tribulations were at an end. The program ran happily and successfully for the next 19 months, and no complaints were heard.

Then, one day, he was sitting quietly in his programming cubicle—Gerry Weinberg would have had something to say about that, I think—reading the job advertisements, when along came the clerk from the user department. "Look," he said, "the last group has been left off the printout again." And indeed it had. The diagnosis was easy. Somehow the program library had been messed up, and it was an old, incorrect version of the program that had been run that week. But not so. After a couple of days of detective work Fred established beyond doubt that it was the current version that had been run. However, he also established that the program had been recently recompiled with the new version 6 compiler, for which the installation was a field-test site. It must have been the compiler that was at fault! With the help of the systems programmer, Fred went through the object code hexadecimal character by hexadecimal character, and related it to the source code. The job took only nine hours, which they did in one marathon stretch, thus earning a bonus from their appreciative management. But the result was to prove that the object code was a perfectly reasonable compilation of the up-to-date cobol source text! Only one possibility was left: it had to be a transient error in the hardware or the operating system. Now, people don't like to come to that conclusion if they can avoid it; but I have to say that I have never found a programmer who, in private conversation, alone with only one fellow programmer, could not remember at least one occasion in the past when an obviously correct program did something funny that had to be put down to that cause. And this seemed to be one of those occasions.

Certainly the error hadn't occurred before—at least, since the "end last group" statements were added to the program. And it didn't happen again.

However, something funny did happen recently. The clerk from the user department came to see the programmer. "I've been wondering," he said "about that week we lost the last group from the printout. I got hold of the card input—which we always keep for a few months—and I discovered that there were exactly 843 cards."

"So?" said the programmer. "Well," the clerk went on, "there were 842 group totals on the printout that week, and there should have been 843." "I don't see that that's relevant," said the programmer, "but it's kind of you to mention it. Thank you for taking the trouble to tell me." That night he took the program listing home secretly, and looked it over carefully. Suddenly the answer dawned on him. Of course! If there were 843 cards and 843 groups, then each group contained exactly one card; so the condition "new group" would be true on every card, and it would always be the "if" that was executed and never the "else." But the instruction to set switch2 was only in the "else" clause! So switch 2 was never set on, and the last group was never ended.

The problem, once identified, was easily solved. In accordance with the principles of defensive programming and incremental change, another statement "move 1 to switch2" was added to the first clause of the "if-else", leaving the original statement untouched in the "else" clause. So the program was now:

```
PA:    open INFILE; display 'SUMMARY'; read INFILE;
       move 0 to switch1; move 0 to switch2;
       do while not eof-INFILE
             if new group
                   move 1 to switch2;
                   if switch1 = 1
                         end old group
                   else move 1 to switch1
                   endif;
                   start new group with record data;
                   move 1 to switch2;
             else add record data to group;
                   move 1 to switch2;
             endif;
             read INFILE
       enddo;
       if switch2 = 1
             end last group
       endif;
       display 'END SUMMARY';
       close INFILE
end PA;
```

We can be confident that the program is now perfect and correct. But, of course, it has been running only for three months in its new form, and I will let you know if there are any new developments.

And the moral? Well it's this. The basic structure of the program, as originally designed, looks like this:

The program structure is a loop over single records; the condition "new group"

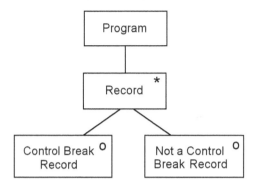

in the pseudocode tests each record to determine whether it is a 'control break' record or not. This structure is wrong. Not inferior; not inelegant; just plain wrong.

Here's why. The difficulties were all caused by the "start group" and "end group" instructions. Now, how often should we start or end a group? Why, once per group! Where, in this program structure, is there a component that processes each group? There is no such component, and the "start group" and "end group" instructions cannot therefore be correctly allocated to the program structure. That's what all the difficulty was about.

Now, I'm sure all of you readers are experienced folk, and you wouldn't have made these mistakes — not, at least, on this small and well-known problem, and certainly not if you have read *Principles of Program Design*. But I know some very experienced programmers who have made just this kind of mistake on bigger and more obscure programs; in fact, a lot of the mistakes they make are of exactly this kind—having the wrong program structure. But I don't suppose that any of those programmers are reading this cautionary tale, are they?

Chapter 4

JSP in Perspective

Michael Jackson

1. Introduction

JSP is a method of program design. Its origins lie in the data processing systems that grew up in the 1960s, when reliable, relatively cheap, and adequately powerful computers first became generally available. The fundamental abstraction in JSP is the sequential data stream. Originally, this abstraction was inspired and motivated by the sequential tape files that characterised data processing in the 1960s, but it quickly became clear that it had a much wider applicability. Today the JSP design method is valuable for such applications as embedded software and handling network protocols.

JSP arose from efforts by a small group of people in a data processing consultancy company to improve their programming practices, and to make their programs more reliable and easier to understand and to modify. In 1971 it became the core product of a very small new company, Michael Jackson Systems Limited, which offered development services, training courses, consultancy, and—from 1975—software to support JSP design of COBOL programs. The name JSP—'Jackson Structured Programming'—was coined by the company's Swedish licensee in 1974. In the commercial world, IBM had appropriated the name 'Structured Programming' in the early 1970s, and Yourdon Inc started offering courses in 'Structured Design' around 1974. A distinctive name was a commercial necessity. It was also technically appropriate to choose a distinctive and proprietary name: the JSP method was very different from its competitors.

2. 1960s data processing systems

Data processing systems of the early and middle 1960s were chiefly concerned with the processing of sequential files held on magnetic tape. Reliable tape drives had become widely available and commonly used in the late 1950s; exchangeable disk drives first became available when IBM introduced the 1311 drive in 1963. Disk was a very limited and expensive medium compared to tape. At 1965 prices a 1311 disk pack cost about £200 and held 2 million characters; a 2400-foot tape reel cost about £7 and held between 20 million and 60 million characters. For large files, which might contain millions of records, tape was the only realistic choice. Most data processing systems had large files.

Because tape is an inherently sequential medium, updating a single record of a master file could be done only by reading the whole file and copying it, updated, to a new tape. This very slow process was economical only if many records were to be updated, so tape systems were almost inevitably batch systems. Transactions— for example, payments received—were recorded daily or weekly on a transaction tape file. The transaction file was then sorted into the same sequence as the file of master records—for example, customer accounts—to which the transactions were to be applied; it was then used in a batch update program to produce a new version of the master file whose records reflected the effects of the transactions.

It was always necessary to process the whole master file and to produce a complete new version, even if the batch contained transactions for very few master records. Processing a file that occupied one full tape might take an hour or more; some master files occupied dozens of tapes. Even worse, there might be several master files to be processed—for example, customers, orders, invoices, and products. The transaction file would then be sorted successively into the different sequences of the different master files, executing a batch update program for each master file and carrying partial results forward to the next update program in a transfer file that would also require to be sorted. To minimise processing time master files were amalgamated where possible. For example, the orders, instead of being held in a master file of their own, might be held in the customer master file, the order records for each customer following the customer record in the combined file. These choices resulted in a database with a hierarchical structure, held on magnetic tape: this was the kind of database for which IBM's database management system IMS was originally designed around 1966 in cooperation with North American Rockwell [Blackman 98].

3. The basic JSP idea

A common design fault in batch update programs was failure to ensure that the program kept the files correctly synchronised as it traversed their hierarchical structures. A read operation performed at the wrong point in program execution might read beyond the record to which the next transaction should be applied. The result would be erroneous processing of that transaction and, often, of the following transactions and master records. Another common design fault was failure to take account of empty sets—for example, of a customer with no outstanding orders. How could one design a program that would not have such faults?

In commercial and industrial programming in the 1960s, the program design question was chiefly posed in terms of 'modular programming': What was the best decomposition for each particular program? The primary focus was on the decomposition structure, not on encapsulation. A 1968 conference [Barnett 68] dedicated to modular programming attracted the participation of George Mealy, the computer scientist who gave his name to Mealy machines. The Structured Design ideas of coupling and cohesion [Stevens 74, Myers 76] took shape as an approach to modularity: it was claimed that a good design could be achieved by ensuring that the modules have high cohesion and low coupling.

The fundamental idea of JSP was very different: program structure should be dictated by the structure of its input and output data streams [Jackson 75]. If one of the sequential files processed by the program consisted of customer groups, each group consisting of a customer record followed by some number of order records, each of which is either a simple order or an urgent order, then the program should have the same structure: it should have a program part that processes the file, with a subpart to process each customer group, and that subpart should itself have one subpart that processes the customer record, and so on. The execution sequence of the parts should mirror the sequence of records and record groups in the file. Program parts could be very small and were not, in general, separately compiled.

The resulting structure can be represented in a JSP structure diagram, as in Figure 1. The diagram is a tree representation of the regular expression

(CustRecord (SimpleOrder | UrgentOrder) *) *

in which the expression and all of its all subexpressions are labelled. Iteration is shown by the star in the iterated subexpression; selection is shown by the circle in each alternative.

The structure is simultaneously the structure of the file and the structure of a program to process the file. As a data structure it may be verbalised like this:

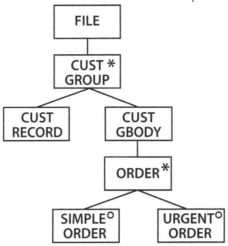

Figure 1. Structure of a File and a Program

"The *File* consists of zero or more *Customer Groups*. Each *Customer Group* consists of a *Customer Record* followed by a *Customer Group Body*. Each *Customer Group Body* consists of zero or more *Orders*. Each *Order* is either a *Simple Order* or an *Urgent Order*."

As a program structure it may be understood to mean:

```
program =
    { /* process file */
      while (another customer group) do
      { /* process customer group */
        process customer record;
        { /* process customer group body /*
          while (another order) do
          { /* process order */
            if simple order then
            { /* process simple order */ }
            else
            { /* process urgent order */ }

    } } } }
```

4. Multiple streams

The JSP program design method insisted that the program structure should reflect all the stream data structures, not just one. Its first steps, then, are to identify the data structure of each file processed by the program, and to form a program structure that embodies them all. Such a program structure allows the designer to ensure easily that program execution will interleave all the file traversals correctly and will keep them appropriately synchronised. Figure 2 shows an example of a program structure based on two data structures.

For brevity, the example is stylised and trivial. The program processes an input file *IN* and and output file *OUT*. The successive *OPAIRs* of *OUT* are constructed from the successive *IPAIRs* of *IN*: that is, the *IPAIRs* and *OPAIRs* 'correspond functionally'. Similarly, the *d* and *e* records are computed from the *b* and *c* records respectively: that is, the *b* and *d* records correspond and the *c* and *e* records

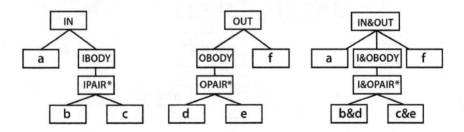

Figure 2. Two File Structures and a Program Structure

correspond. In this trivial example it is easily seen that the program structure embodies both of the file structures exactly. In more realistic examples, a program structure embodying all the file structures can be achieved by permissible rewritings of the file structures. Two such rewritings are shown in Figure 3.

The data structure A1 can be rewritten as A2, and A2 as A3. Permissible rewritings preserve the set of leaf sequences defined by the structure: A1, A2 and A3 all define the sequence <B,C,D>. They must also preserve the intermediate nodes of each structure: A2 may not be rewritten as A1, because the node CD would be lost. The eventual program structure must have at least one component corresponding to each component of each data structure.

5. Operations and conditions

The prime advantage of a program structure that embodies all the file data structures, respecting the correspondences among their parts, is that it provides an obviously correct place in the program text for each operation that must be executed. It also clarifies the conditions needed as guards in iteration (loop) and selection (if-else or case) constructs.

The operations to be executed are file traversal operations, such as *open, close, read* and *write*, and other operations that compute output record values from values of input records. For example, in the trivial illustration of Figure 2 the operations may be:

open IN, read IN, close IN, open OUT, write OUT record, close OUT, d := f(b),

and so on. Each operation must appear in the program component that processes the operation's data. The *read* operations are a special case. Assuming that the input files can be parsed by looking ahead one record, there must be one *read* operation following the *open* at the beginning of the file, and one at the end of each component that completely processes one input record. So, for the example of Figure 2, the operations must be placed as shown in Figure 4.

The correspondence of program and data structures, together with the scheme of looking ahead one record, makes it easy to determine the iteration and selection conditions. For example, the condition on the iteration component *I&OBODY* is

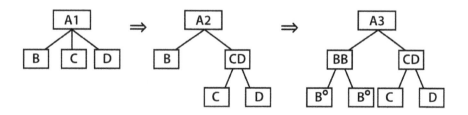

Figure 3. Examples of Regular Expression Rewritings

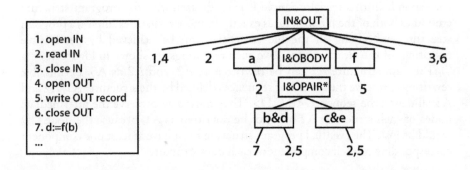

Figure 4. Placing Operations in Program Structure

while (another *I&OPAIR*)

which translates readily into

while (*IN* record is *b*)

in which 'IN record' refers to the record that has been read ahead and is currently in the IN buffer.

6. Difficulties

The development procedures of a method should be closely matched to specific properties of the problems it can be used to solve. The development procedures of basic JSP, as they have been described here, require the problem to possess at least these two properties:

+ the data structures of the input and output files, and the correspondences among their data components, are such that a single program structure can embody them all; and
+ each input file can be unambiguously parsed by looking ahead just one record.

Absence of a necessary property is immediately recognisable by difficulty in completing a part of the JSP design procedure. If the file structures do not correspond appropriately it is impossible to design a correct program structure: this difficulty is called a *structure clash*. If an input file can not be parsed by single look ahead it is impossible to write all the necessary conditions on the program's iterations and selections: this is a *recognition difficulty*.

Although these difficulties are detected during the basic JSP design procedure, they do not indicate a limitation of JSP. They indicate inherent complications in the problem itself, that can not be ignored but must be dealt with somehow. In JSP they are dealt with by additional techniques within the JSP method.

7. Structure clashes

There are three kinds of structure clash: *interleaving clash, ordering clash*, and *boundary clash*.

In an interleaving clash, data groups that occur sequentially in one structure correspond functionally to groups that are interleaved in another structure. For example, the input file of a program may consist of chronologically ordered records of calls made at a telephone exchange; the program must produce a printed output report of the same calls arranged chronologically within subscriber. The 'subscriber groups' that occur successively in the printed report are interleaved in the input file.

In an ordering clash, corresponding data item instances are differently ordered in two structures. For example, an input file contains the elements of a matrix in row order, and the required output file contains the same elements in column order.

In a boundary clash, two structures have corresponding elements occurring in the same order, but the elements are differently grouped in the two structures. The boundaries of the two groupings are not synchronised.

Boundary clashes are surprisingly common. Here are three well-known examples:

+ The calendar consists of years, each year consisting of a number of days. In one structure the days may be grouped by months, but by weeks in another structure. There is a boundary clash here: the weeks and months can not be synchronised.
+ A chapter of a printed book consists of text lines. In one structure the lines may be grouped by paragraphs, but in another structure by pages. There is a boundary clash because pages and paragraphs can not be synchronised.
+ A file in a low-level file handling system consists of variable-length records, each consisting of between 2 and 2000 bytes. The records must be stored sequentially in fixed blocks of 512 bytes. There is a boundary clash here: the boundaries of the records can not be synchronised with the boundaries of the blocks.

The difficulty posed by a boundary clash is very real. The clash between weeks and months causes endless trouble in accounting: in 1923 the League of Nations set up a Special Committee of Enquiry into the Reform of the Calendar to determine whether the clash could be resolved by adopting a new calendar [Achelis 59]. The clash between records and blocks affected the original IBM OS/360 file-handling software: the 'access method' that could handle the clash— software that supported 'spanned records'—proved the hardest to design and was the last to be delivered.

The JSP technique for dealing with a structure clash is to decompose the original program into two or more programs communicating by intermediate data structures. A boundary clash, for example, requires a decomposition into two programs communicating by an intermediate sequential stream. The structure

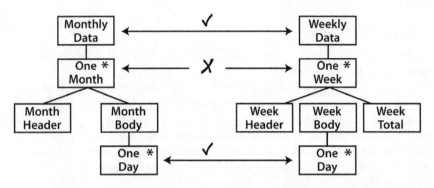

Figure 5. Structures Exhibiting a Boundary Clash

of the intermediate stream is based on the 'highest common factor' of the two clashing structures. For example, an accounting program may have a boundary clash between an input file structured by months and an output file structured by weeks. Figure 5 shows the data structures.

The solution to the difficulty is to decompose the program into two: one program handles the *Months*, producing an intermediate file that is input to a second program that handles the *Weeks*. For the second program the intermediate file structure must have no *Month* component: any necessary information from the *MonthHeader* record must therefore be encoded in the *OneDay* records of the intermediate file.

8. Recognition difficulties

A recognition difficulty is present when an input file can not be unambiguously parsed by single look-ahead. Sometimes the difficulty can be overcome by looking ahead two or more records; sometimes a more powerful technique is necessary.

The two cases are illustrated in Figure 6. The structure on the left can be parsed by looking ahead three records: the beginning of an *AGroup* is recognised when the third of the lookahead records is an *A*. But the structure on the right can not be parsed by any fixed look-ahead. The JSP technique needed for this structure is *backtracking*.

The JSP procedure for the backtracking technique has three steps:

♦ First, the recognition difficulty is simply ignored. The program is designed, and the text for the *AGroup* and *BGroup* components is written, as usual. No condition is written on the *Group* selection component. The presence of the difficulty is marked only by using the keywords *posit* and *admit* in place of *if* and *else*.

♦ Second, a *quit* statement is inserted into the text of the *posit AGroup* component at each point at which it may be detected that the *Group* is, in fact, not an *AGroup*. In this example, the only such point is when the *B* record is encountered. The *quit* statement is a tightly constrained form of GO TO: its meaning is that execution of the *AGroup* component is abandoned and

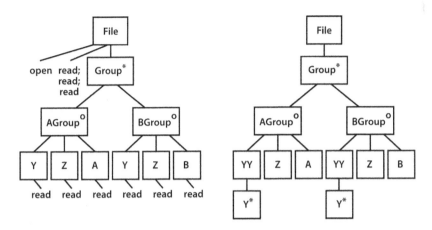

Figure 6. *Structures Requiring Multiple Read-ahead and Backtracking*

control jumps to the beginning of the *admit BGroup* component.

✦ Third, the program text is modified to take account of side-effects: that is, of the side-effects of operations executed in *AGroup* before detecting that the *Group* was in fact a *BGroup*.

9. Program inversion

The JSP solution to structure clash difficulties seems, at first sight, to add yet more sequential programs and intermediate files to systems already overburdened with time-consuming file processing. But JSP provides an implementation technique—*program inversion*—that both overcomes this obstacle and offers other important positive advantages.

The underlying idea of program inversion is that reading and writing sequential files on tape is only a specialised version of a more general form of communication. In the general form programs communicate by producing and consuming sequential streams of records, each stream being either unbuffered or buffered according to any of several possible regimes. The choice of buffering regime is, to a large extent, independent of the design of the communicating programs. But it is not independent of their scheduling. Figure 7 shows three possible implementations of the same system.

In the upper diagram two 'main' programs, P and Q, communicate by writing and reading an intermediate tape file F. First P is run to completion; then F is rewound; then Q is run to completion. In the lower left diagram the intermediate tape file has been eliminated: the 'main' program Q has been *inverted with respect to F*. This inversion converts Q into a subroutine Q' invoked by P whenever P requires to produce a record of F. Q functions as a 'consume next F record' procedure. Similarly, in the lower right diagram the 'main' program P has been *inverted with respect to F*. This inversion converts P into a subroutine P', invoked by Q whenever Q requires to consume a record of F. P' functions as a 'produce

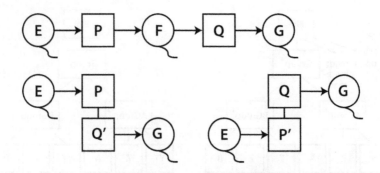

Figure 7. Using Inversion to Eliminate an Intermediate File

next F record' procedure. Both inversions interleave execution of P and Q as tightly as possible: each F record is consumed as soon as it has been produced.

Two or more programs may be inverted in one system. Inverting Q with respect to F, and P with respect to E, gives a subroutine P″ that uses the lower-level subroutine Q′; the function of the two together is to consume the next record of E, producing whatever records of G can then be constructed.

Inversion has an important effect on the efficiency of the system. First, it eliminates the storage space and device costs of the intermediate tape file. It eliminates the time required by the device to write and read each record of F, and also the 'rewind time' to reposition the newly written file for reading: for a magnetic tape file this may be many minutes for one reel. Second, it makes each successive record of G available with the least possible delay: each G record is produced as soon as P has consumed the relevant records of E.

Inversion also has an important effect on the program designer's view of a sequential program. The 'main program' P, the subroutine 'P inverted with respect to F', and the subroutine 'P inverted with respect to E', are seen as identical at the design level. This is a large economy of design effort. The JSP-COBOL preprocessor that supports JSP design for COBOL programs allows the three to differ only in their declarations of the files E and F.

The effect on the program designer's view goes deeper than an economy of design effort. An important example of the distinction between design and implementation is clarified; procedures with internal state can be designed as if they were main programs processing sequential message streams; and JSP design becomes applicable to all kinds of interactive systems, and even to interrupt handlers. Program inversion also suggests the modelling of real-world entities by objects with time-ordered behaviours: this is the basis of the eventual enlargement of JSP to handle system specification and design [Jackson 83].

10. A perspective view of JSP

Although JSP was originally rooted in mainframe data processing, it has been applied effectively in many environments. For applying JSP, the necessary problem characteristic is the presence of at least one external sequential data stream, to provide a given data structure that can and should be used as the basis of the program structure. Many programs have this characteristic. For example:

+ a program that processes a stream of EDI messages;
+ an automobile cruise control program that responds to the changing car state and the driver's actions;
+ a program that justifies text for printing;
+ a file handler that responds to invoked operations on the file;
+ a program that generates HTML pages from database queries.

JSP was developed in the commercial world, often in ignorance of work elsewhere. Some of the JSP ideas were reinventions of what was already known, while others anticipated later research results. The JSP relationship between data structures and program structure is essentially the relationship exploited in parsing by recursive descent [Aho 77]. Some of the early detailed JSP discussion of recognition difficulties dealt with aspects that were well known to researchers in formal languages and parsing techniques. The idea of program inversion is closely related to the Simula [Dahl 70] concept of semi-coroutines, and, of course, to the later Unix notion of pipes as a flexible implementation of sequential files. There was also one related program design approach in commercial use: the Warnier method [Warnier 74] based program structure on the regular data structure of one file. Program decomposition into sequential processes communicating by a coroutine-like mechanism was discussed in a famous early paper [Conway 63]; it was also the basis of a little-known development method called Flow-Based Programming [Morrison 94].

The central virtues of JSP are two. First, it provides a strongly systematic and prescriptive method for a clearly defined class of problem. Essentially, independent JSP designers working on the same problem produce the same solution. Second, JSP keeps the program designer firmly in the world of static structures to the greatest extent possible. Only in the last step of the backtracking technique, when dealing with side-effects, is the JSP designer encouraged to consider the dynamic behaviour of the program. This restriction to designing in terms of static structures is a decisive contribution to program correctness for those problems to which JSP can be applied. It avoids the dynamic thinking—the mental stepping through the program execution—that has always proved so seductive and so fruitful a source of error.

Acknowledgements

The foundations of JSP were laid in the years 1966-1970, when the author was working with Barry Dwyer, a colleague in John Hoskyns and Company, an English data processing consultancy. Many of the underlying ideas can be traced back to Barry Dwyer's contributions in those years. Refining the techniques, and making JSP more systematic and more teachable in commercial courses, was the work of the following four years in Michael Jackson Systems Limited.

The JSP-COBOL preprocessor was designed by the author and Brian Boulter, a colleague in Michael Jackson Systems Limited. Brian Boulter was responsible for most of the implementation.

Many other people contributed to JSP over the years—John Cameron, Tony Debling, Leif Ingevaldsson, Ashley McNeile, Hans Naegeli, Dick Nelson (who introduced the name 'JSP'), Bo Sanden, Peter Savage, Mike Slavin and many others. A partial bibliography of JSP can be found in [Jackson 94].

Daniel Jackson read a draft of this paper and made several improvements.

References

[Achelis 59]   Elisabeth Achelis; *The Calendar for the Modern Age*; Thomas Nelson and Sons, 1959.

[Aho 77]   A. V. Aho and J. D. Ullman; *Principles of Compiler Design*; Addison-Wesley, 1977.

[Barnett 68]   Barnett and Constantine eds.; *Modular Programming: Proceedings of a National Symposium*; Information & Systems Press, 1968.

[Blackman 98]   K. R. Blackman; IMS celebrates thirty years as an IBM product; *IBM Systems Journal*, Volume 37, Number 4, 1998.

[Conway 63]   Melvin E. Conway; Design of a separable transition-diagram compiler; *Communications of the ACM*, Volume 6, Number 7, 1963.

[Dahl 70]   O.-J. Dahl, B. Myhrhaug, and K. Nygaard; *SIMULA-67 Common Base Language*. Technical Report Number S-22, Norwegian Computer Centre, Oslo, 1970.

[Jackson 75]   M. A. Jackson; *Principles of Program Design*; Academic Press, 1975.

[Jackson 83]   M. A. Jackson; *System Development*; Prentice-Hall International, 1983.

[Jackson 94]   Michael Jackson; Jackson development methods: JSP and JSD; in *Encyclopaedia of Software Engineering*, John J. Marciniak, ed., Volume I; John Wiley and Sons, 1994.

[Morrison 94]   J. Paul Morrison; *Flow-Based Programming: A New Approach to Application Development*; Van Nostrand Reinhold, 1994.

[Myers 76]   Glenford J. Myers; *Software Reliability: Principles & Practices*; Wiley, 1976.

[Stevens 74]   W. P. Stevens, G. J. Myers, and L. L. Constantine; Structured design; *IBM Systems Journal*, Volume 13, Number 2, 1974.

[Warnier 74]   Jean-Dominique Warnier; *Logical Construction of Programs*; H. E. Stenfert Kroese, 1974, and Van Nostrand Reinhold, 1976.

Chapter 5

The Michael Jackson Design Technique: A Study of the Theory with Applications

C.A.R. Hoare
edited and introduced by Daniel Jackson

Abstract: This paper reproduces a report written by Hoare in 1977, in which he explains the fundamental ideas of Jackson's programming method, JSP. The notions that Hoare uses for this purpose—program traces, selective traces, and combination of selective programs—appeared in the following years in the conceptual foundation of his process algebra, CSP. Hoare shows that the key step in the JSP method, in which multiple stream structures are merged to form a single program structure, can be viewed in two phases. First, each stream—represented as a regular expression—is transformed by applying simple algebraic equalities into an equivalent structure, matching the structures obtained from the other streams. Second, these structures are merged. The paper also includes a wider discussion about the scope and nature of JSP. A new introduction provides some context, and presents in full the examples that Hoare alludes to in his report.

Introduced by Daniel Jackson

1. Introduction

In March 1977, Tony Hoare wrote a short paper explaining the essence of JSP, the program design method presented two years earlier in Michael Jackson's book, *Principles of Program Design* [4].

Hoare and Jackson had studied classics together at Merton College, Oxford, twenty years earlier, and both had subsequently worked on large software projects and had become dissatisfied with existing programming methods. Hoare was appointed professor at Queen's University in Belfast in 1968, and over the next few years developed the seminal ideas in semantics and verification for which he was to receive the Turing Award in 1980.

Jackson remained in industry (at the consultancy John Hoskyns & Company), and began work on a new method. In 1970, he left Hoskyns and founded his own firm, Michael Jackson Systems Limited, to develop the method fully. By 1977, JSP—standing for 'Jackson Structured Programming', a name coined by the company's Swedish licensee in 1974—was widely known, used in the United States, Europe and Asia, taught in several universities, and had been adopted (under the name 'SDM') by the UK government as its standard program design method.

JSP is unusually rigorous, not only amongst the approaches known as 'methods' at the time of its invention, but even by comparison with programming methods today. Indeed, for most problems, JSP is systematic enough that two programmers can be expected to produce identical solutions to a given problem. This rigour— demanded also by the tools built to support JSP—relied on the notation having a simple and precise semantics. Jackson had provided such a semantics informally; JSP diagrams, it turned out, were essentially regular grammars. There was, however, no mathematical theory of JSP that might explain why the steps were sound, and what kinds of programs could be handled. It is these questions that Hoare began to answer in his short paper.

The paper is interesting for another reason too. Hoare's explanation of JSP in terms of traces and projections connects it to his own work on CSP (Communicating Sequential Processes). The same year that he wrote this paper, Hoare returned to Oxford, becoming head of the Programming Research Group—following the death of Christopher Strachey (who, incidentally, had introduced Jackson to programming as his teacher at Harrow School in the early 1950s). Over the next few years, Hoare developed CSP, culminating in the book of 1985 [3].

2. The contributions of JSP

Because JSP advocated basing the structure of a program on the structure of the *data* that it processes, it has often been misunderstood. In JSP, 'data' does not mean the internal data structures representing the state of the program. Nor does it refer to the processing of inputs that are in-memory data structures (although JSP can be used effectively in this way, as for example in a current approach to functional programming [1] that it inspired). Rather, 'data' in JSP refers to a stream being processed, and its structure is that imposed on it when parsed as input or generated as output.

The premise of JSP is that any sequential stream of data can be treated in the same way, whether it consists of records read from a file on disk or a magnetic tape (dominant when JSP was invented), or of events from a user interface or network. The developers of Unix, in which the sequential stream plays a fundamental role, had the same idea. In fact, one of the features of JSP-COBOL, the preprocessing tool sold by Jackson's company, was its decoupling of programs from the physical properties of the devices, in just the same way that Unix's 'special files' allowed tape drives, network cards and other peripherals to be accessed as if they were disks, through a single API [10].

In this sense, JSP was a precursor not only to CSP but more generally to the view of programs as stream processors. The key insight of JSP is that a program to process a stream is best structured in the same way as the stream itself. When only the input stream has significant structure, JSP reduces to recursive descent parsing: a grammar is written for the stream and the code traverses the grammar in the (now) obvious way. Even today, this simple idea is not always well understood, and it is common to find programs that attempt to parse iterations of iterations without nested loops, or that become contorted with jumps, flags and exceptions because read operations are not placed early enough in the stream to resolve ambiguities.

JSP was more than this though. It identified the source of many of the difficulties that plagued data-processing programs as incompatibilities between stream structures. A program that processes (as inputs or outputs) streams with distinct structures cannot be structured on the basis of one stream alone (although a related method [11] attempted to do exactly that). Instead, a program structure must be found that generalizes over all the streams, reducing to the structure of each stream when projected onto its events.

This idea is the focus of Hoare's paper. He gives both a semantic view—in terms of 'selective traces'—of how a single program structure can be compatible with multiple streams, and an operational view—in terms of algebraic identities on regular expressions—of how the stream structures are manipulated to obtain the merged program structure.

Many aspects of JSP are not addressed by the paper. In some cases, the stream structures are fundamentally incompatible, and cannot be reconciled by the kinds of transformations that Hoare formalizes. JSP calls these situations *structure clashes*, and classifies them into three classes: *ordering clashes*, in which streams share elements but the elements occur in different orders; *boundary clashes*, in which the elements occur in the same order but are grouped differently; and *interleaving* or *multithreading clashes*, in which one stream can be split into (sequential) components, with the elements of each component corresponding to a subsequence of the elements of another stream.

JSP prescribes a solution for each kind of clash. For an ordering clash, the program is broken into two phases, connected by a sort or by a data store that can be accessed in either order. For a boundary clash, an intermediate stream is created, and the program is either run in two phases, or two programs are run in parallel with a stream between them. To eliminate the stream, one program can be run as a coroutine of the other. COBOL, of course, did not provide coroutines, so JSP offered a program transformation (automated by the JSP-COBOL tool) that converted stream reads and writes into calls, and let the programmer choose whether the reader or writer had initiative without changing to the code.

For an interleaving clash, a separate thread was executed for each interleaving. Jackson discovered (as he explained in the penultimate chapter of the JSP book [4]) that most information systems could be viewed as stateful transformers that generated reports from interleaved event streams. These streams could be grouped according to type. The input stream presented to a banking system, for example, might include events related to accounts, and events related to customers, and could thus be viewed as an interleaving of a set of account streams (each containing updates to a particular account) and a set of customer streams (each containing updates regarding a particular customer). Thus Jackson's system development method, JSD, was born [7]. Each type of stream became a process type; instances of a process could be executed concurrently, or could be scheduled on demand, with their states frozen in a database between uses.

This is, of course, much like object-oriented programming (OOP), but with some important distinctions. JSD was more flexible than OOP in terms of scheduling and concurrency. The treatment of scheduling issues as secondary (and their implementation by program transformation) provided an important decoupling. It also made JSD suitable for the design of real-time systems. Moreover, JSD insisted on a clean separation between the objects that represented the state of the world, and the processes that computed functions for output. In OOP, the coupling between these has been an endless source of difficulties that patterns such as *Visitor* [2] and strategies such as aspect-oriented programming [9] try to mitigate. (The 'join points' of aspect-oriented programming are perhaps just indications of how to form JSP correspondences between a base program and its aspects.)

Another major focus of JSP was its treatment of recognition problems—when a record's interpretation could not be resolved until after reading (sometimes an unbounded number of) subsequent records. To handle this difficulty, JSP prescribed multiple readahead, and when this was not feasible, positing a certain interpretation and backtracking if it turned out to be incorrect (an idea due to Barry Dwyer, who worked with Jackson early on in the development of JSP).

Perhaps, however, none of these particular technical ideas was the essential contribution of JSP—nor even the part of the book most widely quoted, namely Jackson's optimization maxim ('Rule 1: Don't do it. Rule 2 (for experts only). Don't do it yet—that is, not until you have a perfectly clear and unoptimized solution.') [4, p. vii]. Rather, the key contribution was the idea that a programming method should identify *difficulties* inherent in the class of problems addressed. The difficulties provide not only a rationale for the method's prescribed solutions, but a measure of progress. Partly in reaction to those who believed that a successful method was one that made all difficulties magically vanish, Jackson formulated this idea explicitly (many years after JSP) as the *Principle of Beneficent Difficulty* [8]:

> "Difficulties, explicitly characterized and diagnosed, are the medium in which a method captures its central insights into a problem. A method without limitations, whose development steps are never impossible to complete, whose stages diagnose and recognise no difficulty, must be very bad indeed. Just think about it. A method without limitations and difficulties is saying one of two things to you. Either it's saying that all problems are easily solved. You know

that's not true. Or else it's saying that some problems are difficult, but the method is not going to help you to recognise or overcome the difficult bits when you meet them. Take your choice. Either way it's bad news."

So the identification of difficulties marks progress not only in a single development, but in the field as a whole. A method's difficulties characterize the class of problems it addresses. In Jackson's view, the limitations of JSP are not an embarrassment to be hidden from potential users. On the contrary, the fact that its limitations are so clearly spelled out—in terms of the difficulties the method addresses, and by omission the difficulties it fails to address—makes it a worthy tool in the software developer's repertoire.

3. An outline of Hoare's paper

Hoare's paper starts by connecting the structure of a program to the structure of its executions. A program's behaviour is represented by its possible executions, called *traces* (later to become the semantic foundation of CSP); and a program with a regular structure defines a regular language of traces. Hoare defines a program as *annotated* if mock elementary statements have been inserted that have no effect on the state when executed, but which indicate, when they occur in a trace, the beginning or end of a structural block (according to whether the program is 'left' or 'right' annotated). The trace of an annotated program thus reveals the structure of the program that generated it, and by this means, Hoare is able to express the idea of structural correspondence between programs entirely semantically.

Hoare then introduces the *selective trace*, in which only some subset of statements appear—such as the reads of a particular input stream, or the writes of an output stream, or the updates of a particular variable—and the *selective program* in which all but the chosen statements have been deleted. By postponing consideration of conditions and treating them as non-deterministic, Hoare ensures that the selective traces obtained by filtering the traces of the complete program are exactly those obtained from the full executions of the selective program. This notion of selection becomes a principal means of abstraction in CSP (where it is referred to as 'restriction' when applied to traces and 'hiding' when applied to processes).

JSP, Hoare explains, can be viewed as a reversal of this selection process. Instead of obtaining selective programs from a complete program, the complete program is synthesized by merging its selective programs. Since the selective program for a stream is exactly that stream's grammar, the selective programs are readily available. To obtain the complete program, the selective programs have to be brought into *correspondence*. Hoare defines correspondence as a simple property on the traces. Two elementary statements a and b correspond if they strictly alternate a; b; a; b; … etc; similarly, two larger structures correspond if the start of the first alternates with the end of the second. (By left-annotating the first selective program and right-annotating the second, this correspondence of structures becomes a simple alternation of the annotation events.)

Two selective programs can be brought into perfect correspondence by manipulating their structures until they match. These manipulations can be expressed as simple transformations on regular expressions, each based on a well-known algebraic identity. Because these transformations preserve the meaning of the regular expression, the changes made to the selective programs do not affect their trace sets.

This formalization does not tell the whole story. As Hoare notes, correspondences have a deeper semantic significance. Two elementary statements a and b can only be paired if, in addition to strictly alternating, the data required to generate each b can be computed from the a's and b's that preceded it. In JSP, the programmer determines this informally.

The contribution of Hoare's paper is not only an elegant and compelling formalization of the basic concept of JSP. From his formalization emerge some concrete proposals for the method itself:

(a) In Jackson's approach, the merging of selective programs is accomplished often in a single step, which can be justified by a check that applying each selection to the merged program recovers the original selective program. Hoare prefers the merging to be performed in a series of small steps, each formally justified, so that the resulting merged program is correct by construction.

(b) JSP postpones the listing and allocation of operations until the merged program has been obtained. Hoare notes that a selective program could be written not only for each stream, but also for each *variable*. Allocation of operations then becomes just another merging step. As Hoare suggests, this could be a useful teaching tool. Whether it would work well in practice is less clear. The usage pattern of a variable—unlike the structure of an input or output stream—is not given but rather invented, is often guided by the structure of the merged program, and is dependent on the usages of other variables. So it may be hard to describe the variables independently before considering their inter-relationships.

(c) Whereas Jackson sees the notion of structure clash as *absolute*—two selective programs clash if the only possible merge places one in its entirety before the other—Hoare prefers to see the notion as *relative*. Whenever correspondences cannot be established all the way down to the leaves of the structure tree, some state must be retained in memory to record the effect of multiple events. Hoare notes that the programmer may have a choice about how far down to go, and might choose to read an entire structure from one stream before writing the entire corresponding structure to another, even if a finer-grained interleaving were possible. Jackson would view this as undesirable, since it sees a structure clash where one does not really exist, and would prefer a tighter program, applying the standard JSP strategy of establishing correspondences as far down as possible. But Hoare's proposal is nevertheless compelling, because it adds some flexiblity to JSP, allowing greater use of intermediate structures. And by JSP standards, most programs written today are quite loose, and take liberal advantage of Hoare's proposal.

Hoare's paper was written not for an academic audience, but as a consulting report. It references example problems (taken from contemporary course materials) and assumes a knowledge of the basic JSP method. To make it more accessible,

I have added brief presentations of these problems, based on the versions that appeared in Jackson's book. The paper was written in Hoare's elegant long hand. Beyond typesetting it, I have made only a few changes: notably updating the code fragments to a more modern idiom, inlining some footnotes, and adding section headings.

4. Multiplication table problem

The *Multiplication Table* problem is the first appearing in Jackson's book [4, pp. 3–7]. It is used not so much as an illustration of how to apply the JSP method, but rather to show the difference between a well-structured program, in which the program structure matches the stream structure, and a poorly structured program obtained by coding from a flowchart (a popular technique back in the 1970s). With the correct structure, a variety of simple modifications are straightforward to apply. With the wrong structure, even the most simple modification is awkward: a change to how a line is displayed, for example, cannot be made locally, because no program component corresponds exactly to the displaying of a single line.

The problem is to generate and print a multiplication table in this form:

```
1
2 4
3 6 9
4 8 12 16
5 10 15 20 25
...
10 20 30 40 50 60 70 80 90 100
```

JSP proceeds by representing the streams as regular grammars, forming a merged program structure from the stream structures, and then allocating operations to it. In this case—somewhat unusually for JSP—the only stream to consider is an output stream, and no merging will be needed. Its structure is simply an iteration of lines, each being an iteration of numbers (Figure 1).

Using a variable r to count rows, and c to count columns, the operations required are the initializations:

1. r = 1
2. c = 1

the updates:

3. r = r + 1
4. c = c + 1

and operations to clear a line, append a number to it, and write the line to output:

5. clear ()
6. append (r × c)
7. write ()

Each operation is allocated (Figure 2) by finding its appropriate component

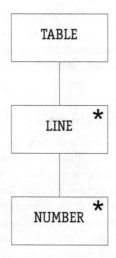

Figure 1: Structure of Multiplication Table

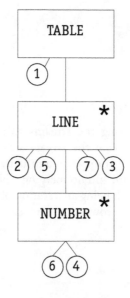

Figure 2: Multiplication Table structure with allocated operations

(by asking how often the operation should be applied), and placed in a position relative to the other operations to ensure the required dataflow. So, for example, to place operation (3) that updates the row, we ask: 'how many times is the row variable updated?' The answer is 'once per line', so we allocate it to LINE, placing it at the end since the new value will be used for the next iteration. Similarly, we place the row initialization at the start of the table; the line-clearing, column initialization and line-writing once per line; and the adding of a new entry and the column update once per number. Although, as Hoare will note, placing the operations requires programmer intuition, it is usually easy; if not, the program structure is almost certainly wrong.

Finally, the conditions for the iterations are identified—c <= r for number iteration and r <= 10 for the line iteration—and the code is transcribed from the diagram:

```
r = 1;
while (r <= 10) {
        c = 1;
        clear ();
        while (c <= r) {
                append (r × c);
                c = c + 1;
                }
        write ();
        r = r + 1;
        }
```

(I have chosen the operations to match the original COBOL program, which is not so different from the program one might write today in Javascript, for example, in which clear () might be written as document.write ("<tr>"), append (r × c) as document.write ("<td>", r*c, "</td>"), and write () as document. write ("</tr>"). In a language such as C# or Java, the need to write a tab before each number would require a small elaboration of the output stream structure, to distinguish the first number on each line, since otherwise an extra tab would appear the end of each line.)

5. Stores movement problem

The *Stores Movement* problem [4, pp. 59–63] is a more typical JSP problem, in which the program structure is derived from the structure of a single input stream.

In the 1960s, magnetic tape was the only realistic choice for large files. A 2400-foot tape cost about $10 and held 20-60MB; a hard disk that held only 2MB cost about $400. Consequently, company data was typically stored on one of more 'master files' held on tape, with records sorted, for example, by customer number. Transactions were held on a separate tape as a stream of records sorted on the same key, and were applied in batch by reading both tapes and writing a new tape for the updated master file.

Although such programs were standard, errors—such as mishandling an empty set of records or mistakenly reading beyond a record—were common, and many of the techniques used at the time encouraged the use of flags and complex control flow, resulting in a bug-ridden program with little semblance of structure. JSP identified the essential difficulties and prescribed simple and systematic remedies for them: readahead for recognition difficulties; interposed streams for structure clashes; inversion for overcoming lack of multithreading, etc.

In the *Stores Movement* problem, a file of transactions is to be summarized. The file contains records for orders of parts received and issued by a factory warehouse, each record consisting of a code indicating receipt or issue, a part number, and the quantity. The file has already been sorted into part-number order. The problem is to generate a report with one line for each kind of part, listing the part number and net movement (total received minus total issued). The reader is encouraged to sketch a solution to this problem before proceeding.

The input file is an iteration of groups (one per part number), each group being an iteration of movement records, and each record being an issue or a receipt (Figure 3a).

The operations are:

1. smf = open (...)
2. close (smf)
3. rec = read (smf)
4. display (pno, net)
5. pno = rec.part_number
6. net = 0
7. net = net + rec.quantity
8. net = net - rec.quantity

The program structure is just the input stream structure. Each operation (as explained before) is allocated (Figure 3b) by finding its appropriate component and placing it in a position relative to the other operations that respects dataflow dependences. So, for example, to place operation (1) that opens the file, we ask: 'how many times is the file opened?'. The answer is 'once per stores movement file', so we assign the operation to the top level node, and knowing that the file must be opened before reading, we place it at the start. Operation (7), which increments the net movement, must be executed once for each receipt record, so we assign it to RECEIPT. To place the read operation (3), we ask how much readahead will be required. Since we only need to determine whether the next record is a receipt or an issue record (and whether it belongs to the group currently being processed) single readahead will do, so a read is allocated once immediately after the open, and once after each record is consumed.

The resulting program is:

```
smf = open (...);
rec = read (smf);
while (!eof (rec)) {
        pno = rec.part_number;
        net = 0;
        while (!eof (rec) && pno == rec.part_number) {
                if (rec.code == ISSUE)
                        net = net - rec.quantity;
                else
                net = net + rec.quantity;
```

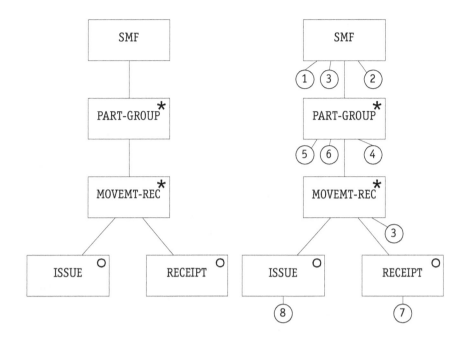

Figure 3: Stores Movement Problem.
3a (left): Structure of input stream; 3b (right): With operations allocated

```
        rec = read (smf);
        }
    display (pno, net);
    }
    close (smf);
```

This example, although simple, illustrated an important point. The double iteration is essential to match the structure of the input; without it, getting a clear and maintainable program is impossible. And yet the traditional approach to writing such programs at the time ignored this simple observation, and, in place of the nested iteration, used a 'control break' to separate the record groups. Although the term 'control break' is no longer used, the same mistake is still made today. Few programmers would solve the *Multiplication Table* problem with only one loop, but many would fail to see the same nested structure in this case.

Hoare's reference to this problem was actually to a version appearing in course notes (Figure 4b), which differed slightly from the version appearing in the book (Figure 4a), by having the report include a heading. This hardly complicates the problem, but it illustrates an important point from a theoretical perspective: that formalizing the merging process would require, in this case, an additonal elaboration that Jackson skips.

6. Magic mailing problem

The *Magic Mailing* problem appears in the chapter of the book [4, pp. 70–74] that shows how to construct programs that handle multiple streams, and is an example of a 'collating' or 'matching' problem.

Here is the description of the problem from Jackson's book:

"The Magic Mailing Company has just sent out nearly 10,000 letters containing an unrepeatable and irresistible offer, each letter accompanied by a returnable acceptance card. The letters and cards are individually numbered from 1 to 9999. Not all of the letters were actually sent, because some were spoilt in the addressing process. Not all of the people who received letters returned the reply card. The marketing manager, who is a suspicious fellow, thinks that his staff may have stolen some of the reply cards for the letters which were not sent, and returned the cards so they could benefit from the offer.

The letters sent have been recorded on a file; there is one record per letter sent, containing the letter-number and other information which need not concern us. The reply cards are machine readable, and have been copied to tape; each reply card returned gives rise to one record containing the letter-number and some other information which again does not concern us. Both the letter file and the reply file have been sorted into letter-number order.

A program is needed to report on the current state of the offer. Each line of the report corresponds to a letter-number; there are four types of line, each containing the letter-number, a code and a message. The four types of line are:
NNNNNN 1 LETTER SENT AND REPLY RECEIVED
NNNNNN 2 LETTER SENT, NO REPLY RECEIVED
NNNNNN 3 NO LETTER SENT, REPLY RECEIVED
NNNNNN 4 NO LETTER SENT, NO REPLY RECEIVED"

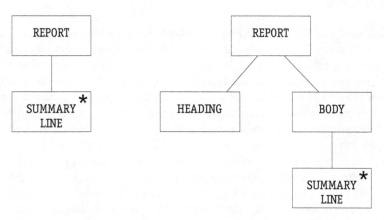

Figure 4: Structure of output stream for Stores Movement Problem
4a (left): Version appearing in book [3]; 4b (right): Version appearing in course notes

When there is more than one stream, JSP proceeds by identifying *correspondences* between the elements of the structures of the various streams. Corresponding elements then become a single element in the program structure. The programmer can check that the program structure is correct by taking each stream in turn, and projecting the program structure onto the elements of that stream. If the program structure has been obtained correctly, this will recover for each stream a structure equivalent to the original one.

Collating problems such as *Magic Mailing* present a complication. The input streams—here, one for letters and one for reply cards—cannot be understood in isolation from one another; we need to impose a structure on each stream based on its relationship to the others. In the *Magic Mailing* solution in Jackson's book, each stream is represented as an iteration of matched or unmatched records (Figure 5). The report is just an iteration of lines, each having one of the four forms (Figure 6).

To obtain the correspondences (Figure 7), we match each type of output record to its corresponding inputs: type 1 when both input files have matched records, type 2 when a letter record is unmatched, and type 3 when a reply record is unmatched. A type 4 output has no correspondence in the input, since it represents the case in which a record is missing from both files.

The operations are easily identified, and allocated using single readahead, resulting easily in the final program:

```
lrec = read (lfile);
rrec = read (rfile);
n = 1;
while (n < 9999) {
        if (lrec.num == n == rrec.num) {
                write_type_1 (n);
                lrec = read (lfile);
                rrec = read (rfile);
        }
        if (lrec.num == n != rrec.num) {
                write_type_1 (n);
                lrec = read (lfile);
        }
        if (lrec.num != n == rrec.num) {
                write_type_1 (n);
                rrec = read (rfile);
        }
        if (lrec.num != n != rrec.num) {
                write_type_1 (n);
        }
        n = n + 1;
}
```

Although this final program is correct, the method is not, strictly speaking, applied correctly. As Hoare notes, there is no correspondence between LREC, RREC, and LINE, since there may be more lines that letters or reply cards. The correct solution is to elaborate the input structures further, to distinguish records that are present from records that are missing. Jackson does in fact show how to perform this elaboration [4, p.72], but appears not to insist on its use.

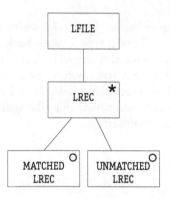

Figure 5: Structure for letter file of Magic Mailing Problem

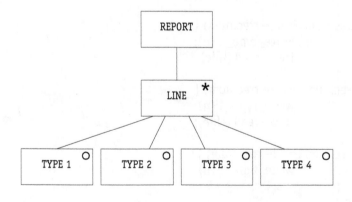

Figure 6: Structure for report of Magic Mailing Problem

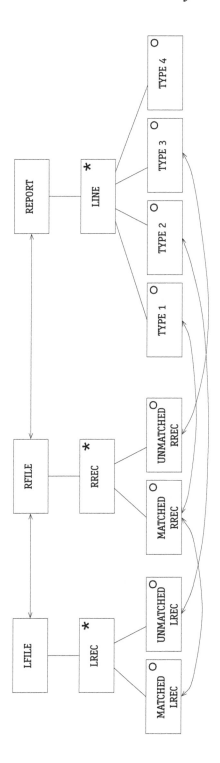

Figure 7: Correspondences for Magic Mailing Problem

The Original Paper by C. A. R. Hoare

1. Programs, traces and regular expressions

The execution of a computer program involves the execution of a series of elementary commands, and the evaluation of a series of elementary tests (which, in fact, the Michael Jackson technique tends to ignore). It is in principle possible to get a computer to record each elementary command when it is executed, and also to record each test as it is evaluated (together with an indication whether it was true or false). Such a record is known as a 'trace'; and it can sometimes be helpful in program debugging.

It is obviously very important that a programmer should have an absolutely clear understanding of the relation between his program and any possible trace of its execution. Fortunately, in the case of a structured program, this relation is very simple—indeed, as Dijkstra pointed out, this is the main argument in favour of structured programming. The relation may be defined as follows:

(a) For an elementary condition or command (input, output, or assignment), the only possible trace is just a copy of the command. This is known as a 'terminal symbol', or 'leaf', of the structure tree.

(b) For a sequence of commands (say P ; Q), every possible trace consists of a trace of P followed by a trace of Q (and similarly for sequences longer than two).

(c) For a selection (say P ∪ Q), every possible trace is *either* a trace of P or a trace of Q (and similarly for selections of more than two alternatives).

(d) For an iteration (say P*), every possible trace is a sequence of none or more traces, each of which is a (possibly different) trace of P. Zero repetitions will give rise to an 'empty' trace <>. Thus it can be seen that a program is a kind of regular expression, and that the set of possible traces of the program is the 'language' defined by that expression. In fact, the 'language' will contain many traces that can never be the result of program execution; but for the time being it will pay to ignore that fact.

Of course, a complete trace of *every* action of a program will often be too lengthy for practical use. We therefore need a *selective* trace, which is a record of all actions affecting some particular variable, or some particular input or output file. (Note that a complete trace is a merging of all the selective traces derived from it; but it is not possible to work out which merging it was from the selective traces alone.)

A record of all input instructions on a particular input file will be effectively the same as a copy of the particular data presented to the program on that particular execution of it; and similarly a selective trace of output instructions will be nothing but a copy of the output file. For program debugging such traces would never be required. But the idea of the selective trace is the basis of the whole Michael Jackson Design Technique.

2. Extracting selective programs

The theoretical foundation for the technique is that there is a very close relation between a complete program, defining a set of complete traces, and the 'selective' or 'partial' programs defining the sets of all selective traces; indeed, a selective program can be derived automatically from a complete program by the following algorithm:

(a) An elementary command is retained if it refers to the selected variable or file; otherwise, it is replaced by the empty trace <>.

(b) A sequence P ; Q is replaced by P'; Q', where P' is the selective program derived from P and Q' is the selective program derived from Q. If P' is <>, then it may be omitted (leaving Q'), and similarly if Q' is <>.

(c) A selection P ∪ Q is replaced by P' ∪ Q' where P' and Q' are the corresponding selective programs. In this case, an empty program element must not be omitted. However, if P' and Q' are *identical*, then one of them can be suppressed.

(d) An iteration P* is replaced by (P')* where P' is the selective program derived from P. If P' is <>, then (P')* should be taken simply as <> instead of <>*. In P*; P*, the second P* can be suppressed.

Let us taken an example, the *Multiplication Table* problem. The complete program is:

```
r = 1;
(
     c = 1;
     clear ();
     (
              append (r × c);
              c = c + 1
     )* ;
     write ();
     r = r + 1
)*
```

The selective program for r is:

```
r = 1; (r = r + 1)*
```

The selective program for c is

```
(c = 1; (c = c + 1)*)*
```

The selective program for output is

```
(clear (); append ()*; write ())*
```

Jackson recommends that all these programs should be written as tree diagrams, which can easily be done. The main advantage of doing so is that every part of the regular expression must be given its own name. This can also be done by splitting the definition of the regular expression, for example: TABLE ≜ r = 1; LINE*

LINE $\triangleq$ c = 1; clear (); NUMBER*; write (); r = r + 1
NUMBER $\triangleq$ append (r × c); c = c + 1

But there remains the advantage of the tree-picture, since it avoids repetition of the 'nonterminal symbols' (LINE, etc); and it prevents recursion.

Now let us suppose that the non-terminal symbols are included in the program, as 'commands' without any effect, except that they are recorded as part of the trace of program execution. We say that a program is *left annotated* if the nonterminal symbol precedes the expression which defines it, and that it is *right annotated* if the nonterminal symbol follows the expression which defines it. These concepts correspond to preorder and postorder traversal of the corresponding tree. For example, the left-annotated version of the *Multiplication Table* problem would be:

```
TABLE;
r = 1;
(
     LINE;
     c = 1;
     clear ();
     (
            NUMBER;
            append (r × c);
            c = c + 1;
     )* ;
     write ();
     r = r + 1
)*
```

And the right–annotated version would be:

```
r = 1;
(
     c = 1;
     clear ();
     (
            append (r × c);
            c = c + 1
            NUMBER
     )* ;
     write ();
     r = r + 1;
     LINE
)* ;
TABLE
```

The advantage of these annotated programs is that we can obtain selective traces and corresponding selection programs that print out only selected *nonterminal* symbols; and thereby we greatly shorten the traces we need to consider. For example, a selective program for LINE and NUMBER would be

(LINE; NUMBER*)*

which is identical to the tree diagram on which the original structure was based.

Consider now a selective trace containing just two commands (or nonterminals) a and b. It may happen that the occurrences of a and b strictly alternate, thus:

a; b; a; b; ...; a; b.

A selective program for this trace is simply (a; b)*. If *every* such selective trace of a program displays this behavior, we say that the actions a and b *correspond* in that program. The correspondence of actions is indicated in Michael Jackson's diagrams by drawing a double-ended arrow between boxes containing the actions a and b.

3. Merging selective programs

The basic insight of the Michael Jackson Design Technique is that in the design phase of the program construction, the selection algorithm for regular expressions can profitably be *reversed*; that is that the programmer should first design his *selective* programs, and then he should arrange them to obtain the complete program. The important selective programs are those relating to the input and output files; fortunately, these can usually be designed quite simply, given the specification of the problem to be solved. There remains only the task of merging them, together with the necessary operations on internal variables.

We shall consider the task of merging only *two* selective programs at a time. We will call these the *left* program (usually the input) and the *right* program (usually the output). We shall assume that these are fully annotated, like Michael Jackson's trees; and in considering the traces, we will assume that the left program is left-annotated, and the right program is right-annotated.

Consequently if two nonterminal symbols (internal nodes in the tree) are found to correspond, this means that the *start* of execution of the left subtree below the left node will always strictly alternate with *completion* of the execution of the subtree below the right node of the pair.

In principle, it is always possible to solve the merging problem in the wholly trivial fashion, by putting the entire left program (for input) before the entire right program (for output), thus: INPUT; OUTPUT. This would mean that the entire input file is read and stored in internal variables of the program; and only when input is complete does the output start. But this trivial solution will usually be totally impractical, since there will not be sufficient room in internal storage to hold the entire input file before output starts. We therefore wish to obtain a program that economises on space by reusing internal storage occupied by input data as soon as possible after the data has been input.

In principle, the best way to ensure this is to move the *output* instructions as *early* as possible in the merged program, because in general it is possible to overwrite input data immediately after execution of the last output instruction that actually *uses* the data.

So it is a good idea to try to plan for early output even before designing the storage layout of the input data, or how it is going to be reused. (Of course, early output doesn't guarantee success; but success will depend on it).

The basis of the technique recommended by Michael Jackson is the recognition of correspondences between the paired actions, in which an action of the left program is paired with some action from the right program. Recall that corresponding actions alternate in every execution of the program. As explained above, the *entire* input program can *always* be paired with the *entire* output program, since the start of the top nonterminal symbol of the one is always followed (exactly once!) by the end of the top nonterminal of the other. So the essence of the technique must be to find paired actions lower *down* in the tree as well, because this is what is required to permit output operations to be more tightly interleaved with input.

There are two conditions necessary for successful interleaving of a left and right program:

(a) the structures of the two programs must match;

(b) the proposed correspondences between the actions must be feasible.

The second of these conditions is the more difficult. Consider, for example, the *Matrix Transposition* problem (Figure 8). Here we seem to have a good 'structural' match (condition (a)): as always, the top level nodes—here INPUT-MATRIX and OUTPUT-MATRIX—can be paired. Apparently also, INPUT-ROW can be paired with OUTPUT-COLUMN. Of course, this would not work for a non-square matrix, which has more rows than columns, or *vice versa*. But this possibility cannot be detected from the diagrams; it must be supplied by the intuition of the programmer. Suppose the programmer *knows* that the input matrix is square, with the same number of rows as columns. Even so, the pairing won't work, because it is *impossible*

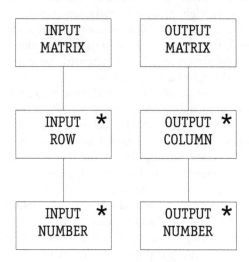

Figure 8: Structures for Matrix Transposition Problem

to print the first column after input of only the first row, simply because there is not yet enough input information available to do so. In fact, output of the *first* column cannot take place until after input of the *last* row. (This example is well explained in Jackson's book [4, pp. 151–153]). The point that I wish to make here is that the identification of the corresponding pairs requires considerable insight from the programmer, and an understanding of what input data is required for the calculation of the value of each item of data output.

When the conditions cannot be satisfied and no interleaving is possible, we have, in Jackson's terminology, a *structure clash*. This is, in fact, a relative term. A structure clash can occur anywhere in the tree, when it proves impossible to perform an output instruction until a whole group of input instructions has been completed. If there is enough room in main store to hold a sufficiently detailed summary of the input data, then the structure clash causes no problem, and can be ignored. If there is *not* enough room, other measures must be adopted: for example, the use of an intermediate data file, sorting, program inversion, etc. But these are just more sophisticated methods of saving main storage, which must be used when the simpler method of interleaving has failed (at any level). They will not be further mentioned in this study.

Let us move away from the extreme of structural mismatch to the other extreme of perfect structural match, in which every component of the left program is paired with some component of the right program, and *vice versa*, and furthermore every member of a sequence is paired with a member of a sequence, every member of a selection is paired with a member of a selection, and every iteration is paired with an iteration. Actually, it does not matter if there are some completely unmatched subtrees in either of the programs; e.g., the structures of Figure 9, for example, are perfectly matched.

It is now a completely mechanical task to construct a merged program from the left and right programs, together with their pairings. First draw an identical copy of either tree, as far as it matches the other (Figure 10); the two trees are, of course, identical up to that point. Then extend each leaf of the tree as a sequence of two elements, the left one taken from the left program, and the right one from the right program (Figure 11). Any subtrees should be copied too.

4. Transformations

The merging we have considered so far is only the simple case. In general, the left program will have quite a different tree structure from the right program. In this case, it is impossible to apply the simple procedure described above, even when the pairing lines can validly be drawn between the boxes. The solution to this problem is to transform one or both the programs to an equivalent program in such a way that there is an exact match between the paired items. We are therefore interested in transformations that preserve the meaning of a program. In general, the transformations will be the *reverse* of the simplifications that can be made when a program is separated by the process described above (in Section 2). Let us try to catalogue such transformations.

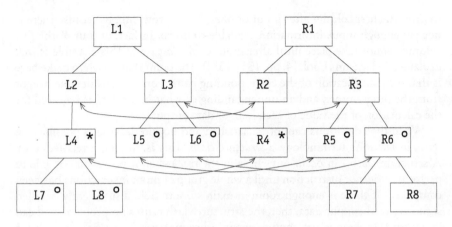

Figure 9: Structures that are perfectly matched despite unmatched subtrees

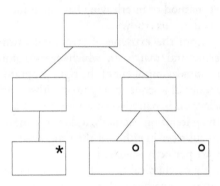

Figure 10: Constructing a merge: first step

The simplest transformation is just the insertion of an extra box on a line (Figure 12). This is required in the *Stores Movement* problem (Figure 13). Of course, after a bit of practice, one would not always wish to make this elementary transformation explicitly; but to begin with, it may be a good idea to realize the necessity for it.

Another very common transformation is the introduction of a selection, by simply copying complete subtrees (as in Figure 14, where B′ and B″ are identical copies of the subtree B). This transformation is required when the output selective program makes a distinction (like MATCH and NOMATCH) that is not made explicitly in the definition of the input. This technique is the converse of the simplification Q ∪ Q → Q in regular expressions, and relies on the fact that the same set of languages is defined before and after the transformations.

In general, multiple structures must be brought into correspondence together.

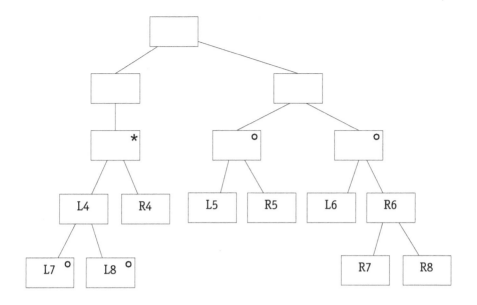

Figure 11: Constructing a merge: second step

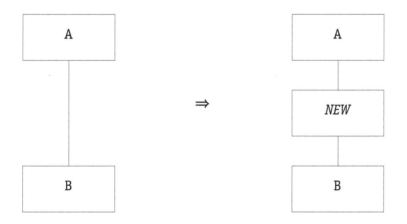

Figure 12: Simple transformation: adding structure
Before transformation (left); After transformation (right)

In the *Magic Mailing* problem, for example, there are three structures: the letter file, the reply file, and the report. Here, we shall deal with only two of the tree structures at a time. This is always a valid simplification, and will always find a successful solution if one exists—though it might be a good idea to get a rigorous proof of this fact.

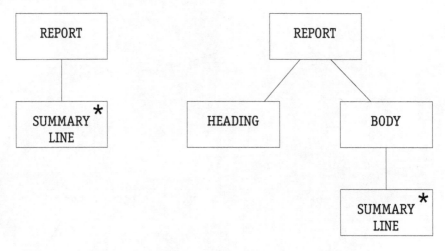

Figure 13: Applying transformation to Stores Movement Problem
Before transformation (left)
After transformation (right), with correspondences to output stream shown

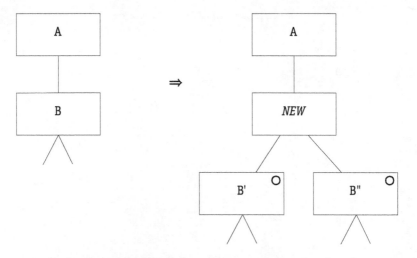

Figure 14: Introduction of a selection, based on the identity $Q = Q \cup Q$
Before transformation (left); After transformation (right)

Consider the reply file and the report (Figure 15). It is clear that RREC cannot be paired with LINE, since there are *more* lines than RRECs. The *only* solution to this problem is to introduce a selection (Figure 16), with an empty alternative to correspond to the lines which are written *without* reading an RREC.

This transformation can be made without looking any further down the tree from the LINE* component. The validity of the transformation relies on the fact that the languages defined by

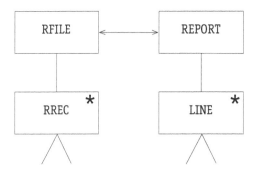

Figure 15: Unmatched structures in the Magic Mailing Problem

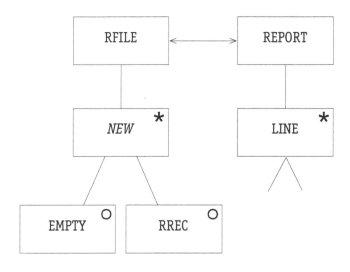

Figure 16: Applying the transformation based on the identity R* = <> ∪ R*
to the Magic Mailing Problem

R*
and
<> ∪ R*

are identical. (Perhaps this is a simple case of Jackson's 'interleaving clash' and its resolution). In the *Magic Mailing* problem, it turns out that two further copies of the empty alternative must be made to match the structure of the line. This splitting of alternatives has already been justified by the fact that (R ∪ R) = R. Then exactly the same transformations must be made in the letter file. In Jackson's solution, all these transformations are made implicitly and simultaneously on both files, thereby obscuring the essential simplicity of the operations.

These two examples of identities over regular expressions can be used to transform the left and right selective programs to make them match prior to merging. It might be interesting to list some of the simpler identities, and construct examples of their useful application; eg.

(P; Q); R = P; (Q; R) = P; Q; R

which is shown diagramatically in Figure 17. Similar diagrams can be drawn for the following:

$$(P \cup Q) \cup R = P \cup (Q \cup R) = P \cup Q \cup R$$
$$P; <> = <> ; P$$
$$P \cup P = P \cup P \cup P = P$$
$$P \cup Q = Q \cup P$$
$$R^* = (R \cup <>)^*$$
$$R^* = (R \cup <>); R^* = R^*; (R \cup <>)$$
$$P; (Q \cup R) = (P; Q) \cup (P; R)$$
$$(P \cup Q); R = (P; R) \cup (Q; R)$$

and so on.

The correct application of these rules could, of course, be checked by computer. But, unfortunately, the computer cannot help in applying the rules in finding correspondences, because this depends intensely on the programmer's intuition about what needs to be done before what. Nevertheless, we can now give the programmer very much more explicit advice about how to apply Michael Jackson's Design Technique.

(a) Initially, one need consider only two partial programs at a time; any others can later be merged with the result of the first two, one after the other.

(b) Start by drawing the correspondence between the root nodes of the tree. Then consider only *one pair of nodes* at a time, one from the left program and one from the right. Check that all nodes higher than the considered nodes have already been successfully paired (that is, all nodes on the path back to the root have been paired). 25

(c) If the nodes cannot be paired, try transforming one or both of the nodes by any of the valid transformations listed above.

(d) If you can't succeed, abandon this pair of nodes, and try any other possible pair.

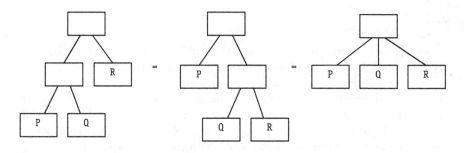

Figure 17: Transformations based on the identity (P; Q); R = P; (Q; R) = P; Q; R

(e) When the tree of paired nodes has been extended as far as possible, check that there is enough room in main storage to accommodate the input data before it is output. This must be done at every point where it was impossible to obtain a correspondence.

(f) If not, try to establish *further* pairs, even though the parent nodes have not been paired. If this can be done, then we have an example of Michael Jackson's 'structure clash' (in this case, a 'boundary clash') which can be resolved by his technique of an intermediate working file, and by program inversion.

Here again, the establishment of the pairs requires an understanding of the nature of the problem, and cannot be done automatically. For example, in the *Telegrams Analysis* problem [4, pp. 155–160] the 'words' of the input file are in the same order as the 'words' required by analysis; but in the case of the numbers of the *Matrix Transposition* problem, this is not so (even though there are the same number of them!). Only the human programmer can distinguish between the two cases.

5. Summary

To summarise this rather rambling discourse, I will give brief answers to a number of questions which were posed before the start of the study.

What is the meaning of a structure diagram?

It is a pictorial representation of a regular expression; the language defined by the regular expression contains all possible traces of execution of the commands which feature as terminal nodes of the tree.

Are there any other programs that cannot be written by the Michael Jackson Design Technique?

In principle there are not; because every program trace is a repetition of the union of all the terminal commands (ie, the regular expression comprising the set of *all* strings over the given alphabet). But this description would be extremely unhelpful. The Michael Jackson Technique is most useful when it is possible to construct rather deep structure trees, and when the structure of the program execution is determined by the structure of its input/output data. It is less useful for the development of clever algorithms, where the content of the program is difficult to determine, and the course of the calculation is dominated by tests on the internal data (ie, while-conditions and if-conditions).

What is the meaning of the 'correspondences' drawn as horizontal double-ended arrows between nodes in two structure diagrams?

A pair of nodes correspond if for *every* execution of the program, the start of execution of the left node alternates strictly with end of execution of the right node.

What is the taxonomy of tricks available to transform a structure to bring it more into correspondence with some other structure?

It is possible to use any valid identity between regular expressions. A number of these identities can be listed and illustrated by example.

Is it possible to write a computer program that will check whether an original and a transformed structure diagram describe the same data or program?

Yes; but the program would be polynomial space-complete (see [12, 13]). This means that there is no efficient algorithm known; the best known algorithms are based on an exhaustive search of all possible methods of matching, which will be quite inefficient in many cases. But perhaps a more serious problem is that we probably do not want an *exact* isomorphism between the languages described; there is no unique way of describing a program as a regular expression; and the programmer should be at complete liberty to give slightly more accurate or less detailed descriptions of his data, if this will help him to find useful correspondences.

Is it possible to detect whether correspondences have been correctly filled in?

Yes. It is trivial, provided that *all* the needed extra nodes have been inserted. All that is necessary to check is that whenever two nodes correspond,
   (a) Their parent nodes correspond.
   (b) They are the same kind of nodes (o , * , or plain).
   In fact, Michael Jackson does not usually put in all the extra nodes and lines that are needed. Presumably it would be possible to define some machine-checkable conventions which would permit these extra nodes to be omitted. But for teaching purposes, it might be better to make the students write them in, to begin with.

What is a structure clash?

A structure clash is whatever prevents the chain of correspondences between branches of two diagrams to be extended.
   (a) Some structure clashes can be resolved by making valid transformations on one or both structures.
   (b) Some structure clashes can be tolerated because there is room enough in main store to hold all of the data required.
   (c) In some cases the clash is not resolvable, since the required output data simply cannot be computed from the preceding input data. There is no automatic way of detecting this case; it must rely on the programmer's judgment.
   (d) In case (c) it sometimes happens that a correspondence *can* be established lower down in the tree. In this case we have a definition of a boundary clash, for which Jackson's methods provide an excellent solution.

How do you list all the executable operations which will be required, and how do you put them in the proper place?

This is in principle the same task as finding correspondences between two structure diagrams. I would recommend that a structure diagram should be drawn for each in ternal variable of the program, just as it is for the input and output. For example, in the *Multiplication Table* problem, we could construct diagrams for c and r; and then establish the correspondences and merge the diagrams in the same way as any other structure diagrams (see Figure 18).

How much of the Michael Jackson Technique relies on programmer judgment, and how much is just routine formal manipulation?

All the part that involves construction of structure diagrams, and established of correspondences, relies on the judgment of the programmer. The great advantages of the Michael Jackson Technique are that:

(a) It provides a framework within which the programmer can make *one decision at a time,* with high confidence that all decisions will mesh properly with each other.

(b) It provides a framework within which he can describe and justify his decisions to his managers, colleagues, subordinates, and successors; and gives these the ability to understand them.

(c) It provides a framework within which alternate decisions can be easily seen, and cheaply explored, until the best decision is recognized and adopted.

(d) It ensures that program documentation is constructed during *program design,* when it is most useful. The usual practice of documentation after testing is *guaranteed* to be useless. If the documentation is not a help to the program writer himself, it will hardly be helpful to the unfortunate maintainer!

Nevertheless, there are several aspects of the Michael Jackson Technique that are routine:

(a) Given a program, it is possible to work back to the original structure diagrams from which it was created. This is a useful check on the correctness of the program, before it is tested.

(b) The final construction of a COBOL program is fairly routine; though there are still good opportunities for skill in local optimization. This task can therefore be delegated to coders, who do not have the necessary judgment to design the program, or to postpone their passion for optimization to a stage when it is relatively harmless.

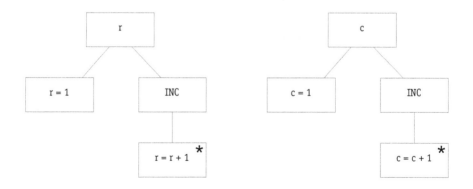

Figure 18: Structure diagrams for variables

Are there any suggestions for shortening the learning time for the Michael Jackson's Technique?

I think it may help to give exercises which show how the structure diagram 'generates' the input data, the output data, and the traces of program execution. Also, perhaps some exercises in constructing selective traces, and selective programs *from* the complete ones. I believe that it is useful in teaching to show how to *check* the solution to a problem *before* trying to get the student to find his own solution. Similarly for correspondences, a list of permissible transformations to a structure should help considerably.

The consideration of only *two* structure diagrams at a time, and only *one* pair of nodes at a time should be helpful. The use of the *same* technique of structure diagrams and correspondences for internal calculations should help too.

Are there any improvements in the Michael Jackson technique that you could recommend before it is packaged for use in the U.S.A.?

Apart from the possible changes in teaching strategy listed in my answers above, I would be very reluctant to suggest any changes without considerable further thought and experience. The fact is that Michael Jackson is one of our most brilliant original thinkers in the field of programming methodology. Not only is his academic distinction of the highest; he also has long experience of commercial data processing, and has seen his ideas tested in practice over a wide range of environments and applications. Finally, he is a brilliant and experienced teacher; and he has as good understanding of the capabilities and limitations of his likely audience, and he has adapted his material to meet them. That is why I am not qualified to make authoritative suggestions for change in his Technique. If I were so bold to suggest a change, I would very much prefer to discuss the suggestion thoroughly with Michael Jackson himself, not only because he would be the most qualified to comment, but because I have always found in him the true scientific spirit, which is eager to understand and evaluate ideas different from his own; and admit freely if he finds them better.

References (Introduction)

1. Matthias Felleisen, Robert Bruce Findler, Matthew Flatt and Shriram Krishnamurthi. *How to Design Programs: An Introduction to Programming and Computing.* MIT Press, 2001.

2. Erich Gamma and Richard Helm and Ralph Johnson and John Vlissides. *Design Patterns: Elements of Reusable Object-Oriented Software.* Addison-Wesley Professional Computing Series, 1995.

3. C.A.R. Hoare. *Communicating Sequential Processes.* Prentice Hall, 1985.

4. Michael Jackson. *Principles of Program Design.* Academic Press, 1975.29

5. Michael Jackson. The origins of JSP and JSD: A personal recollection. *IEEE Annals of Software Engineering*, Volume 22, Number 2, pp. 61–63, 66, April–June 2000.

6. Michael Jackson. JSP in perspective. *SD&M Pioneers' Conference*, Bonn, June 2001.

7. Michael Jackson. *System Development.* Prentice Hall, Englewood Cliffs, New Jersey, 1983.

8. Michael Jackson. *Software Requirements and Specifications: A Lexicon of Principles, Practices and*

Prejudices. Addison-Wesley and ACM Press, 1996.

9.   Gregor Kiczales, John Lamping, Anurag Mendhekar, Chris Maeda, Cristina Videira Lopes, Jean-Marc Loingtier, John Irwin. Aspect-oriented programming. *Proceedings of the 11th European Conference on Object-Oriented Programming*, Mehmet Aksit, Satoshi Matsuoka (Eds.), Jyväskylä, Finland. *Lecture Notes in Computer Science*, Vol. 1241. Springer-Verlag, June 1997, pp. 220-242.

10.   Dennis M. Ritchie and Ken Thompson. The UNIX time-sharing system. *Bell System Technical Journal 57*, 6, Part 2 (1978) pp. 1905–1930.

11.   Jean Dominique Warnier. *Logical Construction of Systems*. John Wiley & Sons, Inc., 1981.

References (Original Paper)

12.   Alfred V. Aho, J.E. Hopcroft, Jeffrey D. Ullman. *The Design and Analysis of Computer Algorithms*. Addison-Wesley, 1974. Page 403, Exercise 10.28.

13.   L. Stockmeyer & A.R. Meyer. Word problems requiring exponential time. *Proc. 5th Annual ACM Symposium on Theory of Computing*, May 1973, pp. 1–10.

Acknowledgments (Introduction)

Thank you to Maria Rebelo for entering the text of the original manuscript; to Dick Nelson (the originator of the name 'Jackson Structured Programming') for retrieving old course notes; and to Tony Hoare for his encouragement in the publishing of this wonderful piece. I am grateful to my father, Michael Jackson, not just for his immediate help on this project—for answering questions about JSP and its history, and for pointing me to earlier papers [5, 6] from which the historical comments in the introduction are partly drawn—but more broadly for the inspiration and encouragement that he has provided over the years in my own career. Since the first time I applied it (as a programmer working for Logica UK), JSP has always represented, for me, the programming method par excellence, showing what it means to bring clarity to a class of problems, and to solve them in a way that is truly rigorous—not in the shallow sense of using notations with mathematic semantics, but in the deeper sense of making the solution process systematic and predictable.

4.2   Text - Correspondence

The following is a simple problem involving two data structures - one input data structure and one output data structure.

'The stores section in a factory issues and receives parts. Each issue and each receipt is recorded on a punched card: the card contains the part-number, the movement type (I for issue, R for receipt) and the quantity. The cards have already been copied to magnetic tape and sorted into part-number order. The program to be written will produce a simple summary of the net movement of each part. The format of the summary is:

STORES MOVEMENTS SUMMARY

```
A5/132      NET MOVEMENT      -450
A5/197      NET MOVEMENT      1760
B41/728     NET MOVEMENT         7
                   .
                   .
                   .
```

No attention need be paid to such refinements as skipping over the perforations at the end of each sheet of paper.'

The first step of the design procedure, the data step, is to draw data structures of all the files in the problem. The result of the data step is:

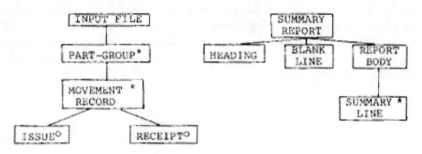

Figure 19: Sample page from original course notes

The Michael Jackson Design Technique (0164)

A study of the theory with applications.

C. A. R. Hoare

March 1977.

The execution of a computer program involves the execution of a series of elementary commands, and the evaluation of a series of elementary tests.*
It is in principle possible to get a computer to record each elementary command when it is executed, and also to record each test as it is evaluated,* (together with an indication whether it was true or false). Such a record is known as a "trace"; and it can sometimes be helpful in program debugging.

It is obviously very important that a programmer should have an absolutely clear understanding of the relation between his program and any possible trace of its execution. Fortunately, in the case of a structured program, this relation is very simple — indeed, as Dijkstra pointed out, this is the main argument in favour of structured programming. The relation may be defined as follows:

* In fact the Michael Jackson techniques tends to ignore these tests.

Figure 20: Sample page from Hoare's original report

Chapter 6

A System Development Method

Michael Jackson

1. Introduction

1.1. The nature of method

A development method may be regarded as a path or a procedure by which the developer proceeds from a problem of a certain class to a solution of a certain class. In trivial cases, the method may be fully algorithmic; for example, there is an algorithmic procedure for obtaining the square root of a nonnegative number to any desired degree of accuracy. In more interesting cases, such as the development of computer-based systems for purposes such as data processing or process control, we do not expect to find an algorithmic method: the goal of the development is not precisely defined, and neither the problem nor the set of possible solutions is sufficiently well understood. But a method, to be worthy of the name, must at least decompose the development task into a number of reasonably well-defined steps which the developer can take with some confidence that they are leading to a satisfactory solution.

The steps of a method impose some ordering on the decisions to be taken during development. Here we are using the term "decision" in a wide sense: it may denote a decision to state explicitly some *a priori* truth about the subject matter of the system, or a decision to define a certain abstract data type, or a decision to store certain variables on disk, or a decision to decompose some system function into three parts, or any of a wide range of possible actions whose result contributes to the final solution. Some decisions will be easy to take, especially where they involve little more than the recording of already known facts: for example, the decision that a multiple of a prime number cannot itself be a prime number. Some will be hard to take, perhaps because they require great foresight on the part of the developer. Some will be highly error prone, and some will be taken in confidence of their correctness. Some will have very limited consequences for the work that follows, some will have wide consequences.

From this viewpoint, we can discern some inchoate principles of methodology (a much misused word, denoting the study or science of method). Decisions about the subject matter of the computation should be taken before decisions about the computation itself. Decisions about implementation should be taken after decisions about what is to be implemented. Decisions which are error-prone should be taken as late as possible, when the developer is most likely to make them correctly. Decisions which have wide consequences should not be highly error-prone. The more error-prone a decision, the more important that the method should provide an early confirmation or disproof of its correctness.

These principles suggest strongly that those methods which can broadly be described as "top-down functional decomposition" are to be avoided. In such a method, the developer begins by deciding the structure of the highest level of the system, viewed as a hierarchy. This decision has the widest possible consequences, because it conditions everything that follows. It is highly error-prone, because it concerns the system itself, which, by definition, is as yet unknown. It is placed at the very start of the development procedure, but it may be invalidated at the end. We may suspect that developers who purport to be using such methods for development. are, in fact, using them only for description; the development work has already been largely done, informally and invisibly, in the developer's head.

1.2. Scope of this method

The method described in this paper is concerned with those problems for which the subject matter is strongly and inherently sequential, and especially those where the sequentiality is an ordering in time. We will refer to the subject matter of the system as the "real world" for the system. The real world for a payroll system contains the employees, their work, their holidays, their periods of sickness, their promotions, their productivity. The real world for a process control system contains the plant to be controlled, its vessels, pipes, valves, the substances being processed, the flows of those substances, their temperatures and densities. The real world for a telephone switching system contains the subscribers, their telephone apparatus, the calls they make, the trunk lines and relays. For all of these, the real world is strongly time-ordered. The telephone subscriber goes off hook before dialling the first digit; he dials the area code before dialling the exchange number; he converses before going on-hook again. The employee joins the company before he works; he goes on holiday before he returns from holiday; he retires before he receives a pension. An adequate description of the real world must do justice to this time-ordering.

For some problems, which are outside the scope of JSD, there is no time-ordering in the real world. A classic example is the problem of providing a system to answer questions about the results of a national census. The real world for this system is a snapshot of the state of the nation at one moment in time, the moment when the census is taken. There is no time-ordering in this real world:

there are no events occurring in sequence, only a state of reality at one moment. Of course, when the system has been constructed to run on a sequential machine, there will be time-ordering in the operation of the system itself; but this is an artefact of the development, not an aspect of the real world. JSD is concerned only with systems for which the real world is sequential.

1.3. Principles of this method

The first principle of JSD is that development must begin by describing and modelling the real world, not by specifying, describing or structuring the function which the system is to perform. A system developed according to the JSD method embodies an explicit simulation of the real world; this simulation is specified before any direct attention is paid to the function of the system. Of course, the developer must have in mind a general idea of the system's function and purpose, to guide the modelling activity; but, just as in the construction of a simulation program, the model is built first and the parts of the system which produce output are added later.

The decisions to be taken in the modelling steps of JSD are, in general, likely to be easier than decisions about the system function. Often (though not always) the real world already exists and is well known to the intending users of the system. In modelling this real world, the developer captures the users' view of the world they inhabit; although the developer must provide the power of abstraction, he will be able to look to the users for authoritative guidance in many of the decisions he must make. These decisions will therefore be easier and less prone to error. Later, when the system functions are specified, decisions will again be easier: an agreed model of the real world provides a sound basis for clear and unambiguous discussion of functions. We may go further: the explicit statement of a model defines a universe of possible functions; every function to be performed by the system must be capable of specification in terms of the model.

The second principle of JSD is that an adequate model of a time-ordered real world must itself be time-ordered. In particular, a database model of reality is not adequate. An appropriate modelling medium is provided by communicating sequential processes, in which the ordering of events in the real world is directly represented in program texts for the processes. We may adapt a statement made by Dijkstra in a different context [2]:

> "... we should restrict ourselves in all humility to the most systematic sequencing mechanisms, ensuring that 'progress through the computation' is mapped on 'progress through the text' in the most straightforward manner."

Our purpose is to map progress through the real world on progress through the system that models it. A model consisting of sequential processes allows this to be done in the desired straightforward manner.

The third principle is that the system should be implemented by transforming the specification into an efficient and convenient set of processes, adapted to running on the available hardware and software. A central concern in the implementation stage is process scheduling; a small number of available processors must be shared among a large number of specification processes, and it is highly desirable to determine and bind the scheduling of processes when the system is constructed, rather than waiting until it is run. The transformations are therefore chiefly concerned with process activation and suspension.

The advantages of transformation as an implementation method are obvious, and have been explained often (see, for example, [1]). JSD specifications are highly explicit; they describe very directly the real world to be modelled and the outputs to be derived from that model. Being in the form of communicating sequential processes, they are amenable to a powerful yet simple set of transformations that suffice to give several different implementations of the same specification.

2. The development medium

2.1. Sequential processes

A sequential process is an execution instance of a program text. The text is a tree structure of sequence, selection, iteration and elementary components; both diagrammatic and textual representations are used for these tree structures, but the usual diagrammatic representation is incomplete (it does not, for example, show the conditions on selections and iterations). By definition, there is only one instance of the program text pointer for a sequential process, and hence there is no concurrency or parallelism within one process.

The control flow constructs of sequence, selection and iteration are augmented by backtracking versions of the selection and iteration constructs. A *quit* statement is provided which may be written within the body of an iteration or within the first part of a two-part selection; execution of the quit statement transfers control to the end of the iteration component or to the beginning of the second part of the selection. Use of this quit statement, which is equivalent to a limited form of GOTO, is considered highly preferable to the use of local variables for the same purpose; control flow should be explicit, and should not be hidden in Boolean variables. The appropriate design discipline for use of these backtracking constructs is discussed in [4], where it forms a part of a general design method for sequential processes.

2.2. Data stream communication

One process may communicate with another process by operations on a named data stream. The operations on a data stream are open, close, write, and read. For any data stream there is a writer process and a reader process. The writer process executes the operations

```
open, write, ..., write, close
```

and the reader process executes the operations

```
open, read, ..., read, close.
```

The close operation executed by the writer process embodies an implicit write operation which writes a special end-marker record.

The data stream is considered to be an unbounded buffer in which writing and reading obey the FIFO rule. When the reader process reaches a read operation in its text, and the data stream from which a record is to be read is empty (the number of records previously written is equal to the number previously read), the process is blocked; its execution cannot continue until another record is written to the data stream. A writer process is never blocked, because the buffering in the stream is unbounded.

A process which is the reader of two or more data streams may determine the interleaving of read operations on those streams by the sequencing of the read operations in its text. Alternatively the interleaving may be determined by the order in which records become available on the data streams. The reader process of a data stream may test the value of a Boolean predicate *empty*, which indicates whether or not the stream is empty and hence whether a read operation would cause the process to become blocked. This interleaving scheme is called a rough merge; its effect depends in general on the implementation of the system, and thus introduces indeterminacy into the specification. Where a rough merge occurs in a JSD specification, the developer has the option of writing an explicit merging process using the empty predicate, or of leaving the merge implicit.

2.3. State vector communication

The state vector of a process consists of its local variables together with its text pointer. The value of a process's state vector can be changed only by execution of the process itself: it is strictly an own variable from this point of view.

In one respect the state vector of a process in JSD is not strictly an own variable: it can be directly inspected by other processes. A process P may execute the operation

```
getsv (Q)
```

Having executed this operation P may then inspect and use the current values of Q's local variables.

The value of a state vector obtained by a getsv operation is always a value at an open, write, read, close, or getsv operation in the process whose state vector is obtained. This rule may be satisfied by the use in Q of a private copy of its state vector, assignments to the public copy being made only at the appropriate points in its execution; although Q's state vector is a shared variable for P and Q, only the lowest-level mutual exclusion is required.

State vector communication, like rough merge, introduces indeterminacy into the specification. The value of Q's state vector obtained by P will depend on the implementation of the system; only the implementation will determine the relative scheduling of P and Q.

3. JSD development procedure

3.1. Development steps

There are six steps in the JSD development procedure:

+ Entity/Action step,
+ Entity Structures step,
+ Initial Model step,
+ Function step,
+ System Timing step and
+ Implementation step.

In the Entity/Action and Entity Structures steps, an abstract description of the real world is made; the world is described in terms of entities which perform and suffer actions. The entities and their actions are listed in the Entity/Action step, and the constraints on the time ordering of the actions (for example, the constraint that a library book must be lent before it is returned) are expressed in the Entity Structures step. This abstract description is realised in the Initial Model step. For each structure specified in the Entity Structures step, a sequential process is specified and a mechanism for connecting that process, directly or indirectly, to the real world entity which it models. The connections between the real world and the model, like the internal connections of the system being developed are by data stream or state vector.

The Initial Model step specifies a simulation of the real world; the Function step adds to this simulation the further executable operations and processes needed to produce the outputs of the system. Because of the indeterminacy in the system, due to the rough merges and state vector connections which it may use, it is necessary to consider explicitly whether the values of system outputs are sufficiently constrained. For example, the user of an accounting system may be satisfied if answers to account enquiries are based on information that may be as much as one day out of date, or he may not. These constraints are partly specified in the Function step, by choosing appropriate connections among processes; they may require further consideration in the System Timing step, where tighter synchronisation among processes can be specified.

The specification produced at the end of the System Timing step is, in principle, capable of direct execution. The necessary environment would contain a processor for each process, a device equivalent to an unbounded buffer for each data stream, and some input and output devices where the system is connected to the real world. Such an environment could, of course, be provided by suitable software running on a sufficiently powerful machine. Sometimes, such direct execution of the specification will be possible, and may even be a reasonable choice. More often, the mismatch between the specification and the available hardware/software machine will be too severe. A data processing system specification may contain hundreds of millions of processes: a social security system for a nation must have at least one process for each member of the nation. But no available hardware system contains hundreds of millions of processors, nor is any available operating system capable of scheduling so many processes with reasonable efficiency.

It is therefore necessary to reduce the number of processes from the large number contained in the specification to a much smaller number, so that a real or virtual processor can be provided for each process to be executed. This is the central concern of the Implementation step. By suitable transformations, processes are combined so that their number is reduced to the number of processors: execution of the combined processes is interleaved, so that they appear to their processor to be a single process.

3.2. Entities and actions

The ideas of entity and action are closely related in JSD. An action is an atomic event, occurring at some point in time, and considered to be instantaneous. One or more entities participate in an event, either performing or suffering the action. Over its lifetime each entity participates in a number of events, the ordering of the events being subject to certain predetermined constraints. This participation is the defining characteristic of an entity in JSD.

It is the real world which is described in terms of entities and actions, not the system itself. In the early steps of JSD development, attention is focused entirely on the real world outside the system. We are therefore careful to exclude from the lists of entities and actions any object or event which belongs to the system being developed rather than to its subject matter in the real world. Thus, for example, in developing a system to control a chemical plant we would regard the plant as a part of the real world, but the control mechanism as a part of the system; there would therefore be no entity "controller" in the abstract description of the real world, and there would be no action "output control signal to valve" or "turn on warning light".

This view of entities and actions is close to the view underlying Hoare's CSP [3]. It is radically different from the view taken in database design. Because a JSD entity must have a significant time-ordered history of actions, there will be many fewer entity types in a JSD description than in a typical database definition; a JSD entity does not correspond to an owner or member of a set in a network database, to a segment in a hierarchical database, or to a 3rd or 4th normal form relation in a relational database.

The guiding principle in choosing entities and actions is that the description must be able to support the functions to be provided by the system. Even when the system is intended to function as a control system, the criterion is simple: will the system need to produce or use information about this event or about the history of this person or object? Putting the same criterion in a negative form, if this putative action or entity is omitted, are there any required functions that cannot then be provided?

In the Entity Structures step it may become apparent that more than one structure specification (and hence, eventually, more than one sequential process) is needed to describe the behaviour of an entity. The structure specifications are regular expressions, eventually to be translated directly into process structures. It will often happen that one regular expression is not enough to describe the constraints on the ordering of the actions of an entity. Consider, for example the following two cases. In the first case, we wish to describe the behaviour of a library book, whose actions are lend (i.e., the book is lent) and return (i.e., the book is returned). The necessary constraints are that lend and return actions must alternate, the first action of the book being a lend action. Diagrammatically we represent the lifetime of the book as:

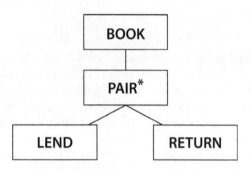

The asterisk in the box PAIR indicates that BOOK is an iteration of (consists of zero or more instances of) PAIR. In the second case, we wish to describe the behaviour of a customer of the same library. The actions are BORROW and RETURN, with obvious meaning; the constraint is that each BORROW must precede the corresponding RETURN, but BORROW and RETURN need not alternate. We must represent this constraint by two structures:

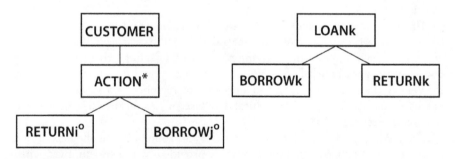

The CUSTOMER structure shows that the behaviour of CUSTOMER is an iteration of ACTION, each ACTION being a selection of RETURN and BORROW (indicated by the circles in those boxes). Each RETURN and BORROW is associated by its index with a particular LOAN and the behaviour of a LOAN is a sequence of BORROW followed by RETURN.

The developer might arrive at the two structures, CUSTOMER and LOAN, by either of two paths. He might start, as suggested above, with only CUSTOMER as an entity; in the Entity Structures step he is then forced to introduce the LOAN structure to describe the constraints on the ordering of CUSTOMER actions. Or he might start with both CUSTOMER and LOAN as entities, BORROW and RETURN being actions common to both.

3.3. Functions

The result of the Initial Model step is a specification of a workable simulation of the real world; for each structure showing the time-ordered actions of an entity, there is a sequential process driven by the real world actions. In the Function step, the developer adds to this simulation the operations and processes required to produce the system outputs.

In the simplest case, an output may be provided simply by embedding a write operation in an appropriate process of the model. For example, an exception report to be produced whenever a customer has more than 10 books on loan can be embedded in the CUSTOMER process directly. A function specified in this way is called a simple embedded function.

A more complex function may require the addition of a new process to the specification, connected to one or more model processes by data stream or state vector connection. For example, a report listing the library's books and showing for each one how many times it has been lent would be provided in this way. Such a function may also require input, if the report is to be produced on demand. If the function process is connected by state vector connection to the model processes, it is called an imposed function; it uses the model by inspecting its state, and may be thought of as being imposed on the model as another level of the system.

The most complex functions are those which change the state of the model, as neither embedded nor imposed functions do. Suppose, for example, that a customer may perform the action of requesting a book which is out on loan, and that the system is to contain an allocation process which reserves the book for loan to that customer when it next becomes available. Then the state of the book process must be changed by the allocation process. The allocation process will he connected to the book process by two connections: it will inspect the state vector of the book process, and it will also write a data stream of reservation records which is input to the book process. The allocation process is called an interacting function because it interacts with the model instead of merely receiving input from it.

3.4. Process scheduling

Suppose that in a very simple system we have a process P and a process Q, connected by a data stream B; P has an input data stream A and Q has an output data stream C. We represent this system diagrammatically as:

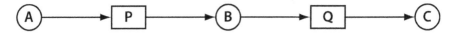

Suppose also that we wish to implement this system on a single processor, and must therefore combine P and Q into one process from the execution point of view. (We would, of course, regard the use of multi-programming or multi-tasking facilities as the use of two processors.)

To combine P and Q into a single process we must choose a scheduling scheme for sharing the processor between them, and implement this scheduling scheme as an explicit interleaving of the execution of P and Q. One possible scheme is to suspend and activate each process once for each record of B, and to activate them alternately. The necessary transformation of P and Q is to transform them into procedures which may be invoked respectively to produce and consume one record of B. This transformation is called "inversion with respect to B"; it consists essentially of implementing the "write B" and "read B" operations as:

```
save process text pointer;
return to invoking program;
label:
```

where the saved value of the text pointer is the value of label. At the entry point of the transformed procedure is a suitable mechanism for resuming execution at the next invocation:

```
entry: GO TO (text pointer);
```

The process state is held in own variables within the process; the text pointer must be set to its initial value before process execution begins, and this can be done conveniently at compile time.

We now design a special-purpose scheduling process which invokes P and Q according to the chosen scheme:

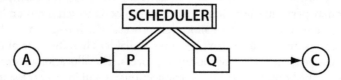

The scheduler itself is, in outline

```
while true do
  call P;
  call Q;
od
```

We could, of course, replace this scheduler by another which implemented a different scheme; for example, we might provide the scheduler with a buffer for 10 records of B, and activate P and Q alternately 10 times each. More ambitiously, we could invert P and Q with respect to all of their data streams:

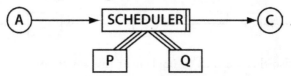

The scheduler may now buffer records of A, B and C, and may therefore implement quite elaborate schemes. For example, it might buffer all records of A until a record of a certain type appears; then it might activate P and Q alternately, buffering the records of C; it might produce records of C in batches of 100. Batch data processing systems may be regarded as the product of this kind of implementation.

Notice that inverting a process with respect to more than one data stream requires a more complex interface with the scheduler: the scheduler must be able to determine whether the suspended process P is suspended at a "read A" or at a "write B" operation.

For the simplest scheme mentioned above, in which P and Q alternate on each record of B, we could have used one of the system processes itself as the scheduler:

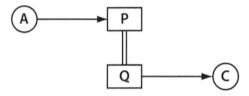

The "write B" operations in P are implemented as calls to Q. It is possible to implement systems of several processes in this way. A sufficient condition for such an implementation is: the system forms an acyclic undirected graph when each process is regarded as a node and each data stream connecting two processes is regarded as an arc.

3.5. State vector handling

If there are several processes modelling several entities of one type, they will have a common program text. An obvious implementation device is to use only one copy of the program text and to associate the appropriate state vector with the text when a process is activated. In a data processing system, the state vectors of processes, treated in this way, become data records corresponding to the entities modelled by the processes. It is necessary to handle these state vectors explicitly as data objects in the scheduling processes.

Consider the very simple system discussed above, with the elaboration that there are multiple instances of the process Q and hence of the data stream B. Diagrammatically we represent this system as:

The double bars on the arrow from B to Q indicate that the relationship between P and Q is one to many.

Suppose now that Q is inverted with respect to B, and that P is to be used as the scheduler process. The state vectors of the Q processes are held in an explicit direct-access store which is accessible to P:

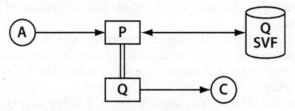

Each "write Bi" operation in P is implemented as

```
obtain state vector of Qi;
call Q (Brec,state-vector);
replace state vector of Qi;
```

The file handling and data base accessing programs of a typical data processing system may be regarded in this light. The access paths to data records are then determined by the choice of process scheduling.

3.6. Process dismembering

All transformations considered so far have kept the program text of a process in one piece. Sometimes it is necessary to dismember the text of a process into several pieces for greater convenience of execution.

One important reason for process dismembering is the need to limit the elapsed execution time of the longest process. In a data processing system, the model processes will typically have execution times measured in years or even decades, because they model in real time the behaviour of real world entities whose lifetimes are long. The use of program inversion allows these processes to be suspended and reactivated almost at will, but this merely transfers the difficulty to the scheduling process. If the execution time of P and Q in the simple system discussed above is, say, ten years, we can break this execution time into small periods by inverting both P and Q and placing them under control of a scheduler. But now the scheduler has an execution time of ten years. This is clearly unacceptable in the execution environments available today.

The solution to the difficulty depends on the scheduler having a structure which admits of convenient decomposition. Suppose, for example that the scheduler has the structure:

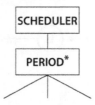

in which one PERIOD component is executed, say, each day. Then we may dismember the scheduler into two parts: one part is the PERIOD component, and becomes a batch program or a day's running of an on-line system; the other part is the iteration SCHEDULER itself, which may be implemented by instructions to the computer operators ("each day, please run the program PERIOD"). Clearly, if the state vector of SCHEDULER contains variables which must be remembered from one PERIOD to another (i.e. are not local to the PERIOD component), provision must be made for the storage and retrieval of these variables between executions of PERIOD.

4. A simple example

4.1. The starting point

A system is required to control the operation of a simple elevator in a building. The building has six floors, and there is one elevator shaft only. The control requirement is to provide a reasonable service to people who want to use the elevator to travel from floor to floor. Some other functions may be needed, but nothing further is yet known.

This starting point, of course, is not a specification; nor should it be. Our purpose in JSD is to develop the specification, no less than to develop a system to satisfy it.

4.2. Entities and actions

Examining the real world with which the system will be concerned, we may identify several candidate entities: the elevator, the shaft, the floors, the people who use the elevator, the motor which raises and lowers the elevator, the call buttons, the various lamps, the. sensors which sense whether the elevator is positioned at a floor. Applying the criterion discussed in section 3.2 above, we decide that we are interested only in the elevator and the people: we do not expect to provide functions which will produce or require information about the behaviour of the motor, the lamps, the buttons, or the sensors. We expect to provide functions which can be expressed in terms of the actions of the elevator and its users: "when the elevator reaches a floor, if some person wishes to enter or leave at that floor, then ...".

However, some intelligent anticipation suggests that we should not choose "person" as an entity type, because it will not be possible to identify individual people and their actions: to do so, we would need to provide users with identity cards, and require them to insert these cards in a slot beside the call button before pressing the button, since only in this way could we obtain the information necessary to model the behaviour of each user correctly. We therefore decide to abandon "person" as an entity type, and to reintroduce "button"; in some sense, each button abstracts from the set of people who have, or might have, called the elevator by pressing that button.

The actions of the button entity are very simple there is only one type of action, namely "be pressed", which, for convenience, we will call PRESS. The actions of the elevator are also simple: they are only LEAVE FLOORj and ARRIVE AT FLOORj. We might have wished to include such actions as "start" or "stop", but the sensor equipment provided is too crude to detect these actions.

4.3. Entity structures

The structure of BUTTON is:

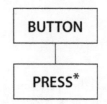

The structure of ELEVATOR is:

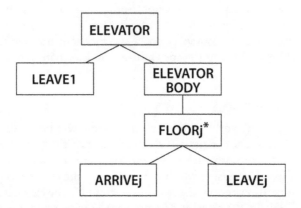

The limitations of the regular grammars we are using prevent us from expressing in the diagram the fact that the successive floor numbers are constrained: $1 \leq j \leq 6$; and, from floor to floor, j can change only by 0, +1, or −1. We expect to use a local variable in the model process, if necessary, to express these constraints. We are assuming, for simplicity, that the elevator begins its life at floor 1, which is the ground floor.

4.4. Initial model

The elevator engineers have arranged each button so that, when pressed, it sends a signal to the computer. The sensors which detect the positioning of the elevator at the floors, however, are simple make/break switches, whose state can be directly inspected by the computer. The sensor switch at a floor is open when the elevator is not within 6 inches of the home position at that floor, and is closed otherwise. We may regard the set of six sensors as a single variable of 6 bits: at any time, either one or none of the 6 bits is set to 1, indicating that the corresponding sensor switch is closed.

Diagrammatically, we represent the initial model in a System Specification Diagram:

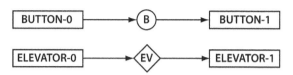

BUTTON-0 is the real button in the real world; it is connected by data stream connection to BUTTON-1, which is the process in the system which models its behaviour. There are sixteen instances of BUTTON-0 and hence of BUTTON-1: 6 within the elevator itself, 5 "up" buttons at floors 1 to 5, and 5 "down" buttons at floors 2 to 6.

ELEVATOR-0 is the real elevator in the real world; it is connected to ELEVATOR-1, which is the process in the system which models its behaviour, by state vector connection. ELEVATOR-1 inspects directly the state of ELEVATOR-0, by examining the value of the set of 6 sensors. The BUTTON-1 process is trivial. It has the same structure as BUTTON-0, and contains operations to read the data stream B. Synchronisation between BUTTON-1 and BUTTON-0 is achieved by these operations BUTTON-1 is blocked at each read B operation until the real BUTTON-0 is next pressed.

The ELEVATOR-1 process is a little more complicated: it must model the actions of ELEVATOR-0 by repeatedly inspecting the state of ELEVATOR-0 and detecting changes of state from which the occurrence of an action can be inferred. Thus, for example, occurrence of the LEAVE1 action is detected when the state changes from "100000" to "000000"; the subsequent ARRIVE2 is detected when the state changes again to "010000", and so on. ELEVATOR-1 is, effectively, in a busy wait loop, waiting for a change of state in ELEVATOR-0. We are using the state vector connection, somewhat reluctantly, to achieve the same effect as would be obtained more easily by the preferable data stream connection.

We may observe that the processes in the initial model are not connected to one another in any way; this is typically, though not universally, the case. The behaviour of each button is certainly independent of the behaviour of other buttons; the behaviour of the elevator will become dependent on the buttons only when we provide some function of the system which will affect the elevator. In this modelling stage, we are concerned only to capture the real world events which we have chosen to model, describing only those constraints which exist separately from the system we are developing.

4.5. Functions: Embedded and imposed

We are now in a position to provide functions which can be specified in terms of BUTTONs being PRESSed and of the ELEVATOR LEAVING and

ARRIVING.

A very simple embedded function might be the following. There is a set of lights inside the elevator, one light for each floor. We are required to turn these lights on and off, by issuing outputs ONi and OFFi respectively for the light associated with floor i. When the system begins execution, ON1 must be issued; subsequently, OFFj must be issued when the elevator LEAVEs floor j, and ONj when it ARRIVEs at floor j. These outputs can be produced by operations embedded directly in the elevator process:

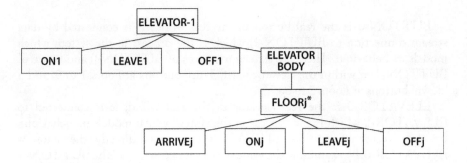

A very simple imposed function might be the following. To cater for nervous or impatient customers waiting at the ground floor for the elevator, a special button is to be provided. When this button is pressed, an indicator beside the button shows which floor the elevator is now at, or, if it is not at any floor, which floor it has most recently visited.

If the ELEVATOR-1 process does not already contain a variable maintained at the required value, we must now provide one. In addition, we must provide a function process ENQF, which will inspect the state of the ELEVATOR-1 process whenever the enquiry button is pressed, and will issue the required output to the indicator:

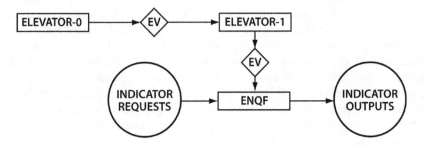

The ENQF process is trivial. It is important to note that it is a process, not a procedure: the lifetime of ENQF spans all the indicator requests that are ever made, not merely one such request.

4.6. An interacting function

We now turn to the requirement of controlling the elevator. The system must issue commands to the motor to cause the elevator to service users' requests in a reasonable way. The motor commands are GO and STOP, and UP and DOWN, with obvious meanings. In addition, the system must turn on and off the lamp which is beside each button: the lamp is to be turned on when a request is recognised, and off when the request is serviced. The lamp commands are UONi, UOFFi, DONi, DOFFi, EONi, and EOFFi: U, D and E refer respectively to up, down and elevator buttons (i.e., the six buttons inside the elevator). Clearly, we will need to introduce a function process ELCONTROL to produce the motor commands: the ELEVATOR-1 process does not have the necessary structure.

Clearly, also, the ELCONTROL process must inspect the states of the buttons, to determine whether or not a request is outstanding for a particular floor. However, the BUTTON-1 process models only the PRESS actions, and this is insufficient for the purpose: we need a process which models also the servicing of a request made on the button, that is, one whose state is affected by ELCONTROL itself. This is the classic situation requiring an interacting function: the ELCONTROL process must both inspect the state of a button and change that state. Avoiding the destruction of our model processes BUTTON-1, we introduce BUTTON-2 processes:

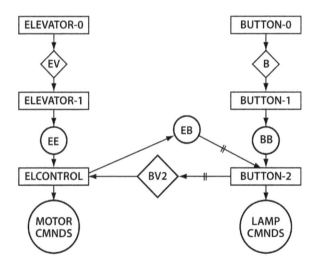

The data streams BB are copies of the streams B. The data streams EB have the structure:

where ELCONTROL writes a VISIT record to a stream EB when it causes the elevator to visit the associated floor in the direction which services requests on the associated button. The data stream EE may contain records for both LEAVEj and ARRIVEj actions of the ELEVATOR-0, or, perhaps, for ARRIVEj actions only.

The BUTTON-2 process merges its input streams BB and EB. This merge is achieved by BUTTON-2 testing whether a record is available in each stream, and reading accordingly from one or the other. Such a merge depends on the eventual implementation of the system: if the BUTTON-1 process runs faster, or is scheduled more favourably, than the ELCONTROL process, then BB records may overtake EB records; and vice versa. The resulting indeterminacy is an unwelcome, but inevitable, feature of the system. The structure of the merged input stream to BUTTON-2, which we will call EB&BB, is then:

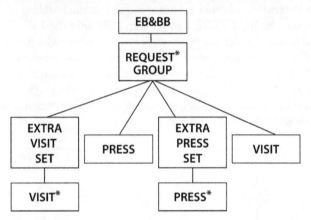

which accommodates any degree of "unfairness" in the merge, and also any possible algorithm, however unreasonable, in the ELCONTROL process.

The structure of BUTTON-2 is essentially that of EB&BB; the operations to output lamp commands are easily allocated to this structure. BUTTON-2 must maintain a variable OS, indicating whether a request is outstanding for the button. A request is outstanding after PRESS and before VISIT, and not outstanding after VISIT and before PRESS.

ELCONTROL may have any structure that gives a reasonable servicing of requests. It is important to recognise that we are still developing the specification during the function step: the structure and detail of ELCONTROL will contain the substance of our specification of the control function.

4.7. Implementation

Considering the implementation of the System Specification Diagram shown in section 4.6 above, we need to decide how many processors we will use.

One option is to use one processor for each process. There are 34 processes (16 BUTTON-1, 16 BUTTON-2, ELEVATOR-1, and ELCONTROL), so we would need 34 processors. We would also need a suitable implementation of the data stream and state vector connections, perhaps by use of shared storage locations which are accessible to both the writing and the reading processes of each connection. We can readily convince ourselves that no deadlock is possible even if the implementation provides only one record buffer for each data stream.

Another option is to simulate the provision of 34 processors by using one hardware processor and a time-slicing supervisor. In JSD we take the view that this is strictly a 34-processor solution. We need to convince ourselves that the time-slices provided to each process give it the equivalent of a processor fast enough to execute the process correctly. For example, the ELEVATOR-1 process must inspect the state of ELEVATOR-0 often enough to ensure that no change of state goes undetected; similarly ELCONTROL must respond sufficiently quickly to the availability of an ARRIVE record in EE to issue the STOP command to the motor in time to halt the elevator at the desired home position.

A more interesting implementation, for our present purposes, is one which uses only one processor: the whole system is arranged so that, from an execution point of view, it is a single sequential process.

A first step in this direction is to consider whether each process contains suitable points in its execution at which it may be suspended by the inversion transformation. Neither ELCONTROL nor ELEVATOR-1 has enough suitable suspension points in this sense. If ELEVATOR-1 is given control, it will enter a "busy wait" loop, inspecting the state of ELEVATOR-0, and will not relinquish control until ELEVATOR-0 changes states. If the elevator is stationary, control will never be relinquished. Similarly, ELCONTROL contains a loop in which it inspects the states of the BUTTON-2 processes, waiting for any request to be made. If ELCONTROL is in this loop, it will never relinquish control because no BUTTON-2 process can change state until it receives control. We therefore introduce additional data streams, SE and SC, which are input to ELEVATOR-1 and ELCONTROL respectively; each process reads a record from the additional data stream once in each iteration of its busy loop, and will thus be suspended at the point where the read operation ELCONTROL is inverted with respect to SC and EE; ELEVATOR-1 is inverted with respect to SE and EE.

A possible System Implementation Diagram, after introducing these additional data streams, is:

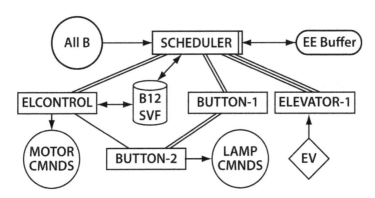

The state vectors of the BUTTON-1 and BUTTON-2 processes have been separated from the executable text, and have been combined into one state vector for each pair, stored in a directly accessible store B12SVF. BUTTON-1 is inverted with respect to its input stream B, and BUTTON-2 with respect to its merged input stream EB&BB.

The merging of the EB and BB streams for each BUTTON-2 process is implemented by making BUTTON-2 a subroutine of both ELCONTROL and BUTTON-I: this is the "fairest" possible implementation of a merge, since the records are read by BUTTON-2 strictly in the order of their writing by BUTTON-1 and ELCONTROL. The buffer for EE is shown, since we do not know *a priori* whether the scheduler will always activate ELCONTROL immediately after ELEVATOR-1 has written a record of EE, nor whether ELCONTROL will always then be suspended at a read EE operation.

The scheduler itself may be quite simple. If a B record is available in its input stream, it may activate the appropriate BUTTON-1 process; otherwise it may activate ELCONTROL and ELEVATOR-1 alternately. This simple scheme may require some modification, depending on the detailed structures of ELCONTROL and ELEVATOR-1, if the processor used has little spare processing capacity: it will then become necessary to consider the execution time for each process activation and, perhaps, to favour one process over another under certain circumstances.

5. Summary

The purpose of this short paper has been to give the flavour, rather than the full detail, of the JSD development method.

The primary advantages claimed for the method are that it structures the development decisions in a sensible way, it leads to systems that can be adapted at reasonable cost when their specifications are changed, and it bridges the uncomfortable gap between specification and implementation.

The small example shown illustrates many of the steps in the method, and some of the relevant considerations at each step. One important point which it does not illustrate is the power of the method to overcome severe mismatching between the dimensions of the specification and the dimensions of the available hardware/software machine. A control system of the kind discussed fits quite well the machine that is, or can be made, available. There are only a few processes, and their demand for machine time is relatively dense. Indeed, there are various operating systems which can execute such a system without discomfort, providing the mechanisms necessary to run such a set of communicating processes.

In a typical data processing system, however, the mismatching would be too great to be overcome by any available, or even conceivable, operating system. Millions of processes, with very long elapsed execution times and very sparse demand for machine time, give a system that is difficult to schedule in an effective manner; the difficulty is compounded by requirements—arbitrary from the point of view of a general purpose operating system—for particular batching of input and output. The transformations used in JSD then provide the opportunity, which is absolutely essential, of defining explicit scheduling rules for the processes of the specification; and they do so without leading to confusion of specification with implementation.

References

1. R. Burstall and J. Darlington, Some transformations for developing recursive programs, SIGPLAN Notices 10, 6, pp. 465-472.
2. E. W. Dijkstra, Notes on structured programming; in O.-J.Dahl, E. W. Dijkstra, and C. A. R. Hoare, *Structured Programming*, p. 22, Academic Press, 1972.
3. C. A. R. Hoare. Communicating sequential processes. *Communications of the ACM* 21, 8, pp. 666-677.
4. M. A. Jackson, *Principles of Program Design*, Academic Press, 1975.

PART 3
DERIVING SOFTWARE
SPECIFICATIONS
FROM SYSTEM
REQUIREMENTS

Chapter 7

Deriving Specifications from Requirements: An Example

Michael Jackson and Pamela Zave

Abstract: A *requirement* is a desired relationship among *phenomena* of the *environment* of a system, to be brought about by the hardware/software *machine* that will be constructed and installed in the environment. A *specification* describes machine behaviour sufficient to achieve the requirement. A specification is a restricted kind of requirement: all the environment phenomena mentioned in a specification are *shared* with the machine; the phenomena constrained by the specification are *controlled* by the machine; and the specified constraints can be determined without reference to the future. Specifications are derived from requirements by reasoning about the environment, using properties that hold independently of the behaviour of the machine. These ideas, and some associated techniques of description, are illustrated by a simple example.

1. Introduction

Software development is concerned with the construction of machines of a particular kind: those that can be implemented by a general-purpose computer, which then becomes the desired machine. Many problems can be solved by these means [Jackson 94], including problems in process control, message switching, text manipulation, decision support, and other fields. For example, an information system is a machine that models a real world outside itself and produces information about it based on the model; a word-processing system is a machine that offers its user a repertoire of operations on texts held within the machine; a control system is a machine that interacts with its environment to bring about or maintain relationships in that environment. We call the hardware/software to be developed the *machine*, preferring this term to the more common *system*, which we consider to be open to too many interpretations. For example, the term *system* may be used to denote the hardware/software machine; or the machine together with the part of the environment with which it interacts directly; or the machine together with its users and the whole environment.

Although the different kinds of problem, and the appropriate methods, have much in common, we focus in this paper on control systems, and on their functional requirements. They seem to offer the cleanest and most concise illustration of the points that we want to make.

A *requirement* states desired relationships in the environment—relationships that will be brought about or maintained by the machine. The requirement is concerned entirely with the environment, where the effects and benefits of the machine will be felt and assessed: the machine is purely a means to the end of achieving the required effect in the environment.

A *specification* describes the behaviour of the machine at its interface with the environment. Like a requirement, it is expressed entirely in terms of *environment phenomena*. Seen from the machine, a specification is a starting point for programming; seen from the environment, it is a restricted kind of requirement.

A specification is derived from a requirement. Given a requirement, we progress to a specification by purging the requirement of all features—such as references to environment phenomena that are not accessible to the machine—that would preclude implementation. The derivation is made possible by environment properties that can be relied on regardless of the machine's behaviour. These properties must, of course, be explicitly described if they are to be exploited.

Such derivation of specifications from requirements is loosely analogous to program refinement [Morgan 90]. In program refinement the purpose is to refine a specification to a program. Program specifications and programs are expressed in the same language, which contains both non-executable elements and executable code. Refinement is complete when all non-executable elements have been removed. The result is a program, because it contains only executable code. The refinement steps must ultimately be justified by appeal to the properties of the computer, as embodied in the semantics of the specification and programming language.

In refining requirements to specifications, we begin with requirements expressed in terms of the environment phenomena. Just as program specifications may contain non-executable elements, so requirements may refer to phenomena that are inaccessible to the machine. Refinement is complete when all references to inaccessible phenomena have been removed. The result is purely a description of machine behaviour. The refinement steps must ultimately be justified by appeal to the properties of the environment.

In this paper we present some elements of a method for describing requirements and for deriving specifications from them. We explain certain distinctions that we regard as essential to a sound treatment, and we show how they guide us in bridging the gap between requirements and specifications. We also show how certain real-time considerations can be handled in a simple and direct way.

We illustrate our points chiefly by means of a very small example. Our intention in using this small example, rather than something more substantial, is to ensure that as little detail as possible is left to the reader's imagination. In presenting the example we rely on finite-state automata and predicate logic as descriptive languages. This choice is meant to simplify the presentation: it should be taken neither as a recommendation nor as an intended contribution.

2. Designating environment phenomena

Our small example concerns the control of a turnstile at the entry to a zoo. The turnstile consists of a rotating barrier and a coin slot, and is fitted with an electrical interface. This mechanical apparatus has already been chosen, and the development job is to write the controlling software. The software will run in a small computer: this is the *machine*. The *environment* is the turnstile mechanism itself and its use by visitors to the zoo. To enter the zoo, a visitor must first push on the turnstile barrier, moving it to an intermediate position from which it will continue rotating of its own accord, returning to its initial position and gently pushing the visitor into the zoo. The turnstile is equipped with a locking device; when locked it prevents the barrier from being pushed to the intermediate position.

The first step is to decide what environment phenomena are of interest (we consider entity classes to be phenomena too). We capture these decisions by writing a *designation set*. Each designation of the set gives a careful informal description by which certain phenomena may be recognised in the environment; it also gives a term by which the phenomena may be denoted in requirement and specification descriptions:

in event e a visitor pushes the barrier to its intermediate position $\approx$ Push(e)

in event e a visitor pushes the barrier fully home and so gains entry to the zoo $\approx$ Enter(e)

in event e a valid coin is inserted into the coin slot $\approx$ Coin(e)

in event e the turnstile receives a locking signal $\approx$ Lock(e)

in event e the turnstile receives an unlocking signal $\approx$ Unlock(e)

The terms on the right hand sides of the designations are predicates. Push(e) is a predicate that is true of e if and only if e is an event in which a visitor pushes the barrier to its intermediate position. In this small example, all the designated phenomena are unary predicates characterising sets of events. This is not typical: in general, designated terms are n-ary predicates. However, it is fully typical that we choose to refer to the designated phenomena by predicates. Our phenomenology is based on facts about individuals; predicates are regarded as generalisations of such facts, and hence as the appropriate vehicle for denoting phenomena [Jackson 92].

By deciding on the designations that are specific to the environment—Push(e), Enter(e), Coin(e), Lock(e) and Unlock(e)—we are not only laying down a basis for description. We are also identifying the phenomena in terms of which we will express the requirement and specification. This is an important decision, and must be made consciously and explicitly. It is often claimed that requirements are relative: one person's requirement is another's implementation, and one person's what is another's how. Without the clear statement that designations provide, it is easy to vacillate about the subject matter of the requirement. Is the requirement really about controlling a turnstile, or is it more generally about admitting and excluding visitors? Or is it about the zoo's profitability? Or perhaps about the profitability of the company that owns the zoo? Might the developers legitimately recommend that entry should be free? Or that the zoo be sold and its real estate redeveloped? Writing a designation set locates the requirement unambiguously in the world.

We must also state explicitly that we are adopting our usual phenomenology of time [Jackson 92, Zave 93]. Like most researchers in formal specifications and requirements engineering, we usually regard events as atomic and totally ordered. We also regard both events, and intervals between successive events, as individuals. Each event begins one interval and ends another. Predicates associated with time-varying phenomena must have interval arguments. The appropriate designations for our view of time are:

e is an atomic instantaneous event $\approx$ Event(e)

v is an interval in which no event occurs $\approx$ Interval(v)

event e occurs before event f $\approx$ Earlier(e,f)

event e begins interval v $\approx$ Begins(e,v)

event e ends interval v $\approx$ Ends(e,v)

These temporal phenomena are general, being recognisable in many different environments. We will assume in this paper that the appropriate assertions about them—for example, that Earlier(e,f) is a total ordering on events—have been made.

3. Shared phenomena

If the machine is to interact with the environment, some phenomena must be *shared* by both. Investigation of the turnstile mechanism and its electrical connections shows that Push(e), Coin(e), Lock(e), and Unlock(e) are shared phenomena; Enter(e) is not shared. (Sharing phenomena does not imply sharing control. Rather, the shared phenomena may be regarded as constituting the interface between the machine and the environment, and control may reside on either side of the interface. We return to this point in Section 4 below.)

By identifying certain events as shared we are choosing to regard them as occurring both in the machine and in the environment. Since events are atomic and instantaneous, this means that we are ignoring any delay involved in transmission of the electrical signals. This decision is reasonable in the context of the turnstile. If we were to decide that the delay is not ignorable, we would treat the electrical channel as another part of the environment, distinguishing the events at the machine end of the channel from those at the turnstile end. The shared events would then be those at the machine end of the channel; the events at the other end would not be shared.

The underlying basis of shared phenomena is shared individuals: the event individuals appear in both the environment and the machine. But this is not enough. It is also necessary that the facts about those individuals, generalised in the predicates, are shared. Push and Coin events are clearly distinguished in the environment. But if, perversely, they were identically signalled by the turnstile, then they would still be shared individuals, but the distinction captured in the two predicates would not be accessible to the machine.

Similar considerations apply to shared state phenomena. In a lift control system, the sensors at the floors may be shared individuals. For the information from the sensors to be accessible to the machine, the facts that particular sensors are associated with particular floors, and that a particular sensor is On or Off in a particular time interval, must also be shared.

4. Control of phenomena

We must also determine where *control* of the shared phenomena resides. Investigation—confirming everyday expectations of turnstiles—shows that Push and Coin events are *environment-controlled*, while Lock and Unlock events are *machine-controlled*. Push and Coin events are environment-controlled because they are *initiated* by the environment. Approaches based on the identification of agents [Feather 87, Johnson 88, Feather 91] would identify agents in the environment rather than in the machine for these events: if there are no visitors to the zoo, no Push or Coin event will ever occur, regardless of the machine's behaviour. Conversely, Lock and Unlock events are initiated by the machine, which sends electrical signals to the turnstile. Regardless of the behaviour of the environment, no Lock or Unlock event will occur unless the machine causes it. Environment phenomena that are not shared are necessarily environment-controlled. (Machine phenomena that are not shared are, of course, of no interest in requirements or specifications. They are significant only in programming.)

Control of an event is the power to perform it spontaneously, but only when it is not precluded by other constraints on its occurrence. Some environment-controlled events may be constrained by environment properties; the machine can exploit these constraints to prevent the events from occurring. For example, Push and Enter events are environment-controlled; but, as we shall see, the machine can prevent their occurrence by locking the turnstile. Coin events are also environment-controlled, but their occurrence, by contrast, can be neither prevented nor stimulated by the machine.

Control of state phenomena is associated with control of events. To say that the environment in a lift scheduling problem controls the state of the floor sensors is to say that the environment controls those events that cause the sensor states to change. The lift scheduling machine can access the sensor states, but only the movement of the lift car in the environment can change them.

In our view, control of events is always unilateral: it is never shared. We consider shared control to be unrealistic: it is rarely found in the real world

[Feather 87, Abadi 93]. If some kind of event is sometimes initiated by the machine and sometimes by the environment, we separate it into two kinds by designating the machine-controlled and the environment-controlled events as different phenomena. In some cases shared state phenomena may be changed either by the machine or by the environment.

5. Indicative environment descriptions

In developing requirements we are interested in two distinct kinds of environment description. The first kind describes the properties we would like the machine to bring about or maintain. These descriptions are in what grammarians would call the optative mood: they express our wishes. The second kind describes the properties that the environment has, or will have, regardless of the behaviour of the machine. These are in the indicative mood: they express what is the case whether we wish it or not.

We avoid descriptions of mixed indicative and optative mood. This separation allows the mood of a description to be determined by its context rather than by its contents. We adopt this approach for two reasons. First: reliance on internal syntactic distinctions, whether formal or informal, between the two moods would cause great linguistic difficulty and would exclude many languages from effective use. Second: when a system has been successfully built and installed the optative descriptions become indicative—the wishes come true. It would be very inconvenient if the descriptions themselves then had to be rewritten. The contextual information on which we rely is, so far, quite informal; but in a practical development environment it should be formalised. In this paper we distinguish the moods of descriptions by giving indicative descriptions names of the form INDn, and optative descriptions names of the form OPTn. We also use definitions of new (undesignated) terms. Definitions may appear in indicative descriptions, where they may rely on the truth of the indicative assertion. They may also appear in separate, purely definitional. descriptions, whose names are of the form DEFn.

We begin here with two indicative properties. The first of these properties is that Push and Enter events alternate, starting with Push. A visitor can not Enter without first Pushing; the next visitor can not Push until the first has Entered. This property is described in a Finite-State Automaton:

(IND1)

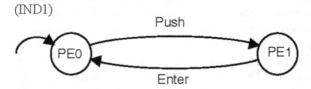

The state names PEO and PE1 do not refer to designated phenomena: they are *defined* in this indicative description. The description *asserts* only a constraint on the ordering of Push and Enter events. It could be falsified by observation of the environment—for example if the sequence <Push,Push> were found to be possible. The property asserted is purely a safety property: the description would still be true if no Push or Enter event ever occurred.

The second indicative property is that if Lock and Unlock events alternate, starting with Unlock, then a Push event can occur only after an Unlock and before the next Lock. This too is a safety property, but its description needs a little care. We do not know, and therefore must not describe, what will happen if Lock and Unlock events do not alternate in the stated way. Possibly the turnstile mechanism will break; perhaps events not fitting the pattern will be ignored; perhaps the mechanism will become permanently locked or permanently unlocked.

So we make this description in two stages. In the first we define three states of the mechanism. LU2 is the state reached when the alternation has been broken. LU0 and LU1 are the two alternating states in which the alternation has been (so far) maintained:

(DEF1)

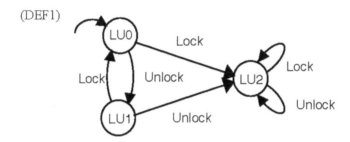

This description is purely definitional. It has an outgoing arc in each state for each kind of event, and so imposes no safety constraint on the event occurrences. Nor is it intended to express any liveness property: there is no implication that the initial state, or any other, will not persist indefinitely. The states LU0, LU1 and LU2 do not appear in the designation set. Nothing in this description DEF1 could be falsified by observation of the environment.

These definitions can now be exploited to assert a safety property:

(IND2) $\forall\ e,v \cdot (LU0(v) \wedge Ends(e,v)\,) \rightarrow \neg\ Push(e)$

This description asserts that if LU0 holds in interval v, and v is ended by an event e, then e can not be a Push event: in other words, Push events are impossible in state LU0. The assertion could be falsified by environment observation—for example, if a Push were found to be possible before the first Unlock. The description exploits the definition of the states, both to assert the safety property concerning Push events and to limit the assertion to the known cases. If we later discover that Lock or Unlock events not fitting the alternating pattern will be ignored, we can add further definition and description to capture the resulting properties without changing or contradicting what we have already said. This kind of technique is essential to effective separation of concerns.

6. Requirements

It is the customer's prerogative to determine the requirements. Essentially, there are two simple requirements: that no-one should enter without paying; and that anyone who has paid should be allowed to enter.

Our customer does not require that payments alternate with entries: that would inconvenience school teachers in charge of groups of children. So the first requirement is simply that entries should never exceed payments. Assume that we have defined predicates Push#(v,n), Enter#(v,n) and Coin#(v,n), meaning that the count of Push, Enter and Coin events respectively preceding interval v is n. (Like the states PE0 and PE1, and LU0, LU1, and LU2, these are not newly designated environment phenomena: their definitions are based purely on the previously designated phenomena.) The first requirement can then be stated:

(OPT1) $\forall$ v,m,n ♦ (Enter#(v,m) $\wedge$ Coin#(v,n)) $\rightarrow$ m $\leq$ n

The second requirement is that visitors who pay are not prevented from entering the zoo. Strictly interpreted, this requirement is unimplementable: they may be prevented by other visitors ahead of them in the queue, or by a police cordon, or by their own inability or unwillingness to perform the Push action that must precede the Enter event that admits them. Intuitively, it means that the machine will not prevent their entry. For now, we can state this requirement very informally as:

(OPT2) $\forall$ v,m,n ♦

(Enter#(v,m) $\wedge$ Coin#(v,n) $\wedge$ m $<$ n) $\rightarrow$

` the machine will not prevent another Enter event'

Later we will make it precise in the form of a specification of the machine behaviour. Like many requirements, this requirement seems very difficult to formalise solely in terms of phenomena that are important to the customer [Johnson 88]. A precise statement must await refinement in terms of the turnstile mechanism.

7. Specifications

A requirement describes a desired relationship among environment phenomena; a specification describes a desired behaviour of the machine in the environment. To be a specification, a requirement must observe at least these rules:

(a) All environment phenomena mentioned in the requirement are shared with the machine. That is, the specification is located entirely at the interface between the machine and the environment.

(b) All phenomena required to be constrained are directly machine-controlled. That is, the implementor will not need to reason about environment properties to achieve execution or inhibition of events: the machine can execute, or refrain from executing, the actions directly.

(c) All required constraints on events are expressed in terms of preceding events or states in preceding intervals. That is, the conditions for executing, or not executing, an event can be evaluated in a suitably defined current state and do not involve reasoning from a subsequent state.

The two requirements stated in the descriptions OPT1 and OPT2 express the customer's intention, but they are not specifications. Both are expressed in terms of Enter events, which are not shared: so they break rule (a).

To realise OPT1 the machine must either compel Coin events or prevent Enter events. Coin events are shared phenomena, but they are environment-controlled. If, then, we interpret OPT1 as requiring the machine to enforce Coin events, it fails as a specification by rule (b): it requires constraints on phenomena that are not machine-controlled.

OPT1 also constrains the state in every interval, including those that are still in the future. When the machine executes, or refrains from executing, any event, it must ensure that OPT1 will hold *afterwards*. A requirement based in this way on a future state, even if refined to a form in which it infringes neither rule (a) nor rule (b), can not be a specification by rule (c).

Our strategy for obtaining a specification from a requirement is to make explicit use of the indicative environment properties. Denoting the requirement, specification, and environment properties by R, S, and E respectively, for a given R and E we seek S such that:

$$S, E \vdash R$$

Satisfaction of the requirement can be deduced from satisfaction of the specification together with the indicative environment properties.

Considering OPT1, we know of no environment property by which the machine could ensure the occurrence of Coin events. Therefore it must instead act to prevent Enter events. We must rely on the safety properties described in IND1—the alternation of Push and Enter events, and in IND2—the impossibility of Push events occurring after certain sequences of Lock and Unlock events. Our specification will require the machine to perform Lock and Unlock events so that certain Push events, and hence the undesired Enter events, do not occur.

The first step is to obtain a form of OPT1 that does not involve Enter events. From the indicative description IND1 we can immediately derive:

(IND3) ∀ v,m,n ◆ *(Enter#(v,m)* ∧ *Push#(v,n))* → $n-1 \leq m \leq n$

That is: at all times Push#$-1 \leq$ Enter# $\leq$ Push#. This property allows us to obtain OPT1a, expressed in terms of Push# (whose definition depends on shared phenomena), rather than of Enter# (whose definition depends on unshared phenomena):

(OPT1a) ∀ v,m,n ◆ *(Push#(v,m)* ∧ *Coin#(v,n))* → $m \leq n$

OPT1a is a strengthening of OPT1. The requirement OPT1 is, informally, that at all times Enter# $\leq$ Coin#. OPT1a specifies the stronger condition that at all times Enter# ≤ Push# ≤ Coin# (the first part of the inequality being guaranteed by IND3). The strengthening is inevitable. If Push# > Coin# were ever allowed to hold, the environment possesses no properties by which Enter# > Coin# could then be prevented: once a Push has occurred the subsequent Enter can not be stopped; and a further occurrence of Coin can not be enforced.

To satisfy the requirement OPT1, then, the machine must ensure that Push# *never exceeds* Coin#. By an obvious piece of reasoning necessitated by rule (c), we refine this to the requirement that when Push# *already equals* Coin# the machine must prevent a *further* Push at least until after a further Coin event. How can Push events be prevented by the machine?

IND2, together with the definitional description DEF1, constrains Push events *provided that the alternation of Lock and Unlock events is maintained*: in the absence of this alternation we can say nothing. So we require the machine's behaviour to satisfy the following safety specification:

(OPT3)

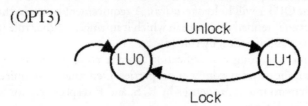

If the machine behaviour has this property, we can be sure that LU2 will never hold. In any interval either Pushes are impossible because LU0 already holds, or LU1 holds and the machine can reach LU0 by causing a Lock event.

Now we can refine OPT1 (in its strengthened form OPT1a). The refinement is to a safety property and a liveness property. The safety property is:

(OPT4) ∀ *v,e,n* ◆

   (LU0(v) ∧ Push#(v,n) ∧ Coin#(v,n) ∧ Ends(e,v)) → ¬ Unlock(e)

If LU0 holds and Push# equals Coin#, the machine must not unlock the turnstile. Push events are impossible while LU0 holds, so the turnstile will eventually be unlocked only after another Coin event, as we might expect.

The liveness property is that the machine must perform a Lock event in certain states. The relevant states are defined by a predicate on intervals:

(DEF2) *ReqLock(v)* ≜

   LU1(v) ∧ ∃ n ◆ (Push#(v,n) ∧ Coin#(v,n))

The liveness property is that if ReqLock holds—that is, if the turnstile is unlocked and Push# equal Coin#—the machine must perform a Lock event in time to prevent a further Push (and thus a further Enter) event.

If we were to adopt the reactive systems hypothesis (the commonly adopted assumption that the machine will react to each stimulus from the environment before the next stimulus occurs), we would say simply that in state ReqLock the machine must perform a Lock event. But there are important real-time considerations here. We will return to this point—and state the liveness property exactly—in the next section.

The refinement of OPT2 is somewhat analogous to that of OPT1. The machine must ensure that the indicative safety property IND2 does not prevent Push events when there is a coin in credit. Again there is both a safety property and a liveness property. The safety property is:

(OPT5) $\forall$ v,e,m,n ·

$\quad$ (LU1(v) $\wedge$ Push#(v,m) $\wedge$ Coin#(v,n) $\wedge$ (m < n) $\wedge$ Ends(e,v))

$\quad$ → ¬Lock(e)

If LU1 holds—the turnstile is unlocked—and there is a coin in credit, the machine must not lock the turnstile. The condition in which Lock events are forbidden will cease to be true when an excess of subsequent Push events over Coin events uses up the credit. The liveness property is that the machine must perform an Unlock event in certain states. The relevant states are defined by a predicate on intervals:

(DEF3) ReqUnlock(v) ≜

$\quad$ LU0(v) $\wedge$ $\exists$ m,n · (Push#(v,m) $\wedge$ Coin#(v,n) $\wedge$ m < n)

The liveness property is that if ReqUnlock holds—that is, if the turnstile is locked and there is a coin in credit—the machine must perform an Unlock event. Again, there is a real-time consideration, and we will state the liveness property exactly in the next section.

8. Real time

We return now to the point deferred above in discussing the statement of the liveness properties in the refinements of OPT1 and OPT2.

The refinement of OPT2 must be more than a specification that in state ReqUnlock the machine will *eventually* perform an Unlock. It must ensure that that state, in which some visitor has paid but has not yet been enabled to Push, does not persist unreasonably long. We may express this quite directly in an optative description:

$\quad$ (OPT6) Duration[ReqLock] < 250

The visitor must be enabled to Push within 250 msecs of paying. OPT6 specifies that the machine must terminate a ReqUnlock state within the time limit. Its only means of doing so, by virtue of DEF3, is to exit from state LU0. By DEF1 and OPT3, that means it must execute an Unlock event. (The environment can not terminate a ReqUnlock state: it can not initiate an Unlock event to terminate LU0; and while LU0 holds it can not initiate a Push.)

The refinement of OPT1 discussed above led us to the specification that in state ReqLock the machine must perform a Lock event soon enough to prevent another Push event: that is the whole point of the requirement. Clearly, we can satisfy this requirement only if the environment guarantees a sufficient real-time delay for the machine to respond. Further investigation of the turnstile reveals that hydraulic damping guarantees delays of at least 750 msecs between a Push and a following Enter, and at least 10 msecs between an Enter and a following Push:

(IND4) *Duration[PE0]* $\geq$ *10* $\wedge$ *Duration[PE1]* $\geq$ *750*

At least 760 msecs will therefore intervene between successive Push events, and the necessary refinement of the liveness part of requirement OPT1 is:

(OPT7) *Duration[ReqLock]* $<$ *760*

The freedom to delay the Lock event is important for smooth and efficient working of the turnstile. The machine may wait in state ReqLock, within the limit of 760 msecs, in order to increase the probability that another Coin event will intervene to cause an exit from the ReqLock state and so make the Lock unnecessary. A machine that does so is preferable to a machine that performs the Lock event immediately.

The preferable machine is not readily specifiable under the reactive system hypothesis. The virtue of the reactive systems hypothesis is that we can avoid real-time considerations in writing requirements and specifications. Everything that the machine must do to satisfy the requirement is assumed to be done fast enough. Or, equivalently, everything that the environment might do to frustrate the requirement is assumed to happen too slowly to do so. The disadvantage is that it becomes very inconvenient to specify that the machine should wait in case another stimulus arrives to countermand the effect of a previous stimulus. Our technique of defining states avoids this disadvantage, and allows us to deal reasonably directly with real-time considerations.

9. Satisfaction of the requirement

In the entailment

S, E ⊢ R

mentioned in Section 7 above, the requirement R is OPT1 and OPT2. The specification S is OPT3, OPT4, OPT5, OPT6, and OPT7. The environment properties E are IND1, IND2 and IND4 (IND3 being deduced from IND1). Assuming the definitions DEF1, DEF2, DEF3, the entailment is therefore

IND1,IND2,IND4,OPT3,OPT4,OPT5,OPT6,OPT7 ⊢ OPT1 $\wedge$ OPT2

To prove satisfaction of the requirement is to prove this entailment. OPT1a will be a lemma in this proof.

The derivation steps presented in this paper are, of course, somewhat too informal to constitute a proof of satisfaction. Most notably, some subtleties in the relationship of Push and Enter events were ignored in the refinement of OPT2. The requirement 'The machine will not prevent another Enter event' is satisfied by a specification in which the machine unlocks, or refrains from locking, the turnstile, thus enabling the visitor to perform a Push event, following which the visitor is automatically enabled to execute an Enter event.

10. Related work

Many researchers in requirements engineering are interested in achieving a fuller understanding of the relationship between requirements and specifications. In this section we compare our ideas to those of four closely related papers.

[Feather 91] is agent-oriented; it envisions systems that are mixtures of human, software, and hardware agents, taking responsibility for various goals and subgoals. We recognize only two agents—environment and machine—and their multiple agents are clearly a decomposition of our two. We emphasise a fixed environment that must be fully accommodated by the machine, while Feather, Fickas, and Helm emphasise a environment that is "designed" along with the machine. Both are legitimate viewpoints for requirements engineering (and we certainly don't intend to limit ourselves to only one of them), but they are irrelevant to this comparison. We are concerned here chiefly with the technical issue of how requirements and specifications differ, and how are they related. For a precise comparison, it is necessary to factor out this difference in viewpoint.

They mention four key transformations by which agent specifications are obtained from requirements or goals:

(a) *Brinksmanship*: identify actions that could cause a constraint to be violated, add components to exert control over these actions, assign some agent to be the controller.

(b) *Spatial split*: split goal responsibility into pieces assigned to separate agents.

(c) *Indirect access*: agent B needs some information it does not have direct access to; agent A gets it and communicates it to B.

(d) *Responsibility accumulation*: assigning multiple responsibilities to the same agent.

Spatial split and responsibility accumulation concern a level of detail that is lower than our scheme—decomposition of the environment and machine agents. We would expect such separations of concerns to be reflected in separate descriptions; but these separations are not needed to explain the difference between requirements and specifications.

Brinksmanship is reminiscent of our rule concerning requirements that are not specifications because they constrain environment-controlled phenomena. But brinksmanship concerns only safety properties, while our rule includes liveness.

Indirect access is reminiscent of our rule concerning requirements that are not specifications because they use unshared phenomena; but it requires the use of an active operational agent to maintain the relation ship between the unshared and the shared phenomena In our view this relationship must be described explicitly, but need not be attributed to an active agent.

In summary, we find our scheme simpler because it does not depend on decomposition of agents, and does not introduce them when not needed. It seems to be more comprehensive because it includes such things as liveness requirements on environment-controlled phenomena. It also seems to be more systematic because it is not an empirically discovered collection, but rather is based on the exhaustive classifications into shared and unshared, and environment-controlled and machine-controlled phenomena.

[Feather 94] extends the work reported in [Feather 91], concentrating on bringing a number of formal techniques to bear on the derivation of specifications from requirements. In particular, Feather exploits a finite differencing transformation, calculation of weakest preconditions, weakening of invariants, and the unfolding of invariants into guarded commands. Use of such formal techniques assists refinement by reformulation of previously stated requirements. It complements the exploitation of indicative environment properties that is a central feature of our approach.

Feather also discusses a form of our distinction between shared and unshared phenomena. Agents in the environment—in his example, railway trains—may be unable to evaluate a predicate that guards one of their actions. For example, a train does not 'know' whether there is another train in the next track segment.

The scheme of [Dubois 89] is based on bilaterally controlled actions, which we consider unrealistic. They are also prone to unnecessary semantic complications, such as the distinction between external and internal (hidden) nondeterminism in [Abadi 93]. Further, Dubois's scheme requires a cumbersome and nonstandard logic.

In many ways, Johnson's work on deriving specifications from requirements [Johnson 88] is the closest to ours philosophically. Johnson's transformation of "removing the perfect knowledge assumption" has exactly the same purpose as our rule about requirements that are not specifications because they use unshared phenomena. Also, his transformation of "defining capabilities" has exactly the same purpose as our rule about requirements that are not specifications because they constrain environment-controlled phenomena. (Incidentally, these transformations have roughly the same purpose as the "operationalization" goals *IsEvaluable* and *IsAchievable* in [Mostow 83]. But Mostow's work focuses on automated problem solving, and thus assumes—if applied to requirements engineering—that the domain is as malleable as the machine.)

One difference is that [Johnson 88], like [Feather 91], is agent-oriented rather than description-oriented. Also, Johnson describes requirements as being edited until they become specifications. Our characterization of requirements and specifications as distinct optative descriptions, linked by the indicative descriptions that cause the specification to imply the requirement, is more general: it embraces other considerations such as the reuse of existing specifications.

We feel that we have added significantly to Johnson's notion of "defining capabilities" by explaining the precise circumstances under which agents have the wrong capabilities (an optative description constrains environment-controlled phenomena) and the precise remedy for the problem (there must be indicative descriptions linking machine-controlled phenomena to the relevant environment-controlled phenomena).

11. Conclusions

We have explained a distinction between requirements and specifications. Both are expressed in terms of environment phenomena. A requirement is expressed in terms of phenomena and relationships that are of direct interest to the system's customers and users, while a specification is restricted to implementable behaviour of a machine that can ensure satisfaction of the requirement. The gap between the two is bridged by reasoning based on environment properties that can be relied on independently of the machine's behaviour.

This view leads to an emphasis on careful expression of environment properties. We separate indicative from optative properties—those that can be relied on from those that the system must bring about. We separate definition from assertion, and designated phenomena from defined terms. We pay explicit attention to control, and express liveness properties in terms of real time.

We have illustrated our ideas with a simple control system example. We believe that other kinds of problem will demand application of the same ideas, albeit in different contexts and expressed in different languages. In some cases a structuring of the environment into domains will be necessary. Larger problems, of realistic complexity, will additionally demand a decomposition into simple problems, and a recombination of the resulting solutions.

Acknowledgement

Martin Feather read an earlier version of this paper and gave us many detailed and helpful comments.

References

[Abadi 93]   Martín Abadi and Leslie Lamport; Composing specifications; *ACM TOPLAS* Volume 15, Number 1, pp. 73-132, January 1993.

[Dubois 89]   Eric Dubois; A logic of action for supporting goal-oriented elaboration of requirements; in *Proc. IWSSD-5*; IEEE CS Press, 1989.

[Feather 87] M. S. Feather; Language support for the specification and development of composite systems; *ACM TOPLAS* Volume 9, Number 2, pp. 198-234, April 1987.

[Feather 91] Martin S. Feather, Stephen Fickas, and B. Robert Helm; Composite system design: The good news and the bad news; in *Proc. 6th RADC KBSE Conference*; IEEE CS Press, 1992.

[Feather 94] Martin S. Feather; Towards a derivational style of distributed system design—An example; *Automated Software Engineering* Volume 1, Number 1, pp. 31-60, March 1994.

[Jackson 92] Michael Jackson and Pamela Zave; Domain descriptions; in *Proc. RE'93*; IEEE CS Press, 1992.

[Jackson 94] M. A. Jackson; Software development method; in *A Classical*

Mind: Essays in Honour of C. A. R. Hoare; A. W. Roscoe, ed; Prentice-Hall International, 1994.

[Johnson 88]   W. Lewis Johnson; Deriving specifications from requirements; in *Proc. ICSE-10*; IEEE CS Press, 1988.

[Morgan 90]   Carroll Morgan; *Programming from Specifications*; Prentice-Hall International 1990.

[Mostow 83]   Jack Mostow; A problem-solver for making advice operational; in *Proc. AAAI-83*, pp. 279-283; William Kaufmann Inc, 1983.

[Zave 93]   Pamela Zave and Michael Jackson; Conjunction as composition; *ACM Transactions on Software Engineering and Methodology*, Volume 2, Number 4, pp. 379-411, October 1993. Also Chapter 10 of this volume.

Chapter 8

E=mc² Explained

Anthony Hall

Abstract: The paper *Deriving Specifications from Requirements: an Example* [1] is one of the publications in which Jackson and Zave put forward a theory of requirements engineering in the form of a simple sequent S,E ⊢ R. I believe that this theory gives us an insight into many aspects of requirements engineering: it is the E=mc² that suddenly explains what was previously obscure. In this commentary I give some personal thoughts on applying this theory to practical requirements engineering.

1. A personal introduction

In the early 1990s my colleagues and I faced a seemingly intractable difficulty. Our job was to specify and develop operational systems, for example support tools for air traffic controllers. I was proud of the fact that, over the previous decade, we had learned how to specify such systems very precisely and that working with these specifications allowed us to develop systems with defect rates that were, for the time, extremely low. Of course we were aware that the specification techniques we were using, and the tools to support them, were a long way from perfect; but we felt that we had, at least in part, cracked the problem of rigorous specification.

In truth, though, we knew there was a huge gap in our understanding. Everyone agreed that there was a progression that went something like: requirements, then specification, then design then implementation. We knew how to do specification, and that, we felt, was a big step forward. But we didn't really have any better idea than anyone else what these mysterious things called requirements were. Where did they come from? What should they say? Indeed, not only did we not know what sort of statements to put in a requirements document, we didn't even know what sort of object we should talk about. Should requirements be some sort of highly abstract description of the software? Or should they describe the ambitions of the customer? And if requirements were indeed descriptions of what the customer really wanted—for example "increase the number of aircraft that can be handled by each air traffic controller" – how on earth did that relate to the nuts and bolts of the software specification?

The answer to this question came with blinding clarity in 1995. Early that year I attended the IEEE International Symposium on Requirements Engineering and heard Michael Jackson's keynote talk on *Problems and Requirements* [3]. In this talk he gave a clear and convincing answer to the problem that we'd been wrestling with. Yes, requirements are indeed about the customer's ambitions. And yes, there is a perfectly precise relationship between these ambitions and the software specification. And here, in the concept of domain knowledge, is the key to that relationship. Best of all, there is a simple formula that encapsulates the whole relationship: the now-famous sequent S,E ⊦ R.

This was the first of several talks and papers that Michael and Pamela Zave published that year. I was lucky enough to attend ICSE where two more papers were presented, including *Deriving Specifications from Requirements: an Example* [1], which gives a beautiful exposition of the method through a simple case study.

I was enthused by this work. It answered a question that had been puzzling me for years, and offered a degree of rigour in the early stages of the lifecycle to match the formality we had been using from the specification onwards. I immediately went back to spread the word, and my colleagues and I developed a requirements engineering training course based round the method. We found that not only could we understand the nature of requirements, but we could give a rationale for many of the practices that we knew from experience were important. This course developed into a whole requirements engineering process, which we called REVEAL [2]. As we applied REVEAL within many projects we learned a lot about the subtleties of finding and classifying domain knowledge and requirements. The more we applied it, the more we realised the key role of the fundamental logic—that S,E ⊦ R is truly the $E=mc^2$ of requirements engineering.

In the rest of this commentary, I want to say a little more about three of the four components of this sequent. I am not going to talk about specifications, because they are relatively well understood. I do want to explore some of the subtleties of E, the environment, of R the requirements and of ⊦, the argument that binds them together.

2. What is the environment?

2.1. Does the environment exist?

The central idea in [1] is that requirements and specifications exist in the environment. The machine is an aid to meeting the requirements, but it cannot usually meet them on its own. This is illustrated by a machine that controls a zoo turnstile: the requirements are to do with preventing people who have not paid entering the zoo, and allowing people who have paid to do so. Entering the zoo is not a phenomenon that can be controlled or even observed by the machine, so we need to understand the relationship between the events that the machine can observe and control, and the events that we are really interested in. We assert, for example, as a fact, that once a visitor has pushed the turnstile he or she necessarily then enters the zoo. This property is supposed to be guaranteed by the mechanics of the turnstile.

There is, however, a subtlety here. In [1] it is assumed that this turnstile pre-exists in the environment, independent of the machine. But this is not, in practice, a realistic assumption. Why would anyone invent a mechanical turnstile with this property? Precisely because they expect to control it with a machine of the sort that we are describing. We may believe that such a turnstile mechanism will exist when our machine goes into service, but unless we are replacing an existing machine of the same type it is unlikely that it exists now.

In other words, the environment properties that we use to derive a specification are not necessarily properties that the environment possesses today (although of course some of them, such as the laws of physics, may well be). Rather, they are properties that we *expect the environment to have in the presence of our machine.*

This point is particularly important where the machine has a user interface. Satisfaction of the requirements in that case usually depends on the operators using the machine correctly. Knowing how the operators behave in the absence of the machine does not give us all the domain knowledge we need to determine whether the machine is satisfactory. We may be able to predict the operator behaviour using, for example, cognitive models or experience of similar machines; more likely, we will have to build prototypes of the machine to investigate how well its proposed user interface works. Once we understand that we are talking about the *future* environment we can thus explain well-known requirements engineering practices like prototyping in terms of the underlying model proposed by Jackson and Zave.

2.2. What is the boundary?

We must also beware of assuming that the boundary between the environment and the machine is either sharply defined or obvious a priori. In practice neither of these is usually true.

The fuzziness of the boundary is closely related to the preceding observation: that we are talking about a future environment. On the one hand, we would like to make a clear distinction: the machine is what we are building, and we have total control over it; the environment, by contrast, is outside our control. On the other hand, once we accept that the environment will adjust to the machine, we admit that we do have some control over the environment: building different machines will bring about different environment behaviour. The turnstile provides some interesting illustrations of this. Consider, for example, the issue of whether we should require payments to alternate with entries. In [1] it is supposed that this is not what is desired, since there are cases where one person should be able to pay for several entries at once. Now consider whether this will be useful: does the teacher in charge of the school party know that she can pay in this way? Perhaps her experience of other turnstiles tells her that she needs to wait for one pupil to enter before paying for the next. We might propose, therefore, that in order to take advantage of this advanced feature of our machine, the zoo proprietor should put up a notice explaining how to use the turnstile. Furthermore we might point out that to avoid misuse of this feature it would be well to arrange the entrance so that opportunistic visitors could not push past the school party and gain free admission. Are these measures part of our machine? Probably not, but they may be necessary for its successful operation. This sort of situation, where there are many ancillary changes that must be made to accommodate a machine, is typical in operational systems where user training, operating procedures, accommodation and so on all have to be considered. Some of these may be part of the scope of supply and thus in the machine; others may not and may thus be part of the environment. They are all, however, more or less under the control of the machine designers.

2.3. Where is the machine?

There is a related and apparently paradoxical fact: not only is the boundary between the machine and the environment fuzzy, but the machine itself becomes part of the environment. For example requirements for an operational system will include not just requirements relating to its day to day use, but also requirements for its maintenance and even its disposal. The subject of these requirements is the machine itself, which is inevitably part of the new world that it has brought about. Such requirements, of course, mean that we need to delve inside the otherwise inaccessible world of "Machine phenomena that are not shared"—for there are many phenomena (such as internal test points) that are irrelevant to the everyday user but shared with the maintainer of the machine. Jackson might treat these as different problem frames [4], but one way or another they need to be considered.

2.4. Can we predict the future?

Finally, of course, we need to recognise that introducing our machine may change the environment in completely unanticipated ways. The "law of unintended consequences" is just one statement of this fact. We know that building new roads can increase congestion, and that whole new industries have come into being as a result of the little-considered GSM feature that provided short messages for service purposes. Recognising that requirements engineers are always describing an unpredictable future helps us understand why even now requirements engineering is a major engineering challenge.

In pointing out these subtleties, it is not my intention to imply that they are weaknesses in [1]. On the contrary, I suggest that understanding the complexity of the relationship between the machine and the environment allows us to recognise the full power and applicability of the ideas presented there.

3. Where are the requirements?

3.1. Where do requirements come from?

At first sight, [1] does not address the question of where requirements come from in the first place, although that is possibly the biggest difficulty in requirements engineering. Insofar as the question is discussed at all, it is treated as a matter of designations—of deciding what phenomena are of interest and characterising them with sufficient precision. In reality, of course, the choice of relevant phenomena is the outcome of a long process that identifies both the phenomena of interest from the point of view of the requirements and the shared phenomena that define the interface of the machine. [1] touches on, but does not elaborate, the problem to be solved: "Is the requirement really about controlling a turnstile, or is it more generally about admitting and excluding visitors?...."

The scope of the machine—how much it does and therefore its interface with the environment—is never obvious at the start of a project. Furthermore the interface is not *discovered*—it is *negotiated*. As Robertson and Robertson [5] point out "The further away from the anticipated automated system you look, the more useful and innovative your product is likely to be" On the other hand, of course, the more radical a change you make, the more risk you incur.

I suggest that, although [1] does not tackle this question head on, it does provide a framework in which we can understand and rationalise the process of requirements negotiation. Although it implicitly assumes that such a process has taken place, and is somewhat dismissive of the "claim" that one person's requirement is another's implementation, I think that it is possible to give a clear account of the recursive layering of requirements, specification and design that characterises real projects.

3.2. Requirements depend on the machine

The key, once again, is the notion of control: what is it within our power to change? Of course the answer to that question depends on who "we" are. If we are the contractor providing the turnstile controller, then as far as we are concerned it is already given that entrance to the zoo is going to be paid for and controlled by a turnstile. It is not our place to suggest that the zoo should be free, or redeveloped for housing, because our machine would have no place in such a scenario. It is, however, within our remit to negotiate whether payments and entries should alternate strictly, because that is within the control of our machine and we may well have expertise in the advantages and problems of different answers to that question.

Let us, however, step back. Suppose that we are the zoo owner. Now we are looking at the same world from a completely different perspective. Our "machine" is the zoo. Our requirements come from our paying customers, local authorities, national regulations and so on. We have the power to change some things: our charging policies, opening times, exhibits and so on. Other things are given: the availability and behaviour of animals, the local climate and many others. All these are much less easy to pin down and formalise than the behaviour of a mechanical turnstile: but there is, I suggest, no difference in principle at all between the way we should understand the requirements for the zoo and the way we should understand requirements for the turnstile controller.

3.3. Machines contain other machines

This perspective also helps to understand the duality between requirements and design. For the zoo owner has another role, more relevant to our original problem. Having answered the larger questions about the requirements for the zoo as a whole, the owner decides how to meet those requirements by acting as design authority for the zoo machine. As part of that role, the owner negotiates the requirements for the subsystems that make up the zoo machine. One of these subsystems is the entry control subsystem, and part of that is the turnstile controller. The design authority for a machine is free to choose the components of that machine and the interfaces between them. For example, the entry control design authority can choose whether to use a turnstile or a manually controlled door, and can decide what payment and entry regime the turnstile should enforce. Every machine has smaller machines within it: the supplier of one machine is the customer for its component machines. In both roles, that person performs requirements engineering, but from different perspectives.

It is, therefore, indeed true that one person's requirement is another person's implementation.

It is also true that one person's requirement is another person's domain knowledge. In procuring the mechanical turnstile, the design authority will place requirements on it that ensure its behaviour is exactly that described in the paper. From the point of view of the turnstile supplier these are requirements; from the point of view of the control system supplier, they are domain knowledge.

This duality, where a given statement may play the role of a requirement, a specification or a piece of domain knowledge is emphatically not an excuse to blur the distinction between requirements and implementation or to abandon the requirements engineering exercise as ill founded. On the contrary, it is another dimension to the requirements process that is illuminated by the insights of [1].

4. Satisfaction arguments

4.1. The meaning of requirements tracing

The central thesis of [1] is the idea that the relationship between requirements and specifications can be expressed formally, as the entailment $S, E \vdash R$. This suggests a role, not just for the descriptions S, E and R but for the argument $\vdash$ that captures the relationship between them. This idea too can be seen as giving a sound basis for an existing, previously ill-defined, practice in requirements engineering: requirements tracing.

Traditional requirements tracing records the relationships among requirements and design statements: for example, the relationship between "user requirements" and the corresponding "system requirements". Tracing is a notoriously difficult and tedious activity and anyone reading the result is faced with trying to understand why particular relationships have been recorded and what they actually mean.

S,E ⊢ R, however, gives us a very clear meaning for our tracing. What we are doing is recording the particular specification statements (aka "system requirements") that contribute to a particular requirement (aka "user requirement"). Furthermore, it suggests two improvements that should be made to the tracing process. First, we should record not only the relevant specification statements S but also the domain knowledge E that contributes to each requirement. Second, we should record the reason that we believe that the particular S and E are indeed necessary and sufficient to ensure R.

When we developed REVEAL, we drew on this idea, together with existing work in safety management systems, to develop the idea of a *satisfaction argument* [2]. Each requirement is associated with an argument that explains why the proposed machine satisfies the requirement: the argument is supported by tracing links to the relevant parts of the specification S and the domain knowledge E. Jeremy Dick gave this idea the more catchy title "rich traceability", which expresses well its relationship to existing tracing practice.

4.2. The role of formality

The possibility of satisfaction arguments raises the question of how these arguments should be expressed and, in particular, how formal they could and should be. One of the major contributions of [1] is that it demonstrates that environment phenomena and requirements are just as much capable of formal description as machine behaviour. Until this paper was published I believed, and I'm sure I was not alone, that formal notations could only be used effectively to write specifications. The sequent S,E ⊢ R, however, demands that we formalise each of the terms within it if we are to have confidence in our argument.

In [1] the relevant environment properties and one of the requirements are stated completely formally, without recourse to any machine description at all. It is, therefore, a little disappointing but typical of real developments that one of the two requirements, (OPT2), is stated informally ("...the machine will not prevent another Enter event") and its formalisation postponed to the machine specification. It is worth examining why this is so and whether it is inevitable. I suspect that there are two different factors at work.

The first difficulty is that, although the notion of control is central to the method, the formal notation does not contain that notion at all. It is therefore difficult to formalise statements, like "the machine will not prevent another enter event", which include a notion of responsibility. This limitation could be overcome perhaps by using a deontic logic or possibly by a branching time temporal logic which allowed us to assert the *possibility* of events. Without such a logic it seems inevitable that a formal description has to refer to just one agent—either the environment or the machine—otherwise we do not know what it is intended to constrain.

The second difficulty is illustrated by the refinement of OPT2 into a specification OPT6: "Duration[ReqUnlock]<250". Magically a constant 250 has appeared. Where did this come from? On the face of it we have no more reason to put a particular value in the specification than in the original requirement. In practice this sort of situation happens a lot. The reason is that requirements, especially performance requirements like this one, are not absolute—they are the result of negotiation depending on what the customer would like and what is technically possible. It's unlikely that the figure 250 has any particular significance: the customer really wants zero, but probably wouldn't notice if the delay were 500; the implementers are probably reasonably confident that they can achieve 250. In other words we do need to understand something about the machine to understand what can reasonably be expected of it. However having understood that, we could still express the requirement at the top level:

(OPT2a) $\forall$ v,m,n •
$\quad$ ((Enter#(v,m) $\wedge$ Coin#(v,n) $\wedge$ $(m < n)$)
$\quad$ → 'the machine will not prevent entry for more than 250 ms')

Is this worth doing? The answer depends on how far removed the specification is from the requirements. In this case the relationship between the 250ms in the requirement and the 250 ms in the specification is obvious. More commonly, however, performance requirements like this are budgeted between several subsystems and in that case it is essential to state the overall requirement, specify the individual machine budgets, and explain the apportionment in a satisfaction argument. The process is not top down, because the requirement is in some sense derived from the design; but it has an essential role, nevertheless, in recording an agreement that is acceptable to all the stakeholders.

5. Conclusion

Every branch of engineering aspires to be the application of scientific knowledge and principles to solving problems, and every branch needs both an underlying theory and a body of practical experience. In [1], Jackson and Zave supply the underlying theory that had been lacking from the discipline of requirements engineering. Theory is not everything, but it is an essential framework for understanding and improving practice. Knowing that $E=mc^2$ does not on its own make anyone competent to design a nuclear power station, but we would not get very far without it. We will not make much progress in requirements engineering unless we understand that S,E ⊢ R.

References

1.　Michael Jackson and Pamela Zave, Deriving Specifications from Requirements: an Example, *Proceedings of ICSE 95*, pp 15-24, ACM, 1995. Also Chapter 7 of this volume.

2.　Jonathan Hammond, Rosamund Rawlings, Anthony Hall, Will it Work?, *Proceedings of the*

5th IEEE International Symposium on Requirements Engineering, pp102-109, IEEE Computer Society, 2001.

3. Michael Jackson, Problems & Requirements, *Proceedings of the IEEE Second International Symposium on Requirements Engineering,* pp2-8; ACM Press, 1995.

4. Michael Jackson, *Problem Frames,* ACM Press, ISBN 0-201-59627-X, 2001.

5. Suzanne Robertson, James Robertson, *Mastering the Requirements Process,* ACM Press, ISBN 0-201-36046-2, 1999.

PART 4
DESCRIPTION
TECHNIQUES
AND
DISCIPLINE

Chapter 9

Aspects of System Description

Michael Jackson

Abstract: This paper discusses some aspects of system description that are important for software development. Because software development aims to solve problems in the world, rather than merely in the computer, these aspects include: the distinction between the hardware/software machine and the world in which the problem is located; the relationship between phenomena in the world and formal terms used in descriptions; the idea of a software model of a problem world domain; and an approach to the decomposition of problems and its consequences for the larger structure of software development descriptions.

1. Introduction

The business of software development is, above all, the business of making descriptions. A program is a description of a computation—or, perhaps, of a machine behaviour. A *specification* is a description of the input-output relation of a computation—or, perhaps, of the externally observable behaviour of a machine. A *requirement* is a description of some observable effect or condition that our customer wants the computation—or the machine—to guarantee. A *software design* is a description of the structure of the computation—or, perhaps, of a machine that will execute the computation.

In spite of its importance, we pay surprisingly little attention to the practice and technique of description. For the most part, it is treated only implicitly and indirectly, either because it is thought too trivial to engage our attention, or because we suppose that all software developers must already be fully competent practitioners. In the same way, the great universities in the eighteenth and early nineteenth century ignored the study of English literature. It was a truth universally acknowledged that anyone qualified to study Latin and Greek and mathematics in the university must already know everything worth knowing about the subject of English literature.

But the discipline of description, like the study of English literature, is neither trivial nor universally understood. Many aspects of description technique are important in software development and merit explicit discussion. The following sections discuss particular aspects, setting them in the context of some simple problems. A concluding section briefly discusses the relationship between the view presented here and a narrower view of the scope of research, teaching, and practice in software development.

2. Symbol manipulation

It has often seemed attractive to regard software development as a branch of pure mathematics. The computer is a symbol-processing machine. Each problem to be solved is formal, drawn from a pure mathematical domain. The development methods to be used are largely formal, with the addition of the intuitive leaps that are characteristic of creative mathematical work. And the criterion of success—correctness with respect to a precise program specification—is entirely formal.

This view has underpinned some notable advances in programming. It has led to the evolution of a powerful discipline based on simultaneous development of a program and its correctness proof, and a clear demonstration that, for some programs at least, correctness is an achievable practical goal. The class of such programs is large. It includes a repertoire of well-known small examples—such as GCD and searching or sorting an array—and many substantial applications—such as compiling program texts, finding maximal strong components in a graph, model-checking, and the travelling-salesman problem.

These are all problems with a strong algorithmic aspect. Their subject matter is abstract and purely mathematical, even when the abstraction and the mathematics have clear practical application. This is what allows the emphasis in software development to be placed on symbol manipulation. As Hermann Weyl expressed it [Weyl 40]:

> "We now come to the decisive step of mathematical abstraction: we forget about what the symbols stand for.... [The mathematician] need not be idle; there are many operations he may carry out with these symbols, without ever having to look at the things they stand for."

He might have gone further. We can't look at what the symbols stand for, because they don't stand for anything outside the mathematics: they are themselves the subject matter of the computation. The task of relating the mathematics to a practical problem is not part of the software developer's concern: it is someone else's business. Although our problem may be called *the Travelling Salesman problem* we are not really interested in the real salesmen and their travels, but only in the abstraction we have made of them.

2.1. The specification firewall

But even in the most formal problems an element of informality may intrude. A useful program must make its results visible outside the computer; most programs also accept some input. So questions of external representation and of data formats, at least, must be considered. How, for example, should we require our program's user to enter the nodes and arcs of the graph over which the salesman travels?

These less formal concerns arise outside the core computation itself, in the world of the software's users and the software developer's customers. In many cases they can relegated to a limbo beyond a *cordon sanitaire* by focusing on the *program specification*. As Dijkstra wrote [EWD 89]:

"The choice of functional specifications—and of the notation to write them down in—may be far from obvious, but their role is clear: it is to act as a logical 'firewall' between two different concerns. The one is the 'pleasantness problem,' i.e. the question of whether an engine meeting the specification is the engine we would like to have; the other one is the 'correctness problem,' i.e. the question of how to design an engine meeting the specification. . . . the two problems are most effectively tackled by . . . psychology and experimentation for the pleasantness problem and symbol manipulation for the correctness problem."

Figure 1 pictures the situation. The specification interface *a* is an interface of shared physical phenomena connecting the customer to the machine. At this interface the customer enters input data, perhaps by keyboard, and receives output data, perhaps by seeing it displayed on the screen. The shared phenomena for the input are the keystrokes: these are shared events controlled by the customer. The shared phenomena for the output are the characters or graphics visible on the screen: these are shared states, controlled by the machine.

The specification firewall is erected at this interface. It enforces a fruitful separation of the 'hard' formal concerns of the software developer and computer scientist from the 'soft' concerns of the 'systems analyst,' addressing informal problems in the world outside the computer. The software developers are relieved of responsibility for the world outside the computer: they need no more discuss the external data format for a graph than automobile engineers need discuss the range of paint colours for their cars' bodywork or the choice of upholstery fabric

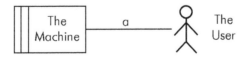

a: The Specification Interface: {keyboard,screen}

Figure 1. The Machine and the user

for the seats. The subject matter for serious attention and reasoning is restricted to the mathematics of the problem abstraction and of the computation that the machine will execute.

The 'soft' concerns, then, are relatively unimportant; they are relegated to a secondary place. The customer—who may well be the developer or another computer scientist with similar concerns and interests—may be slightly irritated by an inferior choice of input-output format at the specification interface, but is not expected to regard it as a crucial defect. The essential criterion, by which the work is to be judged, is the correctness and efficiency of the computation.

3. The machine and the world

Not all customers will be so compliant. For most practical software development the customer's vital need is not to solve a mathematical problem, but to achieve specific observable physical effects in the world. Consider the very small problem of controlling a traffic light unit. The unit is placed at the gateway to a factory, and controls incoming traffic by allowing entry only during 15 seconds of each minute. The unit has a Stop lamp and a Go lamp. The problem is to ensure that the light shows alternately Stop for 45 seconds and Go for 15 seconds, starting with Stop. We can picture the problem as it is shown in Figure 2.

In addition to the machine, we now show the *problem domain*: that is, the part of the world in which the problem is located. There is no user: in this problem—as in many others—it is not clear who is the *user*, or even whether the notion of a user is useful. But there is certainly a *customer*: the person, or the group of people, who pay for the development work and will look critically at its results.

3.1. The specification interface

As before, the specification interface *a* is an interface of phenomena shared by the *machine domain* and the *problem domain*. Here the problem domain is the lights unit, and the shared phenomena are the signal pulses *RPulse, GPulse* by which the machine can cause it to switch on and off its Stop and Go lamps. The lights unit itself is on the other side of the specification interface.

a: The Specification Interface: {RPulse, GPulse}
b: The Requirement Interface: {Stop, Go}

Figure 2. The machine, the world, and the customer

3.2. The requirement interface

The customer is more remote from the machine than the user in a symbol manipulation problem. The customer's need is no longer located at the specification interface: the customer is interested in the regime of Stop and Go lamps, not in the signal pulses. So a new interface has appeared in the picture. The requirement interface *b* is a notional interface at which we can think of the customer as observing the world outside the machine. The phenomena of interest at this interface are the states of the Stop and Go lamps of the lights unit; these are, of course, quite distinct from the signal pulses at the interface with the machine.

The problem is about something physical and concrete. The externally visible behaviour of the machine, and the resulting behaviour of the lights unit, are not matters of pleasantness: they are the core of the problem.

3.3. A system description

Figure 3 is a description of the system as it might be described using a currently fashionable [UML] diagrammatic notation derived from Statecharts [Harel 87]. In the transition markings the external stimulus, if any, is written before the slash ('/'), and the sequence of actions, if any, taken by the machine is written after it.

The initial state is 1, in which neither lamp is lit. Immediately the machine emits an RPulse, causing a transition to state 2, in which Stop is lit but not Go. 45 seconds after entering state 2, the machine emits an RPulse followed by a GPulse, causing a transition to state 3, in which Go is lit but not Stop. 15 seconds later the machine emits a GPulse followed by an RPulse, causing a transition back to state 2, and so on.

3.4. Purposeful description

It is always salutary in software development to ask why a particular description is worth making, and what particular purpose it serves in the development. In this tiny problem we can recognise three distinct roles that our system description is intended to play:

The requirement The requirement is a description that captures the effects our customer wants the machine to produce in the world. When we talk to the

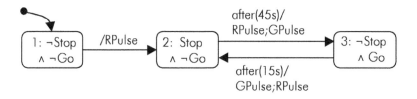

Figure 3. A system description

customer, we treat the description as a requirement. We ignore the actions that cause the pulses, and focus just on the timing events and the states. "To begin with," we say, "both lamps should be off; then, for 45 seconds, the Stop lamp only should be lit; then, for the next 15 seconds, the Go lamp only should be lit;" and so on. The requirement that emerges is:

```
forever {
    show only Stop for 45 seconds;
    show only Go for 15 seconds;
}
```

The machine specification The *specification* describes the behaviour of the machine in terms of the phenomena at the specification interface. It provides an interface between the problem analyst, who is concerned with the problem world, and the programmer, who is concerned only with the computer. When we talk to the programmer, we treat the description as a specification of the machine. We look only at the transitions with the timing events and the pulses. "First the machine must cause an RPulse," we tell the programmer, "then, after 45 seconds, an RPulse and a GPulse;" and so on. The Stop and Go states have no significance to the programmer, because they aren't visible to the machine; at best they are enlightening comments suggesting why the pulses are to be caused. The specification that emerges is:

```
{   RPulse;
    forever  {
        wait 45 seconds; RPulse; GPulse;
        wait 15 seconds; GPulse; RPulse;
    }
}
```

The domain description The *domain description* bridges the gap between the requirement and the specification. The customer wants a certain regime of Stop and Go lamps, but the machine can directly cause only RPulses and GPulses. The gap is bridged by the properties of the problem domain. Here that means the properties of the lights unit. When we talk to the lights unit designer to check our understanding of the domain properties, we focus just on the pulses and the way they affect the states. "In the unit's initial state both lamps are off: That's right, isn't it? Then an initial RPulse turns the Stop lamp on; then an RPulse followed by a GPulse turns the Stop lamp off and lights the Go lamp, doesn't it?" and so on. The domain properties description that emerges[1] is shown in Figure 4.

---

[1] In fact, Figure 4 asserts much more than can be seen from the System Description given in Figure 3. For example: that it is possible to return to the dark state; that the first lamp turned on from the initial dark state may be the Go lamp; and that the RPulses affect only the Stop lamp and the GPulses only the Go lamp. Nothing in Figure 3 warrants these assertions.

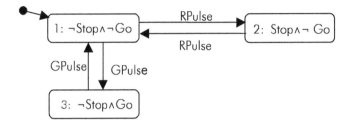

Figure 4. A partial domain description

3.5. Why separate descriptions are needed

Combining the three descriptions into one is tempting, but in a realistic problem it is very poor practice for several reasons. First, if the description were only slightly more complex it could be very hard to tease out the *projection* needed for each of the three roles.

Second, the adequacy of our development must be shown by an argument relating the three separate descriptions. Our goal is to bring about the regime of Stop and Go lamps that our customer desires. We must show that a machine programmed according to our specification will ensure this regime by virtue of the properties of the lights unit. That is:

specification $\wedge$ *domain properties* $=>$ *requirement*

In other words: if the machine meets its specification, and the problem world is as described in the domain properties, then the requirement will be satisfied.[2] The combined description does not allow this argument to be made explicitly.

Third, the single description combines descriptions of what we desire to achieve—the *optative* properties described in the requirement and specification—with a description of the known and given properties relied on—the *indicative* properties described in the domain description. It is always a bad idea to mix indicative and optative statements in the same description.

Fourth, the combined description is inadequate in an important way. Being based on a description of the machine behaviour, it can't accommodate a description of what would happen if the machine were to behave differently—for example, by reversing the order of GPulse and RPulse in each pair. Figure 5 shows what a separate, full description of the domain properties might be.

Each lamp is toggled by pulses of the associated type: RPulse for Stop and GPulse for Go. The designer tells us that the unit can not tolerate the illumination of both lamps at the same time. We show state 4 as the unknown state, meaning

---

[2]A fuller and more rigorous account of the relationship among the three descriptions is given in [Gunter 00].

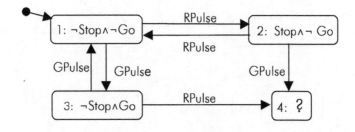

Figure 5. Lights unit domain properties description

that nothing is known about subsequent behaviour of the unit once it has entered state 4. Effectively, the unit is broken.

Fifth, the combined description isn't really reusable. Because the embodied domain description, in particular, is merged with the requirement and the specification, it can't easily be reused in another problem that deals differently with the same problem domain.

4. Describing the world

The three descriptions—requirements, domain properties, and machine specification—are all concerned with event and state phenomena of the world in which the problem is located. But the first two are different from the third. The specification phenomena, shared with the machine, can properly be regarded as *formal*. Just as the machine has been carefully engineered so that there is no doubt whether a particular keystroke event has or has not occurred, so it has been carefully engineered to avoid similar doubt about whether an RPulse or a GPulse event has or has not occurred. The continuous underlying physical phenomena of magnetic fields and capacitances and voltages have been tamed to conform to sharply-defined discrete criteria.

But in general the phenomena and properties of the world have not been tamed in this way, and must be regarded as *informal*. The formalisation must be devised and imposed by the software developer. As W. Scherlis remarked [Scherlis 89] in his response to Dijkstra's observations [EWD 89] cited earlier:

"One of the greatest difficulties in software development is formalization—capturing in symbolic representation a worldly computational problem so that the statements obtained by following rules of symbolic manipulation are useful statements once translated back into the language of the world."

This task of formalization, along with appropriate techniques for its successful performance, is an integral, but regrettably much neglected, aspect of software development. Two important elements of this task are the use of *designations*, and the use and proper understanding of *formal definitions*.

4.1. Designations

Because the world is informal it is very hard to describe precisely. It is therefore necessary to lay a sound basis for description by saying as precisely as possible what phenomena are denoted by the formal terms in our requirements and domain properties descriptions. The appropriate tool is a set of *designations*. A designation gives a formal term, such as a predicate, and gives a—necessarily informal—rule for recognising instances of the phenomenon.

For example, in a genealogical system we may need this designation:

Mother(x, y) ≈ *x is the mother of y*

Probably this is a very poor recognition rule: it leaves us in considerable doubt about what is included. Does it encompass adoptive mothers, surrogate mothers, stepmothers, foster mothers? Egg donors? Probably we must be more exact. Perhaps what we need is:

Mother(x, y) ≈ *x is the human genetic mother of y*

Even this more conscientious attempt may be inadequate in a future world in which genetic engineering has become commonplace.

Adequate precision of the underlying designations is fundamental to the precision and intelligibility of the requirement and domain descriptions that rely on them. If it proves too hard to write a satisfactory recognition rule for phenomena of a chosen class, that chosen class should be rejected, and firmer ground should be sought elsewhere.

This harsh stipulation is less obstructive than it may seem at first. The designated terminology is intended for describing a particular part, or domain, of the problem world for a particular problem. As so often in software development, we may be tempted to multiply our difficulties a thousandfold by trying to treat the general case instead of focusing, as practical engineers, on the particular case in hand. The temptation must be resisted.

For example, in an inventory problem for the OfficeWorld Company, whose business is supplying office furniture, we may need to designate the entity class Chair. Perhaps we write this designation:

Chair(x) ≈ *x is a single unit of furniture whose primary use*
is to provide seating for one person

Philosophers have often cited 'chair' as an example of the irreducibly uncertain meaning of words in natural language. In the general case no designation of 'chair' can be adequate. Is a bar stool a chair? A bean bag? A sofa? A park bench? A motor car seat? A chaise longue? A shooting stick? These questions are impossibly difficult to answer: there are no right answers. But we do not have to answer them. The OfficeWorld Company has quite a small catalogue. It doesn't supply bar stools or park benches or bean bags. Our recognition rule is good enough for the case in hand.

4.2. Using definitions

Another factor mitigating the severity of the stipulation that designations must be precise is that the number of phenomenon classes to be designated usually turns out to be surprisingly small. Many useful terms do not denote distinctly observable phenomena at all, but must be *defined* on the basis of terms that do and of previously defined terms. For example:

Sibling(a, b) =
    $a \neq b \wedge \exists \, p, q \bullet Mother(p, a) \wedge Mother(p, b) \wedge Father(q, a) \wedge Father(q, b)$

The difference between definition and designation is crucial. A designation introduces a fresh class of observations, and thus enlarges the scope of possible assertions about the world. A definition, by contrast, merely introduces more convenient terminology without increasing the expressive power at our disposal.

In an inventory problem, suppose that we have designated the event classes[3] *receive* and *issue*:

Receive(e, q, t) $\approx$ *e is an event occurring at time t*
    in which q units of stock are received

Issue(e, q, t) $\approx$ *e is an event occurring at time t*
    in which q units of stock are issued

Then the definition:

ExpectedQuantity(qty, tt) =

    $(\Sigma \, e \mid ((Receive(e, q, t) \vee Issue(e, -q, t) \wedge t < tt) : q) = qty$

defines the predicate *ExpectedQuantity(qty,tt)* to mean that at time *tt* the number *qty* is equal to a certain sum. This sum is the total number of units received in *receive* events, minus the total number issued in *issue* events, taken over all events *e* occurring at any time *t* that is earlier than time *tt*. Being a definition, it says nothing at all about the world. By contrast, the designation and assertion:

InStock(qty,tt) $\approx$ *At time tt qty items are in the stock bin in the warehouse*

$\forall \, qty, tt \bullet InStock(qty,tt) <=>$

    $(\Sigma \, e \mid ((Receive(e, q, t) \vee Issue(e, -q, t) \wedge t < tt) : q) = qty$

say that initially *InStock(0,t0)* and that subsequently stock changes only by the quantities issued and received. There is no theft, no evaporation and no spontaneous creation of stock. The definition of *ExpectedQuantity* expressed only a choice of terminology; the designation of *InStock*, combined with the accompanying assertion, expresses a falsifiable claim about the physical world.

---

[3]For uniformity, it is convenient to designate all formal terms as predicates. For any set of individuals, such as a class of events, the formal term in the designation denotes the characteristic predicate of the set.

4.3. Distinguishing definition from description

Many notations commonly used for description can also be used for definition, distinguishing the two uses by certain restrictions and by suitable syntactic conventions.

For example, it is often convenient to define terms for state components by giving a finite-state machine. Since mixing definition with description—like mixing indicative with optative—is very undesirable, the state-machine description should be empty *qua* description.[4] That is, in defining states it should place no constraint on the described sequence of events. Suppose, for example, that in some domain the sequence of events is

$<a, b, a, b, a \dots >$

and that we wish to define the state terms *After-a* and *After-b*. Figure 6 shows the definition: it avoids assuming that the sequence of events is as given above. *After-a* is defined to mean the state identified as state 2 in this state machine, and *After-b* is defined similarly. Of course, if the meanings are intended to include the clause ". . . and the given sequence of events has been followed so far," then a different definition is necessary.

5. Descriptions and models

An important aspect of description in software development is clarity in the distinction between a *description* and a *model*. Unfortunately, the word *model* is much overused and much misused. Its possible meanings[5] include:

+ An *analytical* model of a domain: that is, a formal description from which further properties of the domain can be inferred. For example, a set of differential equations describing a country's economy, or a labelled transition

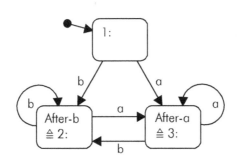

Figure 6. Defining states in a FSM

---

[4] A term defined in a non-empty description is undefined whenever the description is false. It then becomes necessary either to use a three-valued logic or to prove at each of its occurrences that the term is well-defined.

[5] This distinction among the three kinds of model is due to Ackoff [Ackoff62].

diagram describing the behaviour of a vending machine.

♦ An *iconic model* of a domain: that is, a representation that captures the appearance of the domain. For example, an artist's drawing of a proposed building.

♦ An *analogic model* of a domain: that is, another domain that can act as a surrogate for purposes of providing information. For example, a computer-driven wall display showing the layout of a rail network in the form of a graph, and the current train traffic on the network in the form of a blob for each train moving along the arcs of the graph.

Much difficulty arises from confusion between the first and third of these meanings. It is a common and necessary device in software development to introduce an analogic model, in the form of a database or other data structure, into the solution of an information problem or subproblem. Such an analogic model domain is to be regarded as an elaboration of a certain class of local variables of the machine. Descriptions of this model domain are often confused with descriptions of the domain for which it is a surrogate.

5.1. A model of a lift

A small hotel has an old and somewhat primitive lift. Now it is to be fitted with an information panel in the lobby, to show waiting guests where the lift is at any time and its current direction of travel, so that they will know how long they can expect to wait until it arrives.

The panel has a square lamp for each floor, to show that the lift is at the floor. In addition there are two arrow-shaped lamps to indicate the direction of travel. The panel display must be driven from a simple interface with the floor sensors of the lift. A floor sensor is on when the lift is within 6 inches of the rest position at the floor.

Figure 7 is the problem diagram. Here the customer manikin is replaced by the more impersonal dashed oval, representing the requirement. The requirement is that the lamp states of the lobby display (the phenomena *d*) should correspond in

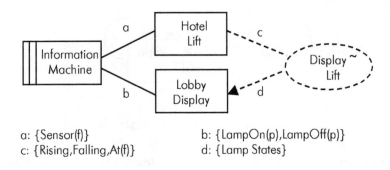

a: {Sensor(f)}
c: {Rising,Falling,At(f)}

b: {LampOn(p),LampOff(p)}
d: {Lamp States}

Figure 7. Lift position display problem

a certain way to the states of the lift (the phenomena c). The arrowhead indicates that the requirement constrains the display, but not the hotel lift itself.

This simple information problem presents a standard *concern* of problems of this class [Jackson 00]. The information necessary to maintain the required correspondence is not available to the machine at the specification interface a at the moment when it is needed. The requirement phenomena include the current lift position and its current direction of travel; the specification phenomena include only the floor sensor states. To satisfy the requirement as well as possible, the machine must store information about the past history of the lift, and must interpret the current state and events in the light of this history.

The local phenomena of the machine in which this history is stored— perhaps in the form of program variables, or a data structure or small database —constitute an *analogic model domain*. If these local phenomena are not totally trivial it is desirable to decompose the original problem into two subproblems: one to build and maintain the model, and one to use the model in producing the lobby display. This problem decomposition is shown in Figure 8.

As the decomposed problem diagram shows clearly, the lift model and the hotel lift itself are disjoint domains, with no phenomena in common. In designing the lift model, the developer must devise model state phenomena f to correspond to the lift domain requirement phenomena c. These model phenomena might be called *MRising* and *MFalling*, corresponding to the lift states *Rising* and *Falling*,

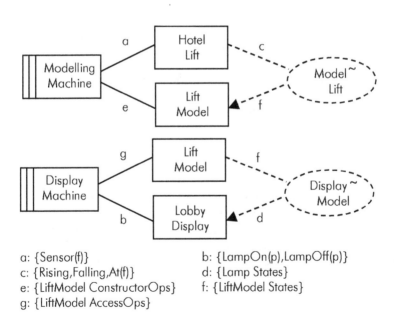

a: {Sensor(f)}   b: {LampOn(p),LampOff(p)}
c: {Rising,Falling,At(f)}   d: {Lamp States}
e: {LiftModel ConstructorOps}   f: {LiftModel States}
g: {LiftModel AccessOps}

Figure 8. Lift position display problems decomposition

and $MAt(f)$, corresponding to $At(f)$.

The modelling subproblem is then to ensure that $MRising$ holds in the model if and only if the lift is rising, that $MAt(f)$ holds in the model if and only if the lift is at floor f, and so on. The model constructor operations—the phenomena e—will be invoked by the modelling machine when sensor state changes occur at its interface a with the hotel lift domain.

The display subproblem is much simpler: the display machine must ensure that the Up lamp is lit if and only if $MRising$ holds; the floor lamp f is lit if and only if $MAt(f)$ holds; and so on.

5.2. The modelling relationship

The desired relationship between a model domain and the domain it models is, in principle, simple. There should be a one-to-one correspondence between phenomena of the two domains and their values. For example, the lift has state phenomena $At(f)$ for $f = 0 \ldots 8$ and the model has state phenomena $MAt(f)$ for $f=0 \ldots 8$.[6] For any f, $MAt(f)$ should hold if and only if $At(f)$ holds.

Because of this relationship it seems clear that a description that is true of one domain must be equally true of the other, with a suitable change of interpretation. For example, the description:

> "in any trace of values of $P(x)$, $0 \leq x \leq 8$ for each element of the trace, and adjacent values of x differ by at most 1."

is true of the lift domain if we take $P(x)$ to mean $At(f)$, and must be true also of the model domain if we take $P(x)$ to mean $MAt(f)$.

It therefore seems very attractive and economical to write only one description. In a further economy, even the work of writing the two interpretations can be eliminated by using the same names for phenomena in the lift and the corresponding phenomena in the model. Unfortunately, this is usually a false economy. Although almost universally attempted, both by practitioners and by researchers, it can work well only for an ideal model in which the desired relationship to the model domain is known to hold; practical models are almost never ideal.

5.3. Practical models

The lift domain phenomenon $At(f)$ means that the lift is closer to floor f than to any other floor. However, it is not possible to maintain a precise correspondence between $At(f)$ and the model phenomenon $MAt(f)$, because the specification state phenomena $Sensor(f)$ do not convey enough information. The best that can be done is, perhaps, to specify the modelling machine so that $MAt(f)$ is true if and only if $Sensor(f)$ is the sensor that is on or was most recently on. So the correspondence between $At(f)$ and $MAt(f)$ is very imperfect. When

---

[6]Floor 0 is the lobby. In Europe floor 1 is the first above the ground floor; in the US the floors would be numbered $1 \ldots 9$.

the lift travels from floor 1 to floor 2, $MAt(1)$ remains true even when the lift is six inches from the floor 2 home position and the state $Sensor(2)$ is just about to become true.

The *Rising* and *Falling* phenomena are even harder to deal with. Once again, the modelling machine has access only to the $Sensor(f)$ phenomena, and must maintain the model phenomena *MRising* and *MFalling* from the information they provide. Initially the lift may be considered to be *Rising*, because from the Lobby it can go only upwards; subsequently, when it reaches floor 8 (or floor 0 again) it must reverse direction. But it may also reverse direction at an intermediate floor, provided that it makes a service visit there and does not simply pass it without stopping.

Investigation of the lift domain shows that on a service visit the floor sensor is on for at least 4.8 seconds, allowing time for the doors to open and close. Passing a floor takes no more than 1 second. The model phenomena *MRising* and *MFalling* will be maintained as follows:

◆ Initially: $MRising \land \lnot MFalling$

◆ Whenever $MAt(n+1)$ becomes true when $MAt(n)$ was previously true, for (n = 0 ... 6): $MRising \land \lnot MFalling$

◆ Whenever $MAt(8)$ becomes true when $MAt(7)$ was previously true: $MFalling \land \lnot MRising$

◆ Whenever $MAt(n-1)$ becomes true when $MAt(n)$ was previously true for (n=2 ... 8): $MFalling \land \lnot MRising$

◆ Whenever $MAt(0)$ becomes true when $MAt(1)$ was previously true: $MRising \land \lnot MFalling$

◆ Whenever $MAt(n)$ has been true for 2 seconds[7] continuously, for (n = 1 ... 7): $\lnot MFalling \land \lnot MRising$

These practical choices represent unavoidable departures from exact correspondence between the model and the lift domain. For example, during the first two seconds of a service visit either *MRising* or *MFalling* is true, although neither *Rising* nor *Falling* is true. Also, when the lift has reversed direction at an intermediate floor but has not yet reached another floor, either *Rising* or *Falling* is true, but neither *MRising* nor *MFalling* is true. Speaking anthropomorphically, we might say that the modelling machine is waiting to discover whether the next floor arrival will invite the inference of upwards or downwards travel.

5.4. Describing the model and modelled domains

Other factors that may prevent exact correspondence in a practical model include errors and delays in the interface between the modelling machine and the modelled domain, and the approximation of continuous by discrete phenomena.

---

[7] A compromise between the limits of 1.0 and 4.8 seconds, affording an early but reasonably reliable presumption that the lift has stopped to service the floor.

A further factor is the need to model the imperfection of the model itself. For example, NULL values are often used in relational databases to model the absence of information: a NULL value in a *date-of-birth* column indicates only that the date of birth is unknown. In the presence of such discrepancies it may still be possible to economise by using the same basic description for both domains and noting the discrepancies explicitly.

Another factor militating against a single description is that a model domain itself usually has additional phenomena that correspond to nothing in the modelled domain. The source of these phenomena is the underlying implementation of the model. A relational database, for example, usually has delete operations to conserve space, indexes to speed access to particular elements of the model, and ordering of tuples within relational tables to speed *select* and *join* operations. These discrepancies between the model and modelled domains can sometimes be regarded as no more than the difference between abstract and concrete views of the model. Introduction of the additional model phenomena is a refinement: the resulting implementation satisfies the model's abstract specification. This view applies easily to the introduction of tuple ordering and of indexing. It is less clear that it can apply to record deletion.

The use of only one description for the two domains fails most notably when the modelled domain has phenomena that do not and can not appear in the model. For example, the lift domain has the moving and stationary states of the lift car, and the opening and closing of the lift doors during a service visit to a floor. These phenomena can not appear in the model because there is not enough evidence of them in the shared phenomena of the specification interface. They are completely hidden from the modelling machine, and can enter into the model only in a most attenuated form—the choices based on assumptions about them. But they must still appear in any careful description of the significant domain properties.

In sum, therefore, it is essential to recognise that a modelled domain and its model are two distinct subjects for description. Confusion of the two results in importing distracting irrelevancies and restrictions into the problem domain description. For example, in UML [UML] descriptions of a business domain must be based on irrelevant programming concepts, such as *attributes*, *visibility*, *interfaces* and *operations*, taken from object-oriented languages such as C++ and Smalltalk. At the same time, UML notations provide no way of describing the syntax of a lexical problem domain, other than by describing a program to parse it.

This vital distinction between the model and the modelled domain is difficult to bear in mind if the verb *model* is used where the verb *describe* would do as well or better. The claim "We are modelling the lift domain" invites the interpretation "We are describing the lift domain," when often it means in fact "We are not bothering to describe the lift domain: instead we are describing a domain that purports to be an analogical model of it."

6. Problem decomposition and description structures

Realistic problems must be decomposed into simpler subproblems. Almost always, the subproblems are related by having problem domains in common: that is, they are not about disjoint parts of the world. The common problem domains must, in general, be differently viewed and differently described in the different subproblems. This section gives two small illustrations of this effect of problem decomposition.

6.1. An auditing subproblem

A small sluice, with a rising and falling gate, is used in a simple irrigation system. A control computer is to be programmed to raise and lower the sluice gate: the gate is to be open for ten minutes in each hour, and otherwise shut.

The gate is opened and closed by rotating vertical screws. The screws are driven by a small motor, which can be controlled by *Clockwise, Anticlockwise, On,* and *Off* pulses. There are sensors at the top and bottom of the gate travel; at the top the gate is fully open, at the bottom it is fully shut. The connection to the computer consists of four pulse lines for motor control and two status lines for the gate sensors.

The requirement phenomena are the gate states *Open* and *Shut.* The specification phenomena are the motor control pulses, and the states of the *Top* and *Bottom* sensors. A mechanism of this kind moves slowly and has little inertia, so a specification of the machine behaviour to satisfy the requirement is simple and easily developed. Essentially, the gate can be opened by setting the motor to run in the appropriate sense and stopping it when the *Top* sensor goes on; it can be closed similarly, stopping the motor when the *Bottom* sensor goes on.

The domain properties on which the machine must rely include:

+ The behaviour of the motor unit in changing its state in response to externally caused motor control pulses;
+ the behaviour of the mechanical parts of the sluice that govern how the gate moves vertically, rising and falling according to whether the motor is stopped or rotating clockwise or anticlockwise;
+ the relationship between the gate's vertical position and its Open and Shut states; and
+ the relationship between the gate's vertical position and the states of the Top and Bottom sensors.

To develop a specification of the control machine it is necessary to investigate and describe these domain properties explicitly.

6.2. Fruitful contradiction

Being physical devices, the sluice gate and its motor, on whose properties the control machine is relying, are not so reliable as we might wish. Power cables can be cut; motor windings burn out; insulation can be worn away or eaten by rodents; screws rust and corrode; pinions become loose on their shafts; branches and other debris can become jammed in the gate, preventing it from closing. The behaviour of the control computer should take account of these possibilities— at least to the extent of stopping the motor when something has clearly gone wrong.

Possible evidences of failure, detectable at the specification interface, include:

* the *Top* and *Bottom* sensors are on simultaneously;
* the motor has been set to raise the gate for more than m seconds but the *Bottom* sensor is still on;
* the motor has been set to lower the gate for more than n seconds but the *Top* sensor is still on;
* the motor has been set to raise the gate for more than p seconds but the *Top* sensor is not yet on;
* the motor has been set to lower the gate for more than q seconds but the *Bottom* sensor is not yet on.

Detecting these possible failures should be treated as a separate subproblem, of a class that we may call *Auditing problems*. The machine in this auditing subproblem runs concurrently with the machine in the basic control problem. The two subproblem machines are connected: the control machine, on detecting a failure, causes a signal in response to which the control machine turns the motor off and keeps it off thereafter.

The particular interest of this problem is that in a certain sense the domain property description of the auditing subproblem contradicts the description on which the solution of the control subproblem must rely. The indicative domain description for the control subproblem asserts that when the motor is set in such-and-such a state the gate will reach its *Open* state within p seconds; but the description for the auditing problem contradicts this assertion by explicitly showing the possibility of failure.

At a syntactic level, this conflict can be resolved by merging the two descriptions to give a single consistent description that accommodates both the correct and the failing behaviour of the gate mechanism. This merged description might then be used for the control subproblem, the auditing subproblem being embedded in the control subproblem as a collection of local behaviour variants. But this merging is not a wise strategy. It is better to solve the control subproblem in the context of explicit appropriate assumptions about the domain properties, leaving the complications of the possible failures for a separate concern and a separate subproblem.

6.3. An identities concern

In the lift display problem it was necessary to pay careful attention to the gap between the requirement phenomena (the *At(f)*, *Rising* and *Falling* states) and the specification phenomena (the *Sensor(f)* states) of the lift domain. But we were not at all careful about another phenomenological concern in the problem. We resorted—naturally enough—to the standard mathematical practice of indexing multiple phenomena: we wrote f for the identifier of a floor, and used that identifier freely in our informal discussion and—by implication—in our descriptions.

This was too casual. The use of 'abstract indexes' in this way is sometimes an abstraction too far: it throws out an important baby along with the bathwater. Essentially, it distracts the developer from recognising an important class of development concern: an *Identities* concern [Jackson 00]. The potential importance of this concern can be seen from an anecdote in Peter Neumann's book about computer risks [Neumann 95]:

"A British Midland Boeing 737-400 crashed at Kegworth in the United Kingdom, killing 47 and injuring 74 seriously. The right engine had been erroneously shut off in response to smoke and excessive vibration that was in reality due to a fan-blade failure in the left engine. The screen-based 'glass cockpit' and the procedures for crew training were questioned. Cross-wiring, which was suspected—but not definitively confirmed—was subsequently detected in the warning systems of 30 similar aircraft."

'Cross-wiring' is the hardware manifestation of an archetypal failure in treating an identities concern.

6.4. Patient monitoring

In the well-known Patient Monitoring problem [Stevens 74] the machine is required to monitor temperature and other vital factors of intensive-care patients according to parameters specified by medical staff. The physical interface between the machine and the problem world of the intensive-care patients is essentially restricted to the shared register values of the analog-digital sensor devices attached to the patients. A significant concern in this problem is therefore to associate these shared registers correctly with the individual patients, and to describe how this association is realised in the problem domain. The complete chain of associations is this:

+ each patient has a name, used by the medical staff in specifying the parameters of monitoring for the patient;
+ each patient is physically attached to one or more analog-digital devices;
+ each device is plugged into a port of the machine through which its internal register is shared by the machine;
+ each port of the machine has a unique name.

To perform the monitoring as required, the machine must have access to a data structure representing these chains of associations. This data structure is a very specialised restricted *identities model* of the problem world of patients, devices and medical staff. It is, of course, quite distinct from any model of the patients that may be needed for managing the frequency of their monitoring and for detecting patterns in the values of their vital factors. The two models may be merged in an eventual joint implementation of the machines of the constituent subproblems, but they must be kept distinct in the earlier stages of the development process.

There is a further concern. Since neither the population of patients, nor the set of monitoring devices deemed necessary for each one, is constant, there must be an editing process in which the identities model data structure is created and changed. Concurrent access to this data structure by the monitoring and modifying processes therefore raises concerns of mutual exclusion and process scheduling. An excessively abstract view of the problem context will miss the existence of the data structure, and with it these important concerns and their impact on the Patient Monitoring system.

7. The scope of software development

The description concerns raised in this paper are primarily concerns about describing the problem world rather than designing the software to be executed by the machine. It's natural to ask again whether these description concerns are really the business of software developers at all. Perhaps the specification firewall does, after all, divide the business of software development from the business of the application domain expert.

Barry Boehm paints a vivid picture of software developers anxious to remain behind the firewall and not to encroach on application domain territory [Boehm00]:

> "I observed the social consequences of this approach in several aerospace system-architecture-definition meetings ("Integrating Software Engineering and System Engineering," Journal of INCOSE, pages 61-67, January 1994). While the hardware and systems engineers sat around the table discussing their previous system architectures, the software engineers sat on the side, waiting for someone to give them a precise specification they could turn into code."

It's clearly true that software developers can not and should not try to be experts in all application domains. For example, in a problem to control road traffic at a very complex intersection it must be the traffic engineer's responsibility to determine and analyse the patterns of incoming traffic, to design the traffic flows through the intersection, and to balance the conflicting needs of the different pedestrian and vehicle users. Software developers are not traffic engineers. But this is far from the whole answer.

There are several reasons why a large part of our responsibility must lie outside the computer, beyond the specification firewall. Here we will mention only two of them. First, the specification firewall usually cuts the development project along a line that makes the programming task unintelligibly arbitrary when viewed purely from the machine side: effectively, pure specifications are meaningless. And second, having created the technology that spawns huge discrete complexity in the problem domain, we have a moral obligation to contribute to mastering that complexity.

7.1. Meaningless specifications

In the problem of controlling traffic at a complex road intersection the pure specification is an I/O relation. Its domain is the set of possible traces of clock ticks and input signals at the computer's ports; its range is a set of corresponding traces of output signals. These trace sets may be characterised more or less elegantly, but, however described, they are strictly confined to these signals. The specification alphabet will be something like this—

{clocktick, outsignal_XIFF, . . . , insignalX207, . . . }

—where the event classes in the alphabet are events occurring in the hardware I/O interface of the computer. Nothing is said about lights or push buttons, about the layout of the intersection, or about vehicles and pedestrians. These are all private phenomena of the problem domain, hidden from the machine because they are not shared at the specification interface.

It's clear that such a specification is unintelligible. A small improvement can be achieved by naming the signals at the specification interface to indicate the corresponding lights and buttons—

{clocktick, outsignal_red27, . . . , insignal_button8, . . . }

—but the improvement is very small. Further improvement would need additional descriptions, showing the layout of the intersection and the positions of the lights. Then the domain properties of vehicles and pedestrians, existing and desired traffic flows, and everything else necessary to justify and clarify the otherwise impenetrable machine behaviour specification.

In short, the machine behaviour specification makes sense only in the larger context of the problem; and the problem is not located at the specification interface. If we restrict our work to developing software to meet given formal specifications, most of what we do will make no sense to us. We will be deprived of the intuitive understanding of the customer's problem that is essential both as a stimulus to creativity in program design and as a sanity check on the program we write.

7.2. Discrete complexity

Computers frequently introduce an unprecedented behavioural complexity into problem worlds with which they interact. This behavioural complexity arises naturally from the complexity of the software itself, and from its interplay with the causal, human, and lexical properties of the problem domains.

In older systems behavioural complexity was kept under control by three factors. First, the software itself—whether in the form of a computer program or an administrators' procedure manual—was usually smaller and simpler than today's software by more than one order of magnitude. Second, there was neither the possibility nor the ambition of integrating distinct systems, and so bringing about an exponential increase in their combined behavioural complexity. Third, almost every system, whether a 'data-processing' or a 'control' system, relied explicitly on human cooperation and intervention. When inconvenient and absurd results emerged, some human operator had the opportunity, the skill, and the authority to intervene and overrule the computer.

In many application areas we have gradually lost all of these safeguards. The ambitions of software developers increase to keep pace with the available resources of computational power and space. Systems are becoming more integrated, or, at least, more interdependent. And it is increasingly common to find levels of automation—as in flight control systems—that preclude human intervention to correct errors in software design or specification.

A large part of the responsibility for dealing with the resulting increased behavioural complexity must lie with computer scientists and software developers, if only because no other discipline has tools to master it. We can not discharge this responsibility by mastering complexity only in software: we must play a major role in mastering the resulting complexity in the problem world outside the computer.

8. Acknowledgements

Many of the ideas presented here have been the subject of joint work over a period of several years with Pamela Zave. They have also been discussed at length on many occasions with Daniel Jackson. This paper has been much improved by his comments.

References

[Ackoff 62]   R. L. Ackoff, *Scientific Method: Optimizing Applied Research Decisions*, Chichester, England, Wiley, 1962.

[Boehm 00]   Barry W. Boehm, Unifying software engineering and systems engineering; *IEEE Computer* Volume 33, Number 3, pages 114-116, March 2000.

[EWD 89]   Edsger W. Dijkstra, On the cruelty of really teaching computer science; *Communications of the ACM* Volume 32, Number 12, page 1414, December 1989.

[Gunter 00]   Carl A. Gunter, Elsa L. Gunter, Michael Jackson, and Pamela Zave; A reference model for requirements and specifications; *Proceedings of ICRE 2000*, Chicago IL, USA; reprinted in *IEEE Software* Volume 17, Number 3, pages 37-43, May/June 2000.

[Harel 87]   David Harel, Statecharts: A visual formalism for complex systems; *Science of Computer Programming* 8, pages 231-274, 1987.

[Jackson 00]   Michael Jackson, *Problem Frames: Analysing and Structuring Software Development Problems*, Harlow, England, Addison-Wesley, 2000.

[Neumann 95]   Peter G. Neumann, *Computer-Related Risks*, Reading, Massachusetts, Addison-Wesley, 1995, pages 44-45.

[Scherlis 89]   W. L. Scherlis, responding to E. W. Dijkstra "On the cruelty of really teaching computing science;" *Communications of the ACM* Volume 32, Number 12, page 1407, December 1989.

[Stevens 74]   W. P. Stevens, G. J. Myers, and L. L. Constantine, Structured design; *IBM Systems Journal* Volume 13, Number 2, pages 115-139, 1974. Reprinted in *Tutorial on Sofware Design Techniques*; Peter Freeman and Anthony I. Wasserman eds, pages 328-352, IEEE Computer Society Press, 4th edition 1983.

[UML]   James Rumbaugh, Ivar Jacobson, and Grady Booch, *The Unified Modeling Language Reference Manual*, Reading, Massachusetts, Addison-Wesley Longman 1999.

[Weyl 40]   Hermann Weyl, The mathematical way of thinking; address given at the Bicentennial Conference at the University of Pennsylvania, 1940.

Chapter 10

Conjunction as Composition
Pamela Zave and Michael Jackson

Abstract: Partial specifications written in many different specification languages can be composed if they are all given semantics in the same domain, or alternatively, all translated into a common style of predicate logic. The common semantic domain must be very general, the particular semantics assigned to each specification language must be conducive to composition, and there must be some means of communication that enables specifications to build on one another. The criteria for success are that a wide variety of specification languages should be accommodated, there should be no restrictions on where boundaries between languages can be placed, and intuitive expectations of the specifier should be met.

1. Introduction

Many notational styles and many formal languages have been proposed for specification. There are well-known specification paradigms—families of related languages—such as process algebras, temporal and nontemporal logics, algebraic languages, state-based and set-theoretic languages, automata, grammars, and type systems. There are languages in everyday use by software developers, but usually considered too informal or too specialized for purposes of formal specification, such as flow diagrams, decision tables or trees, queuing networks, and Gantt charts. There are also programming paradigms that, when applied in their purest form to carefully chosen problems, make good specification languages. Examples of these are functional programming, logic programming, object-oriented programming, and query/data-definition languages for database-management systems.

There is a reason for much of this diversity. Each language offers a different set of expressive capabilities, appropriate for specifying clearly and concisely a different set of properties. Each language also offers a different set of analytic capabilities, appropriate for rigorous reasoning about a different set of properties.

©1993 ACM Press. Reprinted, with permission, from: Zave, P. and Jackson, M. (1993) "Conjunction as composition", *ACM Transactions on Software Engineering and Methodology* 2(4):379-411, October 1993.

This paper addresses the open question of how to compose partial specifications written in many different languages. An answer to this question would make it possible for specifiers to construct multiparadigm specifications in which each partial specification is written in the specialized language best suited to expressing and analyzing the properties it is intended to describe. The ability to compose partial specifications could also contribute to specification reuse, simpler specification languages, better understanding of software-development methods, and increased automation [34].

Our basic approach to composition is the straightforward one outlined by Wing [31]: All specification languages are assigned semantics in the same semantic domain, and the semantics of the composition of a set of partial specifications is the set of specificands (members of the semantic domain) that satisfies all of them. [1] A set of partial specifications is consistent if and only if some specificand satisfies all of them.

Although the basic idea is simple, we have found that many details must be worked out correctly for the idea to succeed. The common semantic domain must be very general (Section 2). The particular semantics assigned to each specification language must be conducive to composition with other languages (Section 3). And there must be some means of communication that, without compromising the semantic framework, enables partial specifications to build on one another (Section 4).

What constitutes success? Three criteria have been foremost in our minds:

+ Composition should accommodate a wide variety of specification paradigms and notational styles.
+ It should be possible to compose partial specifications regardless of overlaps or gaps in coverage, regardless of which paradigms they represent, and regardless of where boundaries between languages are drawn. This contrasts with many ad hoc techniques for composition, which rely on strict assumptions about the languages used and the properties specified in each. The most common example of the latter is the control/data partition; it has been proposed in numerous variations, including recently the LOTOS/Act One partnership [13].
+ Intuitive expectations of a composition operator should be met. It should not define as inconsistent sets of partial specifications that are intuitively consistent and meaningful; it should not map intuitively interdependent properties onto spuriously independent (and therefore noninterfering) ones. It should not introduce implementation bias where none existed before.

We believe that we have succeeded in reaching these goals, and offer the examples in Section 5 as evidence.

Checking the mutual consistency of partial specifications must be a major concern of any specifier using a multiparadigm approach. Although a serious

---

[1] When translated into an assertional framework (see Section 2), this definition of composition corresponds to conjunction—hence the title.

treatment of consistency checking is outside the scope of this paper, Section 6 presents our approach to it and explains why we believe it is a tractable problem.

Section 7 surveys related work. Section 8 enumerates the limitations of these results and outlines a program of further research.

Although most of the limitations are simply topics for future research, Section 8 includes one important characteristic of these results that will not change. "Conjunction as composition" works because of the particular way we assign meaning in the common semantic domain to each language. Although we certainly claim to preserve the usefulness of each notation or style, we cannot pretend to duplicate exactly every popular conception of what a notation means, to translate every conceivable language feature, or (for those languages whose semantics has already been formally defined) to produce a completely equivalent formal semantics. We believe that these subtle semantic changes and limitations will eventually be justified by the advantages of compositional, multiparadigm specification. Much more experience than we have now is needed before the argument willl become convincing, however.

2. The semantic domain

2.1. Generality of the domain

Each member of the semantic domain consists of two components. There is a universe, possibly infinite and possibly empty, of distinct and identifiable individuals. (Individuals are equal only to themselves.) There is also a finite set of predicates on individuals, representing properties of individuals and relationships among individuals. Every predicate is defined on all possible instantiations of its arguments by individuals in the universe.

The subject matter of a formal specification is a portion of the real world that is controlled or supported by a computer system (and is sometimes a computer system itself [15]). We have shown elsewhere [16] that this simple semantic domain is sufficient for formalizing a wide variety of phenomena found in the subject matter of formal specifications. It is also sufficient for assigning meanings to a wide variety of specification languages. Three examples of common specification-language features should provide the necessary intuition:

- The semantics of a primitive type in a specification language is simply a unary predicate true only of individuals belonging to that type.
- The semantics of a structure is one or more predicates. For example, the semantics of any container structure (set, queue, stack, etc.) may include a predicate $member(m,c)$ meaning that contained individual m is a member of container individual c. Other predicates will distinguish the different types of container.
- Any kind of action is an individual. Actions can be atomic events, or they can be nonatomic transactions and related to each other by inclusion. Actions are also related to each other by a temporal ordering $earlier(a_1,a_2)$, which can be

partial or total.

For simplicity of exposition, this paper has only examples in which actions are atomic events and the temporal ordering is total.

2.2. The semantics of composition

The meaning of a partial specification, regardless of the language it is written in, is a set of members (specificands) of the semantic domain. These members of the semantic domain are said to satisfy the specification.

Consider, for example, a specification (such as an automaton) concerned with sequences of atomic events, and consider members of the semantic domain having event individuals in their universes and a total event order $earlier(e_1, e_2)$ in their predicate sets. Each member of the semantic domain is an encoding of exactly one event sequence (or "trace" or "behavior"). If this event sequence is in the set described by the automaton, then this member of the semantic domain is one of the automaton's specificands. Adding other predicates and other types of individual to this member of the semantic domain would produce a different specificand also satisfying the same specification.

The meaning of the composition of a set of partial specifications is the set of members of the semantic domain that satisfy all of the partial specifications. The set of partial specifications is consistent if and only if this intersection of specificand sets is nonempty.

2.3. The role of predicate logic

The semantic domain is the set of standard models of one-sorted first-order predicate logic with equality. This is a useful correspondence, because it is difficult to talk directly about members of the semantic domain—they are infinite and have little structure.

For explanatory purposes, instead of using specificand sets, we shall use equivalent assertions in predicate logic. For the remainder of the paper,:

+ the semantics of a specification language is a function for translating specifications in the language to assertions in predicate logic,
+ the semantics of a particular specification is an assertion in predicate logic,
+ the semantics of the composition of a set of partial specifications is the conjunction of their assertions, and
+ a set of partial specifications is consistent if and only if the conjunction of their assertions is satisfiable.

3. The semantics of specification languages

3.1. Simple nontemporal properties

We shall explain the translation of simple nontemporal properties into predicate logic using the Z specification of Figure 1. This description of a state

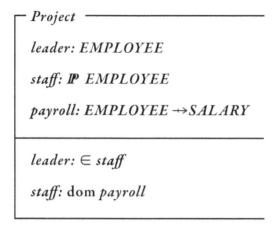

Figure 1. The state space of a Z specification describing a corporation.

space is adapted from Spivey's tutorial example [27], and illustrates the features of Z most commonly used for this purpose.

For each basic type, there is a unary predicate identifying individuals of that type. The basic types in our semantics include the basic types, *EMPLOYEE* and *SALARY*, listed explicitly in Figure 1. We also consider projects to be individuals belonging to a basic type, because any schema (such as *Project*) that declares state-space variables is defining a schema type consisting of all bindings of values to variables in the schema; the project individuals are the members of this type. Finally, our semantics requires that structures be individuals in their own right. Therefore, values of the variables *staff* and *payroll* belong to the basic types *SET-EMPLOYEE* and *SET-EMPLOYEE-SALARY-PAIR*, respectively.

The meaning of Figure 1 includes an assertion that all basic types are disjoint sets.

Each state-space variable such as *leader* translates into a predicate such as *leader(m,p)*, meaning that employee m is the leader of project p. There is always an assertion about such predicates, following the fixed pattern illustrated here:[2]

$$\forall p \ (Project(p) \implies \exists! m \ (leader(m,p) \wedge EMPLOYEE(m) \ ) \ ).$$

This asserts that every project has exactly one leader, which is also an employee. The corresponding assertion for the staff variable is:

$$\forall p \ (Project(p) \implies \exists! s \ (staff(s,p) \wedge SET\text{-}EMPLOYEE(s) \ ) \ ).$$

In our semantics for Z, the individuals that are members of any set are related to the set individual through the standard predicate *member(m,s)*, meaning that individual m is a member of set individual s. Of course, there must be an

---

[2] Following Kleene [19], $\iff$ and $\implies$ have the highest precedence, $\wedge$ and $\vee$ have medium precedence, and $\forall$, $\exists$, and $\neg$ have the lowest precedence. $\exists! x \ p(x)$ means that there exists a unique x such that $p(x)$.

additional type constraint wherever $member(m,s)$ is used, for example:

$\forall s \, \forall m \, (SET\text{-}EMPLOYEE(s) \wedge member(m, s) \implies EMPLOYEE(m))$.

The value of a *payroll* variable is a relation, so it is a set with members belonging to the type *EMPLOYEE-SALARY-PAIR*. In our semantics for Z, the individuals that are components of any pair are related to the pair individual through the standard predicate $pair\text{-}components(c_1, c_2, r)$, meaning that individuals c_1 and c_2, in that order, constitute the pair r. Of course, there must be additional type constraints wherever $pair\text{-}components(c_1, c_2, r)$ is used, for example:

$\forall r \, \forall c_1 \forall c_2 \, (EMPLOYEE\text{-}SALARY\text{-}PAIR(r) \wedge pair\text{-}components \, (c_1, c_2, r)$
$\implies EMPLOYEE(c1) \wedge SALARY(c_1))$.

According to Figure 1, the payroll relation is a partial function. This translates to an additional constraint:

$\forall p \, \forall y \, (Project(p) \wedge payroll(y,p) \implies partial\text{-}function(y))$,

where

$\forall y \, (partial\text{-}function(y) \implies$
$\forall r_1 \, \forall r_2 \, \forall c_{11} \, \forall c_{12} \, \forall c_{21} \, \forall c_{22} \, ($
$member(r_1, y) \wedge member(r_2, y) \wedge$
$pair\text{-}components(\, c_{11}, c_{12}, r_1) \wedge pair\text{-}components \, (c_{21}, c_{22}, r_2)$
$\implies (r_1 = r_2) \vee (c_{11} \neq c_{21})))$.

Obviously total functions, injections, subjections, and bijections would be characterized by stronger assertions.

The *Project* schema contains two assertions in addition to those implicit in the signatures. The first assertion, stating that the leader of a project is a member of its staff, is simply translated as:

$\forall p \, \forall m \, \forall s \, (leader(m,p) \wedge staff \, (s,p) \implies member(m,s))$.

The second asserts that the staff set is the domain of the payroll function. This translates into:

$\forall p \, \forall s \, \forall y \, (staff(s,p) \wedge payroll \, (y,p) \implies$
$\forall m \, (member(m,s) \iff \exists c \, \exists r \, (pair\text{-}components(m,c,r) \wedge member(r,y))))$.

3.2. Sequences

Sequences are ubiquitous in specifications, and this paper contains several examples of them.

It is customary in formal specification languages to regard sequences as partial functions from the natural numbers to the set of sequence elements [18, 27]. Instead, we regard all sequences as totally ordered sets. For one reason, it is more natural for a specification to say "event e is earlier than event f" than for a specification to say "e is the 4,986th event and f is the 4,991st event." Totally ordered sets are also fundamentally simpler, more flexible, and more easily manipulated, as the following examples will show.

We generally use two predicates to establish a sequence, one for membership in the set and one to impose an order, but their exact forms depend on several factors—whether phenomena are formalized as individuals or predicates, where duplications or subsets arise, etc. (This section will illustrate two possibilities, and Section 5.4 will show a third.) Because this section discusses several different membership and ordering predicates specifying different sequences or classes of sequence, the predicates are distinguished from each other by subscripts.

If there is only one sequence in the general category being considered, then the sequence need not have an explicit name. It can simply be described by its membership and ordering predicates. For example, $member_1(m)$ means that m is a member of the sequence, and $precedes_1(m_1,m_2)$ means that m_1 precedes m_2 in the sequence. The order must be irreflexive, transitive, and asymmetric (provable from the first two properties). The order must also be total:

$$\forall m_1 \; \forall m_2 \, (\; member_1(m_1) \wedge member_1(m_2) =>$$
$$precedes_1 \, (m_1,m_2) \vee precedes_1 \, (m_2,m_1) \vee m_1 = m_2).$$

In almost all cases sequences are nondense, meaning that each nonfinal member has a unique successor (i.e., they are like the integers rather than the real numbers). This assertion states that each nonfinal member has a unique successor:

$$\forall m_1 \, ($$
$$(member_1(m_1) \wedge \exists m_2(member_1(m_2) \wedge precedes_1(m_1, m_2)) \,) =>$$
$$\exists! m_2 \, (member_1(m_2) \wedge precedes_1(m_1,m_2) \wedge$$
$$\neg \, \exists m_3(member_1(m_3) \wedge precedes_1(m_1,m_3) \wedge precedes_1(m_3,m_2)) \,) \,).$$

A sequence may have an initial element (with no predecessor), a final element (with no successor), both, or neither. If the set is finite, it obviously must have both.

All nondense sequences with initial members should be well-founded sets, that is, sets such that each subset has a minimal member. This property cannot be stated in first-order logic, and there are nonstandard models of the first-order assertions that do not satisfy it. Nonstandard models are not going to arise in a software development, however, so it is sufficient to state that we intend only standard models of sequences.

A *marked sequence* is a particularly useful variety of sequence. A marked sequence has an initial member. It is also bipartite: Its members fall into two disjoint categories, *items* and *markers*. The sequence is further constrained so that items and markers alternate strictly, beginning with a marker and ending (if there is an ending) with a marker. In a marked sequence, items are like leaves of a book and markers are like positions between the leaves in which a bookmark can be inserted. *premarker(i,m)* means that m is the marker immediately preceding item i. *postmarker(i,m)* means that m is the marker immediately succeeding item

Axioms of a Marked Sequence

event(e)	item(i)		
		initial-marker(m)	initial-interval(v)
interval(v)	marker(m)		
		premarker(i,m)	ends(e,v)
earlier(t_1,t_2)	precedes(x_1,x_2)		
		postmarker(i,m)	begins(e,v)

Figure 2. The temporal predicates are a renaming of the predicates of a marked sequence.

i. Marked sequences are potentially useful whenever a sequence must be explicitly traversed.

In Section 2.1, it was stated that this paper uses for its examples a temporal model in which all actions are atomic, totally ordered events, and all events are individuals. In this temporal model, only an event can cause a state change; in the intervals between events the state is stable and can be observed. Thus, intervals can also be regarded as individuals, since they are distinct and identifiable in the same way that events are.

The two kinds of temporal phenomena, events and intervals, form a marked sequence with events as items and intervals as markers. Because each specificand is an encoding of exactly one temporal marked sequence, the temporal sequence needs no explicit name, and can be specified using predicates like those discussed above. Figure 2 shows the correspondences between the general predicates of a marked sequence and the particular predicates of the temporal sequence. The general predicates are inside the box, the particular predicates are outside the box, and two predicates on the same horizontal line correspond. The arguments of predicates are identified by position, so the mnemonic "role" names of arguments can be changed along with the predicate names.[3]

Note that in renaming *premarker(i,m)* and *postmarker(i,m)*, we have shifted the emphasis. Instead of thinking of intervals as precursors and aftermaths of events, we have found it more natural to think of events as beginnings and endings of intervals of stability.

If we wish to specify properties belonging to all alphabetic sequences (strings), on the other hand, then the sequences themselves must be individuals. As before,

---

[3] The arguments of *precedes* are named x because they may be items or markers. Similarly, the arguments of *earlier* are named t for *temporal phenomenon*, because they may be events or intervals. The notation used in Figure 2 will be explained further In Sections 3.4 and 4.1.

their members are also individuals. The membership predicate $members_2(i,s)$ means that item i is a member of string s. The ordering predicate $precedes_2(i_1,i_2,s)$ imposes a total order on the items in each string s. The alphabetic content of the sequence is captured by the predicate $contents_2(i,c)$, meaning that string item i corresponds to alphabetic character c. Thus, $contents_2(i,``p")$ is true if argument i is instantiated by either the second or third item of "apple;" this indirection solves the problem that strings may have duplicate characters, but there is no notion of duplication in the members of a set.

This view of sequences with duplicate elements may seem unusual, but it is actually only a simplification of the scheme in which sequences are partial functions from the natural numbers to the set of sequence elements. The latter scheme relies on an ordering predicate $precedes_3(i_1,i_2)$ (it is in fact ordinary numerical order) true only of natural numbers—natural numbers are being used in the same role as our sequence items. The membership predicate $member_3(i,s)$ has many constraints on it: The same natural numbers must be reused as items of different sequences, and the members of each sequence must be a contiguous set (adjacent in numerical order) starting from "1." The predicate $contents_3(s,i,c)$ is the partial function from the natural numbers to the sequence elements; it must have one more argument (the sequence individual) than $contents_2$ because the natural numbers are reused as different items with different character attributes. Additions or deletions in the middle of a sequence require a complete reassignment of contents to indices, which is not necessary in our encoding.

3.3. Temporal properties

In this section, we show how temporal properties can be represented in predicate logic. Specificands encode sequences of events and intervals, as described in the previous section. Although this is not the only possible temporal model, its use as an example should make the general style of translation clear enough.

Figure 3 shows a simple deterministic finite-state automaton (DFSA). Its usual[4] semantics can now be given in terms of temporal sequences. Each state label such as *is-off* corresponds to a predicate such as $is\text{-}off(v)$, which is true if and only if v is an interval in which the light is observed to be off. Each transition label such as *press* corresponds to a predicate such as $press(e)$, which is true if and only if e is an event in which the controlling button is pressed.

There are several ways of writing the assertions that capture the meaning of Figure 3; we shall use assertions in five categories. The first category consists exclusively of assertions about states. There is an assertion about the initial state:

$$\forall v\ (initial\text{-}interval(v) => is\text{-}off(v)).$$

There must also be an assertion that in each interval exactly one state predicate holds.

---

[4] The DFSA actually has several different meanings as a specification. Other meanings will be discussed in Sections 3.4 and 4.1.

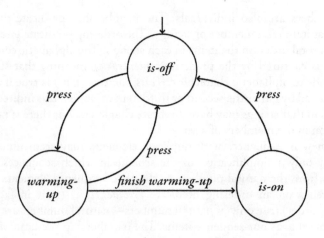

Figure 3. A DFSA describing a fluorescent light.

The second category is an assertion that no event can satisfy both *press(e)* and *finish-warming-up(e)*, This assertion is necessary to make the automaton deterministic.

The third category constrains when events can occur. The fact that there is no out-transition from *is-off* labeled *finish-warming-up*, for instance, means that a *finish-warming-up* event cannot occur in state *is-off*:

$$\forall e \, \forall v \, ((ends(e,v) \wedge is\text{-}off(v)) \implies \neg \, finish\text{-}warming\text{-}up(e)).$$

The fourth category contains assertions about state transitions. For example, this assertion says that when the light *is-on* and a *press* event occurs, the light enters the *is-off* state:

$$\forall e \, \forall v_1 \, \forall v_2 \, (is\text{-}on(v_1) \wedge ends(e,v_1) \wedge press(e) \wedge begins(e,v_2) \implies is\text{-}off(v_2)).$$

The fifth category consists of an assertion that unless an event satisfies *press(e)* or *finish-warming-up(e)*, the state after the event must be the same as the state before it.

Returning to the Z specification, we now see that if the values of state variables can change over time, each state predicate requires an interval argument. For example, now *leader(m,p,v)* means that employee *m* is the leader of project *p* during the interval *v*. The previously stated constraints on state predicates must hold in every interval.

Figure 4 is a Z schema for an operation *AddStaff* to add an employee to a project. Strictly speaking Z has no temporal semantics, but we shall formalize the common convention that a Z operation corresponds to an event type, and that the unprimed and primed variables in the operation schema describe the state before and after events of that type, respectively.

As in Section 3.1, we find that schemas translate into types of individual; there is a predicate *AddStaff(e)*, meaning that event *e* is an *AddStaff* operation. There is also a predicate for each argument of an operation. *AddStaff* operations

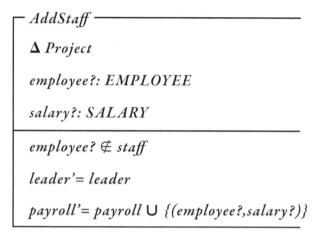

Figure 4. A Z operation.

have two explicit arguments, *employee?* and *salary?*. The predicate *employee?(m,e)* means that *m* is the employee argument of event *e*. It satisfies a constraint much like that associated with every state-variable predicate:

$$\forall e \ (AddStaff(e) => \exists! m \ (employee?(m,e) \wedge EMPLOYEE(m))).$$

The *AddStaff* schema contains the notation Δ*Project*, which indicates that this operation changes a project. Although this fragmentary example does not indicate which project an *AddStaff* operation is applied to (the specification can be completed using the technique of promotion [32]), in the general case an *AddStaff* operation must have a predicate Δ*Project(p,e)*, meaning that *p* is the project to which *AddStaff* operation *e* applies. Its type and uniqueness constraints are similar to those of *employee?(m,e)*.

An *AddStaff* operation cannot occur whenever its employee argument is already a member of the project staff. This constraint is translated:

$$\forall v \ \forall e \ \forall p \ \forall m \ \forall s \ (ends(e,v) \wedge AddStaff(e) \wedge \Delta Project(p,e) \wedge$$
$$employee?(m,e) \wedge staff(s,p,v) => \neg \ member(m,s,v)).$$

Finally, the semantics includes assertions about the states after *AddStaff* events. The *leader* and *payroll* components must be given new values, while the *staff* component retains the fixed relationship with *payroll* specified in Figure 1. This assertion concerns the new addition to the payroll:

$$\forall e \ \forall v \ \forall p \ \forall m \ \forall s \ \forall y \ (begins(e,v) \wedge AddStaff(e) \wedge$$
$$\Delta Project(p,e) \wedge employee?(m,e) \wedge salary?(s,e) \wedge payroll(y,p,v) =>$$
$$\exists r(member(r,y,v) \wedge pair\text{-}components(m,s,r,v))).$$

There are other assertions that the payroll remains the same except for the new addition, and that the leader remains the same.

Borgida et al. [2] have pointed out that in some "object-oriented" specification styles, there may be a problem with expressing what an operation leaves unchanged (as well as what it changes). Their recommended technique for solving this problem works perfectly within the framework of the semantics for Z given here.

Operators of temporal logic have straightforward representations in the common semantics, which is not surprising considering that early formulations of temporal logic encode intervals in a similar way [25]. For example, $\Box P$, read *always P*, is the assertion:

$$\forall v \ (interval(v) \Rightarrow P(v)).$$

The assertion $P \rightsquigarrow Q$ (*P leads to Q*) is translated as:

$$\forall v_1 (P(v_1) \Rightarrow \exists v_2 (earlier(v_1,v_2) \wedge Q(v_2))).$$

Real time can be introduced with a predicate *timestamp(e,t)*, meaning that event *e* occurs at real time *t*.

3.4. Signatures

Each partial specification in a specification has a signature. This is the set of predicates used as primitives in the predicate-logic semantics of the partial specification. In other words, the semantics is a set of assertions over the predicates of the signature.

In the translation of a specification into logic, the names of signature predicates can come from three sources: they may be built into the semantics of the specification language, they may be determined by names or labels written in the specification, or they may be constructed from a combination of the previous two.

Needless to say, signatures are extremely important in understanding the role of each partial specification, its potential inconsistencies, etc. This will be discussed further in Section 6. In the meantime, there are two other reasons for paying careful attention to signatures. One reason is that renaming the signature predicates is a valuable tool for specification reuse.

For example, for full generality the semantics of a DFSA should be defined in terms of predicates characterizing a marked sequence: *item(i)*, *marker(m)*, and *precedes(x_1,x_2)*. An alphabet label always becomes a predicate true only of items, while a state label always becomes a predicate true only of markers. Whenever the DFSA is used, the marked-sequence predicates in its signature can be renamed to be the predicates of the temporal sequence or any other marked sequence.

Another reason for attention to signatures is that they provide new semantic options for old specification languages. We maybe accustomed to thinking that a specification such as Figure 3 has only one meaning, but in fact it can have many. Here are three of them:

- ◆ The signature might consist only of the marked-sequence predicates and the state predicates. In this case, the partial specification makes several assertions about the markers, including that each marker satisfies exactly one of the state predicates, that the first marker satisfies *is-off(m)*, and that an *is-off* marker can never be succeeded immediately by an *is-on* marker without an intervening *warming-up* marker. In this case, Figure 3 is not equivalent to an unreduced DFSA accepting the same regular language, which would have different states and therefore mean something completely different.

* The signature might consist only of the marked-sequence predicates and the alphabet predicates. In this case, the DFSA is constraining only the items of the marked sequence it is describing. It would be equivalent to an unreduced DFSA or regular grammar accepting the same language.

* The signature might consist of the marked-sequence predicates, the state predicates, and the alphabet predicates. The DFSA would then have the meaning given in Section 3.3 (except, of course, that it can describe any marked sequence, not just the temporal sequence as assumed in Section 3.3). Like the first alternative, with this semantics Figure 3 is not equivalent to an unreduced DFSA accepting the same regular language.

There are also some limits on the possible choices of signature. In the case of a DFSA, limits originate in the fact that any reasonable translation of the semantics of DFSAs into predicate logic uses state predicates. If state predicates are not in the signature of the partial specification, as in the second alternative above, then they *must* be fully definable in terms of the predicates that are in the signature. We know from automata theory that the state predicates are definable if all of the alphabet predicates are in the signature, but a subset of the alphabet predicates would not constitute a sufficient signature for the specification.

In general, the definitions of state predicates are mutually recursive and cannot be regarded as shorthands. For example, a paraphrase of the definition of *warming-up(m)* is that it is true if and only if the preceding marker satisfies *is-off* and the preceding item satisfies *press*, or the preceding marker satisfies *warming-up* and the preceding item does not satisfy *press* or *finish-warming-up*. Recursive definitions are not a problem provided that they apply only to well-founded ordered sets, which all marked sequences are.[5]

A description graph, as exemplified by Figures 2 and 5, is a convenient notation for displaying relationships among partial specifications. Boxes represent partial specifications. Lines from the left edge of the diagram into a box represent predicates in the signature of a partial specification. If there are two different predicate labels on a line, one inside the box and one outside, then those labels represent the internal and external (renamed) names, respectively. If a predicate appears in the signatures of two partial specifications, then both specifications constrain the predicate, and there is a potential for interdependence or inconsistency between them.

---

[5] For proving properties of recursively defined predicates, we can add an axiom schema for induction to the other axioms of well-founded ordered sets.

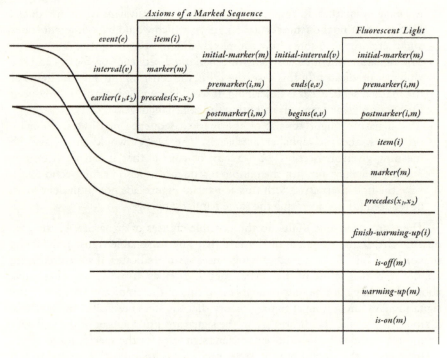

Figure 5. A description graph showing the composition of Figure 3 and the axioms of a marked sequence

4. Definition of predicates

4.1. Definition as communication

So far, the only predicates in signatures are predicates of the semantic domain, which can be viewed as representing relationships that are directly identifiable in the portion of the real world being described. Although partial specifications can "communicate" by constraining the same predicates, this is not enough—there must be a more direct means of communication among partial specifications, enabling them to build on one another.

Section 3.4 showed that the translation of partial specifications into predicate logic sometimes requires definition of new predicates. Although these defined predicates can be kept strictly internal to the semantics of a partial specification (like local variables), they can also be exported for use in the signatures of other partial specifications. Defined predicates provide the needed additional communication among partial specifications.

---

[5] For proving properties of recursively defined predicates, we can add an axiom schema for induction to the other axioms of well-founded ordered sets.

For example, the marked-sequence specification shown in Figures 2 and 5 defines, from the three predicates in its signature, three new predicates *initial-marker(m)*, *premarker(i,m)*, and *postmarker(i,m)*. In a description graph, a line representing an exported predicate passes through the right edge of the box in which it is defined, and may enter the left edges of different boxes in the role of a signature predicate (Figure 5). These figures also show renaming of defined predicates.

Like description of properties, the task of defining a new predicate can be made much easier by exploiting the features of the right paradigm. Just as each language provides concise access to a body of built-in semantics, each language can also provide access to a body of built-in facilities for defining new predicates.

This point is illustrated by the signature options for a DFSA. If state predicates are not observable in the semantic domain but event predicates are, then the definitions of state predicates are automatically part of the translation of the DFSA, and the state predicates can be exported.

Exploitation of the particular features of languages can go further than this. Consider, for example, the augmented DFSA in Figure 6. In addition to an alphabet label, each transition has a unique label that names the meaning or interpretation of the alphabet member in the context in which it is occurring. A press event has three classifications: When the light is off, it is a request to turn it on; when the light is warming up, it aborts the warming-up phase; and when the light is on, it turns it off. Transition labels are a natural extension of the DFSA notation; like alphabet labels, they translate into predicates on items. They can be part of the signature of a DFSA, or they can be defined and exported if the signature predicates are sufficient to do so.

How does definition provide communication? A partial specification with any of *request-on(e)*, *abort-warming-up(e)*, or *go-off(e)* in its signature can describe or

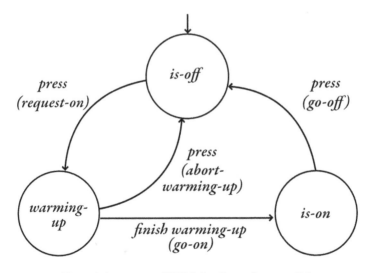

Figure 6. An augmented DFSA describing a fluorescent light

constrain these more precise event categories rather than the coarser classification that the event is a *press*. The result is that it can benefit from the state information encapsulated in the DFSA, without having direct access to it. This is a very general technique—events can belong to any number of classes, that is, be described in any number of ways.

Even though definition of new predicates provides a powerful mechanism for communication among partial specifications, it is declarative and free of operational bias. It is completely compatible with assertional specification and nonoperational semantics.

This point should not be taken for granted. Internal events in Statecharts [9] and *result!* variables in Z [27] both provide versions of event classification—a consummately useful specification technique—but with inherently temporal, operational semantics.

4.2. Extensions to the semantics of composition

The description graph relating a set of partial specifications must be acyclic. This ensures syntactically that all predicates are defined, either directly or indirectly, in terms of predicates in the semantic domain.

A member of the semantic domain (specificand) can be extended by defined predicates, provided that the predicates are defined (directly or indirectly) in terms of predicates found in the specificand. The values of the defined predicates must be consistent with their definitions and the values of the original predicates.

A partial specification with defined predicates in its signature is satisfied by a specificand if and only if the specificand can be extended by the defined predicates, and the extended specificand satisfies the partial specification in the usual way.[6]

5. Examples

5.1. The world information system

The first example is everybody's nightmare: a composition of all the world's computerized information systems (specified in a variety of state-based and database-oriented languages). One of the systems is a corporate information system of which the Z examples in Section 3 are fragments. Its signature includes

---

[6]This explanation assumes global predicate names, that is, the absence of naming conflicts. Conflicts can always be resolved by renaming, as the example in Section 5.1 shows, although it may not be necessary to do so.

[7]Cardelli and Wegner [4] use a framework for discussing type systems in which values may have more than one type. but in their discussion of languages this polymorphic capability is enjoyed only by functions (a special kind of value). In the first-order common semantics functions are represented by predicates rather than by individuals, so polymorphism disappears in the translation altogether. Subrange types are an exception to our claim, but they seem to be a special case without general significance.

the predicates $EMPLOYEE(m)$ and $Project(p)$.

A partial specification written in a strongly typed language such as Z defines a hierarchy of types ordered by inclusion. For all practical purposes,[7] the basic types at the bottom of the hierarchy (of which $EMPLOYEE$ is an example) must be disjoint sets. Within the scope of the strongly typed partial specification, the assumption of disjoint basic types is extremely useful: It is the foundation for type inference and type checking, both important forms of language-specific algorithmic analysis.

Sometimes, however, we want to compose partial specifications whose basic types are *not* disjoint. The world information system may include a specification of a taxation database in which $TAXPAYER$ is a basic type. Obviously, the classes of employees and taxpayers overlap. If these specifications had to be combined in a strongly typed framework, either these partial specifications would be inconsistent, or the sets $EMPLOYEE$ and $TAXPAYER$ would be considered disjoint (falsely independent), or both specifications would have to be rewritten using different basic types.

In our translation semantics, on the other hand, the predicates $EMPLOYEE(e)$ and $TAXPAYER(t)$ have no relationship unless a constraint is asserted explicitly. They can describe overlapping sets of individuals, as is indeed correct. Any partial specification can create and exploit a classification scheme, and partial specifications with different classification schemes can be composed without restriction.

Like classification, the component-of relation forms hierarchies. Because aggregates may be individuals in their own right (with *component* (c,a) predicates expressing the relationships between aggregates and their components), they can participate in many independent component hierarchies.

Individuals of type *Project* are aggregates in the corporate information system. They have components, and may also serve as components of other individuals

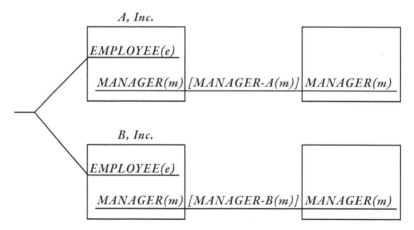

Figure 7. A description graph showing the composition of two corporate information systems with different definitions of a manager.

such as divisions or budgets.

The world information system may also contain systems that use the information in the other systems. A package router, for example, is a system for routing packages to destinations through a tree-shaped network of pipes (with destinations at the leaves of the tree). In the Gist specification of a package router [22], destinations are purely symbolic. For automated support of a business in which incoming packages are sorted by project (and put in a mailbag that is then delivered to the project's central office), we can compose the Z and Gist specifications. All that is required is to use renaming to identify *destination(d)* in the signature of the Gist specification with *Project(p)* in the semantic domain. Now projects/destinations can have attributes in the Gist specification, or be components of other aggregates specified in Gist. A mapping from projects/destinations to street addresses can be shared with an information system from which this information is available (the predicate would appear in the signatures of both specifications).

The administrators of the world information system may wish to integrate the information systems of corporations A and B. Although both may have *EMPLOYEE(e)* in their signatures (see Figure 7), they may both define a predicate *MANAGER(m)*, in different ways.

The partial specifications on the right of Figure 7 use the two different meanings of *MANAGER(m)*. The lines in the description graph make clear which definition is intended in each case. If globally unique names are desired, then the optional renamings *MANAGER-A(m)* and *MANAGER-B(m)* can be introduced, but in either case none of the partial specifications need be rewritten.

5.2. The factory floor

It is commonly recognized that a flow diagram is incomplete with respect to synchronization, and cannot be used for formal specification unless further information is provided [10, 24, 28]. A particular synchronization pattern can be assumed for all nodes of the flow diagram, or the diagram can be composed with other partial specifications. We shall show the semantics of a flow diagram and two Petri nets that can be composed with it to provide different forms of synchronization.

Figure 8 shows a flow diagram describing the layout of a factory floor. There are named machines connected by named conveyor belts.

The signature of this description includes all of the temporal predicates. The signature also includes, for each node of the diagram, a predicate on events. For instance, the predicate *machine1(e)* means that event *e* is an observable action of the first machine. The remainder of the signature of the description is a set of predicates for each queue of the diagram. (Their names have two parts, one built-in and one taken from a label in the diagram.) The predicates in this set describing the queue named *belt1* are:

- *belt1-addition(e)*, meaning that event *e* is an addition operation of the belt,
- *belt1-deletion(e)*, meaning that event *e* is a deletion operation of the belt,

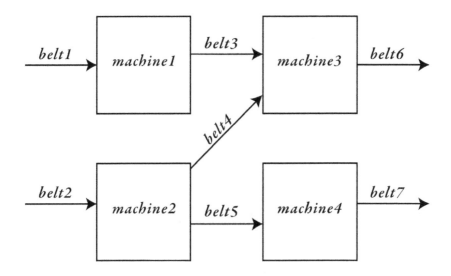

Figure 8. A flow diagram describing the layout of a factory floor.

- belt1-member(i,v), meaning that item i is on the belt during interval v,
- belt1-precedes(i_1,i_2,v), meaning that item i_1 precedes item i_2 on the belt during interval v,
- belt1-size(s,v) meaning that there are s items on the belt during interval v, and
- belt1-event-item(i,e) meaning that item i is being transferred during addition or deletion operation e.

The semantics of the flow diagram includes many assertions obvious enough to be presented informally rather than formally:

- There are type constraints on the arguments of all predicates above.
- One event cannot be both an addition to and a deletion from the same queue. However, this does not preclude the possibility that an event has an effect on more than one queue.
- In every interval, the items on each queue are totally ordered by the precedes predicates.
- Additions and deletions change queues in the obvious way; nothing else can change the contents of a queue.
- A deletion event cannot occur when its queue is empty.
- Initially all queues are empty.
- The size of a queue is equal to the number of items in the queue.

The more interesting part of the semantics concerns the interaction between nodes and queues. For each node of the diagram, there is an assertion that all observable actions of a node are addition or deletion operations of the queues that touch it in the diagram. For the third machine, this assertion is:

$$\forall e\ (machine3(e) \Rightarrow belt3\text{-}deletion(e) \lor belt4\text{-}deletion(e) \lor belt6\text{-}addition(e)).$$

For each queue of the diagram with a source or destination node in the diagram, there is an assertion that all addition or deletion events of the queue must be events of the source or destination node, respectively. Concerning the destination of *belt4* the assertion is:

$$\forall e \ (\textit{belt4-deletion}(e) \Rightarrow \textit{machine3}(e)).$$

Figure 9 is a Petri net providing another description of the third machine. It shows that the machine has no internal buffering or concurrent operation; in one atomic action, it consumes from both input belts and produces for its output belt.

We have shown that the signature of a DFSA must include marked-sequence predicates and may include predicates of three other types associated with parts of the DFSA syntax (states, alphabets, and transitions). Similarly, the signature of a Petri net must include marked-sequence predicates and may include predicates of four other types associated with parts of the Petri-net syntax. For clarity, we shall assume that the marked-sequence predicates are renamed to be the temporal predicates, and explain the semantics in terms of temporal phenomena.

For each transition label, such as *machine3* in Figure 9, there may be a predicate *machine3(e)* meaning that *e* is an event of the third machine. For each place label such as *belt3-size* in Figure 9, there may be a predicate *belt3-size(s, v)*, meaning that during interval *v* the count of this countable phenomenon is *s*. For each place with an out-arrow such as *belt3-size*, there may be a predicate *dec-belt3-size(e)* meaning that event *e* decrements the token count of this place. For each place with an in-arrow such as *belt6-size*, there may be a predicate *inc-belt6-size(e)* meaning that event *e* increments the token count of this place.

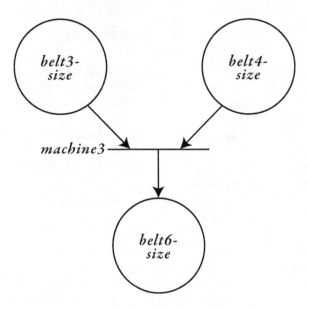

Figure 9. A Petri net describing synchronization in the third machine.

The signature for Figure 9 leaves nothing out: it consists of the temporal predicates, *machine3(e)*, *belt3-size(s,v)*, *belt4-size(s,v)*, *belt6-size(s,v)*, *dec-belt3-size(e)*, *dec-belt4-size(e)*, and *inc-belt6-size(e)*.

Note that all but the decrement and increment predicates are already shared with the signature of Figure 8. To complete the intended composition, the decrement and increment predicates must be renamed to *belt3-deletion(e)*, *belt4-deletion(e)*, *and belt6-addition(e)*, respectively. With these renamings, the decrement and increment predicates have the same names as the predicates in the signature of Figure 8, with the same meanings.

The safety semantics of a Petri net relates transition, place, decrement, and increment predicates in the expected way. Perhaps the most interesting assertion, because of its correspondence with the assertion given above for the semantics of the flow diagram, is the following:

$$\forall e\ (machine3(e) \Rightarrow$$

$$belt3\text{-}deletion(e) \wedge belt4\text{-}deletion(e) \wedge belt6\text{-}addition(e)).$$

In this example, we can see clearly that the composition works as we want it to because the flow diagram and Petri net are making different, complementary assertions about the same event predicates.

We interpret Petri nets as asserting liveness properties as well as safety properties. If a transition is enabled then it will eventually occurs.[8] The translation of this constraint, for each transition, is similar to $P \rightsquigarrow Q$.

Figure 10 shows another Petri net that could be composed with the flow diagram. It differs from Figure 9 in that input and output events of the third machine are separate, so that the node behaves like a concurrent process instead of an indivisible action. Nevertheless, the internal storage capacity of the machine is limited to two items, one from each of the input belts.

The signature of Figure 10 is exactly the same as the signature of Figure 9, and it composes with Figure 8 in the same way, although of course it makes different assertions. For instance, Figure 10 asserts that *belt3-deletion(e)*, *belt4-deletion(e)*, and *belt6-addition(e)* characterize distinct classes of event.

The semantics of Figure 10 is a little more complicated than that of Figure 9, because there are place, increment, and decrement predicates not reflected in the signature. Because our Petri-net semantics relies on having a complete set of place, transition, increment, and decrement predicates, it is necessary to define them from the predicates that are in the signature. This is not a problem, except that they must have names before they can be defined. The Petri-net semantics can supply them with built-in names: from left to right and top to bottom, the unlabeled places are pl, $p2$, $p3$, and $p4$. The increment and decrement predicates are named to match.

Another unusual property of Figure 10 is that all three transitions have the

---

[8]Note that this simple definition works only because these Petri nets are deterministic; there is never more than one transition enabled.

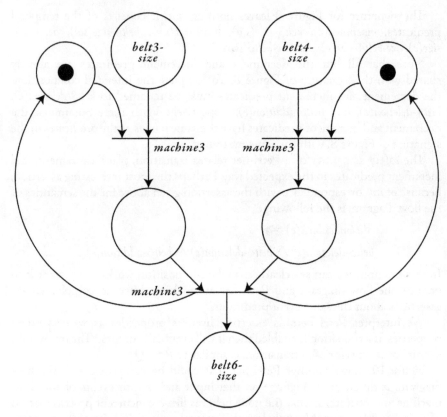

Figure 10. Another Petri net describing synchronization in the third machine.

same label. This is because no finer distinctions about actions of the third machine are directly observable in the domain. The top two transitions can be enabled simultaneously, and since they bo   th have the same label, knowing that an event satisfies *machine3(e)* is not sufficient to determine which transition occurs!

This is not a problem because the signature contains more information about these events than just *machine3(e)*. In particular, it contains the predicates *belt3-deletion(e)*, *belt4-deletion(e)*, and *belt6-addition(e)* that unambiguously identify all three transitions, so that *all* place, increment, and decrement predicates have deterministic definitions in terms of the predicates of the signature. For instance, two related definitions are

$$\forall e \ (dec\text{-}p1\text{-}size(e) \Longleftrightarrow dec\text{-}belt3\text{-}size(e))$$

and

$$\forall e \ (inc\text{-}p3\text{-}size(e) \Longleftrightarrow dec\text{-}belt3\text{-}size(e)).$$

The initial value of each place predicate is determined by the number of tokens visible in the diagram. (Note that the initial values of the belt-size(s, v) predicates, which are all zero, are redundantly specified by the flow diagram.) On the basis

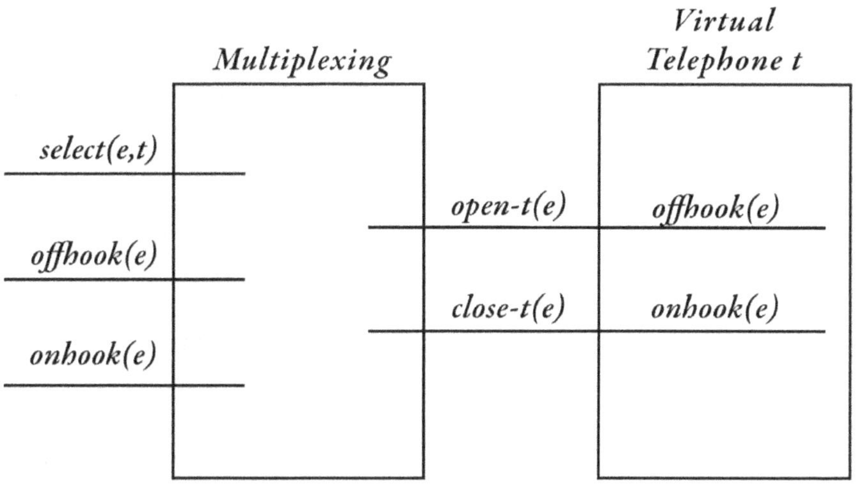

$$Multiplexing \qquad\qquad \substack{Virtual \\ Telephone\ t}$$

Multiplexing		Virtual Telephone t
select(e,t)		
	open-t(e)	offhook(e)
offhook(e)		
	close-t(e)	onhook(e)
onhook(e)		

Figure 11. A description graph for the specification of a multiplexing telephone

of initial values and the increment and decrement predicates, it is easy to write definitions of the place predicates for all unlabeled places.

The translation of Figure 10 shows the value of flexible signature options. Without them we would have had to overspecify by identifying many more predicates in the semantic domain than we wanted or needed.

5.3. The multiplexing telephone

A multiplexing telephone is a modern device with the capacity to participate in many calls simultaneously. It has a set of resources that we have named *virtual telephones* [35] because each resource is similar to an old-fashioned telephone in its capabilities for making and receiving calls (each virtual telephone has a button for selection and several lights for indicating its status). Because virtual telephones share a handset, dialpad, etc., we need some new terminology: an *open* or *close* event is to a virtual telephone what an *offhook* or *onhook* event is to an old-fashioned telephone, respectively.

Figure 11 shows a specification of multiplexing telephone, decomposed for several different reasons into two partial specifications.

The partial specification "Virtual Telephone *t*" is in fact a specification of an old-fashioned telephone, which we are reusing as a description of a virtual telephone. It is a DFSA, and can be used without modification as long as its internal predicates *offhook(e)* and *onhook(e)* are renamed to *open-t(e)* and *close-t(e)*.

The "Multiplexing" specification describes the shared state of the telephone and its relationship to input events. It defines an important predicate *selected(t,v)*, meaning that during interval *v* virtual telephone *t* is in control of the shared resources of the telephone (pressing the selection button of virtual telephone *t* generates an event *e* such that *select(e,t)*. The specification also classifies input events by defining the predicates *open-t(e)* and *close-t(e)*. These predicates have interesting definitions. An *offhook* event is an *open* for the currently selected virtual telephone. An *onhook* event is a *close* for the currently selected virtual telephone. A *select* event has no additional classification if the button pressed was that of the currently selected virtual telephone, or if the telephone is onhook. Otherwise, the *select* event is also an *open* event for the new virtual telephone and a *close* event for the old one. These rules are conveniently expressed in pure Prolog.

Thus, there are three reasons for decomposing this specification:

◆ Different portions are more conveniently written in different languages,
◆ One portion is new while the other is an old specification reused, and
◆ There are two modules encapsulating different portions of the state (the state of a virtual telephone versus the state of the shared resources of a telephone).

State encapsulation is a justifiably popular style of decomposition. Note how conveniently classification provides communication between state-based modules, especially since events are individuals and can be described and classified just as other types of individual can.

5.4. The Shakespeare concordance

Figure 12 is a Jackson diagram (a graphical form of regular expression with labeled subexpressions [14]) describing the text of a play as a sequence of characters. It might be part of the specification of a system computing a concordance of Shakespeare.

Its signature must include *member(i)* and *precedes(i_1,i_2)* predicates defining the sequence being parsed. Its semantics is described in terms of contiguous subsequences of the parsed sequence, of which there are many, so the signature must also include a predicate *subsequence(s)* true of all contiguous subsequences of the parsed sequence, and a predicate *subsequence-member(i,s)* meaning that sequence member *i* is also a member of subsequence *s*. The same ordering predicate applies to both primary sequence and subsequences!

Like the strings in Section 3.2, these sequences and subsequences consist of individual items related to alphabetic characters by the predicate *contents(i,c)*. Relevant character types are distinguished by the disjoint character predicates *letter(c)*, *separator(c)*, and *end-marker(c)*.

Just as any reasonable translation of a nontrivial DFSA into predicate logic uses state predicates, any reasonable translation of a nontrivial regular expression into predicate logic uses subexpression predicates true of subsequences of the described sequence. The subexpression predicates required to translate Figure 12 are *plays(s)*, *non final-part(s)*, *token(s)*, *nonfinal-subpart(s)*, and *space(s)*. Just as with states of a DFSA, they may be part of the signature of the specification, or they may be absent from the signature. Just as with states of a DFSA, if they are absent from the signature, then the predicates present in the signature must be sufficient to define them. And just as with DFSAs, if the subexpression predicates are not in the signature, then a regular expression can be equivalent to a different regular expression (with different subexpressions) that describes the same regular language.

Figure 13 is a description graph for part of the specification of a Shakespeare concordance. The "Lexical Analysis" partial specification is Figure 12, here being applied to describe the text of *Hamlet*.

"Token Identity" is written in pure Prolog. Its purpose is to define when two tokens are to be considered equal for purposes of the concordance—capitalization is irrelevant.

```
word_equal([], []),
word_equal([P|Q], [PIS]) :-word _equal(Q, S).
word_equal([P|Q], [RIS]) :-case_ pair(P, R), word_ equal(Q, S).
case_pair("a", "A").
case_pair("A", "a").
case_pair("b", "B").
case_palr("B", "b"). . . .
```

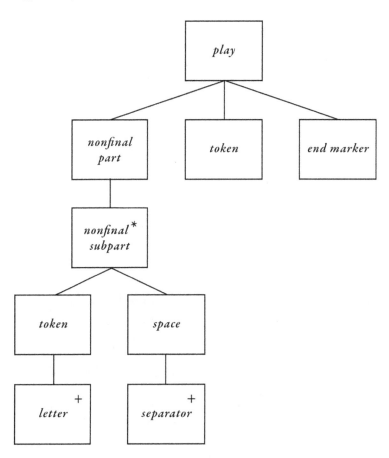

Figure 12. A Jackson diagram describing the text of a play as a character sequence.

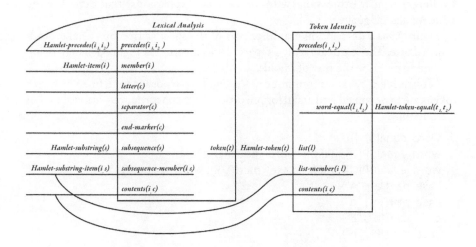

Figure 13. A description graph showing the composition of Figure 12 and a Prolog program.

The Prolog program is concerned with lists of characters. To define its semantics, we need a predicate *list(l)* characterizing the set of lists. In this application of the program, all lists will be tokens of *Hamlet*, so the predicate *list(l)* is renamed as *Hamlet-token(t)*. The latter predicate is also a renaming of the predicate *token(t)* defined by the "Lexical Analysis" specification. The set characterized by *token(t)* is a subset of the set characterized by *Hamlet-substring(s)*, that is, all tokens are substrings of *Hamlet*.

To say that *i* is a member of *l*, that is, *list-member(i,l)*, is the same as to say that *i* is an item of the *Hamlet* substring *s*, that is, *Hamlet-substring-item(i,s)*. The total order on list members ($precedes(i_1,i_2)$ in the signature of "Token Identity") is exactly the same as the total order on sequence members ($precedes(i_1,i_2)$ in the signature of "Lexical Analysis"), which is also the total order on items in *Hamlet* ($Hamlet\text{-}precedes(i_1,i_2)$).

6. Consistency checking across language boundaries

A set of partial specifications is consistent if and only if its composition is satisfiable. Consistency checking is one of the most important kinds of formal reasoning about specifications, and it is closely related to verification in general. With multiparadigm specifications, there is the new challenge of consistency checking across language boundaries.

In theory, the consistency of a multiparadigm specification could be investigated within predicate logic, after translating all partial specifications into that form. In practice, this is obviously infeasible. The logical formulas resulting from the translation are large and incomprehensible, and the complexity of a real specification in that form would be far beyond the capacity of existing automated tools.

We believe that most practical consistency checking must be formulated at the same conceptual level as the specification languages used, and that algorithms for consistency checking will be specialized for particular languages and styles of decomposition.

For an example of a decomposition style, let us consider a multiparadigm specification of a real switching system (with multiplexing telephones as in Section 5.3) [36]. In this specification, one of the principal partial specifications is written in Z. The state of the Z specification includes all configuration information (such as which telephone each virtual telephone is part of), and all information about calls (connections and other relationships among virtual telephones). The Z operations are event classes associated with event predicates, as in Section 3.3.

These event classes are not directly observable in the domain, however, but are defined by other partial specifications as classifications of raw event types such as *offhook*, *onhook*, and *select*. The parsing of the Z operations is actually performed by several layers of partial specifications written using DFSAs, Jackson diagrams, and pure Prolog.

One of the few ways that the Z specification could be inconsistent with these other partial specifications is that one event might be parsed as two distinct Z operations (this occurs in the example of Section 5.3, where under certain conditions a *select* is interpreted as both an *open* and a *close*). This would violate the constraint, written into our version of the Z semantics, that the sets of events identified as Z operations are disjoint. This constraint is necessary because there are no structural limits on which parts of the state a Z operation can modify.

Fortunately, it is easy to show that this potential inconsistency does not occur here. To establish consistency, it is sufficient to prove two properties. No event class (whether identified in the domain, intermediate result of parsing, or Z operation) can be in the signature of more than one partial specification; this is easily determined to be true here from the syntax of the description graph. Also, for the whole specification to be consistent, no partial specification can classify an event of one class as a member of two other classes. For the simple partial specifications we use in parsing, this can be checked algorithmically, and is true of the example discussed here.

The use of a state-based specification whose operations are created by parsing raw inputs is an example of what we are calling a "decomposition style."[9] It prescribes which specification languages (or, in this case, families of languages) are used, which properties are specified in each, and how the specifications interact across paradigm boundaries. This example illustrates several points that we would like to make about consistency checking and the role of the common semantics:

+ A decomposition style may have broad applicability. (This one certainly

---

[9] It might just as accurately be called a "composition style."

does.) Since it is useful in a variety of situations, investments in analyzing it to find sufficient consistency conditions, and in supporting that analysis with automated tools, are practical.

✦ A decomposition style may be amenable to practical consistency checking. (This one certainly is.) In this case, the partial specifications are largely independent, their interdependencies are few, and at least some of the interdependencies can be checked algorithmically.

✦ The proper role of the common semantics is in investigating decomposition styles—in conceiving ways that languages can be used together, in fully understanding the semantics of their composition, and in fully appreciating the interdependencies that arise. For the everyday uses of reading, writing, and checking specifications, the more these underpinnings can be hidden, the better.

✦ Finding good decomposition styles will not be a simple matter, and there are many interesting trade-offs in this area. For example, less redundancy among partial specifications should make checking their consistency easier. At the same time, expanding the signature of a partial specification often makes it self-contained and therefore analyzable with respect to some property, even though more redundancy with other partial specifications is introduced. This effect can be illustrated by deadlock and performance analysis of the same protocol in two different languages [33].

The distinguishing characteristic of our approach to composition is the complete absence of arbitrary restrictions on specification languages and decomposition styles. This means that we have preserved the freedom of specifiers to exploit the potential of multiparadigm specification, and the freedom of researchers to investigate the properties of decomposition styles. It is already common practice for researchers to work on analyzing and verifying specifications within particular application areas or written in particular languages, and they are beginning to work on verifying specifications of popular system architectures [1, 7]. We are not proposing any change to this practice except the use of a small set of complementary languages instead of one language, which should make the overall goal easier to achieve.

7. Related work

Multiparadigm programming and specification have been topics of research interest for some time. In all cases, languages used together must have something in common; much of this work can be compared by noticing where the common ground lies.

By far, the most popular approach to this problem is the design of multiparadigm languages—languages in which several paradigms share a common syntactic and semantic framework (Hailpern's collection [8] provides a good introduction to this work). Wide-spectrum languages, an older idea, are similar in this respect.

Although multiparadigm languages are a practical approach to supporting multiparadigm programming in the near future, they are too inflexible for our goals. Considerations of cost and complexity will limit them to combining particular representatives of a few of the most popular paradigms, while we are interested in experimenting with a wide variety of notations, including those that are highly specialized or similar to each other. Furthermore, merging languages tends to compromise their analyzability, as most algorithmic manipulations of formal languages are quite sensitive to the features of the languages.

Wile's approach to multiparadigm programming [29] is based on a common syntactic framework defined in terms of grammars and transformation. Like multiparadigm languages and unlike our scheme, different paradigms can appear in one partial specification or program. It seems difficult to apply this approach to graphical languages. It also seems difficult to use it for composing multiple descriptions of the same phenomena at the same level of abstraction (as in the factory example), since a certain amount of semantic independence must be maintained.

The Garden project [26] also provides multiparadigm specification by means of a common semantics, but the Garden semantics is operational rather than assertional. In Garden an interpreter for each language is written in a well-integrated object-oriented environment.

"Interoperability" could be described as coarse-grained or loosely coupled multiparadigm programming. Interoperability research tends to assume that programs communicate through procedure calls, and focuses on the problem of sharing data whose types are defined in different languages. At least two interoperability projects [11, 30] provide a partial common semantics for programming languages—covering data types only.

Like our scheme, the transition-axiom method (TAM) [20] provides a common semantics that can serve as a foundation for many different notations. However, the purposes of these two formal systems are very different. TAM is intended to facilitate proofs of the properties of concurrent systems, and all the examples of use of TAM include such proofs. TAM is clearly not intended to facilitate multiparadigm specification. There are no examples of multiparadigm TAM specifications, and TAM's successor, the temporal logic of actions (TLA) [21], has its own specification language.

From our perspective, TAM and TLA should be regarded as a specification paradigm with its own high-level notations, styles, and characteristic proof/analysis techniques. The translation into our semantic domain, for the purpose of composition with other paradigms, should be straightforward.

The ARIES project [17] is closely related to this work in providing a multiparadigm environment based on a common underlying semantics for all paradigms. In the ARIES project, the emphasis is on tool support, however, so only a limited set of specific notations is involved. The common semantics is higher level, richer, and therefore more prescriptive than ours. For example, types, events, temporal operators, components, and roles are all built into the underlying representation. All of these concepts can be represented in our semantics, but since they are not built in it is possible to compose languages based on different versions of them.

Finally, the Viewpoint project [5, 6] is investigating requirements specification in exactly the style we favor: using many languages (some of them graphical) to write overlapping, interdependent partial specifications of different aspects and properties of a specified system. This project has not settled on a formal framework for composition of partial specifications, and could use ours without modification.

8. Limitations and future research

8.1. The semantics of specification languages

At this point, the weakest part of our results is the translation of specification languages into first-order predicate logic. The weaknesses are as follows:

- ◆ We have defined complete, algorithmic translations only for a small number of simple languages.
- ◆ We have no intention of tackling the complete algorithmic translation of large, rich languages such as Z, as it would clearly be beyond our patience.
- ◆ Our semantics for a language does not necessarily have the same properties as the semantics given by the language designers. For example, in the normal Z semantics two instances of the *Project* schema (Figure 1) with the same variable values would be considered equal, just as two data records with the same type and the same field values are equal. In our semantics for the same Z specification, there would be two distinct individuals of type *Project*, which cannot be equal regardless of the values of their attributes.
- ◆ Inevitably, there will be features of specification languages whose semantics have no translation into first-order logic. For example, in Z a non-enumerated set can be declared as finite or infinite.

One issue raised by these weaknesses is that of coverage. Can all specification paradigms be represented in the common semantics? We are fairly confident on this point, having considered a wide variety of notations. In addition, Burstall has shown how to describe a major part of Algol 60 in first-order logic [3]. Many extensions to first-order logic (such as the axiom schema mentioned in Section 3.4) do not compromise this framework, and can be used to cover difficult cases. The only untranslatable language feature we have encountered so far, the example in the fourth point above, does not seem important—computationally there is little difference between an infinite set and a very large finite set.

Another issue raised by these weaknesses is translation complexity. The problem is exacerbated by the fact that we would like to offer various signature options to specifiers, as in Section 3.4, all of which are variations on the basic semantics of a language.

We are optimistic on this point because our experience suggests that multiparadigm specification makes it possible to use much simpler specification languages than are now considered state-of-the-art. There seem to be two reasons for this simplifying trend. One is obvious: if you can compose languages freely, there is no need to extend languages with features that other languages already have. The other reason is that the composition framework subsumes and can replace features, such as composition operators, found in many languages.

For example, the language of Statecharts is rich. The concurrent ("and") decomposition can be replaced by our decomposition into partial specifications. The broadcast communication between concurrent specifications can be replaced by our event classification. The data updates and queries in Statecharts can be replaced by decomposition into a pure DFSA and a data-oriented partial specification. If all of these replaceable features were eliminated, little more than DFSAs with hierarchical states would remain. These remaining features are simply and straightforwardly translatable into the common semantics.

A third issue raised by these weaknesses is the nonstandard semantics we provide for some languages. It is really too early to tell whether this is a significant practical problem. It is important to note that since the standard semantics for many specification languages are incompatible, the only hope of composing such languages lies in providing them with alternative semantics.

However nonstandard, our semantics has the advantages that it facilitates meaningful composition of partial specifications, and that it is based on careful consideration of the relationship between a formal specification and the real world it is describing [16]. For example, with respect to the semantic difference mentioned in the third point above, it certainly makes some sense to assume that two projects are distinct even if their attributes are equal during some interval of time.[10]

In conclusion, there is much work yet to be done in this area. There are difficulties, but little reason to be pessimistic. And it will be impossible to draw firmer conclusions until much more experience with multiparadigm specifications is available.

8.2. Other aspects of specification

There are several other areas in which the work reported here is incomplete.

The major limitation of the semantic domain is that it represents only observable behavior, without any notion of agency, causality, or control. For example, we can duplicate the trace semantics of CSP [12], but cannot represent the stronger semantic domains used by CSP to capture such concepts as hidden internal choices. We are currently extending the semantic domain to include control, but feel that even the limited form discussed in this paper provides useful insight.

The example of Section 5.3 is highly unsatisfactory in one respect: it specifies a single virtual telephone identified as t. What is really needed, of course, is application of the partial specification "Virtual Telephone t" to all virtual

---

[10] This remark is not meant to cast aspersions on any particular specification. A particular specification can only be validated with respect to the semantics in force when it was written.

telephones. We have made some progress on techniques for specification reuse, application of a specification to all members of a set, etc., but they are outside the scope of this paper.

A variety of temporal models are used in specification. We have mentioned atomic versus hierarchical actions, and total versus partial orderings. Time can also be modeled as continuous (there is a nice example by Mahony and Hayes [23]), in which case real instants of time are the interesting individuals, and predicates relate state observations to these instants. Although there is little difficulty in translating any one of these models into the common semantics, it will be very interesting to see how easily partial specifications based on different temporal models can be composed.

Acknowledgements

The presentation of this material has been improved tremendously by the comments of Mark Ardis, Eric Beyler, David Garlan, Tony Hoare, Daniel Jackson, Dick Kemmerer, Jeff Kramer, Peter Gorm Larsen, David MacQueen, David Rosenblum, David Wile, Jeannette Wing, Michal Young, and the anonymous referees.

References

1. Allen, R. and Garlan, D.A formal approach to software architectures. School of Computer Science Tech. Report, Carnegie Mellon University,Pittsburgh, PA, February 1992.

2. Borgida, A., Mylopoulos, J., and Reiter, R. "And nothing else changes": The frame problem in procedure specifications. In *Proceedings of the 15th International Conference on Software Engineering*. IEEE Computer Society, May 1993, 303-314.

3. Burstall, R. M. Formal description of program structure and semantics in first order logic. In *Machine Intelligence 5*, Edinburgh University Press, 1970, 79-98.

4. Cardelli, L. and Wegner, P. On understanding types, data abstraction, and polymorphism. *ACM Computing Surveys 17*, 4 (Dec. 1985), 471-522.

5. Finkelstein, A., Goedicke, M., Kramer, J., and Niskier, C. Viewpoint-oriented software development: Methods and viewpoints in requirements engineering. In *Proceedings of the 2nd METEOR Workshop on Methods for Formal Specification*. Springer-Verlag, 1989.

6. Finkelstein, A., Kramer, J., Nuseibeh, B., Finkelstein, L., and Goedicke, M. Viewpoints: A framework for integrating multiple perspectives insystem development. *Intl. Journal Softw. Engr. Knowledge Engr. 2*, 1 (1992), 31-57.

7. Garlan, D. and Notkin, D. Formalizing design spaces: Implicit invocation mechanisms. In *VDM `91: Formal Software Development Methods (Proceedings of the 4th Intl. Symposium of VDM Europe)*. Springer-Verlag, 1991, 31-44.

8. Hailpern, B. Multiparadigm languages and environments (Guest editor's introduction to a special issue). *IEEE Software 3*, 1 (Jan. 1986), 6-9.

9. Harel, D. Statecharts: A visual formalism for complex systems. *Science of Computer Programming 8* (1987), 231-274.

10. Harel, D., Lachover, H., Naamad, A., Pnueli, A., Politi, M., Sherman, R., Shtull-Trauring, A., and Trakhtenbrot, M. Statemate: A working environment for the development of complex reactive systems. *IEEE Trans. Software Engr. 16*, 4 (Apr. 1990), 403-414.

11. Hayes, R., and Schlichting, R. D. Facilitating mixed language programming in distributed systems. *IEEE Trans. Software Engr. 13*, 12 (Dec. 1987), 1254-1264.

12. Hoare, C. A. R. *Communicating Sequential Processes.* Prentice-Hall International, 1985

13. International Organization for Standardization. Information processing systems—Open systems interconnection—LOTOS—A formal description technique based on the temporal ordering of observational behaviour. ISO 8807, 1989.

14. Jackson, M. A. *Principles of Program Design.* Academic Press, 1975.

15. Jackson, M. Some complexities in computer-based systems and their implications for system development. In *Proceedings of CompEuro 1990.* IEEE Computer Society, 344-351.

16. Jackson, M. and Zave, P. Domain descriptions. In *Proceedings of the IEEE International Symposium on Requirements Engineering, 1992.* IEEE Computer Society, 56-64.

17. Johnson, W. L., Feather, M. S., and Harris, D. R. Representation and presentation of requirements knowledge. *IEEE Trans. Software Engr. 18*, 10 (Oct. 1992), 853-869.

18. Jones, C. B. Systematic Software Development Using VDM. Prentice-Hall International, 1986.

19. Kleene, S. C. *Mathematical Logic.* Wiley, 1967.

20. Lamport, L. A simple approach to specifying concurrent systems. *Communications ACM 32*, 1 (Jan. 1989), 32-45.

21. Lamport, L. A temporal logic of actions. DEC Systems Research Center 57, Palo Alto, CA, Apr. 1990.

22. London, P. E., and Feather, M. S. Implementing specification freedoms. *Science of Computer Programming 2* (1982), 91-131.

23. Mahony, B. P. and Hayes, I. J. A case-study in timed refinement: A mine pump. *IEEE Trans. Software Engr. 18*, 9 (Sep. 1992), 817-826.

24. Plat, N., van Katwlik, J., and Pronk, K. A case for structured analysis/formal design. In *VDM '91: Formal Software Development Methods (Proceedings of the 4th Intl. Symposium of VDM Europe).* Springer-Verlag, 1991, 81-105.

25. Pnueli, A. The temporal logic of programs. In *Proceedings of the 18th Annual Symp. on Foundations of Computer Science.* IEEE Computer Society, 1977, 46-57.

26. Reiss, S. P. Working in the Garden environment for conceptual programming. *IEEE Software 4*, 6 (Nov. 1987), 16-27.

27. Spivey, J. M. *The Z Notation: A Reference Manual.* Prentice-Hall International, 1989.

28. Ward, P. T. The transformation schema: An extension of the data flow diagram to represent control and timing. *IEEE Trans. Software Engr. 12*, 2 (Feb. 1986), 198-210.

29. Wile, D. S. Integrating syntaxes and their associated semantics. USC/Information Sciences Inst. Tech. Rep RR-92-297, Marina del Rey, CA, 1992.

30. Wileden, J. C., Wolf, A. L., Rosenblatt, W. R., and Tarr, P. L. Specification-level interoperability. *Communications ACM 34*, 5 (May 1991), 72-87.

31. Wing, J. M. A specifier's introduction to formal methods. *IEEE Computer 23*, 9 (Sep. 1990), 8-24.

32. Wordsworth, J. B. *Software Development with Z: A Practical Approach to Formal Methods in Sofware Engineering.* Addison-Wesley, 1992.

33. Zave, P. A compositional approach to multiparadigm programming. *IEEE Software* 6, 5 (Sep. 1989), 15-25.

34. Zave, P. and Jackson, M. Composition of descriptions: A progress report. In *Formal Methods in Systems Engineering, 1993*, Springer-Verlag, 41-50.

35. Zave, P. and Jackson, M. Techniques for partial specification and specification of switching systems. In *VDM '91: Formal Software Development Methods (Proceedings of the 4th Intl. Symposium of VDM Europe)*. Springer-Verlag, 1991, 511-525.

36. Zave, P. and Jackson, M. Where do operations come from? A multiparadigm specification technique. *IEEE Trans. Software Engr.* 22, 7 (July 1996), 508-528.

Chapter 11

Distributed Feature Composition: A Virtual Architecture for Telecommunication Services

Michael Jackson and Pamela Zave

Abstract: Distributed Feature Composition (DFC) is a new technology for feature specification and composition, based on a virtual architecture offering benefits analogous to those of a pipe-and-filter architecture. In the DFC architecture, customer calls are processed by dynamically assembled configurations of filter-like components: each component implements an applicable feature, and communicates with its neighbors by featureless internal calls that are connected by the underlying architectural substrate.

1. Introduction

The feature-interaction problem [6, 14, 24] arises from   the incremental, feature by feature, extension of telecommunications system functionality. As new features—especially call-processing features—are added, it becomes increasingly difficult to manage the behavioral complexity of the features and their interactions. Redesign of old features to fit smoothly with the new features is scarcely ever a practical option. Eventually the resulting complexity damages the quality and productivity of all phases of software development. The proceedings of three recent workshops provide a representative sample of research on the feature-interaction problem [3, 7, 9].

This paper introduces a technology, *distributed feature composition* (DFC), for managing the feature-interaction problem. The heart of DFC is a virtual architecture for telecommunications systems in which a feature corresponds to a component type (a few features correspond to two component types—see Section 4.7); each customer call is handled by building a configuration of instances of these components, according to the features to be applied to that particular call. The feature component instances communicate by featureless internal calls that are connected by the underlying architectural substrate. A new feature is specified by describing its corresponding component type (or, occasionally, two component types) and the rules for including the component instances into configurations.

The primary characteristic of the DFC architecture is that each feature is implemented by one or two component types, and each external call is processed by a dynamically assembled configuration of components and featureless, two-port internal calls. The resulting configuration is analogous to an assembly of pipes and filters, and has the typical advantages of the pipe-and-filter architectural style: (1) feature components are independent, they do not share state, (2) they do not or depend on which other feature components are at the other ends of their calls (pipes), (3) they behave compositionally, and (4) the set of them is easily enhanced [12]. These characteristics contribute greatly to the power of the architecture to manage feature interactions. DFC is a virtual architecture, and offers many possibilities of convenient mapping to typical physical architectures.

Section 2 gives a brief overview of the DFC architecture, to convey an intuitive understanding of how it works and how it addresses the feature interaction problem. Section 3 gives a more detailed and formal description, and Section 4 discusses the specification of various features in a DFC setting. In Section 5 we present a summary of the conclusions we draw from our development and study of DFC, and of the contribution that we believe DFC can make to addressing the feature interaction problem.

We have made various simplifying assumptions to avoid complicating our presentation of DFC. We believe that these simplifications are immaterial to the applicability of DFC to a fully realistic context. They are briefly described in Section 5.

2. Overview of the DFC architecture

The fundamental idea is to treat features as independent components—which we call *boxes*—through which calls are routed from caller to callee. The routing of a call reflects the features to be applied to it.

We regard the system as having a *virtual switch* that serves its customers through *line interface (LI) boxes* at its periphery; features are provided by *feature boxes (FBs)*, appropriately interposed on the path between a calling and a callee customer. In general, boxes are not shared among calls: two concurrent collect calls will require two collect feature boxes—that is, two distinct instances of the same *feature box type*. All communication between boxes takes the form of *featureless internal calls* connected by the virtual switch at the command of its embedded *router*. The router and switch, together with the necessary voice and signaling paths, form the substrate of the architecture, routing and connecting these internal calls from box to box.

2.1. Usages

We use the simple term *call* chiefly to denote these internal featureless calls. Episodes of customer service, usually referred to as calls, will here be referred to as *customer calls* or *usages*. We will chiefly use the terms *caller* and *callee* to denote the boxes placing and accepting internal calls. Where there is no ambiguity we will sometimes use *call*, *caller*, and *callee* for a customer call and its originating and terminating customers.

Figure 1 shows a snapshot of one usage in the DFC architecture in a state in which two customers are talking.

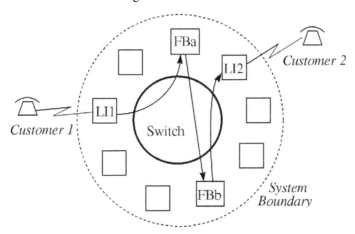

Figure 1. A usage in the DFC architecture.

The customers' telephones are connected to the system at the line interface boxes LI1 and LI2. Two features have been applied to this usage, provided by the feature boxes Fba and FBb. The arrows in the diagram show the routing of calls and the directions in which they were placed. Customer 1's original request was routed as a call from LI1 to FBa; FBa then placed a call that was routed to FBb; FBb placed a call that was finally routed to Customer 2's line interface box LI2. The switch is, therefore, carrying three internal calls in providing the connection between Customer 1 and Customer 2.

Each call is carried by a two-way voice channel and two signaling channels, one in each direction. To complete the connection between LI1 and LI2, the feature boxes FBa and FBb join the voice and signaling channels of the calls in which they are participating. In general, a feature box has full control over the calls to which it is connected. It can coordinate their voice channels in any way desired, freely joining and separating their voice signals, playing announcements and tones, recording speech, and monitoring the in-band signals. Similarly, it can control the out-of-band signaling of its calls by suppressing or passing on messages and by introducing new messages of its own. The order of feature boxes in a usage is, therefore, significant. The behavior of each feature box is independent of the behavior of other boxes; but the effect of its behavior will depend on its position in the usage. Feature box precedence is an important aspect of feature specification in DFC.

A feature box is configured into each usage in which it may possibly be needed.

For example, FBa may be an Originating Call Screening (OCS) box, and FBb a Call Forwarding on Busy (CFB) box, configured into the usage by the DFC router simply because Customer 1 subscribes to OCS and Customer 2 to CFB. If the number dialed by Customer 1 is not in the provisioned screening list, the OCS feature box FBa will behave transparently, the usage proceeding as if the box were not present; similarly, if Customer 2 is not busy, the CFB box FBb will behave transparently. This potentially transparent behavior of feature boxes is an important factor contributing to their independence and to the freedom with which they can be combined and inserted into usages.

When a feature box is actively providing its feature service by nontransparent behavior, it does so without relying on other boxes. For example, if the OCS box finds the number dialed by Customer 1 in the provisioned screening list, the OCS box will not place an outgoing call; instead it may send an *unobtainable* message back to the customer. If the CFB box detects that Customer 2 is busy, it tears down its outgoing call and places another call to the directory number (DN) specified by Customer 2 for such forwarded calls.

2.2. Call routing

The routing of calls from box to box within the system is the responsibility of the router embedded in the DFC switch. The first internal call in a usage is typically placed by the originating customer's line interface box: the box sends the switch a *setup* message containing an empty *routing list* and four fields: (1) a *source* field (whose value is the DN of the originating customer), (2) a *dialed-string* field, (3) an empty *target* field, and (4) a *command* field with an associated *modifier* (which in this case would specify that a new routing list was to be constructed). The router may assign a value to the target field from the dialed string; it then uses the four field values, together with information about customer subscriptions and features, to construct a routing list for the usage. This list is then inserted into the setup message for dispatch to the switch and onward transmission.

To dispatch a call, the router truncates the routing list by removing its head entry, and requests the switch to connect the call to the box specified in that entry. A box that receives a call receives the truncated setup message; in many cases, once that call has been set up, the box will then place a second call whose setup message is a copy of the first. When the switch receives this second setup message, the router again truncates the routing list, and the switch connects the second call to the appropriate box. In this way a chain of calls is formed until eventually the routing list is empty and the last call is routed to the line interface box of its final target.

2.3. Configuring a usage by zones

Features are selected by the router in three *zones:* "Source," "Dialed," and "Target." Intuitively, features in the Source zone are applied to all calls made by the Source caller: for example, the Speed Calling (SC) feature is applied to every call made by its subscriber. Similarly, features in the Target zone are applied to all calls directed to the Target callee: for example, the Call Forwarding on Busy (CFB) feature is applied because the callee subscribes to it. Features in the Dialed zone are applied according to the string dialed by the caller: for example, the prefix '0' causes the Collect feature to be applied. Roughly, the three zones correspond to three obvious subchains in the construction of a usage, as shown in Figure 2.

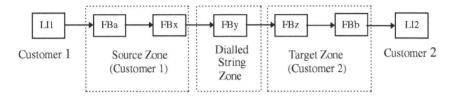

Figure 2. Feature zones in a usage.

The applicable feature boxes are specified in the routing list field of the setup message in zone order. The routing list specifies first the appropriate source zone feature boxes, such as SC and OCS; then the appropriate dialed zone feature boxes, such as Collect; and finally the appropriate target zone callee feature boxes, such as TCS and CFB. Within each of the three zones, the feature boxes appear in the precedence order given by their feature specifications.

Although this arrangement of features in zones may at first sight seem restrictive, we know of no case where it precludes a desirable behavior or obscures or complicates the desired application of features to a usage.

2.4. Routing data

The DFC router uses three sets of global data: *subscription, specification,* and *configuration data.* All of this data takes the form of relations. Subscription and specification data (with one exception) is partitioned by feature, each relational tuple being associated with just one feature.

Subscription data records customer choices to subscribe to optional features, such as OCS and CFB; all subscription data is statically provisioned. Some features are compulsory (for example, the Emergency Break-In feature (EBI) which allows emergency service officials to break into an existing conversation). All customers are considered to subscribe—albeit gratis—to such features, and these subscriptions too are recorded in subscription data.

The *feature specification data* records the general external specifications of individual features: that is, their relationships to usages and to each other but not the behaviors of the feature boxes that provide them. These general specifications describe the applicability of each feature, identify the box types that provide it, and define a precedence order (not partitioned by feature) in which feature boxes are configured into a usage. Feature specification data is written by system engineers when features are introduced or modified.

The *configuration data* records the set of boxes that exist in the system, the

DN of each line interface box, and the internal addresses used for interface and feature boxes. This data provides a part of the underlying mechanism for routing, but does not affect the selection of feature box types to be configured into usages.

2.5. Non-routing data

Another global set of data, not used in routing, is the *feature operational data*. Most of this data is provided by customers and accessed only for reading by the features that use it: for example, a forwarding number for CFB is provided by the customer and read by a CFB feature box. Some of this data may be written and read by different boxes cooperating to provide one feature: for example, the Automatic CallBack (ACB) feature is provided by one box that stores the caller ID for an unanswered call, and another box that later places a return call at the callee's request.

The local state of a feature box may contain data in any necessary form. For example, a Collect feature may allow the caller to record a spoken identification to be played to the callee: the feature box can hold this recorded message as internal data for subsequent playback to the callee.

2.6. More complex routing

In general, the behavior of the router will not be so simple as the sketch above. A detailed description of the routing scheme is given in Section 3; here we mention only some obvious deviations from the simple sketch.

+ Often the target DN cannot be determined from the original dialed string. If the customer is using the Speed Calling (SC) feature, the target DN must be obtained by the SC feature box from the SC feature operational data; if the customer is using the Sequence Credit Card Calling (SCCC) feature, the target DN for follow-on calls must be collected by the SCCC feature box from digits dialed by the customer during the usage.

+ Some features may use the command field of the setup message to change the routing. The Call Forwarding Always (CFA) feature changes the target before the original callee is reached; this change will require reselection of the callee features and hence reconstruction of the unused part of the routing list. A usage resulting from this kind of feature behavior can be regarded as composed of *segments*, each segment having its own "Source," "Dialed," and "Target" zones.

+ Not all usages can be depicted by linear graphs. A usage may *fork* as a result of a customer service request during the usage. A customer who subscribes to Three-Way Calling (3WC) can flash and dial digits to request connection to a third party while maintaining an existing connection to another customer. *Joins*, too, can occur. For example, the Call Waiting (CW) feature joins a new caller customer into an existing connection.

2.7. Routing: Independence of features

Although routing can be quite complex, as indicated above, it does not encroach on the functions of the feature boxes. In particular, it does not access the feature operational data. For example, when the subscription data shows that a callee customer subscribes to CFA, the router merely inserts a CFA box into the usage; it does not examine the operational data and reroute the call to the provisioned CFA destination. Similarly, for a customer subscribing to OCS the router inserts an OCS box into the usage: it does not examine the dialed string and abort the call if the called number is in the OCS customer's screening list.

2.8. Boxes and ports

Calls are connected between *named ports* of boxes. Each internal call that is active at a line interface or feature box requires a dedicated port of that box. In Figure 1, each of FBa and FBb has two active calls; each, therefore, must have at least two ports. A Three-Way Calling (3WC) box must have three ports. A feature box providing Large-Scale Conferencing (LSC) for up to 10 participants must have at least 11 ports: one for each participant and one for the operator.

Each port of a box is statically typed as a *callee, caller,* or *dual* port. A callee port can only receive calls; a caller port can only place calls; a dual port can play either role.

A line interface box communicates through the DFC substrate with other boxes, making and receiving calls on behalf of the customer it serves. It can participate in only one internal call at any time, any multiplexing being handled by boxes that provide call multiplexing features such as CW or 3WC. A line interface box, therefore, has exactly one port, of the dual type. Obviously the interface box must also interact with its own customer line, but these interactions are not constrained by the DFC architecture; rather, they obey the native protocol of the external line or trunk. Since these interactions are not internal calls they do not require a DFC port.

2.9. Connecting internal calls

Calls are carried by the DFC substrate, which consists of the switch, its embedded router, and numerous voice and signaling channels. Each active port in the system is communicating with one port of another box by a two-way voice channel, and with the switch by two reliable FIFO buffered signaling channels *in* and *out*. In addition, each box that has a callee or dual port (and can, therefore, receive calls) is connected to the switch by two reliable FIFO buffered signaling channels *in* and *out*, that are associated with the box itself and not with any port.

Each call is initiated by a dual or caller port of a box sending a *setup* message to the router. The router determines the callee box for the call, and the switch forwards the message to that box. The box might have no idle callee or dual port at which to receive the call, in which case it responds with a *quickbusy* message and the call attempt has failed.

Alternatively, the box might accept the call. In this case, the box reserves an idle callee or dual port for the call, and returns a *reserve* message that names the chosen port in a data field. Upon receiving the *reserve* message, the switch informs the caller and callee ports, and provides a two-way voice channel between them. If every feature box in a linear usage connects its incoming and outgoing voice channels, an unbroken voice path is formed between the originating and terminating customer lines.

Either port can end a call by sending a *teardown* message. The switch will respond by disconnecting the voice channel. The teardown phase of the call protocol ensures that both ports are disconnected from the switch and their signaling channels are flushed.

When a call has been set up between two ports, either participating port can send *status* messages, and the switch will forward them to the other port. For example, the callee port can send a status message indicating that the target destination is busy, or is alerting. The set of possible status messages can be easily extended to meet the needs of new features.

2.10. In-band and out-of-band signaling

Messages sent by a port on its outgoing signaling channel (out-of-band signals) are typically passed from box to box along the chain formed by their configuration into a usage. As a result, the precedence ordering of features and appropriate design of feature boxes can be used to resolve any conflict among boxes awaiting the same signal.

Consider, for example, a customer who subscribes to both CFB and Callee Messaging-on-Busy (CMB). Evidently, there is a conflict between the two feature boxes: if an incoming call, in which both CFB and CMB feature boxes are configured, arrives while the customer is busy, CFB must redirect the call to another DN, while CMB must invite the caller to leave a voicemail message. In the DFC architecture, busy status is signaled out-of-band. Once the usage has been completed as far as the customer's line interface box, a busy signal is sent from that LI box. Whichever of the two feature boxes CFB and CMB is closer to the LI box will receive the busy signal, act on it, and not propagate it further back in the chain; the more distant feature box will not receive the signal at all. Feature precedence determines how the conflict will be resolved.

Conflicts in respect of signals sent on a voice channel (in-band signals) are not so easily resolved. If the LI box were to signal its busy status by emitting an in-band tone, both feature boxes could detect the tone simultaneously. The conflict might then be resolved by the outcome of a race, with all its attendant difficulties. For the most part, then, we prefer to rely on out-of-band status messages. They have the further advantage that they can carry additional information in the message data fields.

One might jump to the conclusion that all voice analysis and generation functions should be performed at line interfaces, so that feature boxes would handle only out-of-band signals. But this is not feasible, because a system's full repertoire of tones, announcements, and recognition vocabularies cannot be anticipated. Our scheme is, therefore, a compromise in which line interface boxes translate the most common in-band signals to and from out-of-band signals. Where feature box processing of in-band signals is inescapable, it is sometimes possible to avoid race conditions, using a technique described in Section 4.9.

2.11. Line interface box behavior

The regime of out-of-band status messages has significant consequences for the specification of line interface boxes. Each LI box translates between its own particular line protocol and the protocol of the virtual network: this translation must include translation from status messages to tones familiar to the human customer. For example, on receiving a busy status message, a calling customer's LI box must place a busy tone on the outgoing voice channel of its line so that the customer can hear it.

The DFC call protocol accommodates, but does not define, a wide range of status message patterns that a LI box must translate into tones. For example, a user of SCCC can make a sequence of customer calls within one usage, dialing '#' instead of going onhook at the end of each call except the last. The subscriber's LI box must produce the appropriate tones—alerting, busy, unobtainable—during each call, mute the alerting tone when a callee answers, and produce dialtone when '#' is dialed. These tones must be produced by the LI box in response to messages sent or passed back by the SCCC feature box. Because a LI box must accommodate sequences of calls, as in the SCCC feature, it never interprets a tone message as a disconnect.

A LI box that receives a setup message when its one port is already active returns a *quickbusy* message. The box whose call attempt has failed will typically pass back a *busy* status message that eventually reaches the calling customer's LI box, where it will be translated into a busy tone on the line. A LI box that sends a setup message and receives an immediate *quickbusy* message in response must translate this *quickbusy* message into a busy tone on the line. (In practice, this can scarcely occur, because a usage with no feature box is unlikely: a setup message sent by a LI box will therefore usually be routed first to a feature box, which will be able to accept the call.)

2.12. Feature box availability

Like conference bridges in a conventional physical architecture, feature boxes in the DFC architecture are regarded as permanent, named individuals. At any particular time, a feature box may be *occupied* or *available*. When a feature is to be inserted into a usage, an available box of the right type is found, and the switch sends the setup message to that box. It is assumed that the population of feature boxes is effectively unlimited: an available box of the right type can always be found when one is needed.

A box may be occupied although it is not currently participating in any call. For example, a box providing a messaging feature may try to deliver a caller's recorded voice message at regular intervals until the intended recipient customer answers the phone. Between attempts, the box is not available: it is occupied waiting for the current interval to elapse before it makes a further attempt.

2.13. Box classes: Free, bound, and addressable

For many features—such as OCS—any available box of the appropriate type may be selected when one is required. Such boxes are called free boxes, because they may be freely selected. Some features—such as Call Waiting (CW)—do not offer this freedom. To provide CW service, a CW box must be inserted into each usage of the subscribing customer; any incoming customer call that arrives while the usage is in progress must then be directed to that particular CW box. Only in this way can the new call be joined into the existing usage.

To handle this kind of requirement conveniently, we classify the CW box as a bound box: it is bound to the line interface of the subscribing customer. Whenever that customer makes or receives a call, the particular CW box bound to that customer will appear in the usage. Essentially, the class of bound boxes is the class of boxes at which a join can occur.

In addition to free and bound boxes there is a third class. Some features are directly addressable by customers through the standard dialing plan. For example, in a Large-Scale Conferencing (LSC) feature, intended participants in a conference may be informed of a special DN to call; the feature box at that DN connects them into the conference after checking a password. Boxes implementing such features are addressable boxes.

3. Description of the DFC architecture

Later, in Section 4, we consider a number of features and show how they may be specified and combined in the DFC environment. First, in this section, we give a more detailed and formal description of the DFC architecture. We begin by describing the configuration: that is, the boxes, their types and classes, and how they are addressed. Then we describe the subscription, specification, and operational data. Then we describe the features, their relationship to the configuration and to the data, and the router's behavior. Next we describe the protocol of internal calls observed by boxes and ports. Finally, we describe the possible behaviors of feature boxes in managing their calls, including the manipulation of voice and signal paths.

In each part, we use a notation convenient for the purpose in hand, connecting our formal descriptions by informal narrative. We write relations indicating their types, in the Z style [23], by distinctive arrow symbols (such as ⇥ for a total surjection). We also use relations as sets of pairs, and vice versa, wherever it is convenient to do so. Appendix A lists the symbols for relations.

3.1. Configuration data: Boxes, addresses, and DNs

The basic sets of the configuration are these disjoint sets:

[LIBox, FFBox, BFBox, AFBox, FFBType, BFBType, AFBType, Port, DN].

They are, respectively: the set of LI boxes; the sets of free, bound and addressable feature boxes; the sets of free, bound and addressable feature box types; the set of ports; and the set of well-formed directory numbers.

Two further sets, the set of all feature boxes and the set of all boxes, are defined from these basic sets:

$FBox \triangleq FFBox \cup BFBox \cup AFBox;\ Box \triangleq FBox \cup LIBox.$

Each feature box has an appropriate (free, bound, or addressable) type, and each type has boxes:

$freeType : FFBox \twoheadrightarrow FFBType;$

$boundType : BFBox \twoheadrightarrow BFBType;$

$addrType : AFBox \twoheadrightarrow AFBType.$

Each port belongs to one box and each box has at least one port:

$portBox : Port \twoheadrightarrow Box.$

Each LI box and each addressable feature box has a unique DN:

$LIbDnum : LIBox \rightarrowtail DN;$

$AFbDnum : AFBox \rightarrowtail DN;$

ran $LIbDnum \cap$ **ran** $AFbDnum = \varnothing.$

Each bound feature box is bound to exactly one LI box:

$boundLI : BFBox \rightarrow LIBox.$

3.2. Specification data: Features, box types, and zones

The additional basic sets for specification data are [*Featr, Zone*]. They are the set of features and the set of zones {*"Source," "Dialed," "Target"*}; they are disjoint from each other and from all other basic sets.

The set *FBoxType* of all feature box types of any class is defined; each box type provides all or part of exactly one feature, and each feature is provided by at least one box type (a feature may be provided by cooperating boxes of different types):

$FBoxType \triangleq FFBType \cup BFBType \cup AFBType;$

$provFeatr : FBoxType \twoheadrightarrow Featr.$

A feature may be associated with more than one zone: For example, 3WC and CW are used in both the outgoing and the incoming calls of their subscribers, and therefore belong to both source and target zones. The association of features with zones is, therefore, many-to-many. However, this association plays no direct part in the formal description of a DFC system: instead, the important association is of feature box types with zones.

For each box type we specify whether it is a source, target or dialed feature box, or more than one of these. (An example of a feature box type associated with more than one zone is a CW feature box: the same type is used for CW on an outgoing customer call as on an incoming call.) Each box type is associated with at least one zone:

    boxZone : FBoxType ↔ Zone;

    ∀*t : FBoxType · t ∈* **dom** *boxZone.*

No bound box type is in the dialed zone:

    BFBType ◁ boxZone ▷ {"Dialed"} = ∅,

but every addressable box type is only in the dialed zone:

    boxZone (|AFBType|) = {"Dialed"}.

3.3. Further specification data: Box applicability and precedence

An element *(t, "Source")* or *(t, "Target")* of the relation *boxZone* given in Section 3.2 indicates that a feature box of type *t* may be applied to a customer call in the source or target zone. Whether it will be so applied to calls made by particular customers is determined by subscription data, as described in Section 3.4. For dialed features, the determination depends on a relation in specification data. This is a relation between sets of strings—for example, all strings beginning with "0"—and feature box types:

    dialSetFBType : ℙ *String ⇸ FBoxType;*

    ran *dialSetFBType = boxZone~ (|{"Dialed"}|).*

The basic set *String* is the set of strings over the characters (0..9, '*', '#') that can be dialed. The relation *dialSetFBType* is given, tuple by tuple, in the specification of the features provided by the boxes (the sets of strings being specified by predicates over strings). One string may cause selection of more than one feature box type. For purposes of explanation it is more convenient to relate strings to feature box types directly:

    stringFBType : String ↔ FBoxType;

    ∀ *s : String, t : FBoxType • (s, t) ∈ stringFBType*

        ⇔ ∃ *ss • s ∈ ss ∧ (ss, t) ∈ dialSetFBType.*

Selection of a box to provide a source or target feature is governed by *boxZone*, by the source or target field in the setup message, and by the relation *subscrip* in the subscription data (see Section 3.4). Selection of a box to provide a dialed feature is governed by *boxZone*, by the dialed-string field in the setup message, and by the relation *stringFBType* in the specification data.

Ordering of feature boxes in a routing list is constrained by a specified precedence relation:

    boxPrec : boxZone ↔ boxZone.

The pair *((fb1, z1), (fb2, z2))* is an element of *boxPrec* iff in any routing list containing both a box of type *fb1* applied as a *z1* feature and a box of type *fb2* applied as a *z2* feature the *fb1* box must precede the *fb2* box. *boxPrec* must be a partial order.

The specified precedence applies to *routing lists* as constructed by the router and held in *setup* messages, not to *usages*. Because usages can be forked and joined, and a new routing list can be constructed for a partially complete usage, the order of boxes in usages is less constrained than their order in routing lists. The informal concept of a *segment* corresponds to the part of a usage in which the feature box order must conform to the precedence specified by *boxPrec*.

Since feature boxes are placed in the routing list in the order source, dialed, target, the partial order *boxPrec* must satisfy:

$\forall$ fb1, fb2 : FBoxType, z1, z2 : Zone •

   ((fb1, z1), (fb2, z2)) $\in$ boxPrec $\Rightarrow$

    (z1 = "Source") $\vee$ (z2 = "Target") $\vee$ (z1 = z2).

3.4. Subscription data: Features, feature boxes, and DNs

A subscriber subscribes to features, ensuring that the appropriate feature boxes are applied to the subscriber's calls in the appropriate zones. However, the effect of a subscription may be different for different subscribers. For example, the Emergency Break-In (EBI) feature is used by privileged emergency subscribers to place calls that will reach even a busy telephone; normal customers are compelled to receive such break-in calls when they are engaged in an outgoing or incoming call of their own. The emergency service subscribes to EBI in the source zone; the normal customer subscribes, compulsorily, in both source and target zones. EBI is provided by two feature box types: a source zone free box for the emergency service, allowing break-in calls ro be made; and a source and target zone bound box for the normal customer, ensuring that incoming break-in calls are always received. Notice that the normal customer's bound EBI box type is in both source and target zones (as is the Call Waiting (CW) box discussed in Sections 4.4 and 4.6).

In this paper, we ignore the process of setting up subscriptions to features, and regard subscriptions simply as subscriptions to feature boxes in zones. The basic sets *[FBoxType, Zone]* were introduced above. The subscription data is the relation *subscrip*, between DNs and *(FBoxType, Zone)* pairs. Since the relation *boxZone* is precisely the set of such pairs (t, z) in which box type t is associated with zone z, we have:

subscrip : DN $\leftrightarrow$ (boxZone $\triangleright$ {"Source," "Target"}).

The relation *subscrip* governs only features in the source and target zones; applicability of features in the dialed zone is governed by the relation *dialSetFBType* described in Section 3.3.

The configuration data relation *boundLI* given in Section 3.1 is constrained by *subscrip*. If the customer at DN d subscribes to a bound feature box type t, then there must be exactly one box of type t bound to the LI at d. The constraint is:

$\forall$ d : DN, i : LIBox, t : BFBType •

   (i LIbDnum d $\wedge$ t $\in$ **dom** subscrip (|d|) $\Rightarrow$

    ($\exists$! b • b boundLI i $\wedge$ b boundType t).

3.5. Operational data: Accessibility

Feature operational data consists of a set of relations [OpernRel]. Each of these relations supports exactly one feature; some features may be supported by more than one relation, some by none:

suppFeatr : OpernRel → Featr.

Each relation is accessible only to feature boxes of the types that provide the feature supported by the data. This constraint contributes importantly to feature independence:

boxRel : FBoxType ↔ OpernRel; boxRel = provFeatr ; suppFeatr~.

3.6. Routing: The setup message

A setup message is sent from a calling box to the switch. The router embedded in the switch modifies the message contents before the switch transmits the message to a callee box; typically, that box will create another setup message by copying all or part of the first message, and send it in turn to the switch.

The full structure of the setup message is:

setup = (source, target : DN ∪ nul;

       dialed : String ∪ nul;

       route : (seq boxZone) ∪ nul;

       command : {"new," "update," "continue," "direct"};

       modifier : ℙ Zone ∪ FBoxType ∪ nul).

The *command* field and its *modifier* are set by the sending box to control the action of the router.

In a setup message sent by an LI box: *source* = DN of the LI; *target* = *nul*; *dialed* = the dialed string; *route* = *nul*; *command* = "new" and *modifier* = *nul*.

In setup messages sent by feature boxes many combinations of values are possible; they must conform to the constraints described in the next section. Further, a box may not access the *route* component except to set it to *nul* or to the value in an incoming setup message previously received by the box.

3.7. Routing: Setting the target and routing list

Initially the router examines the values of *target* and *dialed*. If *dialed* ≠ *nul* and *target* = *nul*, the router sets a value in *target* derived from *dialed* according to the dialing plan; this value may be *nul* when the dialed string does not indicate a target DN (for example, if the dialed string is a speed-calling code, or an 800-number).

Then, after acting on the value of *command*, as described in this section, the router determines the destination box to which the message should be sent by the switch, as described in Section 3.8.

♦ If *command* = "new," the router computes a new routing list, as explained below, for all three zones, and inserts it into *route*.

◆ If *command* = "update," then *modifier* = a subset of {"Source," "Target," "Dialed"} and *route* ≠ *nul*. The router computes a new routing list for each zone specified in *modifier*, and uses it to replace the existing value of route for each of those zones.

◆ If *command* = "continue," then *route* ≠ *nul* (although it may be empty); *modifier* is ignored. The router leaves the existing value of *route* unchanged.

◆ If *command* = "direct," then *modifier* = *bt*, where *bt* is a box type providing the same feature *f* as the box that sent the setup message, and *target* = *dn*, where *dn* is a subscriber to *bt* in zone "Target." The router replaces the existing value of *route* with the singleton sequence <(*bt*, "Target")>.

Each zone of the routing list is computed as follows:

◆ For zone "Source" or "Target" the list is empty if *source* or *target*, respectively, is *nul*. Otherwise the list contains those box types of the zone that are subscribed to by the *source* or *target*, respectively. For "Source" and "Target" these are the following subsets of *boxZone*:

$$(subscrip\ (|\ source\ |)) \rhd \{\text{"Source"}\}$$

and

$$(subscrip\ (|\ target\ |)) \rhd \{\text{"Target"}\}$$

◆ For zone "Dialed" the list is empty if *dialed* = *nul*. Otherwise the list contains the following subset of *boxZone*:

$$(stringFBType\ (|\ dialed\ |)) \lhd boxZone$$

The set *stringFBType* (| *dialed* |) is the set of dialed zone feature boxes to be applied to the string *dialed*.

The router ensures that the complete routing list value set in *route* satisfies the precedence relation *boxPrec*.

3.8. Routing: The destination box

After resetting *target* and *route* as described in Section 3.7, the router chooses the destination box *b* as follows:

◆ If *route* is empty, *b* is chosen according to the value of *target* as follows:
  ◆ If *target* is not the DN of any LI box or addressable feature box, then *b* is any available Dialing Error Response (DER) feature box (a free box).
  ◆ If *target* ∈ *LIbDnum* then *b* = *LibDnum*~(*target*).
  ◆ If *target* ∈ *AFbDnum* then *b* = *AfbDnum*~(*target*).

◆ If *route* is not empty, the head element is (*t*, *z*) of type *FBoxType* × *Zone*. This element is removed from the *route* list, and used to choose *b* as follows:
  ◆ If *t* ∈ *FFBType* then *b* is any available box of type *t*.
  ◆ If *t* ∈ *BFBType* then *b* is the box of type *t* bound to *LibDnum*~(*source*) if *z* = "Source" and to *LibDnum*~(*target*) if *z* = "Target." Such a box necessarily exists, by the constraints given in Sections 3.1 and 3.4, which guarantee the

existence of a bound box for each subscriber to the feature implemented by the box.

After the router has modified the setup message and determined b, the switch transmits the modified setup message to the chosen box.

3.9. Calls: Message types

The message types for internal calls are shown in Table 1, along with their fields, senders, and recipients.

The setup and teardown phase messages are concerned solely with the connection and disconnection of calls; the protocols for their use are given in Section 3.10.

The other messages are status messages, used to communicate between call participants after the setup phase and before the teardown phase. Some messages travel only from a callee to a caller, while others can travel in either direction. The types of status message shown are of basic utility in most systems; additional message types and data fields can be freely defined for the purposes of particular features.

Among the types shown, *busy, alerting, answered, unobtainable, dialtone,* and *quiet* are of particular importance: they are the status messages that a receiving LI box must translate into audio tones (or silence) on the external line to the customer's telephone, as described in Section 2.11. *DTMF* and *flash* status messages originate at a LI box when the customer dials a digit or flashes the switchhook while a call is in progress.

TABLE 1
MESSAGE TYPES IN THE DFC CALL PROTOCOL

Phase	Message Type	Data Fields	From/To
setup and teardown phase messages	setup	(see Section 3.6)	caller to box
	quickbusy	*initiator: DN*	box to caller
	reserve	*reserved: port*	box to switch
	upack	none	switch to caller
	init	none	switch to callee
	teardown	none	caller to callee and callee to caller
	downack	none	caller to callee and callee to caller
status messages	busy	*initiator: DN*	callee to caller
	alerting	*initiator: DN*	callee to caller
	answered	*initiator: DN*	callee to caller
	unobtainable	*unallocated: String*	DER box to caller
	dialtone	none	caller to callee and callee to caller
	quiet	none	caller to callee and callee to caller
	flash	none	caller to callee and callee to caller
	DTMF	*dialed-char: Char*	caller to callee and callee to caller
	...	...	callee to caller and /or caller to callee

3.10. Call protocols

The protocol for calls to be executed by feature boxes is in three parts: a protocol for the caller port; a protocol for the callee box; and a protocol for the callee port. The protocol for the switch is given in Section 3.11.

Each protocol is described below in Promela [16]. A message of type **msg** is sent on channel **out** by the statement **out!msg**. A message of type **msg** is received on channel **in** by the statement **in?msg**. An **if** statement is executed by executing exactly one of its executable alternatives; in these protocols an alternative is executable if it is unguarded or guarded by a send statement or by a receive statement for a message that is available as the next message on the channel. A **do** statement is like an **if** statement except that it continues to execute alternatives until there is an explicit exit from the loop by means of a **break** or **goto** statement.

A callee port on a box is capable of receiving a sequence of calls. Each of its calls must satisfy the following protocol:

```
begin:       in?init; goto linked;
linked:      do
             :: out!status
             :: in?status
             :: out!teardown; goto unlinking
             :: in?teardown; out!downack; goto end
             od;
unlinking:   do
             :: in?status
             :: in?teardown; out!downack
             :: in?downack; goto end
             od;
end: skip
```

A caller port on a box is capable of making a sequence of calls. Each of its calls must satisfy the following protocol:

```
begin:       out!setup; goto requesting;
requesting:  if
             :: in?upack; goto linked
             :: in?quickbusy; goto end
             fi;
linked:      do
             :: out!status
             :: in?status
             :: out!teardown; goto unlinking
             :: in?teardown; out!downack; goto end
             od;
```

```
unlinking:  do
            :: in?status
            :: in?teardown; out!downack
            :: in?downack; goto end
            od
end:        skip
```

A dual port can participate in a sequence of calls. During each call it plays the role of either a caller port or a callee port. Any port is busy when it is in a requesting, linked, or unlinking state, and idle otherwise. Once a call is successfully established the protocols for caller and callee are identical. Because communication is asynchronous a port can receive incoming messages even after it has written a teardown message.

The life history of a box and its own signaling channels (those not associated with particular ports) must conform to the following callee box protocol:

```
begin:      do
            :: in?setup; if
                         :: out!reserve
                         :: out!quickbusy
                         fi
            od
```

If the box sends a **reserve** message, it must be accompanied by the identifier of an idle, unreserved callee or dual port. That port must remain idle and reserved until it receives its **init** message from the switch, at which time it becomes busy and unreserved.

3.11. Switch call protocol

The corresponding protocol to be observed by the switch is more complex because it must take account of the interleaving of many calls and of the connections between them. In the protocol given below, it is assumed that:

+ There are four arrays of signaling channels p_s, s_p, b_s, and s_b used, respectively, for sending out-of-band messages from a port to the switch, from the switch to a port, from a box to the switch and from the switch to a box. They are indexed by port and box identifiers ($[p]$ and $[b]$). Each channel is an unbounded reliable FIFO queue.

+ The switch procedures $CONNECT[p,q]$ and $DISCONNECT[p,q]$ respectively create and destroy a voice path between ports p and q. The order of operands is immaterial.

+ The function $ROUTE: b$ returns the box identifier b of the destination box for the most recently read *setup* message, determined by the router as described in Section 3.8.

+ The switch reads its input channels fairly (in some sense), and is fast enough to ensure that no call suffers any significant degree of starvation.

The switch maintains internal variables whose values represent the connection state:

◆ Current out-of-band signaling connections between ports are represented by elements of an array *WTF* ("where to forward"). If ports *p* and *q* are currently connected in a call then *WTF[p]* = *q* and *WTF[q]* = *p*. If port p is not currently connected to any port, then the value of WTF[p] is not defined.

◆ The array *TDF* has an element for each port; this array is used in the processing of *teardown* and *downack* messages, as explained below. Initially the value of *TDF[p]* is 0 for all *p*.

◆ There is an array of queues containing a queue for each box *b*. The queue for a box holds the port identifiers of senders of *setup* messages that have already been sent to the box but for which the switch has not yet received a *reserve* or *quickbusy* message from the box. The operation *ENQ[x,b]* and the function *DEQ[b]* : *p* have the obvious meanings.

In the protocol we depart from strict Promela in three minor ways. First, the use of parentheses rather than square brackets in the notation

```
:: p_s(p)?msg;...p...
```

occurring in a looping or conditional statement is a shorthand for

```
:: ps[p1]?msg; p=p1;...p...
:: ps[p2]?msg; p=p2;...p...
:: ps[p3]?msg; p=p3;...p...
```

etc. The syntax is reminiscent of

```
:: b_s[b]?reserve(y)
```

in Promela, which assigns to y the value of the data field of the reserve message. The same effect can be achieved in strict Promela with a slight loss of readability. Second, we index arrays by arbitrary box and port identifiers; in strict Promela array index values must be integers. Third, we assume unbounded queues.

The protocol is:

```
/* switch protocol; initially TDF[p]==0 for all
ports p */
do
:: p_s(x)?setup; b=ROUTE; ENQ[x,b]; s_b[b]!setup
:: b_s(b)?quickbusy; x=DEQ[b]; s_p[x]!quickbusy
:: b_s(b)?reserve(y); x=DEQ[b];
   if
   :: TDF[y]==0
   :: TDF[y]==1; z=WTF[y];
      do
      :: p_s[y]?status; s_p[z]!status
      :: p_s[y]?downack; s_p[z]!downack; TDF[y]=0;
         break
      od
   fi;
   CONNECT[x,y]; WTF[x]=y; WTF[y]=x; s_p[x]!upack;
   sp[y]!init
:: p_s(x)?status; y=WTF[x]; sp[y]!status
```

```
:: p_s(x)?teardown; y=WTF[x]; s_p[y]!teardown;
   TDF[y]=1;
   if
   :: TDF[x]==1
   :: TDF[x]==0; DISCONNECT[x,y]
   fi
:: p_s(x)?downack; y=WTF[x]; s_p[y]!downack; TDF[x]=0
od
```

TDF[y] is 1 when (and only when) the switch has sent a *teardown* message to *y* and has not yet received the corresponding *downack* message from *y*; at all other times *TDF[y]* is 0. The global initialization *TDF[p]=0* for all ports *p* is necessary to ensure that if a port *y* is the callee in its first call, then *TDF[y]* is correctly set to 0 when the *reserve(y)* message for that call arrives at the switch. At the completion of every call of port *y* the value of *TDF[y]* is guaranteed to be 0. For a call in which *y* has received a *teardown* message, the assignment *TDF[y]=0* is executed when the *downack* sent by *y* is received at the switch; for a call in which *y* receives no *teardown* message, the value of *TDF[y]* is unchanged from the global initialization *TDF[y]=0* or from the completion of *y*'s preceding call.

When a *reserve(y)* message is received by the switch, port *y* must be idle, since otherwise its box would not have selected it to receive a call. Therefore, it must have received all its incoming messages and written all of its outgoing messages of its immediately preceding call *c* (if there has been such a call). However, there may be some messages of call *c* on the *p_s[y]* channel that have been sent by *y* but not yet received by the switch. If *TDF[y]* is 1, then port *y* has been sent a *teardown* message in call *c*, but its acknowledgment *downack* has not yet been received by the switch. The signal channel *p_s[y]* from *y* to the switch must then be "cleaned," because it is still in use from call *c*. If *TDF[y]* is 0, then the channel *p_s[y]* must be empty. Either the switch has already received a *downack* from port *y*; or else port *y* has itself already received a *downack*, in which case the final message of *p_s[y]* was the teardown of which that *downack* was the acknowledgment.

The first *teardown* message of a call received by the switch causes the switch to disconnect the voice path. When a *teardown* message arrives from port *x*, the guard *TDF[x]==0* correctly specifies the condition that this is the first *teardown* message of the call to pass through the switch. For if *TDF[x]==0* because port *x* has already received a *teardown* message and its acknowledging *downack* has already reached the switch, then that *downack* would have preceded the *teardown* message that has just arrived, contrary to the port protocol.

3.12. Feature box behavior

A feature box and its ports must observe the signaling protocols described in Section 3.10, and must send only correctly formed messages as described in Sections 3.6, 3.7, and 3.9. In this section, we describe the internal voice-processing behavior of a box.

In a legal box state the external output of each port is exactly one of these four alternatives:

+ silence,
+ the external input from another port of the box,
+ the normalized sum of the external inputs from a set of other ports of the box, or
+ a specified sound such as a tone or announcement.

In addition, the external input from a port can be recorded or analyzed for recognition of a specified kind of pattern. Recording and analyzing port states are not mutually exclusive or exclusive of any port-output state.

A language for box programming must make all legal voice-processing states achievable. Its semantics or analysis tools should also help the programmer avoid illegal states and states that waste implementation resources such as mixers.

The language commands for creating active port states must specify certain information. A *record* command must specify where the recording is to be stored. A *play* command must specify the sound to be played; the sound might be given as a tone frequency, a recording, or even as text (in the presence of text-to-speech facilities). An *analyze* command must specify the kind of pattern to be recognized and the place where the result of the recognition is to be stored. The kind of pattern is usually specified in terms of a vocabulary. In the presence of automated speech recognition this will typically be a vocabulary of single word commands.

In addition to these commands, a convenient box-programming language should provide events through which a program can be notified of the status of ports in active states. It should be possible to notify a box program that an announcement of fixed duration has been played completely. It should be possible to notify a box program that recording has been completed, where completion might be defined in terms of a maximum recording time or a minimum interval of silence. It should also be possible to notify a box program that recognition has been completed, where completion might be defined in terms of a maximum sequence length of recognized words, a minimum interval of silence, or recognition of a distinguished "interrupt" word.

4. Feature specifications

In this section, we discuss the specification of various features in a DFC setting: the features and their combinations are chosen to illustrate various aspects of the architecture and its implications. The suggested specifications are neither complete nor in any way definitive: they are intended only to illustrate a possible approach to the features discussed in a DFC setting. The space limitations of this paper preclude the presentation of full programs for feature boxes. Some feature box programs are given in [25]. We, therefore, present only the barest informal sketches, but we have tried to address the chief points likely to cause difficulty in each case.

4.1. The Null feature box: Transparent and end states

We begin by describing a Null feature box. It is completely transparent: its presence has no effect on any usage into which it is configured. The description below should be thought of as that of a process executing in parallel with the protocols on the active ports and sharing events with them.

The Null feature box has a callee port *p1* and a caller port *p2*. It becomes occupied on receiving a *setup* message; it accepts the call on *p1*. It then places a call on *p2*, using a copy of the *setup* message of the *p1* call. If the *p2* call attempt fails, it sends a *busy* status message followed by a *teardown* message on *p1*, and becomes *available* on receiving the corresponding *downack*. If the call on *p2* succeeds, it enters the *transparent* state: that is, it joins the voice channels of *p1* and *p2*, and proceeds to copy all incoming out-of-band signals from each port to the other. When the *teardown* subprotocol on both ports is complete the box enters an *end* state and becomes *available* again.

4.2. Target identity: 800 Service, Speed Calling, and Call Forwarding Always

Three features that change the target of a subscriber call are Speed Calling (SC), 800 Service (800), and Call Forwarding Always (CFA). Each is provided by a feature box which is like the transparent box with one exception. To place the *p2* call, it uses an altered copy, not a true copy, of the *setup* message of the incoming call on port *p1*. In each case the *target* field is altered, and the value of *command* is "update" with a *modifier* {"Target"}, ensuring that the target zone of the route will be recomputed by the switch. Notice that SC, 800 and CFA are, respectively, Source, Dialed, and Target zone features, although each of them changes the target of a call.

The 800 Service feature allows a commercial subscriber to pay for all incoming calls; the calls are placed by dialing an easily remembered string such as 1-800-123-4567. The feature is a dialed zone feature: the string is not a DN, and the 800 feature box determines the required DN from its operational data relation

eightDN : String800 ↦ DN.

The altered value of target is *eightDN (dialed)*, or *nul* if *dialed ∉ dom eightDN*.

The SC (Speed Calling) feature is a source zone feature. It uses an operational data relation

sourceSpeedDN : DN ↦ (SpeedCode ↦ DN)

containing each source subscriber's private mapping from speed-calling codes to frequently called DNs. The altered value of *target* is *nul* if *source ∉ dom sourceSpeedDN* or if *dialed ∉ dom sourceSpeedDN(source)*; otherwise it is *sourceSpeedDN (source)(dialed)*.

Call Forwarding Always (CFA) is a target zone feature. It uses an element of an operational data relation

aForwardDN : DN ↦ DN

mapping the *target* subscriber's DN to a *forward* DN. The altered value of target is *aForwardDN (target)*, or *nul* if *target ∉ dom aForwardDN*.

4.3. Target identity: Originating Call Screening

Originating Call Screening (OCS) is a source zone feature; its function is to prevent calls to barred numbers on a screening list maintained by a subscriber to the feature. Subscribers enter their barred numbers as strings (*DN* is a proper subset of *String*). The operational data is:

screenOCS : DN ↔ String.

For each number *s* barred by *source*, *screenOCS* has an element (*source, s*). The key choice in specifying OCS is: which fields of which messages are candidate values of *s*? Three possible answers are as follows:

- *dialed* in the *setup* message. In this case dialed speed-call codes and 800-numbers can be barred, but forward DNs reached by CFA cannot: a disobedient child whose parents have barred *DN1* simply asks a friend at *DN2* to forward *DN2*'s calls temporarily to *DN1*, and then dials *DN2*.
- *target* in the *setup* message. In this case only DNs occurring in *setup* messages in the source zone can be barred. 800-numbers cannot be barred even if their equivalent DNs are known (because 800-numbers are not DNs and do not appear in the *target* field; they are translated to DNs by an 800 feature box in the dialed zone, too late for OCS to operate). Forward DNs cannot be barred (because CFA is in the target zone, and the forwarding, like 800 translation, operates too late for OCS). DNs accessed by speed-calling codes can be barred provided that OCS has a later precedence than SC: if the OCS feature box precedes the SC box then OCS receives only the *dialed* string, before SC has translated it to a *target* DN.
- *initiator* in an *alerting* or *answered* message. In this case, it is the DN of the LI that is finally reached that is subject to barring by OCS. Forward DNs are barred, but an 800-number cannot be barred unless its equivalent DN is known to the subscriber and entered explicitly in the screening list.

By suitable design of the feature box, OCS can be specified to enforce barring of any or all of these fields. If the *setup* message received at port *p1* is barred neither by its *dialed* nor by its *target* value, the *p2* call is placed with the same *setup* message. If the *p2* call is successful, an *alerting* or *busy* message from the LI finally reached will eventually be passed back by transparent behavior on the part of other feature boxes, and can be checked for a barred *initiator* value.

4.4. Joining usages: Call Waiting

The Call Waiting (CW) feature allows a subscriber to receive an incoming customer call while already engaged on an existing usage. The subscriber can switch to the new call by flashing the switchhook, and back again to the earlier call by flashing again. CW is both a source zone and a target zone feature, because the subscriber may be either the caller or the callee in the existing usage. It must be provided by a bound box, because clearly the second, incoming, call must be routed to the CW box already configured into the existing usage.

Before the second call is received, the CW box behaves transparently. It receives a call, either from the subscriber or from another source. If the call is from the subscriber (in which case the *source* value in the *setup* message is the subscriber's own DN), the call is accepted on port $p1$ and a call placed on port $p2$ with the same *setup* message field values. If the call is not from the subscriber the call is accepted on port $p2$ and a call placed on port $p1$. Both $p1$ and $p2$ are dual ports.

The CW box has a third port $p3$, which is a callee port. If a call arrives at the box while the $p1$ and $p2$ calls are still active, it is accepted at port $p3$, an *alerting* signal is sent from port $p3$, and the call-waiting indication (two short tones) is played on the outgoing voice channel of port $p1$, the speech signal being temporarily interrupted for the purpose. The box then waits for one of the following events:

+ A *teardown* message on port $p2/p3$. The box tears down the call on that port, connects port $p1$ to the remaining port $p3/p2$ if it is active and was not already connected, and is now ready to receive a call on the port $p2/p3$ that has become free. If the remaining port $p3/p2$ was inactive, the call on $p1$ is torn down.
+ A *flash* message on port $p1$. The box disconnects $p1$ from the port $p2/p3$ to which it is connected, and connects it to the other port $p3/p2$, provided that there is an active call on that other port; if not, the flash message is passed on to the connected port $p2/p3$ and is otherwise ignored.
+ A *teardown* message on the port $p1$. If $p1$ was connected to $p2/p3$ and the other port $p3/p2$ is inactive, the box tears down both calls and returns to its initial state. If one of the ports $p2$ and $p3$ is active but has not yet been connected to $p1$, the caller on that port is hearing ringback. The box tears down the call on $p1$ but immediately calls the subscriber back on $p1$ to connect it to the waiting caller at the active port.

In this way the CW box allows the subscriber to multiplex between two calls. Notice that CW does not require an internal three-way connector, because its two calls are multiplexed, not conferenced.

4.5. Splitting a usage: 3-Way Calling

3-Way Calling (3WC) is a feature in both source and target zones, provided by a free box with two dual ports $p1$ and $p2$ and one caller port. Like CW, the box connects the subscribing customer on port $p1$ when first activated. It allows the subscriber, when already engaged in a usage, to make a second, outgoing, call and to conference the two calls together. Like CW it uses *flash* messages to signal the subscriber's intentions. A *flash* while only one call is active indicates that the subscriber wishes to make a second call. The 3WC box then puts the existing customer call on hold, sends a *dialtone* message to port $p1$, collects a dialed string in-band from digits dialed by the subscriber, and places the dialed call on the currently free port. When that call has been set up and the subscriber flashes again, the box conferences the two calls, joining the voice signals at all of its ports at an internal three-way connector.

Disconnection behavior of a 3WC box is as follows:

◆ A *teardown* message on port $p2$ or $p3$ occurring when all three ports are in use makes that port available for placing another outgoing dialed call when the subscriber flashes again.

◆ A *teardown* message on $p1$ occurring when all three ports are in use causes only the call on $p1$ to be torn down, leaving the other two ports connected. The 3WC box is then occupied servicing the calls on ports $p2$ and $p3$ until it receives a teardown message on one of those ports. (The subscriber's LI box, of course, is not involved in this residual connection between ports $p2$ and $p3$ of the 3WC box.) Since 3WC is not a bound box, a fresh 3WC box will be used for a subsequent call to or from the subscriber.

◆ A *teardown* message on any port occurring when only two ports are in use ends both calls and returns the box to the *end* state, where it becomes again available.

4.6. CW and 3WC together

The relationship between CW and 3WC illustrates three DFC principles. The first principle is that a bound box in a usage should always come between its line interface and any free boxes. For CW and 3WC, which are subscribed to in both the source and target zones, this means that (CW, "Source") must precede (3WC, "Source"), and (3WC, "Target") must precede (CW, "Target"). Figure 3a shows why.

If, contrary to the principle, 3WC takes precedence over CW in the source zone, then the configuration in Figure 3a arises when the subscriber has used 3WC to make a second call while one is already in progress. The second outgoing call from 3WC does not go through a CW box, because there is only one such box bound to LI, and it is already fully occupied as far as outgoing calls are concerned. If the first party to which the LI was connected hangs up, then there will be no CW box left in the usage. The second principle then applies: externally initiated modifications of usages are strictly prohibited by the DFC architecture. The CW box, lost from the usage when the first customer call was torn down, cannot be spliced into the usage to become available in the second call. The effect is that subscribers to 3WC are sometimes deprived of CW functionality.

In contrast, Figure 3b and 3c show configurations that arise when the precedence relation follows the first principle. 3WC is a free box, so a separate instance can appear on each fork of the usage.

It is well known that CW and 3WC interact because they both use flashes from the proximate line interface as their control command. This situation invokes a third DFC principle, which is that when two boxes compete for an out-ofband signal, the box closer to the source of the signal has priority access to it. The closer box can respond to the signal and absorb it, or it can ignore the signal and pass it on. Because of the first principle, CW has priority access to the flash, which fortunately is what we want (at least most of the time). The configuration

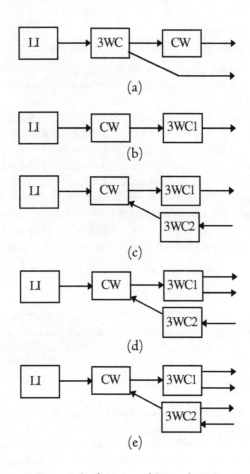

Figure 3. Configurations of CW and 3WC

in Figure 3d arises when the line interface first makes an outgoing call, uses 3WC to create a conference (flashes are forwarded to 3WC1 by the transparent CW box), and then receives an incoming call through CW.

The behavior produced by always giving CW priority access to flashes may or may not be considered acceptable. Even in Figure 3d some aspects of the user interface are awkward, and a configuration such as that shown in Figure 3e, in which all boxes have reached their full potential, is not achievable.

If the default priority scheme for access to flash signals does not yield acceptable behavior, and if enriching the command vocabulary (usually the strategy that yields the best user interface) is impermissible, then it becomes necessary to specify explicit cooperation between two features. It is possible within the DFC architecture to use special status messages between the CW and 3WC boxes to give 3WC priority access to flashes at the appropriate times [25]. Of course, introduction of such special messages is highly undesirable because it compromises feature modularity and independence; but in the circumstances envisaged, such compromise is unavoidable whatever the underlying architecture: the desired behaviors of the two features are in conflict.

4.7. Using the direct routing command

The Emergency Break-In feature (EBI) makes use of the direct routing command in the setup message. An emergency caller, such as the Fire Department, subscribes to EBI as a source feature. An EBIE box is included in the source zone of every outgoing call made by the emergency caller. This EBIE box, perhaps after checking the user's authorization, places a call with a direct routing command. The configuration that results when the callee subscriber is already engaged in a usage is shown in Figure 4.

A customer call is connected between the subscribers at LI1 and LI2. Both LI1 and LI2 have bound EBI boxes. The emergency service places an emergency call to the subscriber at LI2; this call is routed directly from the EBIE box of the emergency service to the EBI box bound to LI2, and that EBI box accepts the call and places the call from LI1 on hold. Evidently a regular subscriber's EBI box must have the highest precedence, ensuring that it is immediately adjacent to the LI box to avoid potential interference from other features.

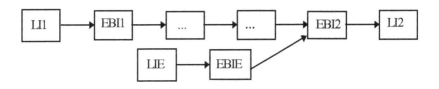

Figure 4. Direct routing.

4.8. Rerouting for a dialed feature

The Directory Link feature (DL) recognizes when a customer has dialed a directory assistance number. It tries to recognize the number announced by directory assistance, and offers to connect the customer to that number directly.

DL is a dialed feature, included in the usage whenever the number dialed (or speed-called) has the form of a directory assistance DN. In the North American long-distance network this form is aaa-555-1212, where aaa is the area code of the destination subscriber for which assistance is needed. A DL feature box has a callee port $p1$ and a caller port $p2$. On receiving a call on $p1$, DL engages in a dialogue in which it offers the DL service to the calling subscriber for a small charge. If the subscriber refuses the service offer, the DL box places a call to directory assistance on port $p2$ and behaves transparently from that point onwards.

If the subscriber accepts the service offer, the call to directory assistance is made on port $p2$. The DL box then monitors the incoming voice signal on $p2$, and will normally detect the number announced by the directory assistance equipment. It then tears down the call on $p2$, and places a new call with the announced number as the dialed string. If DL cannot detect the announced number, it plays a message to the caller (apologizing and saying that no charge will be made for the failed service) and tears down the calls on $p1$ and $p2$.

The performance of DL depends on the intelligibility of the directory assistance announcement of the number and on the quality of the speech analysis used by the DL box. In principle DL can work on any of the following announcements:

+ "The number you require is xxx-ssss." DL places a call to aaa-xxx-ssss, having stored the value aaa from the setup message on $p1$.
+ "The number you require is 800-ppp-qqqq." DL places a call to the announced 800-number. Since this 800-number is the dialed string of the newly placed call, an 800 box will be included in the dialed zone of the new segment.
+ "The number you require is in area code bbb." Please call directory assistance on bbb-555-1212." DL places a call to the announced directory assistance number. Since this number is the dialed string of the newly placed call, a fresh DL box will be included in the dialed zone of the new segment, and the DL service will be offered again in the new call.

4.9. Interactions arising from in-band signaling

The use of voice recognition and other in-band signaling can easily give rise to awkward interactions. Whereas a feature box can absorb an out-of-band signal and prevent it from reaching other boxes simply by not passing it on, it cannot absorb an in-band signal in the same way unless it has previously disconnected the voice channels.

A technique that can be used in the DFC environment is to inhibit recognition of in-band signals by sending out-ofband messages to indicate to other boxes that they should not recognize certain in-band signals until further notice. Call connection between adjacent boxes in a usage uses a pair of voice channels, one in each direction. When a box is about to monitor the signal arriving on an incoming channel from an upstream box, it sends an *inhibit* message to its neighbor or neighbors in the downstream direction, and vice versa; when it ceases to monitor the signal it sends a complementary *uninhibit* message in the same direction. If all boxes observe the obvious discipline, each allowing a box from which an *inhibit* is received to take precedence in monitoring voice signals from the corresponding direction, the in-band signaling difficulty can be overcome.

This discipline allows the same precedence to be enforced for in-band signals as for out-of-band signals. It is also possible to enforce the opposite precedence or even a mixture, at the cost of some complexity and reduction in feature independence. To establish any precedence by such a discipline requires a taxonomy of in-band signals, and the definition of field values in the *inhibit* and *uninhibit* messages to represent the signal classes.

4.10. Addressable boxes and dialed features

Addressable boxes are used only where all customers who dial a given DN must be connected to the same box. By contrast, a dialed feature is merely one that is applied according to the dialed string. Two contrasting examples will make the point clearer.

800 Service (800) is a dialed feature, configured into any usage in which the dialed string begins with the characters '1-800'. But it is not an addressable box: each call dialing an 800 number is routed to a temporarily dedicated free 800 box, which determines a target DN from the operational data of the feature—namely, the relation recording the mapping from 800 numbers to DNs. To make 800 an addressable box would mean having one feature box for each 800 number, and routing all calls to the number through that particular box. While this scheme would have the advantage that the box could contain the maplet for the number, and so would not need to access operational data, it would have a far weightier disadvantage: it would require the box to have enough ports to serve as many customers as could be calling the 800 number at any one time and a corresponding box program able to handle the interleaving of their call protocols.

By contrast, Large-Scale Conferencing (LSC) requires the use of a number of addressable boxes. When a conference is booked, a box of sufficient size to accommodate all participants is assigned; participants who will take the initiative in joining the conference are given this number to call, while other participants may wait for the box to call them and so will not need to know the number.

4.11. Disconnected boxes

Some features are provided by boxes that are temporarily disconnected from all other boxes while engaged in their tasks. Consider, for example, a Wake-Up Call service (WUC). WUC is a dialed feature provided by a free box. On receiving an incoming call the box collects the caller's DN and the desired wake-up time from the caller in local variables. It then tears down the call, and waits until the wake-up time is indicated on the real-time clock to which it has access. During this period of waiting, the box is not connected to any other box; but it is occupied, and not available to service another wake-up call. At the expiry of the period it places the wake-up call to the subscriber whose DN is stored in its local variable.

5. Summary

5.1. Simplifications adopted

In designing and presenting the DFC technology we have adopted several simplifying assumptions in order to clarify and focus our work. Although in themselves these simplifications are unrealistic, we believe that abandoning them would not invalidate the architecture, but merely force the introduction of additional detail that would obscure—but not vitiate—the main ideas. The chief of these simplifications are the following.

* We restrict our consideration to analog phones. The use of ISDN phones would introduce a richer vocabulary of messages that could flow to and from LI boxes, and a richer feature set. But we see no reason to think that the additional features would not fit comfortably into the DFC architecture.
* We assume that each line interface is associated with a single DN, and that DNs are not shared.
* We assume that the interface boxes are all interfaces to telephones, not to trunks. This allows us to ignore the addressing complications that arise with trunks (the relation *trunk* ↔ *DN* is many-to-many), and also the race condition ('trunk glare') that can arise when it is necessary to seize a trunk.

We have also adopted some other simplifications that will take further work to abandon. In particular:

* We do not discuss billing here. However, we have given some consideration to billing issues, and it appears to us that the DFC architecture may offer a helpful environment for specifying billing features.
* We do not consider provisioning, either of subscription data or of feature operational data. Quite apart from the additional detail involved, there are issues of coordination between provisioning and operation. We see no reason to think that these issues would be harder to handle in a DFC setting.
* We assume the absence of resource contention. Although feature boxes are freely conceived as containing dedicated devices such as conference bridges and signal processors, we assume that boxes are always available when needed. We make the same assumption about signaling and voice channels.
* We have ignored broadband and multimedia telecommunications services.

An AT&T Technical Memorandum [25] discusses some aspects of the DFC architecture under less restrictive assumptions.

5.2. Related Work

The most common research approach to the problem of feature interaction is the application of formal verification techniques to system specifications, with the goal of detecting all undesired feature interactions [21]. Velthuijsen concludes:

"None of the approaches have progressed far beyond a mere proof-of-concept result. The approaches show that with the right descriptions and techniques it is indeed possible to detect certain interactions. But the trick is to come up with the right descriptions: the right network and service specifications, and above all, the right properties. This appears very hard to do well and presents for the time being a more urgent challenge than the application of yet another specification formalism to the same general approach."

We agree with Velthuijsen and are trying to find the right (modular, complete, and comprehensible) service specifications. Formal verification and detection of unforeseen interactions are activities we hope to pursue later, building on this new foundation [25].

There are other architectural approaches to service specification, the most well-known being the Intelligent Network (IN) architecture [1, 10, 13, 18, 20]. The major limitation of the IN architecture is that its conceptual model is strongly oriented towards two-party calls, and is difficult to extend to multiparty services. We regard the ease with which DFC handles nonlinear usages and multiparty services as an important advantage, as explained below.

More recently other architectures for telecommunications services have been proposed, for example [15, 22, 26]. In these architectures a typical component is an agent representing a subscriber, resource, common function, or type of connection. These agents determine their call-processing behavior by negotiating with each other, sending messages to each other as needed. The most important difference between these agent-based architectures and the DFC architecture is that agent-based architectures impose little in the way of limits or structure on communication among agents. For example, in [26], communication between agents is presented only loosely and informally, making it hard to see what constraints are imposed by the architecture described. For this reason, it will be very difficult to exploit the modularity of the decomposition into agents to understand feature interactions or determine global system properties.

Another characteristic of the DFC approach is that features are distinct, first-class modules. Many other formalizations of feature behavior have partitioned features into syntactic modules, for example distinct sets of rules [4, 8, 11, 19]. But a set of rules shares unrestricted state with other rules, so the syntactic constraint actually places very little constraint on semantic interaction among modules. All interactions among DFC modules, on the other hand, are strictly limited by the architecture.

The specification technique of [2, 5] is based on layered state-transition machines; it is similar to ours in having feature modules communicating by means of a fixed protocol. Their feature modules may sometimes require knowledge of each others' states, so they are more closely coupled than DFC feature boxes. DFC feature boxes achieve a much looser coupling by means of the pipe-and-filter arrangement, in which each box has a great deal of independent control over the voice channels passing through it.

There are as many possible comparisons to related work as there are research projects on feature interaction, especially since even research that is focused narrowly on detection must start with some specification formalism. In the previous paragraphs we have given a representative sample of comparisons— representative with respect to both similarities to and differences from the DFC architecture.

We know of no specification approach that is closer to the DFC architecture than those we have cited.

5.3. Advantages of DFC

The treatment of features as distinct components is not in itself new. The key novelty of DFC is the choice of an architecture in a dynamic pipe-and-filter style, with the advantages that this brings.

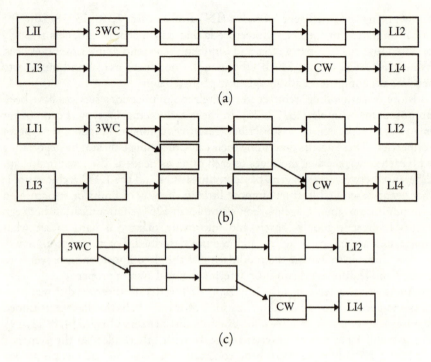

Figure. 5. Usage configurations.

One important advantage already mentioned is the ease with which nonlinear usages can be handled. and represented in graphs. The dynamic configuration and recon-figuration of a usage can be complex. For example, Figure 5 shows a progression through three configurations.

In Figure 5a there are two clearly distinct usages: LI1 is connected to LI2, and LI3 to LI4; in Figure 5b these usages have been joined because LI1 has placed a further call to LI4; in Figure 5c both LI1 and LI3 have dropped out, leaving LI2 connected to LI4. Notice that the final connection of LI2 and LI4 depends on continuing use of the 3WC box originally introduced in LI1's call to LI2; this causes no difficulty because 3WC is a free box.

This complexity of configuration is easily handled in DFC because of its distributed nature. Although the notion of a *usage* is convenient for informal explanation of DFC behavior, it has no formal status in DFC. There are no usage identifiers to be allocated or manipulated; nothing in the DFC architecture depends on identifying and distinguishing individual usages over time. Only individual boxes and individual internal calls are signficant: DFC configurations arise solely from the internal featureless calls, each involving just two parties. DFC can, therefore, exploit the simplicity of POTS, while avoiding the traditional, but obscure and difficult, elaboration of the notion of a *call*, which is central in some approaches. Avoiding this notion eliminates many complications and restrictions that flow from it, and simplifies the specification of feature behavior.

We believe that the DFC scheme of feature communication by featureless internal calls offers several advantages in feature specification, analysis, and implementation. The primary advantage in feature specification is the high degree of separability among features. To a very great extent, at least an initial specification of a feature can be made without consideration of other features that may be present, by assuming that any other feature boxes in the usage are in a transparent state. (Of course, there are some general concerns that must always be taken into account. For example, any feature may find itself in a usage within whose lifetime several customer calls are placed and answered. The OCS feature, for example, must therefore be specified to check a sequence of customer calls, not just one.)

Another specification advantage is the clear separation between the behavior of individual features and the underlying mechanism for their composition. As was pointed out above, the DFC router does not provide any feature functionality, even for features that might perhaps be viewed as essentially routing features, such as 800 Service or CFA. Equally, the individual features play no direct part in determining the routing. Their contribution to the routing behavior is at the more abstract level of indicating that further routing is to be based on a new value of the source or target field in the setup message.

The chief advantage in analysis is that interaction between feature boxes is constrained in a well understood way closely analogous to the interaction between caller and callee in a traditional POTS call. Just as in the approach of [17], behavior of individual boxes and their interactions is susceptible to model checking techniques; properties of the interaction of the caller and callee protocols given in Section 3.10 with the DFC switch protocol and with each other have been checked in Spin [16]. The explicit treatment of voice channels in internal calls allows feature box states and behaviors to be analyzed in terms of voice processing states as well as in terms of sending and receiving out-of-band signals.

Finally, the DFC architecture appears to be relatively easy to implement on a wide variety of physical telecom munications architectures [25]. There is an obvious correspondence between a DFC usage and a voice path through the switches and trunks of a physical network.

Furthermore, we have consciously avoided choices in the definition of the DFC architecture that are likely to be expensive to implement. For example, the constraint that source, dialed, and target zones are configured in that order simplifies the assignment of feature functionality to network nodes. Although the three zones are routed together in the virtual architecture, the routing of the three zones can easily be distributed for the purpose of efficient signaling. Another example is that each feature box has the narrowest possible scope of action: for instance, Wake-Up Call, and 800 Service features are provided by free boxes serving one usage at a time. Engineers are free to implement these and other feature boxes as individual physical components or as processes on a large platform serving many usages concurrently.

5.4. Further work

So far we have programmed sample feature boxes in Promela. Our highest-priority task is the development of a domain-specific language that makes feature boxes easy to program and easy to analyze for unexpected feature interactions and other interesting properties.

At the same time, we are also working on:

+ the extension of the DFC architecture to aspects of telecommunications that it does not currently cover;
+ the systematic implementation of the DFC virtual architecture on a variety of physical architectures; and
+ investigation of further techniques for abstraction, classification, and verification of features.

Acknowledgements

We thank the editor, Yow-Jian Lin, and the anonymous reviewers for many helpful suggestions.

References

1. I. Aggoun and P. Combes, Observers in the SCE and SEE to detect and resolve service interactions, [9], pp. 198-212.
2. P.K. Au and J.M. Atlee, Evaluation of a state-based model of feature interactions, [9], pp. 153-167.
3. Feature Interactions in Telecommunications Systems II, L.G. Bouma and Velthuijsen, eds. Amsterdam: IOS Press, 1994.
4. J. Blom, B. Jonsson, and L. Kempe, Using temporal logic for modular specification of telephone services, [3], pp. 197-216.
5. K.H. Braithwaite and J.M. Atlee, Towards automated detection of feature interactions, [3], pp. 36-59.
6. E.J. Cameron, N.D. Griffeth, Y.-J. Lin, M.E. Nilson, W.K. Schnure, and H. Velthuijsen, A feature interaction benchmark for IN and beyond, [3], pp. 1-23.
7. Feature Interactions in Telecommunications Systems III, K.E. Cheng and T. Ohta, eds. Amsterdam: IOS Press, 1995.
8. P. Combes and S. Pickin, Formalisation of a user view of network and services for feature interaction detection, [3] pp. 120-135.
9. Feature Interactions in Telecommunication Networks IV, P. Dini, R. Boutaba, and L. Logrippo, eds. Amsterdam: IOS Press, 1997.
10. J.M. Duran and J. Visser, International standards for Intelligent Networks, IEEE Communications, vol. 30, no. 2, pp. 34-42, Feb. 1992.
11. A. Gammelgaard and J.E. Kristensen, Interaction detection, A logical approach, [3], pp. 178-196.
12. D. Garlan and M. Shaw, An introduction to software architecture, V. Ambriola and G. Tortora, eds., Advances in Software Eng. and Knowledge Eng., pp. 1-39. World Scientific,

1993.

13. J.J. Garrahan, P.A. Russo, K. Kitami, and R. Kung, Intelligent Network overview, *IEEE Communications*, vol. 31, no. 3, pp. 30-36, Mar. 1993.

14. N.D. Griffeth and Y.-J. Lin, Extending telecommunications systems: The feature-interaction problem, *Computer*, vol. 26, no. 8, pp. 14-18, Aug. 1993.

15. N.D. Griffeth and H. Velthuijsen, The negotiating agents approach to runtime feature interaction resolution, [3], pp. 217-235.

16. G.J. Holzmann, Design and validation of protocols: A tutorial, *Computer Networks and ISDN Systems*, vol. 25, pp. 981-1,017, 1993.

17. F.J. Lin and Y.-J. Lin, A building block approach to detecting and resolving feature interactions, [3], pp. 86-119.

18. J. Kamoun, Formal Specification and Feature Interaction Detection in the Intelligent Network, Dept. of Computer Science, Univ. of Ottawa, Ontario, 1996.

19. T. Ohta and Y. Harada, Classification, detection and resolution of service interactions in telecommunication services, [3], pp. 60-72.

20. S. Tsang and E.H. Magill, Behavior based run-time feature interaction detection and resolution approaches for Intelligent Networks, [9], pp. 254-270.

21. H. Velthuijsen, Issues of non-monotonicity in feature-interaction detection, [7], pp. 31-42.

22. M. Weiss, T. Gray, and A. Diaz, Experiences with a service environment for distributed multimedia applications, [9], pp. 242-253.

23. J. Woodcock and J. Davies, *Using Z: Specification, Refinement and Proof.* Prentice Hall Int'l, 1996.

24. P. Zave, Feature interactions and formal specifications in telecommunications, *Computer*, vol. 26, no. 8, pp. 20-30, Aug. 1993.

25. P. Zave and M. Jackson, The DFC Virtual Architecture: Scenarios for Use and Plans for Future Work, AT&T Research Technical Memorandum HA6164000-971202-18TM, Murray Hill, N.J., Dec. 1997.

26. I. Zibman, C. Woolf, P. O'Reilly, L. Strickland, D. Willis, and J. Visser, Minimizing feature interactions: An architecture and processing model approach, [7], pp. 65-83.

Appendix A—Relation Symbols

Appendix A explains the relation symbols used in this paper. A, B, and C are sets of any elements; R and S are relations.

Relation Symbols	Definition
$A \leftrightarrow B$	The general relation, consisting of any set of pairs (Ai, Bj).
$A \rightarrow B$	A total function. Each element Ai of A occurs in exactly one pair (Ai,Bj).
$A \nrightarrow B$	A partial function. Each element Ai of A occurs in at most one pair (Ai, Bj).
$A \twoheadrightarrow B$	A total surjection. Each element Ai of A occurs in exactly one pair (Ai, Bj). Each element Bj of B occurs in at least one pair (Ai, Bj).
$A \rightarrowtail B$	A total injection. Each element Ai of A occurs in exactly one pair (Ai, Bj). Each element Bj of B occurs in at most one pair (Ai, Bj).
ran R	The range of R. If R consists of pairs (Ai, Bj), **ran** R is the set of Bj occurring in R.
dom R	The domain of R. If R consists of pairs (Ai, Bj), **dom** R is the set of Ai occurring in R.
R~	The inverse of R. If R consists of pairs (Ai, Bj), R~ is the set of pairs (Bj, Ai) such that (Ai, Bj) is in R.
C ◁ R	R domain-restricted to C. If R consists of pairs (Ai, Bj), C ◁ R is the set of pairs (Ai, Bj) occurring in R such that Ai is in C.
R ▷ C	R range-restricted to C. If R consists of pairs (Ai, Bj), R ▷ C is the set of pairs (Ai, Bj) occurring in R such that Bj is in C.
R (|C|)	The relational image of C under R. If R consists of pairs (Ai, Bj), R (|C|) is the set of elements Bj such that at for least one Ai (Ai, Bj) occurs in R and Ai is in C.
R ; S	The relational composition of R and S. If R consists of pairs (Ai, Bj) and S consists of pairs (Bk, Cn), R ; S consists of the pairs (Ai, Cn) such that for at least one Bj (Ai, Bj) is in R and (Bj, Cn) is in S.

Chapter 12

Modularity in Distributed Feature Composition

Pamela Zave

Abstract: Distributed Feature Composition (DFC) is a modular architecture for building telecommunication services. It has been implemented and used to build two industrial-scale voice-over-IP services, as well as many smaller prototype and demonstration services. With all this experience it is possible to assess how and how well DFC modularity works.

1. Introduction

Distributed Feature Composition (DFC) is a modular architecture for building telecommunication services. Michael Jackson and I got the idea for DFC in an "aha!" moment in December 1996. We spent 1997 and 1998 working out the details, and published the original paper on DFC in 1998 [8]. In 1999 a team[1] began working with us to implement DFC. Since then this team, with new additions[2] and occasionally other AT&T colleagues, has worked continuously on DFC-based technology and applications.

Historically, DFC bridges the Public Switched Telephone Network (PSTN) and the Internet. When we invented DFC, Michael and I had been studying the software problems of the PSTN for some time, and we had no other context in mind. Nevertheless, by the time DFC was ready to implement, voice-over-Internet-Protocol (VoIP) was the new technology that researchers wanted to work with. DFC proved to be equally applicable to VoIP, and all of the implementations of DFC have been Internet-based.

The focus of this paper is modularity in DFC, which is an adaptation of the pipes-and-filters architectural style to telecommunication applications. This

---

[1] Gregory W. Bond, Eric Cheung, K. Hal Purdy, and J. Christopher Ramming.
[2] Thomas M. Smith and Venkita Subramonian.

kind of modularity is much less familiar than other kinds of modularity such as object-oriented programming, so the primary purpose of this paper is to explain where, why, and how it works. After 13 years, there is an abundance of experience to draw upon.

DFC was designed to support modular development of *features*; Section 2 explains the significance of this motivation and its history in telecommunications. Section 3 is an overview of pipes-and-filters modularity as realized in DFC.

The benefit of feature modularity comes with the burden of managing interactions among features. This burden is also an opportunity, because each principle for identifying or managing interactions captures important domain knowledge about the organization of features. Section 4 introduces the major categories of feature interaction and how they are managed.

Subsequent sections are based on our experience with implementation of DFC and deployment of services built on our platforms. They evaluate its form of modularity and speculate on its future.

Most of the service examples in this paper come from old-fashioned telephony, because these are simple and easy to discuss. DFC is equally useful, however, for the richer services being built or envisioned today. Contemporary telecommunication services differ from telephony (including mobile telephony) in three ways:

+ Rather than being limited to voice (low-fidelity audio), they also support media such as music (high-fidelity audio) and video. Text, images, and other data can also be treated as media. For example, email fits easily into the DFC architecture, as do home networks.
+ Telecommunication services used to be limited to and by "black" phones, with their very restricted user interface. Now personal computers with Web browsers are common, as are handheld devices with touch-sensitive screens. These devices make it possible for users to interact conveniently with much more elaborate and data-oriented services.
+ Not all telecommunication systems are stand-alone applications. They can also be embedded in applications for multiplayer games, distance learning, collaborative television, networked music performance, and other forms of computer-supported cooperative work and play.

In reviewing the original paper for this volume, I am happy to see how much cleaner DFC has become over time. Since 1997 there have been generalizations for mobile and virtual addresses, for multi-media calls, and for features that reverse caller/callee roles. Numerous complications have been removed from the architecture, as they have been found unnecessary or subsumed by more general improvements. Nevertheless, the DFC concepts today are still very close to our original ideas.

2. Feature-oriented description

DFC was designed to provide feature modularity and to manage the feature-interaction problem, so an explanation of DFC must begin with features.

The behavior of telecommunication software is almost always described in terms of *features*. A *feature* is an optional or incremental unit of functionality. A *feature-oriented description* consists of a base description with additional, optional feature modules.

For example, a traditional informal explanation of telephone service begins with Plain Old Telephone Service (POTS), which has as its primary states idle, dialing, busy, ringing, and talking. This is a base description. The explanation then presents separately a set of features such as Speed Dialing, Call Waiting, and Call Forwarding. Each feature is presented as an addition or exception to POTS, without mentioning or relying on other features.

The modification of POTS by features began in the 1960s, when telephone switches became software-controlled. By the mid-1980s large telephone switches had thousands of features, each described in an informal requirements document. Because there was no feature-oriented programming technique, all of the features had to be implemented in the same piece of software. The size and complexity of this software was making it extremely difficult to add new features and to maintain software reliability.

A *feature interaction* is some way in which a feature or features modify or influence another feature in describing or generating the system's overall behavior. Feature interactions are inevitable in any nontrivial feature-oriented description. The modular nature of the description tends to make interactions (at best) implicit or (at worst) obscure.

For the large telephone switches of the 1980s and later, feature interactions were perceived as a huge problem. It took tremendous skill to predict the interactions implied by multitudes of informal feature descriptions, and arduous labor to specify the desired behavior in all cases. In the implementation, which was not decomposable along feature boundaries, feature interactions were a major source of complexity and software defects.

The primary goal for the design of DFC was to find a feature-oriented way to program telecommunication systems, so that features could be implemented independently and yet composed to produce overall system behavior. We also needed a way to predict potential feature interactions, enable the desired ones, and prevent the undesired ones.

3. Pipes-and-filters modularity

3.1. The signaling protocol

Basic telecommunication service is built into the DFC architecture. Each user device is represented by a persistent software module called an interface box, which has a network address and the ability to translate signals between the DFC protocol and the native protocol of the device.

When one interface box calls another, the DFC protocol forms a connection between them. This connection supports a single two-way, FIFO signaling

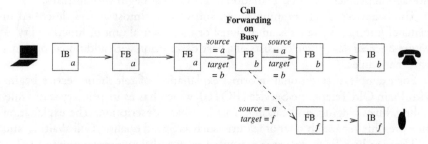

Figure 1: Example of a usage, with interface boxes (IB) and feature boxes (FB). Internal calls are represented by arrows to show the direction in which they are set up.

channel and any number of media channels.

When there are applicable features, telecommunication service is provided by a graph called a *usage*, as shown in Figure 1. The nodes of a usage include *feature boxes* as well as interface boxes. Each feature box is a concurrent software process that implements a separate feature.

The edges of a usage are *internal calls*, each of which is a connection made with the DFC protocol. This means that each feature box is a signaling and media endpoint for the internal calls that it participates in. The term *internal call* is used to distinguish an edge in the graph from the informal, end-to-end meaning of "call" in telecommunications.

In the DFC protocol, an internal call begins when one box sends a *setup* signal to another box. The box acknowledges it by sending an *upack* signal back, thus establishing the connection and its signaling channel. Subsequently the signaling channel can be used to open and close media channels. It can also be used for commands and status signals involved in feature control.

Each setup signal carries a source address and a target address. In simple cases these are the addresses of the interface boxes on the two ends of the usage. However, as we shall see, many features manipulate these addresses.

The two most important status signals are *avail* and *unavail*. The *avail* signal travels from the callee or receiving end of the call to the caller or placing end. It indicates that the entity identified by the target address is available for communication. Its dual is *unavail*, which indicates that the targeted entity is not available. Either box participating in a call can tear it down at any time by sending a *teardown* signal, acknowledged by a *downack*.

A well-designed DFC feature box has the properties of *transparency*, *autonomy*, and *context-independence*. *Transparency* means that when its feature is not active, it is unobservable by other boxes in the graph. It is acting as an identity element, merely relaying signals from one port to another. *Autonomy* means that when it needs to perform some function, it does so without help from other boxes. A DFC feature box can act autonomously because it sits in a signaling path between user devices, where it can observe all the signals that travel between them. Because it is a protocol endpoint, it can absorb or generate any signals that it needs to. *Context-*

independence means that it does not rely on the presence of other features, or contain any knowledge of them. A DFC feature box does not know what is at the other end of the internal calls it is participating in.

These properties are illustrated in a simple way by Call Forwarding on Busy (CFB), which is one of the types of feature box shown in Figure 1. Initially the box behaves transparently, receiving an incoming internal call, and continuing the chain by placing an outgoing internal call with the same setup information. If it receives *avail* from downstream (its outgoing call), then its function is not necessary, and it stays transparent during its entire lifetime. The usage containing this box (the graph connected by solid arrows in Figure 1) persists while the parties are communicating. When they are no longer communicating and the usage is no longer needed, a *teardown* from either end propagates through the usage, destroying internal calls and terminating box programs as it travels.

If the device interface box with address *b* receives a setup signal when the device is already busy, it will generate the status signal *unavail*. If a CFB box receives *unavail* instead of *avail* from downstream, it takes autonomous action. It tears down its old outgoing call, so that the subgraph between CFB and IB(*b*) disappears. It places a new outgoing call with a setup signal containing the forwarding address *f* as its target. This creates the dashed subgraph extending to IB(*f*).

The CFB box is context-independent because the unavail signal that triggers it might have been generated by the user device, or by any feature box between CFB and the device. This point will be illustrated further in Section 4.1.

3.2. The routing algorithm

In Shaw and Garlan's characterization of a pipes-and-filters architecture [11], the graph of pipes (internal calls) and filters (boxes) is pre-configured and static. DFC is more complex because each usage is assembled dynamically and evolves over time.

The mechanism for assembling usages is the *DFC routing algorithm*, executed by a *DFC router*. A DFC router has a different purpose from IP routers. The purpose of an IP router is to find the destination of a message, while the purpose of a DFC router is to insert feature boxes in the path of a setup signal (message).

Each time a box sends a setup signal, that signal goes to a DFC router that chooses a box to receive it, and forwards the *setup* to the receiving box. Then the receiving box sends an upack signal directly to the sending box, and a direct connection is formed between them.

Every continuous routing chain from one interface box to another contains a *source region* and a *target region*. The source region comes first; it contains feature boxes working on behalf of the source address in its role as caller. The target region contains feature boxes working on behalf of the target address in its role as callee. Each address *subscribes* to some (possibly empty) set of feature box types in each region. In the "solid line" subgraph of Figure 1, there are two feature boxes in the source region subscribed to by address *a*, and two feature boxes in the target region (including CFB) subscribed to by address b.

If the CFB box is triggered to take action, its second outgoing call is routed to a box on behalf of the *forwarding address f*, which is the target address in the new setup signal. No additional boxes are routed to on behalf of the original target address b. The same thing can happen in the source region, if a box changes the source address when placing a call that continues the chain. Because of this mechanism of *address translation*, a routing chain can have multiple *source zones* in its source region, and multiple *target zones* in its target region. Each zone contains the feature boxes added to the chain on behalf of a particular address.

Within a zone, the routing algorithm orders the feature boxes by *precedence*. The source and target *precedence relations* are partial orders on feature box types.

Feature box types fall into two categories: *free* and *bound*. When a DFC router is working on a setup signal and selects a free box type as its destination, the router creates a new feature box (program object) as an instance of its type. Thus each free feature box is a transient, anonymous instantiation of its type.

Bound feature boxes are completely different. For each address subscribing to a bound feature box type (in either region), there is a single, persistent instance of that box type. When a router is working on a setup signal and selects a bound box type as its destination, the *setup* goes to the bound box identified with the address on whose behalf it is required. The use and significance of bound boxes are illustrated in Section 4.2.

A simple routing chain from interface box to interface box begins when the calling interface box creates a setup signal with the *new* method and sends it to a DFC router. To continue the chain, a feature box takes a setup signal it has received and applies the *continue* method to it. The *continue* method returns a suitable setup signal, which the box then sends to a DFC router. The continue method gives the box the option to change (translate) the source or target address of the setup. For example, a CFB box may invoke continue twice. The first time there is no address translation, so both addresses of its first outgoing call are the same as the addresses of its incoming call. The second time it exercises its option to change the target address to f.

Like signaling in DFC, routing in DFC supports transparency, autonomy, and context-independence. By using the continue method and no address translation, a feature box can continue a routing chain transparently. A feature box has some autonomy because it can affect routing by address translation or its choice of routing method. (Further uses of the *new* method are discussed in Section 4.4, and there is a third method *reverse* not covered here.) A feature box has context-independence because it never uses or sees the names of other feature box types.

Usage-dependent routing history is carried in setup signals and manipulated by routing methods and DFC routers only. It can be encrypted to enforce the context-independence of feature boxes. DFC routers need subscription and precedence data, but are stateless with respect to individual usages.

3.3 Other

Media and media control are discussed briefly in Section 4.4. The only other aspect of the DFC architecture is *operational data*, which is persistent data used by features. For example, the CFB box gets its forwarding address by retrieving it from operational data. Boxes can write operational data as well as read it. Operational data is usually partitioned by address and feature, so that a box can only access data belonging to its subscriber and feature.

As a result of transparency, autonomy, and context-independence, DFC features can be programmed independently. A particular feature can be present or absent in a usage without requiring changes in other features. Similarly, features can be added to or removed from the system without changing other features. These characteristics are the essence of modularity in DFC.

4. Management of feature interactions

DFC features are supposed to interact through the specified mechanisms of the architecture, and in no other way. By constraining how features can interact, the architecture makes it possible to identify and manage feature interactions in an organized fashion.

Once a class of feature interaction is identified, it is necessary to decide which members of the class are desirable or undesirable. Domain knowledge and experience are the best guides during this task.

Once the potential interactions in a feature set are predicted and evaluated, it is necessary to make adjustments to enable the good ones and prevent the bad ones. The preferred mechanism for managing feature interactions is to make adjustments in the precedence relations.

To illustrate this process, the following subsections introduce the five major classes of feature interaction in DFC. Each subsection attempts to provide a little insight into the nature of the interactions. The subsections also provide some additional explanation of DFC.

4.1. Activation interactions

It is possible for one feature to activate a function of another feature, or to ensure that it will not be activated. Four features illustrate some of that ways that this can happen: Call Blocking, Record Voice Mail, Quiet Time, and Parallel Ringing. All of these features are subscribed to in the target region.

First, I will describe briefly what these features do and how they interact, assuming that they are ordered by precedence as listed above and shown in Figure 2. Then I will show how this precedence relation could be derived from the features themselves.

An instance of Call Blocking (CB) receives a setup signal targeted to its subscriber, and checks whether the source address is on the subscriber's blocking list. If so, it sends unavail upstream, because this subscriber is not available to this caller. CB does not continue the routing chain, but rather tears down its incoming

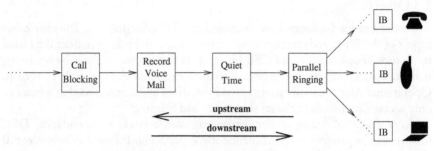

Figure 2: Four features in the target zone of a subscriber.

call and terminates.[3]

If CB does not block its incoming call, then it continues the routing chain transparently by placing an outgoing call. Its behavior is transparent from that point on.

Next in the chain is Record Voice Mail (RVM). RVM is initially transparent, merely placing an outgoing call.

Next in the chain is Quiet Time (QT). If QT is currently disabled by the subscriber, it is transparent and merely places an outgoing call to continue the chain. If it is currently enabled, on receiving a setup signal, it employs a media resource (see Section 4.4) to initiate an interactive voice-response (IVR) dialog with the caller. The media resource (IVR server) announces that the subscriber wishes to be undisturbed, and prompts to ask the caller if the call is urgent. If the call is not urgent, then QT sends *unavail* upstream and terminates, because the subscriber is not available for casual calls. If the call is urgent, then QT places an outgoing call and is transparent from that point on.

If QT sends *unavail* upstream, this signal reaches RVM and triggers it. RVM employs an IVR server to prompt for and record a voice message from the caller to the subscriber. Before doing this, RVM sends an avail signal upstream. Thus RVM has the effect of turning failure (*unavail*) to success (*avail*). From a philosophical viewpoint, this means that recording voice mail is considered to be (almost) as good as talking to a person. From a practical viewpoint, sending *avail* prevents features upstream from behaving as if the call is still ringing and unanswered.

Whether QT is disabled or the user's need is urgent, if QT places an outgoing call, that call is routed to Parallel Ringing (PR). PR places concurrent outgoing calls to a list of addresses supplied by the subscriber, for example the addresses of the subscriber's mobile phone, home phone, and work phone. This is the last box in the target zone of the subscriber, because each outgoing call has a different target address.

---

[3] Because the signaling channel is FIFO, *unavail* will arrive before *teardown*, so that boxes upstream will know why the call is being torn down. Most unavail signals are followed immediately by *teardown*.

Note that an interface box to a phone or similar user device will send an avail signal upstream when the user answers the phone. If PR receives an avail signal from one of its downstream branches, it tears down the other branches and forwards the avail signal upstream. If it receives *unavail* from all branches or times out, it tears down all the branches, sends *unavail* upstream, and terminates. The unavail signal will pass transparently through QT and will trigger RVM to record a message, just as if the usage reached a phone and the phone was busy.

This completes the brief description of the four features. Note that each feature is described strictly in terms of its own concerns. Its function and observable effects make perfect sense if it is the only feature that the target address subscribes to.

The "activation" class of interaction among these features is based on the following feature properties, which are easy to extract from feature programs in the form of finite-state machines [12]:

+ If a feature receives an incoming call and does not place an outgoing call, it *cancels* all features with later precedence, because they will not even appear in the usage for this subscriber.
+ Some functions of some features *are triggered* by receiving *avail* or *unavail* from downstream. For example, *avail* triggers PR to tear down other branches, and *unavail* triggers RVM to record.
+ Some of these features generate unavail signals upstream (CB, QT, PR) and one *generates* an avail signal upstream after receiving an unavail signal from downstream (RVM).

By evaluating the potential interactions caused by canceling, triggering, and generating, we come to the following conclusions:

+ CB should be first. If it blocks, it cancels all subsequent features, which is desirable. If it blocks it generates *unavail*; it would be undesirable for that signal to trigger RVM, which would happen if RVM preceded CB.
+ RVM should precede both Both QT and PR. Both of the latter generate *unavail* and it is desirable for these signals to trigger RVM, which can only happen if RVM is upstream of them.
+ QT should precede PR. If QT is enabled and the call is not urgent, no phones should ring. So it is desirable for QT to cancel PR in this case.

This reasoning provides a total precedence order on the four features that enables all desirable activation interactions and prevents all undesirable ones. The same kind of analysis can be applied to other shared signals.

It is important to note that this is one of many possible examples of target-zone feature sets. The functions of these features could be bundled into features differently. Changes in feature purpose and bundling of functions could result in different decisions about how the features should interact. With very little extra programming, it is possible to generate a wide range of possible and desirable behaviors.

4.2. Multi-party interactions

A free feature box has exactly one incoming call; it cannot have more than one because each incoming call is routed to a fresh instance of the box type. In contrast, if an address subscribes to a bound feature box type, then *all* calls routed to that feature for that address go to the same box. Thus bound boxes make it possible for two separate usages to join into one usage graph.

Bound boxes usually implement multi-party features, such as Call Waiting (CW). A subscriber usually subscribes to CW in both source and target regions, because its function is desired whether the subscriber's phone is busy in a caller role or busy in a callee role.

CW is initially transparent. Its function is triggered when it receives an incoming call for the subscriber when CW is already supporting (transparently) a connection between the subscriber and some far party. At this time it sends an *alerting* signal to the new call as if the subscriber's phone were ringing, and sends a signal to the subscriber that a call is waiting. On the subscriber's command, it will switch the subscriber back and forth between talking to the old party and talking to the new party. If CW receives another incoming call while it already has one call waiting, it will refuse it by generating *unavail* and then *teardown*.

Another multi-party feature much appreciated by our users is Mid-Call Move (MCM). MCM allows a subscriber to move from one device to another during a conversation. For example, a subscriber can be talking on a home phone, realize that it is time to leave the house, and move the call to a mobile phone without interrupting the conversation. On receiving a command from the user, MCM places an outgoing internal call to the new device. When the new device rings, the subscriber answers it and hangs up the other phone. Like CW, a subscriber usually subscribes to MCM in both regions, so that he can use the feature regardless of who initiated the conversation.

A typical multi-party interaction is illustrated by Figure 3. The device with address *a* subscribes to both CW and MCM in both regions. In the left usage, MCM precedes CW in the source region and succeeds it in the target region, so MCM is always closer to the device than CW. If the subscriber triggers MCM when CW has a call waiting, both calls to far parties are carried along to the new connection with the phone having address *b*.

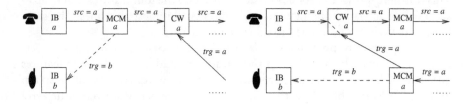

Figure 3: Two compositions of Call Waiting and Mid-Call Move.

In the right usage of Figure 3, the precedence orderings of CW and MCM have been reversed in both regions. Note that MCM is implemented by free boxes, because the function of MCM does not require joins. This is why we see two instances of MCM, both on behalf of a.

The right usage is troublesome when both features are active. The typical default behavior of a feature is to forward unrecognized signals transparently, so that it does not interfere unnecessarily with the functions of other features or devices. If CW forwards unrecognized signals from the subscriber to the far party currently selected, as shown by the dashed line in CW, then a move command goes only to the lower instance of MCM. After the subscriber hangs up phone a and MCM tears down its call to a, the waiting call will be lost. If CW forwards unrecognized signals from the subscriber to both far parties, then a move command goes to both instances of MCM. The resulting behavior (as both MCM boxes try to connect to b) will be time-dependent and probably undesirable.

DFC modularity is especially valuable when it comes to multi-party features. In Figure 3, each of the CW and MCM boxes controls at most three internal calls, which is not difficult to program. If we added Three-Way Calling (TWC) to the feature set, CW and MCM boxes would remain the same, and each TWC box would also control three internal calls.

If these features were programmed monolithically, however, the implementation of CW and MCM would have to control four internal calls simultaneously, and with TWC active there could be six. The complexity of a monolithic program rises very rapidly with the number of simultaneous calls to be controlled. This programming problem is particularly acute when multi-party features are added incrementally.

Multi-party features introduce other issues as well. Here are three in addition to the previously mentioned question of replicating or selectively forwarding signals to multiple far parties:

◆ An internal call linking a feature box to its subscriber may have to multiplex signals from multiple far parties.
◆ Signaling paths between devices may contain irregular patterns. For example, on the left side of Figure 3, the path between device b and the lower far party has two outgoing internal calls joined at MCM, and two incoming internal calls joined at CW.
◆ Different devices may have different user interfaces. A feature box may interact with multiple or changing devices, and therefore have multiple or changing user interfaces.

Modularity in DFC draws attention to these issues, and they can be handled in DFC with relative ease [17]. Without the kind of help DFC offers, such issues are often overlooked or mishandled.

4.3. Interactions caused by address translation

When a feature box in the target region of an address $t1$ uses the option in the continue routing method to change the target address to $t2$, it has an important effect on assembly of the usage. There will be no subsequent boxes on behalf of $t1$, even if some of $t1$'s features have not been included yet. Instead, there will be boxes on behalf of $t2$. The same thing happens when a box in the source region translates the source address.

Address translation is a powerful mechanism. It performs many functions and solves many problems. It can also cause problems, in the form of interactions between features of different zones in the same region. Precedence does not help to manage these interactions, because the relative order of zones in a region is determined strictly by address translation. Precedence can only affect the order of features within a zone.

A feature interaction in this category occurs when a user with address p has Parallel Ringing (PR) as described in Section 4.1, configured to ring several devices including his mobile phone at address d. At the same time, the user's mobile phone has Unconditional Call Forwarding (UCF), which he sets to forward all calls to the address p that subscribes to PR. Since UCF and PR are both implemented by free feature boxes, the initial *setup* for a call to one of these two addresses (d or p) will create a usage in which a new instance of $PR(p)$ translates the target address to d, creating a new instance of $UCF(d)$ that translates the target address to p, creating a new instance of $PR(p)$ that translates the target address to d, and so on until the system runs out of resources. However strange it might seem, many users will do this if given the chance.

The best general approach to managing address translation begins with a recognition of what each address represents [13]. In the example above, p represents a *person* and d represents one of the telecommunication *devices* that the person uses. Other common kinds of address represent *groups* of people, *roles* that a person plays, or *organizations*.

This recognition is useful all by itself because it emphasizes that an address should subscribe to the features that work on behalf of the entity that the address represents. For example, an address representing a person might subscribe in the source region to a feature that allows the person to translate the source address to an address representing his role as an employee. If the employee exercises this option, his outgoing call would be routed through a source feature that charges the call to his employer.

After categorizing addresses, it is next necessary to impose a partial order on

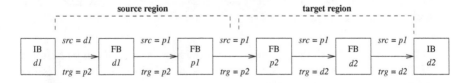

Figure 4: *Proper address translation with device addresses d1, d2 and personal addresses p1, p2. Each zone has one feature box.*

the categories. This order is based on "abstractness" vs. "concreteness" of the thing represented *as a network endpoint*. For example, a device is very concrete, being literally a network endpoint. From this perspective a person is more abstract, being reachable from many network endpoints, and a group of people is more abstract still.

There are three principles, all based on the abstraction hierarchy of addresses, for organizing address translation [13]. The first principle is that source-region features should only translate source addresses to addresses more abstract than their own, and target-region features should only translate target addresses to addresses more concrete than their own. This principle creates the pattern illustrated by Figure 4. It prevents the bad feature interaction above (between UCF and PR) because UCF cannot translate *d* to *p*.

The second principle is symmetry between the source and target regions, which is often required for correct behavior. For example, one of the bad email feature interactions identified by Hall [7] occurs when *user2@host2* is maintaining anonymity in an email conversation with *user1@host1*. User2 is known to *user1* as *anon2@remailer*; email to this address goes through an anonymous remailer, which forwards it to *user2@host2* while retaining the original source address.

The trouble arises when *user2* goes on vacation. On receiving email, his vacation program automatically replies with "vacation" email, reversing the source and target addresses. Thus *user1@host1* receives email directly from *user2@host2*, whose identity is now revealed.

This problem is due to the lack of a source-region feature box to balance the remailer, which is a target-region feature box. A solution is shown in Figure 5. In this figure the mail hosts are interface boxes, and the vacation program is part of the mail host for *user2@host2*. This address subscribes to Anonymize Source (AS) in the source region. AS has in its operational data the correspondents to whom *user2* wishes to be anonymous. When it receives email for one of these correspondents, it translates the source address to *anon2@remailer*.

With this symmetric solution, all the user has to do to create an anonymous conversation is to put the correspondent address in AS data before sending the first email. The rest is automatic.

For simplicity, Figure 5 is somewhat different from the way that real email

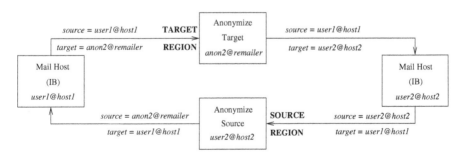

Figure 5: Symmetric feature boxes provide anonymous email.

works. [13] describes several realistic schemes based on the same underlying principle.

The third principle is that internal addresses can be produced and consumed by feature boxes for their own coordination purposes, provided that an abstraction hierarchy is preserved. This principle can be illustrated by the Answer Confirm (AC) feature.

Parallel Ringing (PR), as seen in Section 4.1 and Figure 2, has a serious vulnerability: if it tries to ring a device configured for immediate voice mail (for example, a mobile phone that is turned off), then voice mail will answer immediately, aborting PR's attempts to reach other phones that might have been answered by people. AC removes this vulnerability by reacting to *avail* from downstream. It connects the answered phone to an IVR server, plays an announcement "This is a call for . . . ," and prompts for a touch-tone acknowledgment. If the answering entity is voice mail it will fail this test, and AC will send *unavail* upstream instead of *avail*.

AC is a device feature, in the sense that some devices should have it, and all other devices should be unencumbered by it. We cannot expect device addresses to subscribe to it, however, because it acts on behalf of the personal address subscribing to PR. For a personal address p subscribing to PR and a device address d needing AC when called by PR(p), the best solution is to introduce a new address $p2d$ that PR calls instead of d. The address $p2d$ subscribes to AC. When AC receives an incoming call, it places an outgoing call to d. The address $p2d$ can be described as "internal" because it appears in the usage only between PR and AC, and in the abstraction hierarchy only between p and d.

4.4. Media-related interactions

In Section 4.1, both Record Voice Mail and Quiet Time (QT) used media resources to implement IVR dialogs with callers. To do this, a feature box places an internal call to a suitable media resource (IVR server), which has a DFC interface box just like any other device. The feature box uses the *new* routing method and an empty source address, because this call should not be routed through any of the feature boxes of the caller or callee. It will be routed through target features of the resource, if any.

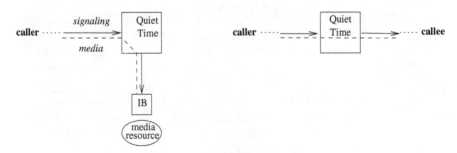

Figure 6: How Quiet Time uses a media resource.

The setup signal of the new call carries the identifier of a script that the resource should work from. The script acts as a flowchart combining announcements and prompts to be played to the caller, decisions made by the caller through touch tones, and recording sessions.

When a QT box has established an internal call to a resource, it connects the voice channel to the caller with the voice channel to the resource, so that voice flows between those endpoints in both directions, as shown in Figure 6 (left). If QT places an outgoing call, then QT tears down the call to the resource and connects the voice channel of its incoming call to the voice channel of its outgoing call (figure right).

A box programmer needs two main primitives to control media channels: a primitive to *link* two media-channel endpoints together within the box, as shown in Figure 6, and a primitive to *hold* a media endpoint within a box, which means keeping the media channel open even though there is no media flow at the moment [16]. Binary links are sufficient even for conferencing, because conferencing applications always connect all the participants individually to a *conference bridge*, as shown in Figure 7. A conference bridge is a media server that mixes all its input channels and sends the mix to all its output channels.

A typical media-related feature interaction in other architectures is as follows. Alice will participate in a conference call today, and asks the conference server to call her at her personal address when the conference begins. This address subscribes to Find Me (FM), which is like Parallel Ringing except that it tries different device addresses sequentially. Because FM can take some time to find Alice, it first plays an announcement to the caller, "Please wait while we find Alice for you."

When the conference server (playing the role of caller) receives the signals to open a voice channel for the announcement, it believes that Alice has answered the phone. It prompts for the callee to enter a conference code, times out, prompts again, and then disconnects the call. Alice misses her conference.

DFC avoids feature interactions in this class by recognizing that opening a voice channel and connecting to a person are two different things. Often the former precedes the latter, because of the use of the voice channel for signaling and control purposes. Confusion between these things is avoided by having

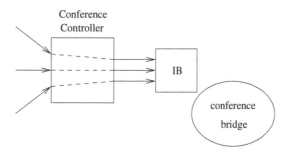

Figure 7: A Conference Controller feature box connects all the participants to a conference bridge.

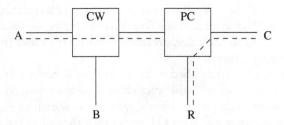

Figure 8: A media feature interaction resolved by proximity in the usage graph.

separate signals for them, with avail being the "connected to a person" signal.[4]

A second class of media feature interaction is caused by the fact that feature boxes use the voice channel for IVR dialogs independently. Consequently, there is a danger that two features in a usage might attempt to use the voice channel to the same user at the same time.

The majority of IVR dialogs are triggered when the box receives a setup signal from upstream or an outcome signal (*avail* or *unavail*) from downstream. Contention for the voice channel is easily avoided by a convention that the triggering signal is a token that confers the right to use the voice channel. If a feature box wants to use the voice channel, it must complete its IVR phase before forwarding the token signal [14].

A third class of media feature interaction is illustrated by Figure 8. A, B, and C are phones, while R is an IVR server; interface boxes are omitted. A subscribes to Call Waiting (CW), and is using it to switch between far parties B and C. The figure is a snapshot in which C is selected, so CW is connecting the voice channel to A with the voice channel to C.[5]

At the same time, C called A with the help of a prepaid card. The account on the card is exhausted, so the Prepaid Card (PC) feature box has interrupted C's voice connection to the far party, put the far party on hold, and is connecting C to an IVR server through which C can authorize payment. This is a feature interaction because, from the viewpoint of CW, A is talking to a far party. It is only because of the presence of PC that A is on hold.

In DFC the management of this feature interaction is automatic and obvious from the figure: PC has priority over CW in controlling the voice channel to C because PC is closer to C in the usage graph than CW is. CW only has the power to connect A to B, or to leave A on hold in the PC box. Note that these feature interactions cannot be resolved by the token convention because they occur after the last token signal (*avail*) has been sent by one device and received by another.

A fourth class of media feature interaction concerns different media channels

---

[4] Being connected to a voice mail recorder is an adequate substitute for a person in most cases (Section 4.1), but is not adequate in the presence of Parallel Ringing (Section 4.3). This is typical of the subtleties of feature interaction.

[5] More precisely, CW is connecting A to the far party reached through the call on its right, as opposed to the far party reached through the call on its bottom.

of the same call. Bandwidth limitations could constrain the number and type of media channels that can be used simultaneously. There is not enough experience with multimedia features to discuss this issue yet.

4.5. Data interactions

Subscription data need not be static. A user could turn a feature off and on by unsubscribing and subscribing, respectively, though a Web interface. The time of day could also be used to alter subscriptions automatically.

To prevent feature interaction through operational data, this data is usually partitioned by subscriber address and feature, so only one feature box type on behalf of one subscriber can access a particular datum.

It is also possible to partition data less strictly, for example by subscriber address only. A subscriber's address book could safely be accessed by all the feature boxes of that subscriber. One feature might even add an entry, which another feature ultimately uses. This is a very indirect and benign feature interaction.

The partitioning constraint is also softened by the fact that, as an increment of functionality, a feature is sometimes implemented by more than one box type. For example, Anonymize Target and Anonymize Source in Section 4.3 are both required for anonymous email.

The current trend is toward *converged* services that have both telecommunication and Web aspects. Web services are naturally data-intensive, and provide the most convenient and popular user interface to data. For example, all the services we have built have Web user interfaces to DFC subscription and operational data.

We plan to investigate converged services, data modularity, and data feature interactions as aspects of a single research topic. This makes more sense than treating DFC operational data differently from Web-services data, especially in a converged environment.

5. Brief notes on implementation

Although this paper is not much focused on implementation, it makes sense to say a little about how DFC is now implemented. These notes will make some comparisons and evaluations more intelligible.

SIP [10] is the dominant signaling protocol for IP multimedia services. Because telecommunication devices and other network elements use SIP, DFC implementations must interoperate with SIP.

DFC is independent of system architecture, because the feature boxes of a DFC usage can be located anywhere. If two adjacent boxes are on the same host, then the signaling channel of the DFC internal call between them will be implemented with software queues. If two adjacent boxes are on different hosts, then the signaling channel between them will be implemented with a network connection.

Consequently, one possible implementation architecture is to implement all the feature boxes subscribed to by a device address in the software of the device itself [3]. But there are many situations in which this architecture is undesirable or impractical, so that device feature boxes must be implemented in network servers called *application servers*. Even if all devices implement their own features, there are many abstract addresses whose features must be implemented in application servers because there is nowhere else to put them. So most usages will be distributed over telecommunication devices and one or more application servers.

Our first implementation of DFC [2] ran in an application server created just for this purpose. Both subsequent implementations of DFC have run within commercial or open-source SIP application servers, to make use of their performance, reliability, and operational conveniences.

The SIP Servlets API is a standardized way of programming SIP application servers, offering "servlets" as functional modules. In our second DFC implementation (the first one on a SIP Servlet container), the entire DFC runtime environment was packaged in one servlet.

In our third and current implementation, individual servlets simulate DFC feature boxes. To implement DFC internal calls between boxes in the same SIP Servlet container, we use SIP in a stylized way that approximates the DFC protocol. We have persuaded the community that a DFC-like router is the best way to perform application composition, so that DFC routing is now enabled by all SIP Servlet containers [9], and an open-source DFC router for SIP Servlet containers is freely available.

By far the most difficult part of implementing DFC on the Internet is implementing media flow and control. DFC conceptualizes media streams as passing through feature boxes, because that is the best way to understand them and to specify what behavior is required. This point is illustrated by Figure 8. On the Internet, however, it is necessary to make a distinction between signaling channels and media channels. Signaling channels need to go through application servers; as they are low-bandwidth, this is not a problem. Media channels are high-bandwidth and should take the most direct route between media devices. It is too inefficient to route media packets through one or more application servers, which may be located far from either media device.

The result of this situation is a difficult problem of distributed control. Media flow must be implemented by instructing the media devices to send media packets directly to one another through the Internet. These instructions come from feature boxes like Call Waiting and Prepaid Card, which prescribe different media flows in their different states. These feature boxes do not know about one another. Yet the instructions received by media devices must correctly reflect the *composition* of the states of all relevant feature boxes.

Our first implementation simplified this problem by solving it in a separate, but centralized, component to which all feature boxes report their states [4]. We have since found an efficient, completely distributed solution for DFC [16], and are adapting it for use within SIP [6].

6. Experience and evaluation

6.1. Experience

Our experience with DFC began with design and implementation of several service prototypes, for demonstration and trial use within AT&T. Lessons from the most ambitious of these are captured in [17].

In 2003 were were given the opportunity to develop the advanced features for AT&T's first consumer VoIP service. For the first trial, we specified, implemented, and delivered eleven features two months from the inception of the project. This feature set included such challenging features as Parallel Ringing, Ten-Way Calling, and Mid-Call Move. We also implemented voice mail. System testing and subsequent trials revealed very few bugs in the feature server. In 2004 the service went public, winning two industry awards citing its voice quality and advanced features. By 2005 the service was supporting close to 100,000 customers [1].

This unprecedented speed and quality of development was possible because of separation of concerns. Different people could safely and independently work on different features at the same time. With the DFC architecture providing structure, overlapping tasks could also be performed in parallel. For example, once we had an informal specification of each feature, feature implementation and analysis of feature interactions could proceed at the same time. Feature interactions were managed mostly by precedence and occasionally by small feature changes.

The second major system built with DFC is the teleconferencing service now used internally by AT&T. On a typical workday, the service handles millions of minutes of calls. It was originally designed for our second implementation of DFC, and is now being re-engineered for our third implementation of DFC, with interesting differences between them. As with the consumer VoIP service, there have been very few post-deployment bugs in the feature code [5].

6.2. Failures of modularity

As anyone with software experience will expect, DFC modularity is not perfect. The independence of features is not always as complete as the overview of Section 3 implies. As an example of a typical exception, consider a Call Log (CL) feature that writes a record of each incoming call to its subscriber's operational data. The record should show if the caller talked to the subscriber, recorded a voice message, or neither.

CL must precede Record Voice Mail (RVM) in the subscriber's target zone, because once RVM receives *unavail* from downstream it tears down its downstream call (if not torn down already) and downstream boxes disappear. However, the *avail* and subsequent teardown signals sent upstream by RVM do not tell CL whether the caller left a message or not. The only way to provide the desired interaction between CL and RVM is for RVM to send a special-purpose signal or signal field to CL indicating whether it recorded a message. In this case interaction between these two features must be programmed explicitly into both features.

This example illustrates the problem of status signals, which is the one part of DFC that does not feel "settled." Built-in status signals such as *avail* and *unavail* provide a common language for communication among features. They support modularity because a feature can react to such a signal without knowing whether it came from a user or another feature. More status signals means more modularity. For example, if "message recorded" were part of the built-in signal vocabulary, then CL and RVM would be independent. On the other hand, the more built-in signals there are, the more work it is to program each feature, and the harder it becomes to give each signal a feature-independent meaning.

Arguably the worst failure of DFC modularity concerns treatments (call forwarding, call queueing, interrupt, voice mail) for failure (busy, no answer) when there are multiple zones within a target region. From Section 4.3, we assume that the zones of more abstract addresses precede the zones of more concrete addresses. Becuse failure signals travel upstream, the most concrete features receive them and act upon them first. Abstract features receive failure signals only when concrete features cannot fix the failures.

Failure treatments, and the situations in which failures arise, are a big subject. Suffice it to say that sometimes the most abstract feature should be triggered first. This behavior can be achieved in various ways (Answer Confirm, shorter timeouts in the more abstract features, explicit cooperation among features at different levels of abstraction), but all of them can be seen as subverting the native mechanisms of the architecture.

Finally, a designer should be able to use any legacy component (with a suitable purpose and interfaces) as a feature box program. This is not always possible, because an unfortunate grouping of functions may include functions with different natural places in the precedence order. The result is that the precedence relation becomes over-constrained, i.e., cyclic. The easy fix is to separate the feature implementation into two box programs.

6.3. Modularity successes

Despite occasional exceptions, DFC modularity has proven to be very successful. All of the experience related in Section 6.1 indicates that it is intuitive and effective from an engineering viewpoint. It supports fast development and quality code.

For evidence of a different kind, consider Hall's study of feature interactions in 10 common email features [7]. Of the 26 undesirable interactions identified by Hall, 14 have something to do with address representation, address translation, or feature application. All 14 of these are diagnosed by, and could be prevented by, the DFC techniques for managing feature interactions caused by address translation [13].

The original purpose of DFC modularity was to support easy development of features as additions or exceptions to a basic telecommunication service. In keeping with common practice, customers could subscribe to features individually, making each one optional. An interesting lesson learned from all our experience is that

DFC seems to provide "all-purpose" modularity: it works fairly well regardless of what functions are being decomposed into modules, or why the decomposition is desired. In addition to the expected purpose, we have so far identified many other (possibly overlapping) purposes served by DFC modularity.

First, a feature can be an addition or exception, not to the basic service, but to another feature. This is illustrated perfectly by the addition of Answer Confirm to solve a problem with Parallel Ringing.

Second, as with other forms of modularity, DFC modularity can insulate a system from the effects of probable change. In our teleconferencing service, we prototyped features that we ended up dropping, because their value was not sufficient to justify their user complexity and resource costs. Because they were optional modules, they were trivial to remove. We also used feature boxes to encapsulate uncertainty concerning which vendor's media resources would be used. The content of these boxes most closely resembles a software library [5].

Third, many box programs are re-usable modules. For example, consider a Call Forwarding on Failure program with two parameters: a forwarding address and a type of failure (because unavail signals can have failure types attached). This program can be used to implement a variety of features, including RVM (on any failure, forward to voice mail resource) and Redirect on No Answer. In both deployed services, we re-used several box programs from earlier prototypes.

Fourth, a feature box can easily be inserted into a usage as an adaptor. Adaptors can enhance the re-usability of other box programs [5]. DFC feature boxes used as adaptors are extremely valuable for solving problems in other technologies, because they are powerful and quick to deploy. Integration testing of the consumer VoIP service revealed many integration problems, due to immature vendor-supplied components, inadequate standardization, and innate deficiencies in other technologies such as SIP [1]. We were able to fix many of these problems immediately by building software adaptors. Having such adaptors as separate modules is advantageous because they can be removed easily from the software when technologies and standardization improve.

Finally, off-the-shelf servers or other components can be treated as feature boxes and composed with other features. When consumer VoIP migrated to a vendor-supplied voice mail server, we were able to improve its integration with other features significantly by treating it as an idiosyncratic DFC resource. A subscriber can call the server, listen to a message, enter a code, and have the voice mail server call the person who left the message. If that call from the server is routed by DFC as coming from the subscriber, then the ensuing usage contains the subscriber's source-region features such as Ten-Way Calling and Mid-Call Move. If the call from the server is not routed by DFC, the subscriber does not have his normal features available.

6.4. Analysis of feature interactions

The first step in managing feature interactions is to analyze each box program in a feature set to see if it has interaction-prone behaviors such as generating signals (Section 4.1) or translating addresses (Section 4.3). Individual box programs are small, and this should be easy to do [12].

The second step is to calculate all potential feature interactions, based on these behaviors. The third step is to classify each potential feature interaction as desirable or undesirable. The fourth step is to derive from this information, if possible, a set of precedence constraints that enables all the good interactions and prevents all the bad ones.

All steps but the third one are easily automatable, while the third one relies on human knowledge of what goals the features are intended to achieve. The real problem with this straightforward approach, however, is that it generates too many potential feature interactions for a person to pass judgment on. A practical approach must combine heuristics, partial constraints, and dependencies to prune the potential interactions. Then requirements engineers will be able to find and consider the important ones.

A typical usage in the consumer VoIP service had at least 20 different feature boxes [1]. The principles in Section 4 separate concerns well enough to make manual analysis practical for this service, but not ideal because of the scope for human error. Other real feature sets could be much larger because they could have many alternative features from which subscribers can choose. Manual analysis will not be feasible for these larger feature sets.

We have not been able to do much work yet on automated analysis of feature interactions, because of our long journey through the SIP jungle. When we emerge from it, analysis will be high on our list of priorities.

Analysis of feature interactions is an opportunity as well as a burden. The structures, properties, and principles used to manage feature interactions are a precious kind of domain knowledge in their own right. Section 4 provides numerous examples of this.

6.5. Performance

Our current implementation of DFC runs on SIP Servlet containers compliant with the new standard [9]. Both our implementation and the containers are too new to say much about performance, except that it does not seem to be a pressing problem.

In general, we expect all forms of modularity to impose overhead, and can accept that overhead if it is not excessive. Early SIP Servlet containers expected to run exactly one servlet per external call, rather than a chain with many servlets, so their descendants may implement servlets in a way that is too heavyweight for DFC modularity. If this proves true, some targeted optimization of servers will be necessary.

From the system viewpoint, a usage is a graph of devices, application servers, and network connections. In this context there is reason to believe that the DFC protocol is considerably more efficient than SIP [16]. The conclusion is drawn from analyzing message traces rather than measuring real deployments, however, so it cannot be considered definitive.

7. Conclusion

For telecommunication systems, DFC's form of modularity is a clear and proven success. Now our most pressing research problem is to understand converged applications, where the DFC architecture must interoperate with Web services, which have a very different architecture. The challenge is to compose the architectures in such a way that each view has its own appropriate form of modularity.

In practice, DFC will live on as an overlay structure imposed on SIP. In containers compliant with the new standard, SIP servlets can be programmed and invoked just like DFC feature boxes, with the sole difference being the protocol they must use. The early work on Boxtalk, a high-level programming language for DFC feature boxes [18], has now evolved into StratoSIP, a high-level programming language for SIP servlets [15]. StratoSIP restores much of the simplicity of the DFC protocol by making the right abstractions of SIP. All of these technologies are available or will be available in the future as open-source software at **echarts.org**.

It appears that there are important Internet design issues, and networked applications other than telecommunications, that could benefit from the ideas in DFC. Investigating these relationships is another compelling area of future research.

References

1. Gregory W. Bond, Eric Cheung, Healfdene H. Goguen, Karrie J. Hanson, Don Henderson, Gerald M. Karam, K. Hal Purdy, Thomas M. Smith, and Pamela Zave. Experience with component-based development of a telecommunication service. In *Proceedings of the Eighth International Symposium on Component-Based Software Engineering*, pages 298–305. Springer-Verlag LNCS 3489, May 2005.

2. Gregory W. Bond, Eric Cheung, K. Hal Purdy, Pamela Zave, and J. Christopher Ramming. An open architecture for next-generation telecommunication services. *ACM Transactions on Internet Technology*, 4(1):83–123, February 2004.

3. Eric Cheung. Implementing endpoint services using the SIP Servlet standard. In *Proceedings of the Fifth International Conference on Networking and Services*. IEEE, April 2009.

4. Eric Cheung, Michael Jackson, and Pamela Zave. Distributed media control for multimedia communications services. In *Proceedings of the 2002 IEEE International Conference on Communications: Symposium on Multimedia and VoIP—Services and Technologies*. IEEE Communications Society, 2002.

5. Eric Cheung and Thomas M. Smith. Experience with modularity in an advanced teleconferencing service deployment. In *Proceedings of the Thirty-First International Conference on Software Engineering*, IEEE Computer Society, 2009.

6. Eric Cheung and Pamela Zave. Generalized third-party call control in SIP networks. In *Proceedings of the Second International Conference on Principles, Systems and Applications of IP Telecommunications*. Springer-Verlag LNCS 5310, 2008.

7. Robert J. Hall. Feature interactions in electronic mail. In M. Calder and E. Magill, editors, *Feature Interactions in Telecommunications and Software Systems VI*, pages 67-82. IOS Press, Amsterdam, 2000.

8. Michael Jackson and Pamela Zave. Distributed Feature Composition: A virtual architecture

for telecommunications services. *IEEE Transactions on Software Engineering*, 24(10):831–847, October 1998. Also Chapter 11 of this volume.

9. JSR 289: SIP Servlet API Version 1.1. Java Community Process Final Release, http:// www. jcp.org/ en/ jsr/ detail?id=289, 2008.

10. J. Rosenberg, H. Schulzrinne, G. Camarillo, A. Johnston, J. Peterson, R. Sparks, M. Handley, and E. Schooler. SIP: Session Initiation Protocol. IETF Network Working Group Request for Comments 3261, 2002.

11. Mary Shaw and David Garlan. *Software Architecture*. Prentice-Hall, 1996.

12. Pamela Zave. An experiment in feature engineering. In Annabelle McIver and Carroll Morgan, editors, *Programming Methodology*, pages 353–377. Springer-Verlag, 2003.

13. Pamela Zave. Address translation in telecommunication features. *ACM Transactions on Software Engineering and Methodology*, 13(1):1–36, January 2004.

14. Pamela Zave. Audio feature interactions in voice-over-IP. In *Proceedings of the First International Conference on Principles, Systems and Applicatons of IP Telecommunications*, pages 67–78. ACM SIGCOMM, 2007.

15. Pamela Zave, Gregory W. Bond, Eric Cheung, and Thomas M. Smith. Abstractions for programmig SIP back-to-back user agents. In *Proceedings of the Third International Conference on Principles, Systems and Applications of IP Telecommunications*. ACM SIGCOMM, 2009.

16. Pamela Zave and Eric Cheung. Compositional control of IP media. *IEEE Transactions on Software Engineering* 35(1), January/February 2009.

17. Pamela Zave, Healfdene H. Goguen, and Thomas M. Smith. Component coordination: A telecommunication case study. *Computer Networks*, 45(5):645–664, August 2004.

18. Pamela Zave and Michael Jackson. A call abstraction for component coordination. In *Proceedings of the Twenty-ninth International Colloquium on Automata, Languages, and Programming: Workshop on Formal Methods and Component Interaction*. University of Málaga, 2002.

Chapter 13

Property-Part Diagrams: A Dependence Notation for Software Systems

Daniel Jackson and Eunsuk Kang

Abstract: Some limitations of traditional dependence diagrams are explained, and a new notation that overcomes them is proposed. The key idea is to include in the diagram not only the *parts* of a system but also the *properties* that are assigned to them; dependences are shown as a relation not from parts to parts, but between properties and the parts (or other properties) that support them. The diagram can be used to evaluate modularization in a design, to assess how successfully critical properties are confined to a limited subset of parts, and to structure a dependability argument.

1. Introduction

A traditional dependence diagram consists of a node for each component, and an arc from A to B when component A depends on component B. Such a diagram has many uses—in reasoning, in guiding division of labor, in determining the impact of changes, in identifying reusable subsets, and so on. Every dependence is a potential liability, so reducing or eliminating dependences is a primary design goal, and the presence (or rather, the absence) of dependences is a key indicator of design quality. Our interest in dependence diagrams is primarily in their application to dependable systems, in determining which components are relied upon in the performance of critical functions.

In their standard form, however, dependence diagrams have two fundamental limitations that prevent them from being as widely applied as they deserve to be.

+ Dependence is a boolean notion. A dependence between components is present or absent, and no account is taken of its extent or purpose. Consequently, a design move that replaces one major dependence with several minor ones—a frequent consequence of the use of design patterns—appears to be bad. Also, a component that uses other components only for relatively unimportant functions will appear to depend on them no less than on components used for critical functions. The dependence diagram will not show that the designer has successfully localized critical functions within a small part of the system.

◆ Dependence does not capture the notion of collaborating components. When two components work together to achieve an effect, their coupling cannot be shown except by making one dependent on the other, or making some other component dependent on both. As a result, dependence diagrams do not extend naturally to system-level interactions, involving a combination of software components and human operators or peripheral devices. At the root of this problem is the implicit assumption that any desired property of a system can be assigned to the interface of a single component that is responsible for ensuring it (with the help of the components on which it depends).

Many of the puzzles that arise when attempting to use dependence diagrams can be traced back to these limitations. For example, related to the first limitation:

· *Cycles in the dependence structure*—which are prevalent in object-oriented code, and the target of elimination in some approaches—are not well explained. If A depends on B, but B depends on A, does that mean that A depends indirectly on itself, and its correct functioning is based on a circular argument? An answer is found by qualifying the dependences. It is possible that A and B implement mutually recursive functions, in which case B will indeed depend on A for the very functionality that A offers in depending on B. But, more likely, A depends on B for one function, and provides a *different* function for the dependence of B.

· *Dynamic linking* is not easily accommodated. A hash table component, for example, will fail if the inserted key objects do not provide appropriate hashing and equality methods. It thus appears that a library component (the hash table) depends on an application-specific component (the one providing the key at runtime) suggesting, incorrectly, that the hash table is not reusable without the key. This conundrum is easily resolved by noting that the hash table depends only on very limited functionality of the key component— namely that it provide equality and hashing methods satisfying a standard contract.

And related to the second limitation:

· *Who depends on whom?* In a system that relies on a function being scheduled at a certain frequency, does the function depend on the scheduler or vice versa? Neither uses the other in a standard sense; the specification of the scheduler does not mention the effects of the tasks that are scheduled, not does the specification of the function mention who often it should be executed. The solution to this dilemma is simply to regard the function and scheduler as working together.

2. A new notation

A *property-part diagram* is a graph of nodes and arcs, much like a traditional dependence diagram. The nodes, however, comprise two separate categories:

parts and *properties*.

A part may be a software component or 'module', a physical component (such as a peripheral device), or a human operator or user. A property is a claim about observable behaviour, for example that some physical phenomenon occurs or does not occur, or that execution of some function has some given effect. We use the term 'property' rather than specification because a property may describe behaviour only partially, and may not be associated with one part alone.

An arc may point to a part or to another property, but always originates at a property. In Alloy:

```
sig Property {
    support: set (Property + Part)
}
sig Part {}
```

The properties and parts that a property p is directly connected to by outgoing arcs (p.support in Alloy) constitute the *support* of p: together, they are sufficient to establish it. This means that if the properties in the support hold, and the parts behave according to their descriptions (in the case of software modules, their code), then p will hold also. When the support of p includes a part or property q, p is said to *depend* on q.

The most common patterns are:

- *Property decomposition* (Figure 1a). A property p depends on properties q and r, making the claim that p is implied by the conjunction of q and r.
- *Domain assumption* (Figure 1b). A property p depends on a single part e representing an aspect of the environment in which the software operates, making the claim that the environment has this property. The property is an *assumption* that should follow from the description denoted by the domain part. In practice, the description may be omitted, and the properties are then not formally justifiable, but are instead confirmed by experiment or by the judgment of domain experts.
- *Satisfaction* (Figure 1c). A property p depends on a single part m representing a module, making the claim that the part m satisfies the property p. One property may be established by more than one module, in which case they are claimed to establish it in combination, and a module may satisfy more

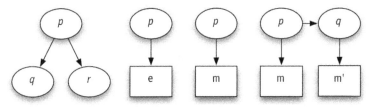

Figure 1: Standard patterns. From left to right: (a) property decomposition, (b) domain assumption, (c) satisfaction, (d) contingent use

than one property.

Note that the domain assumption and satisfaction patterns are drawn in the same way, even though their validation is very different, because the analysis required in both cases is logically the same: determining that some property of a part follows from its formal description.

- *Contingent use* (Figure 1d). A property p depends on a part m and another property q, where q depends on another part m′ used by m. In this case, p is claimed to follow from the combination of m and the property q. Unlike a property decomposition, this claim will not generally be established by showing an implication, but rather by using the property q about m′ in an argument that m satisfies p. This pattern may be counterintuitive at first; readers familiar with traditional dependence diagrams might expect the dependence edge to originate in the part m rather than the property p. Drawn this way, however, the diagram would fail to show that the use of m′ is specific to property p. The property-part diagram shows not only which property of m calls for a use of m′, but additionally which property of m′ is required in that use. (Note that the diagram does not *imply* this use; this pattern is simply a way to express the dependences induced by it.)

From the basic model, some auxiliary notions can be defined:

- The *exposure* of a property p is the set of parts reachable from p in one or more steps (in Alloy, p.^support & Part). These are the parts that are responsible for establishing the property, and whose breakage (or failure to satisfy properties) might undermine p.
- The *argument* for a property p is the subgraph rooted at p (in Alloy, p.*support <: support), namely that containing all parts and properties that p depends on directly or indirectly.
- The *impact* of a part m is the set of properties that a breakage or error in m might compromise (in Alloy, ^support.m & Property).

A primary aim of design is to reduce the exposure of critical properties to a small set of parts that are highly reliable (that is, satisfying their properties with high probability). The argument for a critical property should be small too—not only in the size of the graph, but also in the size of its parts and properties—since the size of the argument is likely to be strongly correlated to the cost of assuring adherence to the critical property. Parts that are unreliable (for example, human operators or complex physical peripherals) should preferably not have critical impacts.

3. Example: Tracking stock quotes

The program of Figure 2 implements a complete stock quote tracker that takes a list of ticker symbols and displays a message when the stock associated with a symbol moves more than some predefined amount. It works as follows:

✦ QuoteApp class. A Java timer object is created (line 3) for scheduling the downloading of quotes. For each ticker symbol presented as a command line argument (line 4), a tracker object is created and registed as a timer task with the timer for invocation every 10,000 milliseconds (line 5).

✦ Tracker class. A tracker object maintains as state high and low watermarks (line 10) on the value of the stock corresponding to the ticker symbol, and declares a constant (line 11) that defines how large a move in the stock spurs an alarm. Every 10,000 milliseconds, the Java timer calls the run method of the tracker, which causes the value of the stock to be obtained (line 14) and the watermarks to be updated. If the gap between the high and low watermarks exceeds the preset constant, a message is displayed on the console (line 18) and the watermarks are brought together so that a subsequent message will be generated only if another such move occurs.

✦ Quoter class. Stock quotes are obtained using the Yahoo quote server. A URL is constructed that includes the ticker symbol and a formatting string indicating what kind of quote is desired (line 26). Using Java's networking and I/O libraries, an HTTP get is then performed and the returned page, which contains only the quote, is stored as a string (line 27). This string is parsed as a floating-point number, multiplied by 100 (to convert from dollars to cents), and then returned as an integer (line 28).

```
1    public class QuoteApp {
2        public static void main(String[] args) throws Exception {
3            Timer timer = new Timer();
4            for (String ticker: args)
5                timer.schedule (new Tracker (ticker), 0, 10000);
6        }
7    }
8    public class Tracker extends TimerTask {
9        String ticker;
10       int hi = 0; int lo = Integer.MAX_VALUE;
11       int MOVE = 10;
12       public Tracker (String t) {ticker = t;}
13       public void run () {
14           int q = Quoter.getQuote(ticker);
15           hi = Math.max(hi, q);
16           lo = Math.min(lo, q);
17           if (hi - lo > MOVE) {
18               System.out.println (ticker + ": now " + q + " hi: " + hi + ", lo: " + lo);
19               hi = lo = q;
20           }
21       }
22   }
23   public class Quoter {
24       static String BASE_URL = "http://finance.yahoo.com/d/quotes.csv?s=";
25       public static int getQuote (String ticker) {
26           URL url = new URL(BASE_URL + ticker + "&f=l1");
27           String p = new BufferedReader(new InputStreamReader(url.openStream())).readLine();
28           return (int) (Float.valueOf (p) * 100);
29       }
30   }
```

Figure 2: Stock quote tracker (import statements omitted)

Although small and crude, this program exhibits three key features that are of interest for dependence analysis: use of libraries, a dynamic call-back mechanism; and reliance on an external service.

The property-part diagram (Figure 3) has eight parts: one for each of the three user-defined modules (6, 7, 14), three for Java libraries—for networking (15), for I/O (16), and for Timer and the classes it uses (5)—one for the Yahoo server (13), and one for the window manager of the local machine (18), whose role will be explained shortly.

The system's requirement (1) is shown as a property at the top of the diagram: that a message will indeed be displayed for any ticker included on the command line if the stock moves by the preset amount in the last 10 seconds. Since our focus is on the structure of the diagram and the relationship between properties and parts, we have not carefully formalized the properties themselves. For a critical system, this would be essential, to make sure the properties are clear and well-defined, and to enable mechanical reasoning. Formalizing the requirement would force us to decide exactly what is meant by a 'move in the last 10 seconds'; our implementation obtains only the current value from the Yahoo server, and thus would fail to catch large fluctuations occurring between checks.

The requirement (1) depends (*property decomposition* pattern) on two properties: that QuoteApp creates a tracker object for each of the ticker symbols whose run method gets called every 10 seconds (3), and that calling run displays a message if a move has occurred since the last time it was called (8). The first property (3) depends (*contingent use* pattern) on the code of QuoteApp (6) and on the properties that the parts it uses meeting their specifications (2, 4). These properties depend only on the parts they describe (*satisfaction* pattern), although in fact, as we shall see later, this is erroneous: the property that registering a timer task with schedule causes its run method to be called at the specified interval (2) actually depends on more than the code of Timer and its associated classes (5).

The property that calling run has the desired effect (8) is decomposed into the properties that the getQuote method of Quoter works (10) and that a call to println causes a message to be displayed on the console (12). The property that getQuote works (10) depends on the code of Quoter (14), on the Java libraries' meeting their specifications (11), and on the property that an HTTP get with an appropriately formed URL containing a ticker symbol will return the value of the corresponding stock (9). This last property depends, of course, on the Yahoo server (13) operating as advertised and being reachable in the network (not shown).

The println property (12) is more subtle than one might expect. It depends not only on the code of the relevant Java library (16), but also on a console window's actually being open (17). The println method writes to the standard output stream. Whether a write to this stream is displayed depends on the state of the window manager; if the console is not showing, the write will not be visible.

Exposure, argument and impact are easily read off the diagram by simply following paths. Thus the argument for property (8)—that run has the desired effect—is obtained by selecting all nodes reachable from it (Figure 4). The impact of a failure in the Yahoo server (13) is obtained by selecting all property nodes

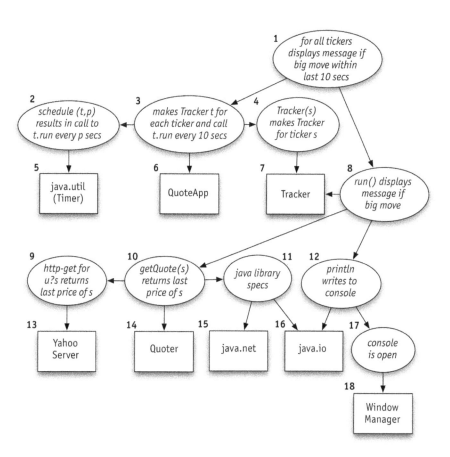

Figure 3: Property part diagram for stock tracker example (Figure 2)

reachable backwards (Figure 5); not surprisingly, these include the requirement (1). Because this particular system is so simple and performs only a single function, these reductions are less useful than they would be in a larger system.

Constructing the dependence diagram and carefully reviewing each property and its dependences revealed, in addition to the issue regarding println mentioned above, a problem with the Timer class. Its official Java documentation warns

"Corresponding to each Timer object is a single background thread that is used to execute all of the timer's tasks, sequentially. Timer tasks should complete quickly. If a timer task takes excessive time to complete, it "hogs" the timer's task execution thread. This can, in turn, delay the execution of subsequent tasks, which may "bunch up" and execute in rapid succession when (and if) the offending task finally completes."

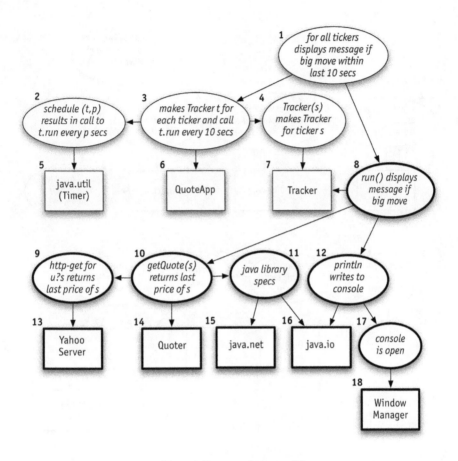

Figure 4: Exposure of property (8)

In short, our property (2) does not depend on the code of Timer alone (5). In addition, it depends on a property we failed to state (shown as 2a in Figure 6): that the run method of the timer task completes quickly.

For comparison, a traditional dependence diagram is shown in Figure 7. To construct such a diagram there needs to be at least an implicit specification of each component (so that A can be said to depend on B when the adherence of B to its specification is required for A's adherence). We therefore assigned each property to a part; the requirement was assigned to QuoteApp. This diagram is appealingly small, but it conveys very little information. The arrow from QuoteApp to Timer is due not only to the explicit calls to its methods, but just as importantly to the fact that QuoteApp uses Timer to make calls to the run method of Tracker. The arrow from Timer to Tracker is not a necessary consequence of Timer calling the run method of Tracker; it would be absent were it not for the fact that Timer relies on Tracker to return quickly in order to meet its specification.

This example reveals a subtlety of traditional dependence diagrams that is

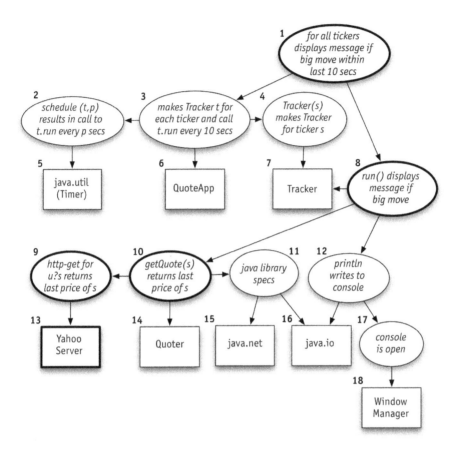

Figure 5: Impact of part (13)

usually not recognized. The specification of Timer promises that calls to the timer task will occur with the given period *contingent* on their completing quickly. If we changed the specification to say that the frequency of execution is the given period *minus* the completion time, we would effectively shift the burden onto QuoteApp, and the dependence arrow from Timer to Tracker would no longer be shown! Dependences, in other words, are *property specific*: whether A depends on B cannot be determined unless we know what property A is expected to meet, and what properties other modules might be providing to A.

4. Related work

Notions of dependence in compilation and parallelization have been widely studied, but notions of dependence in program and system design have received less attention from researchers.

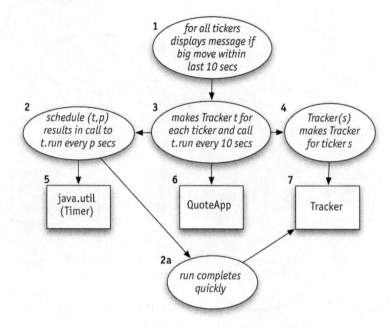

Figure 6: Corrected diagram showing assumption about timer tasks

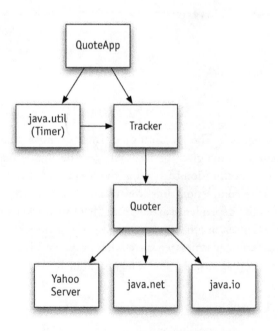

Figure 7: Traditional dependence diagram for stock tracker

4.1. Parnas's uses relation

The dependence diagram appears to have been invented by David Parnas. He defines the *uses* relation as follows [14]:

"A uses B if there exist situations in which the correct functioning of A depends on the availability of a correct implementation of B."

This definition reveals how Parnas must have grappled with the complexities of dependences. Note that the correct functioning of A need not always depend on B; more can therefore be inferred from lack of dependence than from its presence. The significance of the word 'availability' is unclear; perhaps it was intended to allow B to be replaced by an equivalent component, or perhaps it emphasizes the need for not merely the existence of B but its availability in the context of use. Either way, the definition seems to imply that B is a specification but that A is an implementation. 'Correct functioning' of A is presumably with respect to its specification.

Parnas recognized that dependences do not necessarily follow procedure calls: that some calls result in no dependences, and that some dependences are present in the absence of explicit calls.

Despite their enormous value, dependence diagrams appear not to have been widely adopted, and are rarely taught at universities. At MIT, dependence diagrams have been emphasized in software engineering classes for 25 years, due to the efforts of Barbara Liskov and John Guttag who advocated them as a fundamental means for expressing and evaluating designs [11].

Extending dependence diagrams to object-oriented code is not straightforward, for the reason explained in the introduction (with the hash table example).

4.2. Class diagrams

A *class diagram* mixes elements of an object model (how fields of one class point to another, and how classes implement interfaces or subclass other classes) with elements of a dependence diagram (how methods of one class call another). Design patterns are often depicted using class diagrams [5].

Class diagrams are, unlike dependence diagrams, easy to construct (both by programmers and tools), since they capture purely syntactic properties. But this limits their utility. When a field points to a generic class or interface, the class diagram will not show what class it is bound to at runtime. And when a class makes a call to another class through an interface, the actual class called will not be shown. With some amount of fudging, these problems can be overcome. One can replicate interfaces and abstract classes for their different contexts of use, and show, for each context, which concrete classes they are instantiated with. This enrichment of the class diagram makes their extraction from code far more challenging, however, and although tools [6, 13] have been designed to produce diagrams in this form, they may not scale well and even defining correct output turns out to be surprisingly tricky.

4.3. Design structure matrices

The design structure matrix (DSM) is a dependence graph represented as an adjacency matrix. It was introduced by Steward in the 1960s [18]. Various algorithms have been develop for automatically discovering structure in DSMs, for example, by topologically sorting the graph to assign modules to layers, and clustering modules into equivalence classes to eliminate cycles. Until recently, DSMs had been used primarily for streamlining manufacturing processes [4], but there has been increasing interest in using DSMs to capture modularity in design [1]. Lattix has developed a tool [16] (now imitated by offerings from other companies) that can extract a DSM from a large codebase, and help identify dependences that violate the intended architectural structure.

The notion of dependence in a DSM, especially for software, is not precisely defined. Tools tend to rely on syntactic dependences. Sullivan and his collaborators, however, have revisited Parnas's work in the context of DSMs [19], and, using design decisions as the nodes of the dependence graph, have given a formal characterization of dependence in terms of logical constraints [2]. Extending these ideas to graphs in which the nodes are components (rather than design constraints) remains to be done.

4.4. Goal notations

A variety of diagrammatic notations [20, 10, 3] have been invented for depicting goals and their relationships. The initial motivation was to capture the rationale for system requirements, prior to the articulation of the requirements themselves.

Of these, Goal Structuring Notation (GSN) [10] is closest to ours, since it aims to represent the structure of a dependability argument. A GSN 'goal structure' is superficially very similar to a property-part diagram: a key requirement of the system is decomposed progressively, and related to knowledge of the software and its environment. In addition to goals, however, which are similar to our properties, a goal structure includes 'strategies' that represent the activities performed (proof, testing, etc) to establish the goals; and the focus of the structure is not the relationship between the goals and the components, but rather between the goals and the strategies that justify them. Thus the structure of the dependability argument is based not on the structure of the *system*, as in our approach, but rather on the structure of the *process*, which need not be related either to the structure of the system, or to the structure of the argument for its safety. For example [10], a top level goal 'logic is fault free' may be decomposed into 'argument by satisfaction of all requirements' and 'argument by omission of all identified hazards'.

Peter Henderson is currently working on a dependence model that represents argument structure directly. Its elements are claims and evidence, with dependences of claims on the claims and evidence that support them. His purpose is to build tool support to make it easier to navigate and maintain large arguments.

KAOS [3] is a goal notation that supports both behavioural goals (similar to our properties) and soft goals (which are 'satisfied' in Herbert Simon's sense), although, in contrast to GSN, these are usually about the product and not the process. Unlike property-part diagrams, KAOS supports 'or' decompositions, which are useful for showing design alternatives in a single diagram. Whether 'or' decomposition is needed to describe systems that make use of redundancy is not clear. KAOS is backed by a temporal logic and a catalog of refinement patterns which can be used to formally validate a design down to a low level. It seems that KAOS naturally represents the property decomposition and satisfaction patterns, but perhaps not the contingent use pattern.

4.5. Enriched module dependence diagrams

The first author made an earlier attempt at overcoming the shortcomings of traditional dependence diagrams [7]. Modules were viewed as 'specification transducers', mapping specifications they provided (to clients) to specifications they required (as clients of other modules). An additional relation, in the spirit of architectural connection [12], represented the binding of provided 'ports' to required ports.

For example, if a module B provided a service Q so that a module A could provide a service P, the module A would map P to Q, and B's provision of Q would be bound to A's requirement for Q. In contrast, a property-part diagram would show the property P depending on module A and property Q, with a subtle shift in the interpretation of the properties: P and Q are no longer descriptions of anonymously provided services, but assert that modules A and B provide these services. This is what allows the contingent use relationship to be captured without any outgoing dependences from A.

Although this earlier model solved some of the problems, it still required properties to be bound to modules: every property was a specification of a single module. This makes it unsuitable for system-level description, supporting (in Michael Jackson's terminology [8]) only *specifications* and not *requirements*. Moreover, a ternary dependence relation (specification-module-specification) is hard to draw, so in practice the diagrams added specification labels to dependence arcs between modules, but did not show the internal dependences that are essential for fine-grained tracking.

4.6. Frame concern diagrams

The property-part notation was inspired by Michael Jackson's problem frame diagrams [9], which show (requirements) properties explicitly as nodes. Jackson's 'frame concern diagram' shows the archetypal form of an argument for a particular class of property following from properties of the constituent domains. Seater, in his doctoral thesis [17], extended the problem frame diagram to an *argument diagram* that makes explicit the properties of the individual domains, but does not link them together in a dependence structure. Property-part diagrams grew out of his work, and can be seen as an attempt to layer a dependence relation on top of the argument diagram. An early version of the property-part diagram was in fact much closer to the argument diagram, as it included shared-phenomenon links between parts, but these links were dropped as they did not seem to be necessary.

5. Conclusion

Dependences are not innate properties of the parts of a system, but arise from the particular way in which a designer chooses to assign responsibilities. A part's functionality does not determine its responsibility. Just because module A calls module B does not mean that A guarantees to its clients the properties of B; it might instead promise only to call B. This is why we have abandoned the idea of explicit dependences between parts, preferring instead to relate parts and properties. So rather than asking 'does the application depend on the database?', we would ask 'does *this service* provided by the application depend on the database?' If the service is merely to execute certain queries and updates in response to user actions, it will not depend on the database. But if the service is to provide persistent storage and retrieval of data, it surely will.

Including properties in a dependence diagram is not optional; they were there all the time, albeit implicitly. Keeping them implicit had two disadvantages that property-part diagrams overcome: it obscured the rationale for the dependences, and it prevented a more fine-grained analysis that allows different properties to be traced independently. In an analysis of a proton therapy machine, the critical property that pressing the emergency button inserts a beam stop was found to have an exposure very much smaller than the entire system, but still larger than one would ideally want [15]; a traditional dependence analysis would have produced a graph that was close to fully connected.

Much work remains to be done to understand and refine the property-part diagram, to understand what kinds of inferences can be made from the diagram, and how it might be checked mechanically. The claim, for example, that a change to a part can only affect the properties within its impact clearly will not hold if a change to the 'alphabet' of the part is permitted, so that it engages in entirely new phenomena. The property-part diagram makes it easy to see (unlike a traditional dependence diagram) what properties a replacement part should have, but less clear what other parts might be impacted by a replacement. Moreover, the very notion of a 'contingent use' is, as we noted, only partially modelled, and it may be that in some cases a more complete representation of the relationship between modules is needed.

We are also interested in understanding when dependence of a property on multiple parts induces a coupling between them, and in reconsidering the (unjustified?) assumption that a module should be regarded as vulnerable to changes in the modules it uses but not to changes in the modules that use it. We plan also to investigate the notion of information hiding, to see how it might be accommodated, perhaps as properties over uninterpreted functions.

Acknowledgments

Derek Rayside made many suggestions about our ideas and their presentation. Axel van Lamsweerde helped us relate our work to KAOS, and has been generous in his encouragement, and tolerant of our slow recognition that dependences arise from goals. Pamela Zave gave us very perceptive comments on a draft of the paper and helped us clarify some obscure points.

The first author is grateful to Michael Jackson in whose honour this workshop was held, not just for his work on problem frames (whose influence on this work is pervasive), but for many years of wise advice and thought-provoking technical discussions. He continues to be an inspiring model (in the iconic rather than analogic sense) of what it means to be an engineer, a thinker, and a mensch. Ad me'ah ve'esrim shanah!

References

1. Carliss Baldwin and Kim Clark. *Design Rules: The Power of Modularity*. MIT Press, 2000.

2. Yuanfang Cai and Kevin Sullivan. Modularity analysis of logical design models. *Proceedings of 21th IEEE/ACM International Conference on Automated Software Engineering*. Tokyo, Japan, 2006.

3. A. Dardenne, A. van Lamsweerde, and S. Fickas. Goal-directed requirements acquisition. *Science of Computer Programming*, 20(1–2):3–50, 1993.

4. Steven D. Eppinger. Innovation at the speed of information. *Harvard Business Review*, Vol. 79, no. 1, pp. 149-158, January 2001.

5. Erich Gamma and Richard Helm and Ralph Johnson and John Vlissides. *Design Patterns: Elements of Reusable Object-Oriented Software*. Addison-Wesley Professional Computing Series, 1995.

6. Daniel Jackson and Allison Waingold. Lightweight extraction of object models from bytecode. *IEEE Transactions on Software Engineering*, February 2001.

7. Daniel Jackson. Module dependencies in software design. *Post-workshop Proceedings of the 2002 Monterey Workshop: Radical Innovations of Software and Systems Engineering in the Future*. Venice, Italy, 2002. Springer Verlag, 2003. Available at: http://sdg.csail.mit.edu/publications.html.

8. Michael Jackson. *Software Requirements and Specifications*, Addison-Wesley and ACM Press, 1996.

9. Michael Jackson. *Problem Frames: Analysing and Structuring Software Development Problems*, Addison-Wesley, Boston, Massachusetts, 2001.

10. Tim Kelly and Rob Weaver. The goal structuring notation—A safety argument notation. *Proceedings of the Dependable Systems and Networks Workshop on Assurance Cases*, 2004.

11. Barbara Liskov and John Guttag. *Abstraction and Specification in Program Development*. MIT Press, 1986.

12. Jeff Magee and Jeff Kramer. Dynamic structure in software architectures. *Proceedings of the 4th ACM SIGSOFT Symposium on Foundations of Software Engineering*, San Francisco, CA, 1996.

13. Robert O'Callahan. *Generalized Aliasing as a Basis for Program Analysis Tools*. PhD Thesis, Technical Report CMU-CS-01-124, School of Computer Science, Carnegie Mellon University, Pittsburgh, PA, November 2000.

14. David Parnas. Designing software for ease of extension and contraction. *IEEE Transactions On Software Engineering*, Vol. SE-5, No. 2, March 1979.

15. Andrew Rae, Daniel Jackson, Prasad Ramanan, Jay Flanz, and Didier Leyman. Critical feature analysis of a radiotherapy machine. *Reliability Engineering & System Safety*, Volume 89, Issue 1, Elsevier Science, July 2005, Pages 48–56.

16. Neeraj Sangal, Ev Jordan, Vineet Sinha, and Daniel Jackson. Using dependency models to manage complex software architecture. *20th Annual ACM SIGPLAN Conference on Object-Oriented Programming Systems (OOPSLA 2005)*.

17. Robert Morrison Seater. *Building Dependability Arguments for Software Intensive Systems*. PhD Thesis, Dept. of Electrical Engineering and Computer Science, MIT, Cambridge, MA, February 2009.

18. Donald Steward. Design structure system: A method for managing the design of complex systems IEEE *Transactions on Engineering Management*, 28:33, 71–74, 1981.

19. K.J. Sullivan, W.G. Griswold, Y. Cai and B. Hallen. The structure and value of modularity in software design. *Joint Proceedings of the European Software Engineering/ACM SIGSOFT Foundations of Software Engineering Conference (ESEC/FSE)*, Vienna, September 2001.

20. Eric Yu. Towards modelling and reasoning support for early-phase requirements engineering. *Proceedings of the 3rd IEEE Int. Symp. on Requirements Engineering*, Washington, DC, pp. 226-235, 1997.

PART 5
PROBLEM
FRAMES

Chapter 14

Some Principles and Ideas of Problem Frames

Michael Jackson

Abstract: The problem frames approach to software development is primarily—but not exclusively—concerned with computer-based or software-intensive systems. The broad content and nature of the approach are explained, and the underlying ideas and principles are reviewed and discussed. Some familiarity with the approach is assumed, and much detail is omitted. The paper does not aim to offer a tutorial: it presents only enough of the approach to illustrate the ideas.

1. Introduction

The purpose of the problem frames approach to software development is to contribute to improving the dependability of *computer-based* or *software-intensive* systems. These are systems in which the computer—or some assemblage of computers—interacts with other parts of the physical and human world in order to produce some desired effects there. In this sense, a heart pacemaker is a computer-based system, and so are a telephone switch and a system to administer a lending library. But a program to factorise large integers is not, nor is a program to find cycles in a graph, because they are concerned purely with mathematical abstractions and they interact only trivially, if at all, with the human and physical world.

The approach is concerned in particular with designing the software so that the system will satisfy its functional requirements—that is, requirements specifying the observable behaviour of the system in operation: it is not concerned with managerial problems, although its adoption could impinge on the technical content—if any—of any chosen managerial style; nor does it directly address such important tasks as eliciting system requirements from stakeholders or negotiating compromises where requirements are in conflict.

1.1. Computer-based systems

Because Problem frames treat software development as a problem to be solved, the relevant parts of the world outside the computer are referred to as the *problem world*. For a realistic system the problem world is likely to comprise many heterogeneous parts or *problem domains*. These may include: human beings (for example, as operators and users, or as the subject of information that the system must use or produce); inert physical structures (for example, the track layout of a railway); mechanical devices (for example, lift cars, doors, and winding gear in a lift control system); actuators and sensors (for example, motor relays); and concrete realisations of lexical structures (for example, credit cards).

The functionality of the system is likely to support many features, and many local and global modes of operation. For example, a modern phone may combine the functions of a phone, an address book, a diary, an alarm clock, a camera, a GPS device, a web browser and an email client. The interactions among these features are likely to give rise to great complexity in the whole system, and to impinge on every aspect of the development task. The customer or end-user *requirements* of different features may conflict, or they may interact in a way that makes them hard to consider separately and even harder to understand in combination.

The versatility and power of the computer encourages this proliferation of system features. It also encourages complexity in the functionality of the individual features. A central-locking system for a family car must deal with four doors, each with an exterior handle, an interior handle and a button, one or two of the doors also having an external key, a tailgate with an external key and an internal release lever, buttons for locking all four doors or the two rear passenger doors, and interlocks with the ignition control, gearbox and accelerator pedal. This environment has a large number of states and transitions, and its complexity must be related to several functional requirements—child safety, guarding against carjackers, preventing locking of the car while the key is inside, convenience of use in shopping, preventing theft of the car or its contents, and accessibility in the event of a crash.

The computer is installed in the problem world, and interacts with neighbouring problem domains through a narrow interface of shared phenomena—for example, through control lines by which the computer can set the state of a motor or detect whether a sensor is on or off, or at data ports through which it can read the data encoded on a swipe card or entered on a keyboard. The scope of the system requirements is not restricted to these neighbouring domains, but typically stipulates desired properties and behaviours for distant domains that interact with the computer only indirectly, through each other and through the computer's neighbouring domains.

For all but the most critical systems the computer itself may be effectively regarded as a formal system, faithfully exhibiting the behaviour described by the software it executes and interacting with the world through its narrow—and effectively formal—predefined interface. But the problem world, unlike the computer, is not a formal system: it can readily falsify almost any formal assumption about its properties and behaviour. There is, therefore, a mismatch between the formal behaviour described by the software and the effects it can evoke in the non-formal problem world. Many of the system failures, large and small, regularly reported among the copious material published in the Risks Digest [Risks08] and elsewhere, are attributable to this mismatch.

1.2. The nature of the problem frames approach

The problem frames approach addresses some—but not all—of the challenges posed by the development of computer-based systems. It is not yet another development method or process. It rests on the presumption that the system to be developed is a computer-based system; but beyond that it prescribes no software or system architecture, object-oriented or otherwise. It can be regarded as an intellectual structure within which elements of appropriate development techniques—for example, notations and calculi, modelling languages, and repertoires of program and model transformations—can be applied to different parts and facets of the problem in hand. It is not itself a method, because it neither provides nor mandates any particular language or process. It offers no particular notations for describing problems or their solutions, beyond its very simple diagrammatic notation for representing the principal parts of a problem and their relationships, and some accompanying annotations of the diagrams. It is above all a structure of principles and ideas for thinking about problems and solutions in software engineering. Its purpose is to help in mastering complexity, to direct the developers' attention to concerns that should not be neglected, and to ensure clarity in the application of descriptive and analytical techniques, whether formal or informal. Its central goal is human understanding: its basic premise is that increased understanding will prove a powerful tool for increased dependability of the developed system.

The purpose of this paper is to present and motivate the most basic problem frame concepts. The paper is not a tutorial, and it is not in any way comprehensive. In particular, for brevity it includes no detailed treatment of interface phenomena in problem diagrams. Section 2 provides and illustrates a very broad outline of the approach, explaining and illustrating its underlying principles and motivations. A more detailed discussion of some of the ideas and practices that realise or support these principles is given in Section 3. The paper ends with some general reflections on the role of problem frames in the context of a system development.

2. Principles and motivations

The immediate focus of the problem frames approach, as its name suggests, is on software development as a *problem* to be solved. The notion of a problem was originally inspired by Polya's exposition [Polya57] of the work of Pappus and other ancient mathematicians on problems in what today—thanks to their work—we can regard as elementary mathematics. They classified problems in two classes: problems to *find*, and problems to *prove*. An example of a problem to find is: "Find a prime number strictly between 1,000,000 and 1,100,000." An example of a problem to prove is: "Prove that the sum of the angles of a triangle is equal to two right angles."

The key idea in the classification is that problems of different classes have different *principal parts*, and invite different solution techniques specifically adapted to those parts. A problem to find has an *unknown*, a *given* and a *condition* relating them. In the example given earlier: the required prime is the unknown; the given is the specified range; and the condition is that the unknown lies in the range. Polya offers many heuristics for solving such problems—for example: "Could you change the unknown, the given, or both if necessary, so that the new unknown and the new data are nearer to each other?" The heuristics, necessarily, are expressed in terms of the principal parts of the problem. The broad theme of the work is that a firmer grip on a problem's structure and elements provides more specific—and therefore stronger—intellectual tools for its solution.

2.1. Software development as a problem

Polya's understanding of problems can be applied—in spirit, at least— to problems of developing computer-based systems. These problems can be characterised—with some adjustment—as problems to find. The unknown is the software to be developed, for execution by computer; the given is the problem world; and the condition is the functional requirement that the whole system must satisfy. Figure 1 is a *problem diagram*, showing these principal parts for a problem of controlling traffic at a road junction:

Figure 1. A Problem: Controlling Traffic at a Road Junction

The principal parts of the problem are:

+ The *problem world*, represented by the plain rectangle. This is the portion of the human and physical world with which the system is concerned. In the diagram the problem world has been named *Traffic & Junction*.
+ The *requirement*, represented by the dashed ellipse. The requirement is a condition on the problem world. In the diagram the requirement has been named *Safe and Convenient Traffic*. Establishing and maintaining that condition is the purpose of the system. The dashed line shows what the requirement refers to. The arrowhead shows that the requirement does not merely refer to the problem world, but also constrains it: for safe and convenient traffic we must constrain the movement of the people and vehicles using the junction.
+ The *machine*, represented by the doubly striped rectangle. This is the computer, executing the software to be developed. In the diagram the machine has been named *Traffic Controller*.

The solver's task is to find the machine: that is, to develop the software that will be executed. The idea of a machine is quite general—even abstract—here. For example, the eventual implementation may use several computers, one computer, or only a part of a computer shared with another system. These possibilities do not affect the representation of the machine in the problem diagram: it always appears as a single box. The machine interacts with the problem world at the interface of *shared phenomena* represented by the solid line joining them. For example, a shared phenomenon might be an event in which the machine sets one of its output lines high, the line being shared with a traffic light unit for which the high state of the line means 'red light on'.

Identifying the requirement with the condition of a problem to find demands some conceptual licence. This is unsurprising, given that mathematical problems are about an abstract world without time or causality, while computer-based systems are about a changing physical problem world. In particular, the condition is not about a relationship between the unknown and the given. It is a condition that the unknown—the machine—must impose on the given—the problem world.

In problem frames the problem world plays the central role in the problem for two reasons. First, because the whole purpose of the system is located there, and it is there that the success of the software development will be judged. The requirement, expressed entirely in terms of the problem world, is not restricted to interaction with the machine: on the contrary, it is usually concerned with phenomena located deeper into the problem world, sometimes far from the machine. In this problem the requirement is entirely about vehicles and pedestrians. The machine is only an instrumental means of affecting the problem world—for example, by setting the traffic lights. Second, because the machine can ensure satisfaction of the requirement only by respecting and exploiting causal properties which the problem world exhibits independently of any possible behaviour of the machine. The machine exploits the propensity of car drivers to stop at a red light, and must respect the protocol by which it can control the light units. These properties, therefore, play a vital role in the system, providing the necessary causal links that can allow the machine indirectly to monitor and control phenomena to which it is not directly connected.

2.2. The problem world as a given

In the perspective adopted in this paper, the problem world is understood to be given in the sense that the developer is not free to replace or modify the problem world, or any part of it, by introducing a new or substitute domain that will make the problem easier. For example, in the traffic control system, the developer is not free to introduce vehicle-detecting sensors if they are not already a part of the given problem world. Of course, in practice the software developer might well make such a suggestion, and it might perhaps be adopted by the engineer responsible for the electromechanical equipment at the road junction. The result, from the standard problem frames perspective, would be regarded as a substantially modified problem, not as a step, taken strictly within the scope of software engineering, towards solving the original problem.

This assumption of a fixed problem world should not be misunderstood as an attempt to restrict the choices available to the software developer over a whole career or even over a whole development project. It is, rather, an example of the style of separation of concerns that permeates the problem frames approach: the assumption is purely local, adopted for purposes of the problem in hand. Like the problem world properties, the requirement is also assumed to be given, and to bound the developer's concerns accordingly.

If we describe the given properties of the problem world in a description W, and the requirement in a description R, then we can say that the problem is to find a machine whose properties, described in a description M, are such that the developer can argue as follows:

"The machine behaves as described by description M. The problem world has the properties described by description W. When they act together through their interface of shared phenomena, the requirement, described by description R in terms of problem world phenomena, will be satisfied."

We are assuming, then, that the problem world W and the requirement R are given, and that the problem is to devise the machine M. In the present paper, we will assume this perspective throughout. However, at least two other perspectives are possible and may sometimes be useful:

+ If M and W are given the question may be: What will be the effect of the interaction between them? That is, what requirement R'—if any—will they satisfy? If it is different from the proposed requirement R, is it an acceptably close substitute? This question arises, for example, when a software system (M) that has been successfully installed in one branch of an organisation is proposed for installation in another branch having different properties (W).
+ If M and R are given the question may be: In what problem worlds W will M achieve satisfaction of R? More specifically: Will M achieve satisfaction of R in the particular problem world W of interest, and, if not, is there a modified problem world W' in which R will be satisfied? This question arises when a COTS package (M) is considered for use as a system component, and can achieve its desired purpose (R) only if the context is modified (W')to accommodate it.

2.3. Bounding the problem world

The choice of names for the problem world, requirement and machine in the traffic problem is suggestive but no more than that. It is necessary, at the earliest stage, to be more explicit about the structure and content of the problem world. Figure 2 shows a fuller version of the traffic control problem diagram.

The problem world is structured as a collection of *problem domains*, interacting with each other and with the machine at interfaces of shared phenomena. The domains have been named to convey a good general idea of what they are. The Road Layout domain must be included: the control of traffic cannot be achieved

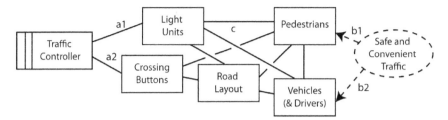

Figure 2. Controlling Traffic at a Road Junction: the Problem World.

without knowledge of where the Light Units and Crossing Buttons are located, and where Vehicles and Pedestrians may be positioned in relation to the lights and buttons. The interfaces also can be named. In a fully detailed problem diagram each interface would be named, and an annotation provided to identify the shared phenomena in each interface. For example, interface C might be annotated specifying that the shared phenomena are *pressButton* events controlled by the Pedestrians. For brevity we will say little about the interfaces in this paper. This omission should not be taken to suggest that they are unimportant. Paying proper attention to the phenomena of the problem world is a fundamental tenet of problem frames, and of requirements engineering more generally [Zave97].

A problem diagram with named problem domains and annotated interfaces bounds the problem world for the developer. What is relevant to the problem— and only what is relevant—is included. From the diagram in Figure 2, for example, it can be inferred that:

- there is to be no provision for manual override of the regime imposed by the Traffic Controller machine: the diagram shows no problem domain that could command an override, and no interface at which the machine could detect such a command; and
- the machine will not take account of varying weather conditions: again, there is no problem domain that can embody the weather, and no interface at which the machine could monitor it; and
- the requirement takes account of pedestrians, and the Traffic Controller machine must accordingly take account of their crossing requests conveyed in *pressButton* events.

2.4. Understanding and describing the problem world

Because all the problem domains shown are relevant to the problem, they will all demand investigation—and, eventually, description—of their relevant properties: each has its own $\mathcal{W}$. For example:

- if the road layout is more complex and irregular than a simple rectangular crossing of two routes, it must be described by some kind of topographical map. The map must show the roads and pedestrian crossings with the positions of all lights and buttons, and dimensions from which the developer can determine sight lines, estimate traversal times for vehicles and pedestrians and calculate the space available for vehicles waiting on intermediate road segments.

+ The light units may be simple reactive devices, changing state by illuminating those lamps that correspond to the control lines currently set *high* by the Traffic Controller machine: they can then be described by a simple mapping from control line states to visible light states.

+ The pedestrians, being human participants in the system, can be expected to behave according to instructions, but not reliably so. There is therefore a stochastic element in their behaviour, demanding estimates of the probability that a pedestrian will start to cross at various times after the 'walk' light has been superseded by the 'wait' light. There are also physical and other constraints on the speed with which a pedestrians can traverse a crossing of a given size (in [Goh04] this is related to the individual pedestrian's age, sex and trip purpose, and to the density of pedestrian traffic crossing in each direction).

+ The vehicles, with their drivers, can be regarded similarly to the pedestrians. They can be expected to obey the traffic lights, but their obedience is not fully reliable, and may vary according to their position on the road: for example, a bend in the road approaching the crossing from one particular direction may make approaching drivers slower to see and respond to a red or amber light.

+ The crossing buttons may be simple devices whose state—*pressed* or *not pressed*—is shared with the Traffic Controller machine.

To investigate and describe the problem world adequately, the developer must maintain a resolute focus on the real physical problem world domains and their phenomena. The machine as eventually designed and implemented may—or may not—include software objects corresponding to some or all of these domains; but software objects are not the subject of the description here.

2.5. Decomposing the problem—1

When a problem is complex—and realistic systems are complex—it must be decomposed into *simpler subproblems*. Both words are important. The decomposed parts must be simpler than the complex whole: otherwise the task may have been made harder, not easier, by the decomposition. They must also retain the form of problems: otherwise the decomposition will have too much of the flavour of solving, rather than structuring and analysing, the original complex problem.

Simplicity in a subproblem has many facets. Problem frame ideas of simplicity in an individual subproblem or problem are discussed and illustrated in Section 3 of this paper. The approach also adopts a radical principle of simplicity in decomposition: the eventual recombination of the decomposed parts should be ignored in their initial definition and analysis. By separating the analysis of each part from the analysis of its composition with other parts, the developer can see its essence more clearly; and analysing the composition task itself becomes easier when the parts to be combined are already understood to an appropriate depth.

The problem shown in Figure 3, derived from a problem discussed in [Jackson01, Hayes03], is small but rich enough to provide a simple illustration

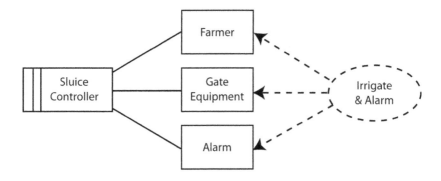

Figure 3. Controlling an Unreliable Sluice Gate.

of decomposition.

The problem is to control the raising and lowering of a sluice gate in a farm irrigation system according to a schedule specified from time to time by the farmer. The operation of the mechanical and electrical equipment of the gate is unreliable, because it is subject to deterioration or failure due to rust and other factors, and because debris from the irrigation channel may clog the mechanism, damage the sensors, or obstruct the gate's vertical travel. The requirement includes the stipulation that when the equipment is faulty, or its operation is obstructed, the machine must sound an alarm to alert the farm engineer to the situation.

The problem frames approach strongly suggests a decomposition into two subproblems: one to raise and lower the gate to satisfy the irrigation requirement as specified by the farmer, and one to monitor the behaviour of the gate equipment and sound the alarm if necessary. The two subproblems are shown in Figure 4.

Each subproblem is a well-formed problem. Each has one machine and one requirement, and a problem world. In the subproblem shown on the left the only requirement is to operate the gate in accordance with the farmer's specified irrigation schedule. The requirement refers to the farmer's instructions, and to the states *open* and *closed* of the gate. It stipulates appropriate open and closed periods for the gate: this part of the requirement can be satisfied only if the equipment is functioning correctly. The motor must respond to *up*, *down*, *on* and *off* from the Irrigation Machine, raising and lowering the gate; and the sensors that indicate when the gate reaches its upper and lower travel limits, going *on* and *off* as they are designed to, allowing the machine to stop the motor at the

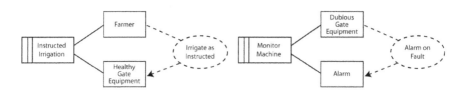

Figure 4. Controlling a Sluice Gate: Decomposition into Two Subproblems.

desired point. In this subproblem, this correct functioning is *assumed* as the given property of the Healthy Gate Equipment domain. That is: in the development of the Irrigation Machine no attention is paid to the possibility of equipment faults.

In the subproblem shown on the right the requirement is not to control the gate, but only to detect possible faults in the equipment and to sound the alarm if a fault is detected. This requirement refers to the Alarm, and it defines *faulty* and *healthy* states of the gate. In this subproblem the Dubious Gate Equipment is regarded as autonomous: the motor states *upward, downward, on* and *off* are assumed to change spontaneously in the domain. The significant given properties of the domain assumed here are those that allow faults to be detected—that is, they relate the *faulty* and *healthy* states to the motor and sensor states shared with the Monitor Machine. For example, if the motor state has been *on* and *upward* for more than some specified time, and the upper sensor is not *on*, then the Dubious Gate Equipment is in a *faulty* state; similarly, there is a fault if both upper and lower sensor are *on* simultaneously; and so on. If the alarm domain allows for the transmission of a message along with the alarm signal, the requirement may also stipulate some diagnosis of the fault. This would necessitate a more detailed investigation and description of the possible faulty states and their symptoms.

In this decomposition, as in all problem frame decompositions, each subproblem is regarded as fully independent of the others. The developer considering one subproblem is not merely permitted to ignore the other problem, but is positively enjoined to ignore it. The left subproblem is not concerned with possible faults; the right subproblem is not concerned with the irrigation schedule. Nor, in principle, is any consideration given to the eventual need to combine the solved subproblems—for example, to ensure that when a fault has been detected the Irrigation Machine does not continue to make fruitless attempts to control the equipment. In the eyes of the developer considering it, each subproblem is located in an independent universe of its own.

2.6. Decomposing the problem—2

The decomposition described in the preceding section can be seen as a decomposition of the requirement: the functional requirement falls naturally into two parts. Another, different, motivation for decomposition can be seen, at least partly, as a decomposition of the undecomposed machine: essentially, the decomposition exposes a local variable of the machine, assigning its writing and reading to separate subproblems. Treating this decomposition as a tool for problem analysis is justified when the local variable is a complex data structure and the relationship between the writer and the reader subproblems can be more easily understood by making the variable visible as a part of the problem.

The two subproblems shown in Figure 4 provide two simple examples of this form of decomposition. The first concerns the farmer's specification of the irrigation schedule, and is discussed in this subsection. The second introduces a *model domain*—a notion of very general importance that demands a separate discussion in the following subsection.

The first example decomposes the problem shown on the left of Figure 4. The problem is to operate the Sluice Gate in accordance with the farmer's instructions. If these instructions are no more than the commands *start_irrigating* and *stop_irrigating*, there is no motive for decomposition. If, at the other extreme, the farmer's instructions can specify an elaborate schedule hour by hour and day by day, there is good reason to decompose the problem.

The appropriate decomposition separates the subproblem in which the farmer specifies the desired schedule from the subproblem in which the gate is operated accordingly. Figure 5 shows the decomposition.

In the subproblem on the lower left the farmer edits the schedule; in the subproblem on the lower right, the Irrigation Machine operates the gate in accordance with the schedule. The single stripe on the boxes representing the schedule indicates that it is a *designed domain*. That is, within the scope of the irrigation problem it must be, or has been, designed by the software developer to satisfy the needs of both subproblems. A designed domain may be realised as a collection of disk records forming a database, an assemblage of program objects, a USB key, a magnetic-stripe card, or any other concrete representation that the machine can read and write. Its concrete properties allow it to be written and read, and they furnish the substrate for representing its lexical content.

The decomposition promotes the schedule from its role in the solution, as a hidden local variable of the Instructed Irrigation machine, to a role in the problem, as a problem domain shared by the two subproblems. This problem domain is not given, but designed. The decomposition exposes both the design of the schedule domain and the development task—here postponed—of designing the recombination of the separated subproblems.

2.7. Decomposing the problem—3

The second example of a decomposition exposing and promoting a local variable of the machine is a decomposition that introduces an *analogical model domain*.

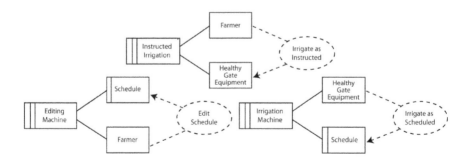

Figure 5. Irrigation as instructed: Decomposition into Two Subproblems.

The word 'model' has at least two senses that are relevant to software development. An *analytical model* of a problem domain is a description of the domain: a description W of the problem world's given properties is an analytical model. Such an analytical model is created and used by the developer, during the development. An *analogical* model of a problem domain, by contrast, is a designed lexical domain. If domain A is an analogical model of domain D, then D is the *subject* domain of A, and for some purpose A is intended to act as a *surrogate* for D. So, for example, a bank account database may be an analogical model of the bank's customers and the states of their accounts: queries about past transactions and balances are answered by inspecting the database, not by asking the customer or the bank manager. The schedule domain in Figure 5 is not an analytical model, because it is not useful to regard it as a surrogate for any physical problem domain.

The decomposition is shown in Figure 6. The upper part shows the Alarm problem of Figure 4. The Monitor machine is required to monitor the behaviour of the gate equipment and sound the alarm when a fault is detected. The decomposition will introduce a model domain whose subject domain is the Dubious Gate Equipment. As in the preceding example, the decomposition is justified only by the degree of complexity of the local variable to be exposed. If the only faults that can arise are simple and of a kind that can be detected without reference to historical data—for example, top and bottom sensors are both *on* simultaneously—then the decomposition is probably unwarranted. If, by contrast, faults can be detected only by checking the present state of the equipment against a record of past behaviour, then the decomposition is likely to be justified.

The lower part of Figure 6 shows the decomposition into two subproblems. On the left is a subproblem that builds the model domain. It creates and maintains the model data structure, continually recording the events and state changes in the subject domain—that is, in the Dubious Gate Equipment—in whatever raw or summarised forms the model design demands. On the right is a subproblem that uses the model, continually scanning the data structure for evidence of the faults that are to be detected. For example: a gradual increase of the upward travel time of the gate implies deterioration of the mechanism; the

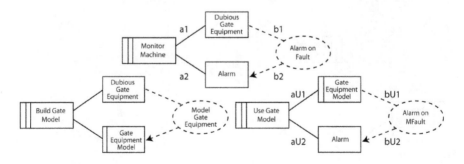

Figure 6. Decomposition Introducing a Model Domain.

lower sensor's remaining in the *on* state when the motor has been *on* and *upward* for more than two seconds suggests a failed motor, a clogged gearbox, or a stuck sensor; and so on.

The requirement for the Build Gate Model subproblem specifies the relationship to be maintained between the Dubious Gate Equipment domain and the model. This is a correspondence between their states, including behaviour histories. If this correspondence is correctly maintained, then a fault in the real gate equipment will be represented by a computed state of the model: the requirement for the Use Gate Model subproblem specifies those model state values for which the alarm must be sounded.

The explicit representation of model and subject domains in the problem diagram for building the model shows clearly that the model and its subject matter are two distinct domains having no common shared phenomena. They are connected only by the behaviour of the Model Builder machine: at interface $aB1$ the machine detects the state changes of the Gate Equipment; at $aB2$ it causes corresponding updates of the model. When the Model User machine examines the state of the model domain at $aU1$, it is not, of course, examining the Gate Equipment itself, but a surrogate. These trivial truths can sometimes be overlooked in developments in which there is no explicit recognition of the nature of analogical models. In particular, when developers describe some of the given properties W of a problem domain in object or class diagrams— notations designed for describing software rather than the physical world— they may be subtly encouraged to forget that the subject matter and its model are distinct realities. It is a conscious intent in the problem frames approach to keep this distinction always clearly present in the developer's mind.

2.8. Recombining subproblems

Recombining the subproblems identified in a decomposition is itself a significant development task. The subproblems are not like the pieces of a well-designed jigsaw puzzle, whose carefully shaped boundaries fit together perfectly to give the whole picture. Instead, because of the simplifications introduced in the decomposition, their boundaries have been shaped with a view to simplicity, not to the eventual need for recombination. Some rework, and even the introduction of additional subproblems, may be necessary to enable the subproblems to fit together without interfering with each other or frustrating each other's purpose. Further, they must be composed in a way that satisfies the requirements of the parent problem from which they were derived.

The recombination process has two facets: reconstructing the whole problem, and implementing its solution. From the problem perspective, composition is bottom-up development: the original whole problem is reconstructed upwards from the leaves of the decomposition tree. The task here is to reconcile and combine the problem domains and requirements, both between sibling subproblems and between a parent and its children. The subproblems are the available parts from which the whole is to be assembled; but some additional parts—that is, additional subproblems—may be needed for the assembly, and some of the available parts may need modification. The implementation perspective, by contrast, focuses on combining subproblem machines—that is, transforming and connecting their program texts to give the desired executable machine. The problem frames approach has less to say about implementation than about problem analysis; but the two are not disjoint, and the approach makes a contribution here too. In this subsection the problem view is discussed; the implementation view is discussed in the following section.

2.9. Readers and writers

A frequent task in subproblem composition arises when two subproblems have a problem domain in common. The resulting considerations are roughly those of shared data in programming. The subproblems shown in Figure 6 have the Gate Equipment Model in common: the model building subproblem is both a writer and a reader; the model using subproblem is a reader only. It is necessary to ensure mutual exclusion, with appropriate atomicity. The reader must always be presented with a version of the model that is sufficiently up to date, and is syntactically and semantically consistent with the given properties of the model domain that have been assumed in the analysis of the reader subproblem. The necessary constraints can be enforced, for example, by a transaction mechanism.

The irrigation and alarm subproblems shown in Figure 4 have the physical gate equipment as a common problem domain. The alarm subproblem monitors the gate equipment, which the irrigation subproblem controls, so they can be regarded respectively as reader and writer. In this case the composition will present no difficulty, provided that all access to each element of the gate equipment state—for example, setting the motor state to *on*, or testing the state of the top or bottom sensor—is atomic. The alarm subproblem makes no assumptions about relationships among the elements of the equipment state: atomicity of access to each element individually is therefore enough to guarantee a valid composite state.

Combining the writer and reader subproblems of the farmer's irrigation schedule, shown in Figure 5, is a little more interesting. By hypothesis the schedule is sufficiently complex to warrant the decomposition: for example, it may be an elaborate program hour by hour, day by day and month by month to reflect the changing seasons and variations in water availability. Clearly at least mutual exclusion is required: the irrigation machine must always see a schedule that satisfies the designed domain's assumed properties. However, because the schedule is complex, the farmer may take a long time to complete the editing of a new version (perhaps even leaving it in a partially edited state for many hours). Depending on whether the partially edited schedule satisfies the domain properties, mutual exclusion may demand that execution of the irrigation machine is suspended during this long time. The obvious solution to this difficulty is to allow the irrigation machine to proceed using the current version while the farmer is editing the new version. When the new version is complete the irrigation machine switches from the old schedule to the new.

Arranging for the switchover of schedules is the requirement for a new subproblem. Clearly, it may be desirable to increase quite radically the separation between creating a new irrigation schedule and applying it: perhaps the farmer should be able to create a whole library of schedules, and to apply any schedule from the library at will. The requirement for this new subproblem will describe the structure and desired management and use of the schedule library.

2.10. Switching a control regime

Switching the irrigation from one schedule to another gives rise to an example of a concern—the *switching concern*—that is important in many compositions. The essence of a switching concern is that a problem domain is passed from the control of one regime to the control of another. In this case the problem domain is the gate equipment, and the regime is the irrigation schedule. When the irrigation machine switches from one version of the schedule to another, it is necessary to ensure that the switchover is properly managed with respect to two concerns. First, the operation of the gate equipment must continue to satisfy the constraints of the breakage concern discussed in the following section. A certain timed protocol must be observed in motor operations, the motor being allowed to come to rest before starting in the reverse direction. The switchover is therefore feasible only in certain equipment states: in effect, each *raise* and *lower* operation must be executed within a critical region that includes the periods necessary for the motor to come to rest. Second, the concatenation of actual behaviour under the old schedule and any prefix of the new schedule must satisfy the general scheduling constraints of the undecomposed problem. Suppose, for example, that it is stipulated that there must never be uninterrupted water-flow for more than five hours. Then if the new schedule begins with a water-flow period of two hours, the switchover must not take place at any point at which water has been flowing continuously for three hours or more under the old schedule.

Switching concerns arise in many diverse situations. Consider, for example, a banking system that manages loans to householders. It may be appropriate to decompose the problem of managing each loan into one subproblem for managing loans in good standing, and another for managing delinquent loans in which the borrower has infringed the terms of the loan. Each particular loan is then under control of either the good or the delinquent regime, and may switch—possibly more than once—between them. Depending on the complexity of the good and delinquent regimes there may be severe constraints on the states in which the switchover is feasible.

2.11. Checking a joint requirement

In the first decomposition, shown in Figure 4, the whole problem was decomposed into the irrigation and alarm subproblems. The requirement of the original problem, shown in Figure 3, no doubt stipulated some relationship between its irrigation and alarm aspects—perhaps that the alarm must sound at least for any fault that makes continued operation of the gate either impossible or very likely to damage the equipment severely, and perhaps for others. After the decomposition has been made, and the two subproblems have been analysed, the equipment assumptions necessary for irrigation, and those necessary for fault detection and diagnosis, are known. Now it is a part of the composition task to check that the stipulated relationship will be satisfied.

If the predicate *Faulty(t)* characterises those behaviours—starting from the beginning of system execution—in which at time t the equipment has exhibited a fault for which the alarm should be sounded, and *Workable(t)* characterises those in which—starting from the beinning of system execution—the equipment properties assumed in the irrigation subproblem have been satisfied up to time t, then we must show that

$$not\ Faulty(t) \Rightarrow Workable(t).$$

That is: if the alarm has not sounded the farmer can assume that the equipment is capable of performing the required irrigation schedule. However, we should not try to show that

$$Faulty(e) \Rightarrow not\ Workable(e)$$

because some detected faults may indicate impending rather than actual failure: in spite of the fault, *Workable* may still hold, and may continue to hold in the future. Nonetheless it is probably required to stop operating the gate when any fault is found. It would then not be good enough simply to halt the Irrigation machine, because it might halt leaving the motor permanently in the on state, damaging the equipment severely. The design of the combination must ensure that this does not happen—perhaps by modifying the Irrigation machine to enclose each raise and lower operation in a critical region, or perhaps by introducing an additional subproblem whose requirement is to put the equipment unconditionally into a stable and safe state when a fault is detected.

3. Ideas and practices

The general conceptual framework described in the preceding section must be fleshed out by specific ideas and practices suited to the particular nature of computer-based systems. In this section, some of these ideas and practices are identified and explained.

3.1. Problem world phenomena

The problem world is central to a computer-based system, and so the task of describing it is central to software development [Jackson93]. A description that can be used for reasoning about the world must use ground terms that denote recognisable *phenomena* in the world: events, states, entities and so on. Two underpinnings are needed. First, a *phenomenology*: that is, a taxonomy of the kinds of phenomena that can be recognised in the problem world and denoted by ground terms in descriptions. Second, a set of *designations*: that is, a mapping of the ground terms to the phenomena they denote, with a *recognition rule* for each term showing how individual instances of the phenomena can be identified in the problem world and distinguished from each other and from phenomena of other kinds.

Sometimes, especially for a problem domain that is itself an engineered artifact of high technical quality, the phenomenology and the designations are provided ready to hand in an instruction manual. But most of the world does not come accompanied by an instruction manual, and there is work to be done. This work demands abstraction and approximation, appropriately judged for the purpose in hand. For example, the proposed designation

LightOn ≈ event: the light comes on

may abstract from a causal chain starting at the movement of a mechanical or electronic switch and progressing through a flow of electricity through wires to the heating of the element of an incandescent bulb. Identifying each traversal instance of this causal chain as a single event is evidently an abstraction: the steps in the chain are ignored. The abstraction is justified when the individual steps are not of interest for the description to be made. The whole chain is considered sufficiently reliable, and the small but inevitable delay in its traversal is considered negligible: so *LightOn* can be properly designated as an event—which in the chosen phenomenology is atomic and instantaneous. Similar issues arise in the designation of phenomena in problem domains of largely human activity. For example, in an e-commerce system it may be appropriate to designate

Deliver(p,c) ≈ event: product p is delivered to customer c.

The designated event is again an abstraction of a causal chain starting perhaps from an instruction to a delivery company and ending at the physical receipt of the product at the customer's location.

The need for designations—whether explicitly considered and recorded, or merely decided tacitly and imperfectly communicated and remembered—cannot be bypassed by basing problem world descriptions solely on the phenomena shared between the machine and its immediately neighbouring problem domains. A developer who decides that *LightOn* means only that the machine has set the appropriate line to high, or that *Deliver(p,c)* means only that the machine has sent an electronic message to the machine of the delivery company's system, is thereby deciding to abandon the task of describing the problem domains. There will be no recorded description *W* of the given properties of the problem world, and therefore no explicit basis for arguing that the developed system satisfies its requirement.

3.2. Problem locality

The designations of the phenomena of a problem domain provide the ground terms for the descriptions of its given properties. In general, the same domain will exhibit different given properties when it appears in different subproblems, and these differences may even demand different choices in the set of designations. The irrigation subproblem shown in Figure 4 relies on the healthy operating characteristics of the physical sluice gate equipment. It is therefore appropriate to designate

GateOpen ≈ state: the gate is open and the top sensor is on

as a simple state value. In the Alarm subproblem, however, the same equipment is assumed to be potentially faulty, and interest centres on the given properties that allow fault diagnosis. For example: after a certain period in which the motor has been driving the gate upwards the gate may be at the top of its travel, but the top sensor may be stuck off. For the purposes of this subproblem it is absolutely necessary to distinguish two distinct state values

GateAtTop ≈ state: the gate is at the top of its travel

TopSensor ≈ state: the top sensor is on

This is just one small illustration of what may be called *problem locality*. The view of the problem world taken in a problem is strictly local, and may differ—sometimes radically—from the view of the same parts of the world in another problem. Another small illustration is the treatment of the *control* of phenomena in the two subproblems. In the irrigation subproblem the event *MotorOn* is shared by the machine and the gate equipment, and controlled by the machine; in the alarm subproblem it is regarded as an unshared phenomenon controlled by the gate equipment itself. A larger illustration of problem locality is that the assumed given domain properties are quite different for the two subproblems.

The assumptions of each subproblem are local, and fully independent of those of the other subproblem. This view of the meaning of problem world properties is strongly influenced by the rely/guarantee structure due to Jones [Jones83]: in *guaranteeing* to satisfy its own requirement, each subproblem machine *relies* on its own problem world assumptions. If the rely condition does not hold—that is, if the problem world's given properties do not satisfy the assumptions—then the guarantee is withdrawn.

3.3. Problem simplicity

The treatment of the given properties of the problem world as local assumptions, rather than truths that hold globally in space for the whole system and in time from the beginning to the end of its operation, is the basis for simplifying the subproblems in a decomposition. Where local assumptions are in conflict it will be necessary to resolve any inconsistency in the design of the recombination of the subproblems. The claim implicit in problem frames is that buying subproblem simplicity at the price of deferring the recombination concerns is, in general, a profitable exchange. In developments that have a substantial ingredient of *radical design*, in which the problem and its subproblems are largely or entirely novel, the recombination concerns reveal inherent difficulties in the overall problem. Addressing them can then be profitably separated from the concerns of the individual simple subproblems.

Subproblem simplicity has many facets: they are all facets of a kind of *uniformity* in the view that the developer is required to take of the problem and of its principal parts. This means that the terms used in the adequacy argument to be made by the programmer—that the proposed machine, installed in the given problem world, will satisfy the requirement—must themselves be sufficiently simple for the argument to go through with one consistent view of the problem world, the requirement, and the machine.

In effect, this is an insistence on simplicity in what the chemist and philosopher, Michael Polanyi, calls the *operational principle* [Polanyi58] of a working system, whether natural or engineered. Drawing on Polanyi's work, the aeronautical engineer Walter Vincenti writes [Vincenti93]:

> "Designers must first of all know what Michael Polanyi calls the 'operational principle' of their device. By this one means, in Polanyi's words, 'how its characteristic parts ... fulfil their special function in combining to an overall operation which achieves the purpose' of the device—in brief, how the device works. Every device, whether a mobile machine such as an aircraft or a static structure such as a bridge, embodies a principle of this kind."

Polanyi stresses that the operational principle of a device is not deducible from scientific or mathematical knowledge, however detailed and exact, of its possible behaviours. It is parallel to, and distinct from, such knowledge. The operational principle of a subproblem must be expressible at its largest granularity. If the problem is simple its operational principle is both concrete enough to embrace the substance of the problem and abstract enough to be easily understood.

We may define a simple problem as one in which the 'purpose of the device', the 'characteristic parts', their 'special functions' and their 'combining' are all easily grasped because each plays a uniform role. Consider, for example, the undecomposed sluice gate problem shown in Figure 3. The requirement, at the largest granularity is something like "irrigate the field, but if that becomes impossible or dangerous to the equipment, then don't irrigate but sound the alarm." This is not a simple problem: the complexity in the requirement lies in the two levels of desired behaviour, corresponding to two levels of given properties in the problem domain. The decomposition shown in Figure 4 separates the two levels, each with a uniform requirement and a problem world with uniform given properties.

In a simple problem each problem domain has a clear and uniform role. Consider, for example, an e-commerce support system in which agents are engaged in responding to customers' email queries. The system must provide an efficient editing tool for the preparation of outgoing emails; it must also provide information to help in managing the relationships between agents and customers—for example, directing a customer's query to an agent who is familiar with that customer's account. For the editing requirement the agent is an active user of the editing tool; for the relationship requirement the agents and customers are part of a problem domain about which information is needed. The agent is therefore playing different roles in these two requirements, and each role should be handled in a distinct subproblem.

Another aspect of uniformity is the need for a simple tempo of the problem world and the requirement. In a simple problem, the interacting given and desired behaviours of the problem domains are all accommodated in one tempo—one synchronous temporal structure. The absence of this kind of uniformity creates what in the JSP program design method [Jackson75] is called a *boundary clash*. The classic illustration is the conflict between months and weeks in the Gregorian calendar: their boundaries are not synchronised, and this lack of uniformity causes serious difficulties in accounting. Essentially, the symptomatic difficulties arise when it becomes necessary to consider explicitly all the cases of interaction between weeks and months: it is a small-scale instance of the combinatorial explosion. A system function that runs at a weekly tempo should therefore be separated in the decomposition from a function that runs at a monthly or annual tempo.

A different, but related, temporal uniformity may be achieved by assuming that some phenomenon is constant that does, in reality, vary over time. Consider, for example, a system to administer a lending library, for which there are requirements about the borrowing and return of books, and also requirements about people joining the library as members, and renewing or terminating their memberships. The temporal cycle of the membership requirement is roughly annual, membership being renewable each year, while the temporal cycle of borrowing and returning may be one, two or three weeks. There is boundary clash here. It is therefore desirable to separate two subproblems: a membership subproblem, in which book borrowing and returning occur only as mutually unrelated atomic events; and a borrowing subproblem, in which library membership is constant, in the sense that only a person who is a member may borrow a book, and it is assumed that their membership remains intact during the whole of the borrowing episode. The predictable complication of dealing with the subproblems' interactions—for example, handling (or preventing) cases in which membership expires during the currency of a loan—is deferred to the task of subproblem recombination.

This notion of simplicity as uniformity may seem imprecise, and indeed it is. That is not surprising: we are concerned here, as everywhere in the problem frames approach, with human capacity for understanding, for which there are no precise criteria.

3.4. Dependability and simplicity

Other things being equal, a simple subproblem is more understandable than a more complex subproblem. In an important sense, simplicity is a fundamental kind of strength in software: a simpler program is stronger because it is less likely to be faulty. This notion of simplicity as software strength implies a decomposition criterion that is an essential contributor to system dependability.

In an imaginary ideal world a system designed for dependability would be perfectly dependable in every part and every respect. In practice this cannot be, because human developers are fallible and resources are limited. A more realistic—and rewarding—ambition is to try to ensure that the most critical system functions are the most dependable. They must therefore be the most simple. An extremely critical function—for example, the shut-down function in a radiotherapy machine, activated by an emergency button—must be allocated to a subproblem of its own, and must be purged of every complication that is not vital to the function.

The appropriate treatment of a critical subproblem in composition is clear. From the problem perspective, in which subproblems are combined, a critical subproblem should be exempt from invasive composition. If an invasive modification is necessary to reconcile it in some way with a less critical subproblem, only the less critical subproblem should suffer the modification. The same principle applies in the implementation perspective, briefly discussed in a later subsection, in which subproblem machines are combined.

3.5. Subproblem concerns

Even the simple subproblems aimed at by problem frame decomposition may present significant difficulties. Depending on the natures of the problem domains, of their interactions, and of the requirement, a simple subproblem will still present concerns that must be addressed by the developer. Every problem, of course, presents the basic concern of satisfying its operational principle—of ensuring that the parts can, indeed, combine successfully to fulfil the overall purpose. This basic concern may be called the *frame concern*. Other subproblem concerns address possible failures that may interfere with the designed success. It is useful to name these concerns, and to address them separately and explicitly.

One subproblem concern is *initialisation*. The programming danger of uninitialised variables is well known. In a computer-based system the danger is greater. Consider, for example, the subproblem shown at the lower left of Figure 6, where the machine is required to build and maintain the model of the gate equipment so that it can act as a surrogate for the equipment itself. The developer might assume that when the machine begins its execution the gate will be in some suitable initial state—for example, with the gate in its lowest position, the lower sensor *on*, the upper sensor *off*, and the motor it its *off* and *upward* states. This assumption may not hold in reality: the machine may be started in some other state and failure is then a likely result. In general, there are many ways of addressing the concern. The machine can be designed to accommodate any possible initial state of the modelled domain; the machine can execute a prologue phase in which it detects the current state of the modelled domain, or brings the domain into a known state; a manual initialisation procedure can be stipulated to be performed when the machine is started; and so on.

Another concern arising when a physical domain is to be controlled is the *breakage* concern mentioned in an earlier section: the system may fail because the machine has damaged the domain. In the irrigation subproblem, the gate is raised and lowered by the machine. The physical gate equipment may have been designed on certain assumptions about the operating protocol—for example, that the motor direction would not be switched between *upward* and *downward* except when the motor is at rest; or that the motor will not be held *on* for long enough to drive the gate hard against its travel limits. The developer must identify such restrictions, and ensure that the machine observes them correctly.

In the Traffic Control problem shown in Figure 2, the machine has an interface of phenomena shared with the Light Units domain. This is a *physically multiple* domain, in the sense that it is populated by multiple instances of a physical type—the individual light units. The machine will be designed to set a particular control line *high* in some particular situation because the physical light sharing that phenomenon is, for example, the north-south red light in the unit at a certain position in the road layout. How can it be known that the actual physical pairing of units with control lines is set up exactly as the developer supposes? This is an *identities* concern, and arises only for physically multiple domains. Like initialisation, it concerns the set-up conditions of the implemented system, but it is nonetheless a software development concern. The developer must consider how to avoid—or tolerate—faulty set-up conditions that might otherwise cause failure.

One final example of a subproblem concern is what we may call the *anomaly* concern. It can arise with any domain of human behaviours, states, and attributes. For such a domain almost every assumed property must be carefully questioned, and measures taken to guard against surprises. It might, for example, be reasonably supposed that a person's date of birth is not subject to change. But there are many reasons why people might misreport their date of birth, especially immigrants from countries with oppressive regimes, and correct this misreporting some time after they have become known to the system. Similarly, changes of name or gender are easily overlooked.

Addressing subproblem concerns is about avoiding failures. After a failure has occurred it may be relatively easy to identify the causes that have contributed to the failure. A commonplace—and superficially reasonable—reaction to a software failure is then to wonder how the developers could have been so negligent. The answer to this question is usually straightforward: the developers lacked the hindsight available to the investigators and critics. A realistically large system provides a very large conceptual space in which potential failures can hide: exhaustive search is not feasible, and teasing out potential failures depends heavily on knowing where they are most likely to be found.

A discipline of identifying and addressing subproblem concerns is an essential part of any serious approach to avoiding system failures. It can be seen as a part of the normal process of constructing a safety case for a system, but it is different in two ways. First, it is integrated into the basic development activity; and second, it takes place at the subproblem level, where the scope to be considered is smaller and the desired goal—with respect to which failure must be avoided—is clearly expressed in a simple operational principle.

3.6. Problem reduction

A problem diagram is simple, but it captures important decisions that will have a large effect on the subsequent analysis and development. The diagram bounds the problem to be solved, both above and below. Everything that is in the diagram is relevant, and everything relevant is in the diagram. In Figure 2 the developer cannot ignore any part of the requirement or any of the pictured problem domains, but is entitled—indeed, obliged—to ignore everything else.

As discussed in an earlier section, acceptance of the problem diagram therefore obliges the developer to document and reason about the given properties of the Pedestrians and Vehicles and of the Road Layout domain. However, the problem can be *reduced* [Rapanotti06] if this obligation is discharged—probably by someone other than the developer—in a preceding phase of work. A reduced problem is shown in Figure 7.

The Pedestrian and Vehicles domains have been removed in the reduction. Their influence on the problem has been precalculated, and their given domain properties, such as speeds and accelerations, have been taken into account in a modified requirement. The modified requirement says nothing about collisions, about speeds of traversing the pedestrian crossings and road segments of the junction, or about how many vehicles can wait in particular controlled segments. Instead it stipulates the permissible patterns of combinations of light settings, specifying for each combination which lights on the Road Layout are red and which are green, the patterns specifying the timed sequencing of combinations and of the intermediate settings when the lights change between successive combinations. Now the developer needs no knowledge of the behaviour of cars and pedestrians, but is still required to understand notions of the Road Layout, positions of Light Units and Crossing Buttons, and to respect the operation protocols for setting the traffic lights. In effect, we may say that the problem has been moved closer to the machine—but not so close that the resulting problem bears no intelligible relationship to the problem world and the requirement.

In an important sense, every computer-based system problem presented to a developer has already been to some extent reduced. The problem of controlling the sluice gate was reduced from a larger problem about crops, fields and water—which was itself reduced from an even larger problem of managing the farm, and so on in an endless regression of purposes and means. Drawing the problem diagram bounds the problem at both ends. The requirement cannot be about the meaning of life; but neither can it be about the behaviour of the machine. The purpose of the machine is specifically to interact with the problem world: in the absence of the problem world the machine's becomes incomprehensible.

3.7. POSE: Problem-Oriented Software Engineering

Problem reduction, discussed in the preceding subsection, is an example of a *problem transformation.* It has been discussed in a formal setting in [Rapanotti06]. Other examples of transformation are problem decomposition and problem recombination, discussed in the preceding section. Even the elaboration of an empty description of a problem domain—consisting only of its name—by discovering and recording relevant given properties can be viewed as a problem transformation. More generally, the whole development activity can be regarded as the execution of problem transformation steps leading eventually to a software specification. (This sense of moving from an initial problem towards a software specification is reflected in use of the term *problem progression* [Seater06] as a synonym of *problem reduction.*)

One of the respects in which the approach described in the earlier sections of this paper is incomplete is the lack of a formally structured framework for the whole development activity. Problem-Oriented Software Engineering [Hall07] offers such a structure. The structure captures the step-by-step solution of a system development problem; it also captures the arguments that must eventually justify the adequacy of the developed system. The framework is itself formal, defining what is essentially a sequent calculus in which each step is regarded as a problem transformation according to a rule. The rules themselves are formally expressed, but the content of the transformations, and the associated arguments that justify their application, can be either formal or informal.

3.8. Implementation aspects of combining subproblems

Eventually the subproblem machines must be composed to give the complete machine, however implemented, that solves the original problem. The subproblem machines are not a set of programs encoded in a specific programming language, in whose texts many problem-independent implementation choices have already been bound. They are to be regarded, in effect, as more abstract than the given domains of the physical problem world, because they are merely projections of the behaviour of the complete machine—a machine domain that has not yet been constructed. The way is therefore open to a range of behaviour-preserving transformations of subproblem machines, and designed domains offer similar opportunities. For example:

✦ Two model domains whose subject is the same underlying problem domain—

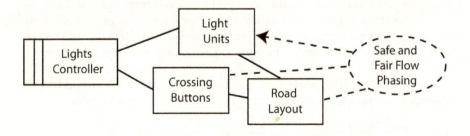

Figure 7. Reduced Problem: Traffic Lights Control at a Road Junction

though with different assumptions—may be merged into a single composite model domain.

✦ Where one subproblem machine takes the initiative in causing certain events or state changes in a problem domain, and another monitors the same phenomena in the same domain, it may be possible to fragment the second machine into a collection of actions that can be inserted into the behaviour of the first machine.

Such transformations embody implementation decisions that are otherwise liable to be taken prematurely in an earlier development phase.

Because the problem frames approach is concerned to structure and analyse problems, it has in general paid less attention to the implementation task of designing the complete machine. However, some specific proposals have been presented for implementation techniques whose basic starting point is a problem structuring:

⸱ *Architectural Frames* [Rapanotti04] are problem diagrams in which the machine is elaborated into a structure of component machines. The component machines have interfaces to each other, and also to the neighbouring problem domains. This technique allows advantage to be taken of appropriate known solution patterns—for example, of the Model-View-Controller pattern, or of a pipe-and-filter machine architecture—both in forming the implementation design and also, at an earlier stage, in guiding the problem analysis and structuring towards a desired solution.

⸱ *Composition Controllers* [Laney07] are machines introduced into the system to take control of subproblem machines. A composition controller interposes itself between each subproblem and its problem domains, and is therefore capable of managing the interactions at that interface. For example, it can cut a subproblem machine off completely from its problem world, thus terminating its ability to affect the world; or it can selectively suppress individual interaction phenomena to resolve a conflict between one subproblem's requirement and another's. An advantage of the composition controller technique, where applicable, is that the controller manages subproblem interactions at execution time, reducing the need for invasive compositions in which the subproblem design is modified.

3.9. Implementation of critical subproblems

Isolation of critical functionality is a criterion of decomposition and of subproblem recombination: a subproblem providing a critical function must not be obscured or complicated by the influence of less critical functions. The same general principle applies in the implementation perspective, when subproblem machines are combined: a more critical subproblem must not be exposed to the consequences of failure of a less critical subproblem.

Here is an example. In a system to control and manage a proton therapy machine, two of the identified subproblems were Emergency Stop and Command Logging. The emergency stop subproblem shuts off the beam and closes down the equipment in response to the operator's pressing of the emergency button. Command logging ensures that every command issued by or through the control system is logged to disk for auditing in the event of any incident demanding investigation. It seemed necessary to the developers that commands issued by the emergency stop function should be routed to the equipment through the logging function, to ensure that they would be logged; that was how the software was originally configured. However, the developer of the logging subproblem had neglected to address a specific subproblem concern: the behaviour of the logging function was unspecified if there was not enough disk space to record the current command. The actual—unintended—behaviour was that the logging function failed to log the command, failed to pass it on to the equipment, and failed to return to the procedure that had invoked it: in the chosen composition the current command would not then be executed. In effect, the emergency button ceases to work if the logging disk is full.

4. The role of problem frames

The emphasis on problem analysis and structuring is in some respects unusual. Ralph Johnson, one of earliest champions of the Design Patterns movement, wrote [Johnson94]:

"We have a tendency to focus on the solution, in large part because it is easier to notice a pattern in the systems that we build than it is to see the pattern in the problems we are solving that lead to the patterns in our solutions to them."

As Johnson points out, it is somehow easier to focus on solutions than on problems. Solutions seem concrete and specific, and constrained by the programming language and implementation environment: problems naturally seem more abstract and general, and relatively unconstrained. In the development of computer-based systems the role of problem frames is first to show that problems too can be concrete and specific—constrained by the properties of the given problem domains—and second to provide an intellectual framework for analysing and structuring them.

A large part of the original motivation [Jackson94] for problem frames sprang from the recognition that inappropriate software development methods are often chosen for the problem in hand. Sometimes the chosen method is too general to provide a good grip on the problem; sometimes it is specific enough, but makes implicit assumptions that do not fit the problem. It seemed clear that realistic software development problems could not be usefully classified as wholes. Most must be seen as complex and heterogeneous assemblages of smaller problems. It is more useful, then, to identify and name different classes of elementary software development problem—*information display, controlled behaviour, transformation, workpieces* and others. Each class can be described [Jackson01] by a *problem frame*. A problem frame is a formalised problem diagram, with formal annotations for interface and requirement phenomena and with each problem domain marked with its type—*causal, lexical,* or *biddable*. A particular small problem fits a class if its actual topology, domain types and interface phenomena can be exactly mapped to their formal equivalents in the class description, and its requirement fits the purpose associated with the class.

Although problem classification has not been emphasised in this paper, it remains a significant aspect of the problem frames approach. It offers a basis for extending the applicability of *normal design* to the development of computer-based systems. A brilliant book [Vincenti93] about engineering points out that normal design is everyday practice in the established engineering branches:

> "[in normal design] ... the engineer knows at the outset how the device in question works, what are its customary features, and that, if properly designed along such lines, it has a good likelihood of accomplishing the desired task."

In *radical* design, by contrast:

> "... how the device should be arranged or even how it works is largely unknown. The designer has never seen such a device before and has no presumption of success. The problem is to design something that will function well enough to warrant further development."

Suitably refined and developed, the classification of elementary problem frames could offer a taxonomy of what Vincenti calls 'devices', and a structure within which accumulating experience and knowledge can be codified and made more easily accessible. The notion of subproblem concerns, discussed in an earlier section, is an example of capturing such knowledge and, to that extent, bringing those subproblems within the ambit of normal design. As knowledge increases, problems that had previously been regarded as composite could come to be regarded as elementary—just as multiplication comes to be regarded as an elementary operation when we learn arithmetic. (The distinction between normal and radical design, and its importance for software development, are discussed more fully in [Jackson 09], also Chapter 2 of this volume.)

Few realistic computer-based systems are the object of purely normal or purely radical design. Vincenti, regarding the engineering process and its product as a hierarchy, goes on to say:

> "Whether design at a given location in the hierarchy is normal or radical is a separate matter—normal design can (and usually does) prevail throughout, though radical design can be encountered at any level."

In computer-based systems, where feature proliferation is the rule rather than the exception, radical design is perhaps most notably encountered in designing the composition of subproblems, especially where solutions to some subproblems are already available. Because much of current software development practice is strongly focused on solutions rather than on problems, it may be difficult to determine exactly what problem is solved by an available component, and what assumptions its designer has made about the problem world. In such an environment, effective analysis of composition concerns may demand some reverse engineering to clarify the subproblems that are to be composed. Problem frames can offer guidance in reverse engineering: the notions of subproblem simplicity are useful in the reverse, as well as in the forward, engineering direction.

Acknowledgements

Cooperation over thirteen years with Pamela Zave laid down an understanding of phenomena and domain descriptions that underpins the whole problem frames approach. Extensive discussion over several years with Cliff Jones and Ian Hayes has illuminated the Sluice Gate problem and its many lessons. Colleagues and postgraduate students at the Open University have contributed greatly to the understanding of the ideas described here and of their enrichment and extension in more than one direction. Notable among them are Charles Haley, Jon Hall, Robin Laney, Zhi Li, Armstrong Nhlabatsi, Bashar Nuseibeh, Lucia Rapanotti, Mohamed Salifu, Thein Than Tun and Yijun Yu. Continual discussions with Daniel Jackson, and his perspicuous comments on many topics, have always been invaluable.

References

[Dijkstra89]   E. W. Dijkstra; On the cruelty of really teaching computer science; *CACM* Volume 32 Number 12, pages 1398-1404, December 1989.

[Goh04]   P. K. Goh and William H. K. Lam; Pedestrian flows and walking speed: A problem at signalized crosswalks; *ITE Journal*, Institute of Transportation Engineers. Jan 2004.

[Hall 07]   J. G. Hall, L. Rapanotti and M. Jackson; Problem oriented software engineering: A design-theoretic framework for software engineering; in *Proceedings of 5th IEEE International Conference on Software Engineering and Formal Methods*, IEEE Computer Society Press, 2007.

[Hayes03]   Ian J. Hayes, Michael A. Jackson and Cliff B. Jones; Determining the specification of a control system from that of its environment; in Keijiro Araki, Stefani Gnesi and Dino Mandrioli eds, *Formal Methods: Proceedings of FME2003*, pages 154-169, Springer Verlag, Lecture Notes in Computer Science 2805, 2003.

[Jackson75]   M. A. Jackson; *Principles of Program Design*; Academic Press, 1975.

[Jackson93]   Michael Jackson and Pamela Zave; Domain descriptions; in *Proceedings of IEEE International Symposium on Requirements Engineering* January 1993, pages 56-64; IEEE CS Press, 1992.

[Jackson94]   M. A. Jackson; Software development method; in *A Classical Mind: Essays in Honour of C A R Hoare*, A W Roscoe ed; Prentice-Hall International, 1994.

[Jackson01]   Michael Jackson; *Problem Frames: Analysing and Structuring Software Development Problems*; Addison-Wesley, 2001.

[Jackson09]   Michael Jackson; Engineering and software; Chapter 2 of this volume.

[Johnson94]   Ralph E. Johnson; Why a conference on pattern languages? *ACM SE Notes* Volume 19 Number 1, pages 50-52, January 1994.

[Jones83]   C. B. Jones; Specification and design of (parallel) programs; *IFIP'83 Proceedings*, pages 321–332, North-Holland, 1983.

[Laney07]   Robin Laney, Thein T. Tun, Michael Jackson and Bashar Nuseibeh; Composing features by managing inconsistent requirements; in *Proceedings of the Ninth International Conference on Feature Interactions in Software and Communications*

Systems, Grenoble, September 2007.

[Polanyi58]   Michael Polanyi; *Personal Knowledge: Towards a Post-Critical Philosophy*; Routledge and Kegan Paul, London, 1958.

[Polya57]   G. Polya; *How To Solve It*; Princeton University Press, 2nd Edition 1957.

[Rapanotti04]   Lucia Rapanotti, Jon G. Hall, Michael Jackson and Bashar Nuseibeh; Architecture-driven problem decomposition; in *Proceedings of the 2004 International Conference on Requirements Engineering (RE'04)*, Kyoto, IEEE CS Press, 2004.

[Rapanotti06]   Lucia Rapanotti, Jon G. Hall and Zhi Li; Deriving specifications from requirements through problem reduction; *IEE Proceedings—Software*, Volume 153 Number 5, pages 183-198, October 2006.

[Risks08]   The Risks Forum; http://catless.ncl.ac.uk/Risks (accessed 19th November 2008).

[Seater06]   Robert Seater and Daniel Jackson; Requirement progression in problem frames applied to a proton therapy system; *Proceedings of the 14th International Requirements Engineering Conference (RE06)*, Minneapolis USA, 2006.

[Vincenti93]   Walter G. Vincenti; *What Engineers Know and How They Know It: Analytical Studies from Aeronautical History*; The Johns Hopkins University Press, Baltimore, paperback edition, 1993.

[Zave97]   Pamela Zave and Michael Jackson; Four dark corners of requirements engineering; *ACM Transactions on Software Methodology* Volume 6 Number 1, pages 1-30, July 1997.

Chapter 15

Abuse Frames: Inferring Security Requirements from Anti-requirements

Bashar Nuseibeh

Abstract: Effective elicitation and precise representation of security requirements offers opportunities for early analysis of security concerns, the discovery and elaboration of additional security requirements, and an exploration of alternative protection solutions. Requirements engineering (RE) is a branch of software and systems engineering concerned with understanding stakeholder goals in the problem domain, and the specification of operational requirements for a system in order to satisfy such goals. This paper explores the application of RE techniques to security engineering, to provide a front-end for security analysis that facilitates the early identification of potential system vulnerabilities and the specification of more robust security requirements. In the particular, the paper investigates the notion of anti-requirements—the requirements of users with malicious intent—to identify potential vulnerabilities not addressed by existing security requirements. The paper makes use of an emerging approach from requirements engineering, problem frames [23], to capture descriptions of an initial problem and its security requirements, and extends the approach by introducing abuse frames that capture the problem of a malicious user and his anti-requirements. The successful composition of a problem frame with an abuse frame identifies potential vulnerabilities. The approach is illustrated with examples, and some abuse frame patterns are suggested to facilitate its application.

Prologue

Although I have known Michael Jackson for almost 20 years, I am one of his more recent collaborators. I met Michael when I was a PhD student at Imperial College London in the early 1990s. I would characterise my relationship with him at that time as being of the "admirer-of"variety. This relationship has persisted and grown over the years, and it is now also my privilege to call him a colleague and a friend.

Soon after I joined The Open University (OU) in 2001, Michael graciously agreed to join me in the role of Visiting Professor in the OU's Department of Computing. It is not an exaggeration to say that Michael's transformative influence on the Department's research agenda was instrumental in the Department's rise to become a leading Computing research department in the UK eight years later.

Michael drew upon his many years of experience as a software engineering practitioner to present my OU colleagues and me with real practical problems that demanded deep study by researchers. He helped us formulate our research questions, suggested ideas for answering them, critiqued our solutions, and co-authored our write ups. Before long, and with Michael's help, the OU's software engineering group was attracting substantial external funding for its research, and publishing prolifically in the area of requirements engineering in general and problem frames in particular.

A major research contribution that Michael helped us develop over the years at the OU was to shed light on the complex relationship between software problem structures and solution structures [18]. Using problem frames as our intellectual tool, my OU colleagues and I were able to develop our research in the areas of problem composition [27], software architecture [39], coordination [7], problem semantics [19] and security requirements [15]. These contributions continue to develop and find applications in areas of feature-based development [47], problem-oriented engineering [20], computer-based security [16, 36], adaptive systems design [42], and the analysis of software-related failures [48]. PhD degrees continue to be awarded at the OU, inspired and guided by Michael, including Zhi Li (2006), Charles Haley (2007), Mohammed Salifu (2008), Derek Mannering (2009) and Armstrong Nhlabatsi (2009).

In this chapter, I provide an overview of a research topic, inspired by problem frames, that Michael and I have discussed for a number of years. I describe Abuse Frames—a kind of problem frame—that can potentially help analyse security problems, by modelling threats, security requirements, and potential security vulnerabilities, long before any commitments to security solutions. I am looking forward to the continued development of the ideas presented with Michael.

1. Introduction

The importance of understanding and specifying precise security requirements for computer-based systems is generally accepted, yet is also recognised as problematic [6, 12, 38]. Security requirements are often expressed informally and most forms of early security specification and analysis assume significant design of a system, as opposed to focusing on the nature of the security problem in which the system might subsequently be installed [8]. Techniques for early risk and threat analysis exist [3, 9, 37, 46], but it is often not clear how these relate to precise specifications of system behaviour.

This paper explores the application of the languages and techniques of *requirements engineering* in the field of security engineering. Requirements engineering is a branch of software and systems engineering concerned with the elicitation, modelling, and analysis of stakeholder goals for an envisioned system, and their specification in a form that permits their validation and their subsequent incorporation into the design and implementation of the system

[35]. The focus of requirements engineering is on the "problem world" in which users, their goals and their assets exist, rather then the "solution world", in which the system designed to meet those goals exists [22]. Thus, the motivation of our work is to inform the security engineering process in its early stages, with a view to discovering *potential* system vulnerabilities before they become more costly to address. We speculate that security requirements analysis could be used forensically to explain existing attacks, although further experience is required to substantiate this claim.

The paper presents an approach using Problem Frames [23] to analyse security threats and derive security requirements. Our approach introduces two conceptual tools—*anti-requirements* and *abuse frames*. A user's malicious intent is captured by an anti-requirement. An anti-requirement is incorporated into an abuse frame in order to represent a threat to the system. Different classes of threats are represented by different classes of abuse frames. A *base system* is an envisioned system bounded by a problem frame. For a threat to be realised in a base system, its abuse frame is composed successfully with the base system to identify the vulnerabilities. The paper illustrates the approach briefly using simple examples, and proposes an agenda for further development of the work and its evaluation.

The paper is structured as follows. The next section discusses a selection of related work, from both security and requirements engineering, that addresses early security requirements analysis. Section 3 provides an overview of problem frames upon which this research builds and illustrates how they may be used to represent security requirements. Our approach based on abuse frames and their analysis is then presented in Section 4, and the paper concludes in Section 5 with a discussion of open issues and future work.

2. Related work

A thorough review of related work is beyond the scope of this short paper, so the intention in this section is to contextualise our work, and identify and distinguish key related contributions.

There is increasing recognition of the importance and role of security requirements [1, 41]. Explicit consideration of security requirements has traditionally fallen in the general areas of risk and threat assessment [3, 9, 37, 46]. Although this work does indeed provide early analysis of security concerns and identifies assets in need of protection, explicit elicitation and specification of security requirements is outside the scope of such activities. The Common Criteria [2] do mandate the consideration of security requirements, but do not provide more then a check list and template structure to document them. Recent security methodologies [13, 33, 40] provide frameworks within which security requirements may be considered, but offer little in the form of rigorous analysis support.

Anderson [5] reports on a study in which a number of analysts (students) investigated a (lottery) system with which they were not previously familiar, and argues that the exercise was equivalent to each student engaging in requirements engineering. However, the students appear to have been searching for system vulnerabilities rather then security requirements.

Abuse cases [32] from security engineering and misuse cases [4, 44] from requirements engineering support the construction of scenarios describing malicious usage of systems, as an inverse to the more common use case [24]. These abuse/misuse cases share much in common with our proposed approach in analysing the intentions of a hostile user, however like use cases they make assumptions about the design and interfaces of a system, whereas our aim is to examine the problem world before a system has been envisioned let alone designed. Similarly, Heitmeyer's work on using the SCR methodology [21] to check security properties automatically assumes a detailed level of specification rather than providing early problem analysis.

Our work is positioned at what Wing [50] calls application layer security and as such is aimed at contributing to analysis to alleviate so-called social engineering attacks [34]. However, our own focus is not on attacks per se [43], but on the social [31], organisational [11, 14] and technical [49] subversion of stakeholder goals.

Finally, our work shares many characteristics with hazard analysis [26] and safety argumentation [25] found in the safety engineering community [28], but is distinguished from that work in its focus on (malicious) intentionality rather then accident.

3. Problem frames and security requirements

Jackson [22] characterises software development problems by distinguishing three kinds of knowledge: knowledge of the problem world and its properties, W; knowledge of the requirements, R, that one wishes to be true in the world; and knowledge of the specification, S, of a machine that when installed in the world, satisfies the requirements. Thus: $S, W \vdash R$; that is, the problem world (with its domain properties) and the specification entail the requirements. Jackson further proposes the notion of *problem frames* [23], an approach and associated graphical notation that captures this entailment relationship. A problem frame defines a pattern of an identifiable problem class in terms of its context and the characteristics of its domains, interfaces, and requirements. Domain and interface characteristics are based on an identification of shared *phenomena*. A phenomenon is an element observable in the world. Jackson suggests four classes of basic problem frames. Each basic frame corresponds to a recognisable and well-understood problem class to which there are standard solutions available. Figure 1 is an example problem frame diagram, illustrating the notation.

In Figure 1, the plain rectangles represent problem domains; the connecting lines represent interfaces (shared phenomena) between them. A rectangle with two double vertical stripes represents the machine to be built. This machine is built in the form of software and deployed by running the software on a general-purpose computer. The job of the software engineer is to derive a specification

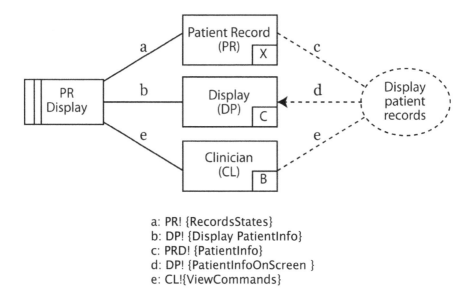

a: PR! {RecordsStates}
b: DP! {Display PatientInfo}
c: PRD! {PatientInfo}
d: DP! {PatientInfoOnScreen }
e: CL!{ViewCommands}

Figure 1. A simple problem frame diagram for a patient record display system

of the machine. The dashed oval represents the *requirement*. The dashed lines connecting the oval to a problem domain represent a *requirement reference*; that is, the requirement refers to certain phenomena of the problem domain. A dashed arrow denotes the requirement reference as a *constraining reference*—meaning that the requirement stipulates some desired relationships or behaviour involving the domain phenomena.

The Display (DP) is a causal domain, meaning that its properties include predictable causal relationships. A causal domain is indicated by a C in the bottom right corner. The Clinician (CL) is biddable, meaning it is a domain consisting of humans, and is indicated by B in the bottom right corner. Finally, the lexical property (physical representation of data) of the Patient Record (PR) domain is indicated by an X.

Interface phenomena are annotated to show the sets of shared phenomena between two domains. For example, the shared phenomenon PR!{RecordsStates} represents the shared state of the PR database and the PR Displayer machine. It also shows that the event is controlled by PR (prefix PR!).

To show that a problem is solved, a software developer needs to address the *frame concerns* associated each problem frame diagram. Addressing frame concerns adequately means that the software developer must produce a *correctness argument* that fits requirements, specification, and descriptions of the problem world properly. This means that the correctness argument needs show that given the machine specification (S) and all modelled behaviour in the world (W), the requirement (R) is always satisfied. That is, $S, W \Rightarrow R$. The notion of correctness argument relies on W being strictly bounded by the problem frame diagram; i.e.

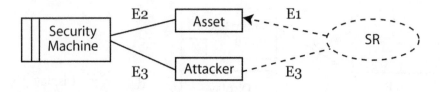

Figure 2. A security problem frame diagram

phenomena that are not explicitly shown on the diagram are not within the scope of the problem world and are not included in W. In Figure1, an example of a correctness argument is that information of patient record (a) will be displayed correctly on the DP (d) as requested by the clinician (e).

3.1. Capturing security requirements using problem frames

A security requirement describes the constraints on some functionality of a system [17]. That is, security requirements must state the system's behaviour in the presence of attackers and their imposed threats.

In Figure 2, we represent a security requirement as a requirement in a problem frame that requires the machine to result in some constrained phenomena in the world in order to protect the Asset domain.

+ The phenomenon E3 identifies the potential shared phenomena between the Machine and a malicious user. E3 can be regarded as the phenomenon that describes the attacks from the attacker.
+ The Machine is the machine to be built that incorporates the security measures to counteract the attacks from the Attacker.
+ E1 identifies the desirable phenomenon of the protected domain in the presence of an attack.

The correctness argument of this problem frame must show that in the presence of attackers, the security measures incorporated into the security machine satisfy the security requirement.

3.2. Example

Consider the following description of a cheque Issue/Approval problem:

A bank has a simple cheque issuing system. A cheque is considered valid if and only if it is issued (printed). A cheque is issued only after a cheque issue request has been made and subsequently approved. A cheque request has to be made for the cheque to be approved. Any cheque approval request made before its issue request is ignored. Any issue requests waiting to be approved are stored in a company database.

This problem statement leads to the following requirement:

Cheque Issue/Approval: Only staff in Group2 shall be allowed to make cheque approval requests and only staff in Group1 shall be allowed to make issue requests.

To prevent loss of money, one of the security objectives is to prevent any unauthorised issuing of cheques. Thus, an additional security requirement is identified (consistent with the separation of duties principle [10]):

Security Requirement: No person shall issue and approve the same cheque.

Figure 3 shows the problem frame diagram of a development problem for a cheque issue and approval system. The Issue_Rq_log stores any cheque issuing request that is waiting to be approved. The Cheque Issue/Approval Machine, M, is the machine to be built, and the descriptions of the phenomena in Figure 3 are:

+ A cheque is issued if and only if only it is printed out; i.e. prt(chq).
+ The check_Group(s) is a query of the membership of s that M sends to the Issue_Rq_log (s = staff).
+ The chequeIssueRq(staff, chq) and chequeApproveRq(staff, chq) represent the issue and approve requests made by the staff, respectively.
+ Issued_Rqd(chq), Issued(chq) and Group(staff, group) are predicates. They describe the states of the IssueRq_log, Cheque, and the Group domain respectively.

To show that the cheque issue/approval problem is solved, a correctness argument must be constructed that fits requirements, specification, and descriptions of the problem adequately. This means that the correctness argument needs show that given the specification of the issue/approval machine, and all

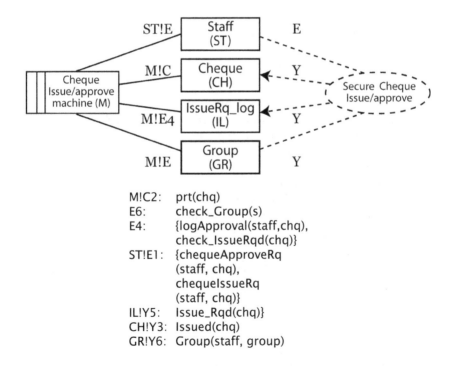

M!C2:   prt(chq)
E6:   check_Group(s)
E4:   {logApproval(staff,chq),
          check_IssueRqd(chq)}
ST!E1:   {chequeApproveRq
          (staff, chq),
          chequeIssueRq
          (staff, chq)}
IL!Y5:   Issue_Rqd(chq)}
CH!Y3:   Issued(chq)
GR!Y6:   Group(staff, group)

Figure 3. A cheque issue/approval problem frame diagram

possible behaviours in the world (i.e. Staff, Cheque, IssueRq_log, and Group domains and their interfaces), the requirement, Secure Cheque Issue/approve, is always satisfied. However, a convincing correctness argument for the cheque issue/approval problem cannot always be constructed if the problem diagram is missing a description of the threat whose satisfaction will result in the violation of the security requirement for the system. Any undesirable behaviour identified has to be addressed appropriately to ensure that the corresponding threats can never be realised. Omitting descriptions of threats from the problem analysis makes the identification of undesirable behaviour more difficult. Thus, an appropriate correctness argument cannot be constructed that demonstrates the machine specification ensures the satisfaction of the requirements. Currently, the problem frame notation does not support the explicit representation of threats in a problem diagram. We now propose an extension to problem frames to enable requirements time modelling and analysis of threats.

4. Anti-requirements and abuse frames

In our proposed approach, problem frames are used as a means of defining system boundaries to provide a focus for early security threat analysis. We further exploit the notion of an *anti-requirement* to capture the intent of a malicious user. An anti-requirement (AR) is the requirement of a malicious user that subverts an existing requirement. That is, an anti-requirement defines a set of undesirable phenomena imposed by the malicious user that will ultimately cause the system to reach a state that is inconsistent with its requirements.

We represent a security threat using an *abuse frame* [29,30] (Figure 4). Abuse frames share the same notation and principal parts as normal problem frames, but each domain is now associated with a different meaning:

+ The Malicious Machine (MM) domain acts as the interface between the attacker and the domain. Its behaviour will allow the attacker to achieve the anti-requirement. The machine is the domain to be specified during *abuse frame analysis*.
+ The Asset is the domain under attack.
+ An anti-requirement is defined in terms of the domain and/or shared phenomenon of the Attacker and Asset domains.
+ The Attacker domain represents the domain that is imposing the threat.

Interface phenomena are annotated to show the sets of shared phenomena between two domains. For example, the shared phenomenon AS!E1 represents the undesirable phenomenon in the victim domain during an attack. It also shows that the phenomenon is controlled by the Asset domain (prefix AS!).

In an abuse frame, a vulnerability is identified as the conditions in the problem world that in conjunction with the malicious machine specification, satisfy the anti-requirements. To show that an abuse frame can be *realised* requires the construction of an *abuse frame argument* that shows that the malicious machine specification (MM) together with some behaviour in the problem world that

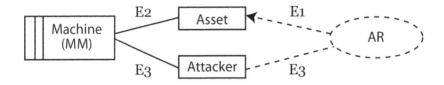

Figure 4. A threat described by a generic abuse frame diagram.

satisfies the vulnerability condition $(v(W))$ will achieve the anti-requirement (AR). That is: $MM, v(W) \Rightarrow AR$. An abuse frame argument relies on the fact that W is strictly bounded by the problem frame diagram; i.e. any phenomena that are not explicitly shown on the diagram are not within scope and are therefore not included in W. The vulnerability condition v, is defined as the relationships between the phenomena within W.

Abuse frames provide an abstract model of the threat imposed by a malicious user within a defined system boundary. Separation of concerns for different threats is achieved by expressing each threat in a different abuse frame diagram. In this way the security analysis focuses on the domains and the shared phenomena shown in each abuse frame diagram.

Abuse frames capture the notion of threats imposed by the attackers on the problem world. A realisable threat defines a sequence of domain phenomena interactions that ultimately cause the problem world to exhibit undesirable phenomena violating the security requirements for a system. In contrast, problem frames describe the desirable phenomenon to be exerted on the problem world. Abuse frames and problem frames are therefore be inherently inconsistent. The inconsistency plays a key role in deciding on the granularity of the anti-requirement. Anti-requirements should always include sufficient details that allow them to be differentiated from the desirable system properties. Describing anti-requirements in this way is important as it separates the undesirable phenomena from the desirable phenomena such that any unnecessary substantial modification to the desirable phenomena from the system may be avoided.

4.1. Abuse frames analysis

In our approach, a *base system* is constructed by building, using problem frames, the bounded context of the system to be protected. The term base system (BS) is used to denote the system under attack. To analyse a security threat to the base system, an abuse frame is *composed* with the base system problem frame to form composed abuse frames, as illustrated shown in Figure 5.

Anti-requirements are captured by generic abuse frames. Generic abuse frames are abuse frames with their problem context partially assigned (instantiated) to the problem world (i.e. some domains remain unassigned). The generic abuse frames are then composed with the problem frame of the BS to obtained fully assigned abuse frames. The fully assigned abuse frames are then analysed to identify the security vulnerabilities. After security threats and vulnerabilities are identified, further security requirements analysis can be undertaken to generate

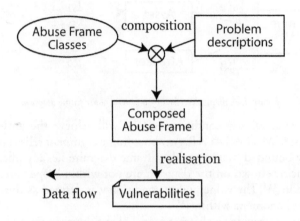

Figure 5. Threat analysis based abuse frames.

additional security requirements in order to counter the identified threats.

A composed abuse frame is *realised* when it can be shown that the anti-requirement in the composed frame is achieved by exploiting the identified vulnerabilities. Since anti-requirements are existentially quantified, a vulnerability is identified as the condition v that defines an instance of the BS, denoted by $v(BS)$. To show that an abuse frame can be realised, an abuse frame argument must be constructed to show that a malicious machine, MM, and the BS that satisfies the vulnerability conditions, $v(BS)$, will satisfy the anti-requirement; i.e. $MM, v(BS) \Rightarrow AR$. The argument relies on the fact that the BS is strictly bounded by the problem frame diagram; that is, any phenomena not explicitly shown on the frame diagram of the BS are not within the scope of the BS.

We also represent classes of threats as classes of abuse frame. Each abuse frame class describes a specific pattern of attack and vulnerabilities from threats belonging to that class. Our abuse frame classes draw on the existing research on security threats classification schemes [45] and include: *interception, interruption, fabrication, modification* and *required behaviour*. Although there is no direct one-to-one mapping, broadly speaking interception compromises confidentiality, interruption compromises availability, fabrication and modification compromise integrity, while required behaviour threats compromise non-repudiation.

5. Conclusions

In this paper, we started from the premise that early identification and thorough analysis of security requirements is a cost-effective approach to engineering secure systems. We suggested that an important (although by no means exclusive) class of security difficulties arise in the problem world in which security requirements reside, rather then the solution world in which systems are installed and operate. We proposed an approach that examined a particular kind of threat: that posed by a malicious attacker. Our approach, derived from requirements engineering, provides an intellectual framework for thinking about security problems and requirements, and allows engineers to analyse a security problem systematically and rigorously, to identify potential system vulnerabilities and to derive improved security requirements.

Our work is preliminary in that it requires validation and evaluation with respect to both scalability and effectiveness. Validating scalability will necessitate undertaking case studies of significant size and realism upon which to apply our approach. Effectiveness is more difficult to evaluate: our approach is not designed to identify vulnerabilities in existing systems, but to help prevent them from arising in systems-to-be. A forensic analysis of existing security failures to assess if our approach would have identified vulnerabilities may prove useful, however, we believe that ultimately, sound engineering practice justifies the need for early analysis of security needs and concerns. More studies applying our approach will consolidate our set of abuse frame classes and provide experience (and heuristics) on their applicability. Finally, integrating early security analysis of the kind we have advocated with other parts of the security engineering process is essential for its effective deployment and uptake.

References

1. CLASP: Comprehensive Lightweight Application Security Process, Technical Report Version 2.0, Secure Software Inc., McLean, VA, USA, 2006.

2. Common Criteria for Information Technology Security Evaluation Part 3: Security assurance components, Version 3.1 Rev 1, Technical Report CCMB-2006-09-003, National Institute of Standards and Technology, Washington DC, USA, Sept 2006.

3. Alberts, C. and A. Dorofee, *Managing Information Security Risks: The OCTAVE (SM) Approach*, 2002: Addison Wesley.

4. Alexander, I., Misuse cases: Uses cases with hostile intent, *IEEE Computer*, 2003, 20(1): 58-66.

5. Anderson, R., How to cheat at the lottery (or, Massively parallel requirements engineering), in *Proceedings of Annual Computer Security Applications Conference (ACSAC'99)*, 1999, Scottsdale, Arizona, USA, IEEE CS Press.

6. Anderson, R., *Security Engineering*, 2001: Wiley.

7. Leonor Barroca, Jose Luiz Fiadeiro, Michael Jackson, Robin C. Laney, Bashar Nuseibeh, Problem frames: A case for coordination, *Proceedings of Coordination 2004*, pp. 5-19.

8. Baskerville, R., Information systems security design methods: Implications for information systems development, *ACM Computing Surveys*, 1993, 25(4): 375-414.

9. Chivers, H. and M. Fletcher, Adapting security risk analysis to service-based systems, in *UK Workshop on Grid Security Experiences*, 2004, Oxford.

10. Clark, D.D. and D.R. Wilson, A comparison of commercial and military computer security policies, in *Proceedings of Symposium on Security and Privacy*, 1987, Oakland, USA, IEEE Press.

11. Crook, R., D. Ince, and B. Nuseibeh, On modelling access policies: Relating roles to their organisational context, in *Proceedings of 13th IEEE International Requirements Engineering Conference (RE'05)*, 2005, Paris, France, IEEE CS Press.

12. Devanbu, P. and S. Stubblebine, Software engineering for security: A roadmap, in *ICSE-2000 Future of Software Engineering*. 2000, Limerick, Ireland, ACM Press.

13. Firesmith, D.G., Common Concepts Underlying Safety, Security, and Survivability Engineering, Technical Report CMU/SEI-2003-TN-033, Carnegie Mellon Software Engineering Institute, December 2003.

14. Giorgini, P., F. Massacci, J. Mylopoulos, and N. Zannone, Modeling security requirements through ownership, permission and delegation, in *Proceedings of 13th IEEE International Requirements Engineering Conference (RE'05)*, 2005, Paris, France, IEEE CS Press.

15. Charles B. Haley, Robin C. Laney, Jonathan D. Moffett, Bashar Nuseibeh, The effect of trust assumptions on the elaboration of security requirement, *RE 2004*, pp. 102-111.

16. Charles B. Haley, Robin C. Laney, Jonathan D. Moffett, Bashar Nuseibeh, Security requirements engineering: A framework for representation and analysis, *IEEE Transactions on Software Engineering*, 34(1): 133-153 (2008).

17. Haley, C.B., J.D. Moffett, R. Laney, and B. Nuseibeh, A framework for security requirements engineering, in *Proceedings of Workshop on Software Engineering for Secure Systems (SESS'06)*, 2006, Shanghai, China, IEEE CS Press.

18. Jon G. Hall, Michael Jackson, Robin C. Laney, Bashar Nuseibeh, Lucia Rapanotti, Relating software requirements and architectures using problem frames, *RE 2002*, pp. 137-144.

19. Jon G. Hall, Lucia Rapanotti, Michael Jackson, Problem frame semantics for software development, *Software and System Modeling*, 4(2): 189-198 (2005).

20. Jon G. Hall, Lucia Rapanotti, Michael Jackson, Problem oriented software engineering: Solving the package router control problem, *IEEE Transactions on Software Engineering*, 34(2): 226-241 (2008).

21. Heitmeyer, C., Applying 'practical' formal methods to the specification and analysis of security properties, in *Information Assurance in Computer Networks (MMM-ACNS 2001)*, 2001, St. Petersburg, Russia, Springer.

22. Jackson, M., *Software Requirements & Specifications: A Lexicon of Practice, Principles and Prejudices*, 1995: Addison Wesley.

23. Jackson, M., *Problem Frames: Analysing and Structuring Software Development Problems*, 2000: Addison-Wesley.

24. Jacobson, I., M. Christerson, P. Jonsson, and G. Overgaard, *Object Oriented Software Engineering - A Use Case Driven Approach*, 1993: Addison Wesley.

25. Kelly, T.P., Arguing Safety—A Systematic Approach to Safety Case Management, in D.Phil Dissertation, Department of Computer Science. 1999, University of York: York, UK.

26. Kletz, T.A., HAZOP & HAZAN: Notes on the Identification and Assessment of Hazards, 1983, Rugby, UK: Institution of Chemical Engineers.

27. Robin C. Laney, Leonor Barroca, Michael Jackson, Bashar Nuseibeh, Composing requirements using problem frames, *RE 2004*, pp.122-131.

28. Leveson, N.G., *Safeware: System Safety and Computers*, 1995: Addison Wesley.

29. Lin, L., B. Nuseibeh, D. Ince, and M. Jackson, Using abuse frames to bound the scope of security problems, Poster Paper in *IEEE Proceedings of 12th International Requirements Engineering Conference (RE'04)*, 2004, Kyoto, Japan..

30. Lin, L., B. Nuseibeh, D. Ince, J.D. Moffett, and M. Jackson, Introducing abuse frames to analyse security requirements, Poster Paper in *11th IEEE International Requirements Engineering Conference (RE'03)*, 2003, Monterey Bay, USA.

31. Liu, L., E. Yu, and J. Mylopoulos, Security and privacy requirements analysis within a social setting, *11th International Requirement Engineering Conference (RE'03)*, 2003.

32. McDermott, J. and C. Fox, Using abuse case models for security requirements analysis, in *Annual Computer Security Applications Conference*, 1999, Phoenix, Arizona, USA.

33. Mead, N.R., E.D. Hough, and T.R.S. I, Security Quality Requirements Engineering (SQUARE) Methodology, Technical Report CMU/SEI-2005-TR-009, ESC-TR-2005-009, CMU/SEI, Pittsburgh, USA, November 2005.

34. Mitnick, K., *The Art of Deception: Controlling the Human Element of Security*, 2002: John Wiley & Sons Inc.

35. Nuseibeh, B. and S. Easterbrook, Requirements engineering: A roadmap, in *ICSE-2000 Future of Software Engineering*, 2000, Limerick, Ireland, ACM Press.

36. Bashar Nuseibeh, Charles B. Haley, Craig Foster, Securing the skies: In requirements we trust, *IEEE Computer*, 42(9): 64-72 (2009).

37. Peltier, T., *Information Security Risk Analysis*, 2001: Auerbach.

38. Pfleeger, C.P. and S.L. Pfleeger, *Security in Computing*, 3rd ed, 2002: Prentice-Hall.

39. Lucia Rapanotti, Jon G. Hall, Michael Jackson, Bashar Nuseibeh, Architecture-driven problem decomposition, *RE 2004*, pp.80-89.

40. Redwine, S.T., Editor, Software Assurance: A Guide to the Common Body of Knowledge to Produce, Acquire, and Sustain Secure Software, Technical Report Version 1.05.245, Dept. of Homeland Security, USA, 15 Aug 2006.

41. Rushby, J., Security requirements specifications: How and what?, in *Symposium on Requirements Engineering for Information Security (SREIS)*, 2001, Indianapolis, USA.

42. Mohammed Salifu, Yijun Yu, Bashar Nuseibeh, Specifying monitoring and switching problems in context, *RE 2007*, pp. 211-220.

43. Schneier, B., *Secrets and Lies: Digital Security in a Networked World*, 2000: Wiley.

44. Sindre, G. and A. Opdahl, Eliciting security requirements through misuse cases, in *Proceedings of IEEE International Conference on Technology of Object-Oriented Languages and Systems*, 2000, Sydney, Australia..

45. Stallings, W., *Cryptongraphy and Network Security: Principles and Practice*, 1999: Prentice-Hall.

46. Swiderski, F. and W. Snyder, *Threat Modeling*, 2004: Microsoft Press International.

47. Thein Than Tun, Tim Trew, Michael Jackson, Robin C. Laney, Bashar Nuseibeh, Specifying features of an evolving software system, *Software- Practice and Experience*, 39(11): 973-1002 (2009).

48. Thein Than Tun, Michael Jackson, Robin C. Laney, Bashar Nuseibeh and Yijun Yu (2009), Are your lights off? Using problem frames to diagnose system failures, *RE 2009*, pp. 343-348.

49. van Lamsweerde, A., Elaborating security requirements by construction of intentional anti-models, in *26th International Conference on Software Engineering (ICSE-04)*, 2004, Edinburgh, UK, IEEE CS Press.

50. Wing, J., A symbiotic relationship between formal methods and security, in *Workshop on Computer Security, Fault Tolerance, and Software Assurance: From Needs to Solution*, 1998, NSF.

Chapter 16

From Problem Frames to HJJ (and its Known Unknowns)

Cliff B. Jones

Abstract. This paper traces the evolving ideas of an approach to "open systems" that interact with the physical world. Such systems nowadays almost always include computers. The design in the simplest cases has a control computer connected to sensors that receive information about the physical world and to actuators that can cause some aspects of that world to change. Jackson's "Problem Frame Approach" is to think about the computer system with respect to the requirement of the desired overall system behaviour; the "Hayes/Jackson/Jones" (HJJ) approach introduces sufficient formalism to support the derivation of the specification of the computer control system.

1. Introduction

This paper is an update of on-going research that Ian Hayes and I have the pleasure of undertaking with Michael Jackson. After the initial letter of each of our family names, the research will be referred to as the "HJJ" approach (citations below). The HJJ ideas owe a huge debt to Michael's "Problem Frame Approach" (PFA) [Jac03] (and PFDs [Jac00] in general). This section sets out the background; Section 2 outlines those parts of the HJJ approach with which we are moderatly satisfied; the problem areas are sketched in Section 3; and our current ideas on filling the gaps are mentioned in Section 4.

The three authors of [HJJ03, JHJ07] share the—not uncommon—view that the process of software development is imperfect. That having been said, it is also our view that the theory for development of "closed" systems is known. By a closed system, we mean one that exists in some neat domain such as number theory or matrix algebra. Here one can write a brief and complete specification of what it means, say, to print all of the primes less than a million or to invert a matrix. Furthermore, ideas like data reification[1] and operation decomposition [Jon90] can be employed to show that steps of design lead from such a specification to code that satisfies the specification. (If this were to be a complete account, we should add comments about compositionality, assumptions

---

[1] I owe thanks to Michael for pointing out that the transition from a clean mathematical abstraction such as sets to a machine implementation based (necessarily) on a mess of pointers should not be considered to be "refinement". Sadly, few others have seen the force of the observation and adopted my use of "reify" as a more appropriate verb.

and acknowledge that real development projects undergo requirements changes during development.)

The situation is rather different with "open systems" where it is the physical world that both sets the context for the system and—in some sense—provides the touchstone of acceptability of the system. A classic example that we have (over) used is that of a "sluice gate".[2] The overall requirement might be that the ratio of open to closed time of the physical gate approximates to some required ratio. A more challenging example might be an advisory system for air traffic controllers whose ultimate responsibility is to achieve minimum vertical and horizontal separation of physical aircraft.

Such open systems are the meat of Michael's Problem Frame Approach (PFA) [Jac03, Jac00]. The insistence in PFA in grounding the requirements of a system in the physical world is central to HJJ.

At most of the points on the complexity spectrum from sluice gates to air traffic control systems, the physical phenomena are likely to vary continuously. Various notations have been used for such descriptions. Perhaps the best known is the "Duration Calculus" [CHR91, CH04]. HJJ has deployed the notation proposed by Ian Hayes and Brendan Mahony [MH91, MH92] (which references also begin to use the ideas in the next paragraph). Key to the usefulness of such notations for continuous variables is the ability to use a form of integration that makes it possible to express things like the amount of time, perhaps over a stated interval, that a value has certain properties.

My own contribution to HJJ derives from earlier work on the development of concurrent programs: [Jon81, Jon83a, Jon83b] show that it is possible to use rely and guarantee conditions to achieve compositional development even in the presence of "interference". The specific rules offered in these early papers are not the point. More recently, what might be called "rely/guarantee thinking" [Jon96, CJ00, CJ07, JP08] generalises the approach to the rather obvious position that if one wants to reason compositionally about interfering systems, one must record something about the interference. We have used rely/guarantee thinking in HJJ to record assumptions about those physical components that are part of the overall system but are not included in the software system that is to be designed.

That's enough background, it is time to outline the HJJ approach in as far as we are confident about its features.

2. What we (think we) know

For open systems, a major issue is how a specification is obtained. Think of a requirement to maintain the temperature in some space within certain

---

[2] For readers unfamiliar with [Jac00] (or the HJJ papers themselves) a few words about this example should suffice. Consider an irrigation channel into which the flow of water is controlled by a sluice gate. This gate has sensors at the extreme positions. There is also a bi-directional motor that will raise or lower the gate. As well as being connected to the gate, the motor has actuators which can set its direction and turn it on or off. The sensors and actuators are connected to a control computer which can thus (indirectly) cause the gate to move safely between extreme positions.

bounds. Software alone can have no affect on the temperature of anything but this does not mean that one should immediately begin writing the specification of a control system as an isolated component. It is basic to PFA to ground the system in its overall physical environment. In HJJ as well, we begin by writing the requirement of the overall system at the level of the physical phenomena: that is, the temperature of the room. If one forgets what one knows about a particular geographic location, it is obvious that it is necessary to make assumptions about how fast the contextual (ambient) temperature can change. So, from the outset, one is faced with recording some assumptions. To arrive at the specification of what Michael calls "the silicon package" (i.e. the control system), it is necessary to record more assumptions.

It is the essence of the HJJ approach to "derive" the specification of the silicon package from that of the overall system. Two of the contributors to HJJ are unreformed formalists so they strive for notations with which all of the specifications and assumptions can be made precise (and tractable) enough that proofs can be written. The extra assumptions that are required to make such a derivation possible are about both the way in which the software can obtain values of things in the physical world and how sending signals might cause other (physical) components to affect the real world. In fact, the assumptions often twine together the outputs and inputs. In the case of a temperature control system, one needs assumptions about sensors that convert the temperature of the physical environment into signals that can be read by the computer on which the software is executed and assumptions about the effect (on the temperature of the room) of sending signals via actuators to heating and/or cooling devices.

The HJJ approach then is to begin with a requirement grounded in the physical world; to record assumptions about how the world can change; to record further assumptions about physical components of the system; to "derive" the specification of the control system (silicon package); and to check that an implementation of the silicon package that fulfils its specification, in an environment that satisfies the assumptions, will indeed keep the overall system within the bounds required in the physical context. (The reader might well wonder what happens if these assumptions are undermined by failure of some physical component; this question is addressed below.)

In nearly all of the systems we have tackled with the HJJ approach, this reasoning ends up being about continuously varying quantities. For example, in the sluice gate problem in [JHJ07], the physical phenomena are indexed by continuous time. Many providers of formal methods tend to what might be termed "premature discretisation"; because their method revolves around discrete operations (or events), they assume some arbitrary polling frequency to reduce the understanding of the continuous phenomena to discrete behaviour. For people who will extol for hours the advantages of formal reasoning this is interesting behaviour. It should be clear that questions like the polling frequency need to be reasoned about in terms of assumed rates of change etc. It is almost inevitable that one ends up at a discrete controller but the derivation of its specification should be part of the (formal) development process.

It is important to note that we are here "preserving the design history" in the same sense that standard formal stepwise refinement leaves behind a record of design steps and their justification.

It is crucial to understand that the HJJ process does not require that the designer build a complete model of the physical components of the system. Again, in the sluice gate example, assumptions are made about the position sensors returning indicators that the gate has achieved a required physical position within a certain period of time from sending a polarity setting signal followed by a start motor signal. This circumvents the need to build a model of motors, gears etc.

So, to return to the issue at the beginning of this section (how to obtain a specification of a control system that is intended to interact with the physical world), the basic HJJ approach can be summarised as:

+ determine the requirements of the overall system with respect to the physical phenomena
+ record assumptions about the way those phenomena can be affected by things beyond the system
+ record assumptions about the physical components of the system (linking the external world to the silicon package via sensors and actuators)
+ "derive" a specification of the silicon package that will achieve the overall requirement if the other system components behave according to their assumptions

Of course, the overall requirement and the assumptions about other components must be agreed with the customer. But it is a key advantage of the HJJ approach that it leaves a record of assumptions for subsequent deployments. In contrast to any approach that tries to build a model of the environment, the HJJ message might be viewed as "how little can we say (about the environment)?".

Interestingly, we have found many examples where rely conditions are used within a development to record assumptions that it is necessary to make for safe use of the physical components of the system. For example, in the sluice gate, one must not reverse the polarity of the gears connecting the motor to the gate whilst the motor is running.

Most importantly, the HJJ approach councils against a premature jump into the specification of the silicon package. Such a jump nearly always results in a confusion about assumptions and requirements. Examples of formal specifications in the literature where this is the case are too numerous to list.

This much of the HJJ approach was fairly well established in [HJJ03] and is most clearly set out [JHJ07]. Both papers use the sluice gate problem which is, among other reasons, interesting because it also has to address fault-tolerant behaviour. At one level, addressing degraded modes of behaviour requires no more than recording weaker assumptions about the environment but as is conceded in the next section, there is a difficulty in knowing the best way to combine the specifications of normal and error recovery modes.

Before moving on to the issues that still need to be resolved, it is worth sketching what the HJJ approach might achieve for one or two aspects of a complex system like an advisory system for air traffic controllers. Suppose that a base air traffic control system is in place: RADAR, displays of aircraft position, etc. are all established; assume further that one then wished to specify a new system that helped Air Traffic Controllers (ATCs) by warning of future approaches within specified distances and—furthermore—to carry out thought experiments like "what are the effects of sending an aircraft on a particular vertical angle and acceleration". Given the large system that already exists, the obvious temptation is to use the expertise of people who know the existing system and the physical behaviour of aircraft and to simply specify the new component. The HJJ approach would advise against this; or rather would suggest that there are advantages in a more circuitous route to the specification of the new component (as a separate silicon package).

What the ATCs are required to achieve is physical separation of aircraft.[3] This is a sobering place to start: an ATC does not, in fact, move aircraft. Thus one sees at once that a fairly simple overall requirement is actually made challenging (to meet) because of the assumptions that have to be made. Interestingly, the assumptions in this case (as in many complex systems) involve some on human players: it is not an actuator that connects the silicon package to the position of the aircraft but rather the ATC sending a voice message to a pilot who might or might not react as intended. Such assumptions must be recorded.

Furthermore, there are many assumptions to be made about the physical ability of an aircraft to achieve particular changes of position. Factors that influence this include type, load and air pressure. Focusing on this last item, the approach of jumping straight to a specification of the new sub-system might well make inadvertent assumptions about the potential rate of change in air pressure at a particular geographic location. This in turn might result in reading air pressure at some fixed intervals.

If, instead, one determines the potential effect of each of the factors on maneuverability of aircraft, one can calculate what might have to be considered to achieve certain tolerances; one can record assumptions about changes in air pressure; and prove that a certain currency of information is adequate. Here again, the recorded assumptions could be invaluable if the same software were to be deployed in another geographic location.

---

[3]Strictly, there are also progress conditions: the easiest way to achieve separation is to have few—or no—aircraft in the sky.

3. What we know that we don't know

Dubium Sapientiae initium[4]

3.1. How far should one push out the boundaries of a system?

We have argued that the HJJ approach (just as PFA) should start by pushing out the boundaries of "the system" to be considered—but how far? This is certainly a valid question about HJJ but it is in some sense unanswerable. To continue with the imaginary air traffic scenario, if one were to regard the system as that of the planet, one might indeed decide that safe aircraft separation was best achieved by flying less planes thus obviating the need for ways to inform ATCs of ways to handle more flights. It is however an answer that is unlikely to impress National Air Traffic Services (NATS is the UK body responsible for air traffic in the UK airspace).

One can see that the approach of recording assumptions comes into play wherever one places the boundary by returning to the example that our papers have analysed in more detail:

+ Setting the boundary at moving the sluice gate prompts the need for assumptions about the relationship between request signals (presumably causing actuators and motors to perform) and return signals from sensors with further assumptions about the relationship between the sensor values and phenomena in the physical world.
+ The sluice gate was proposed by Michael as an object of study in [Jac00] as a way of controlling the irrigation of fields—were one to view the requirements at that level, assumptions would be needed about the presence of water at the gate.
+ Presumably the real reason for releasing the irrigation stream is to achieve a certain moisture level in the soil—one could only achieve a satisfiable specification at this boundary by making assumptions about the weather.
+ One can go yet further and discuss things like farm subsidies if the requirement is about farm profits.

With typical pragmatism, Michael offers the only insight possible as to where one should stop this broadening: if the customer is the farmer—and he says "the job is to achieve a certain gate open/close ratio"—then that bounds the concern of the developer. It is however true that one can sometimes get a clearer view by considering a slight extension that grounds the purpose without undermining the legitimate requests of the paying customer. For example, knowing that the gate is for irrigation might prompt a wise designer to make the actual ratio of open vs. closed times a rather easy parameter to

---

[4] As a classics scholar like Michael can tell you, Descartes was somewhat ahead of Donald Rumsfeld (or even Thoreau "To know that we know what we know, and that we do not know what we do not know, that is true knowledge") in pointing out that "Doubt is the origin of wisdom".

change in the created system. There are also overriding ethical considerations that would, hopefully, prevent most designers building systems whose function was manifestly immoral.

3.2. Linking fault tolerant specifications to the idealised behaviour

A technical challenge that has occupied the three authors for some time is handling the sort of exceptional behaviour that is often seen in fault tolerant systems. For any system there is in our opinion a strong case for recording first its idealised behaviour. The term "idealised" is meant to cover the obvious functionality which is only likely to be achievable under optimistic assumptions such as all of the physical components working without failure. The issue that in a sense represents the difference between the two HJJ papers ([HJJ03] and [JHJ07]) is how one tackles adjoining the specification of the exceptional behaviour to that of the idealised system. Unfortunately, we do not feel that the ideas in the more recent paper are a total solution—see Section 4.

To return to the sluice gate example, suppose the assumption that turning the motor on should achieve a physical change in the gate position appears to be false: after a sensible period, the sensor at the extreme to which the gate was to be propelled has not changed state. In order to avoid burning out the motor by pushing the gate against a physical limit, it is not difficult to add a requirement that the motor should never be run for more than, say, a minute. If one is lucky enough to have a free hand in ordering further sensors, one might track extra phenomena; even if not, a developer might well suggest a warning signal be added to record when normal operation ceases.

This train of thought is what gives plausibility to the statement that handling exceptions just needs weaker assumptions and different (in some sense also weaker) guarantees. But there is a difficult question about handling the handover between normal and exceptional behaviour. If one wants a single specification of the entire system, it is very easy to be inadvertently prescriptive about exactly when the deviation from normal behaviour must be sensed. This key problem is addressed in Section 4 as describing "phase changes".

Michael's relatively small challenge problem offers another sort of exception that has taxed the basic HJJ approach. The other side of the coin on delayed sensor indication is a premature signal. Indeed, what if sensors indicating that the gate is in two different positions are on "together". Clearly, something is amiss. It is tempting to say that a safe system must detect such abnormalities (and again turn on an alarm). But here again, stating the precise timing can result in unrealisable specifications. For example, if the eventual program is to poll two sensors, it cannot possibly detect that the two sensors are on at precisely the same time because the polling events will be separated by an—admittedly very small—interval. In fact, two such positive sequential sensor readings (separated perhaps by a thread interruption) do not constitute proof that the sensors were on unacceptably close together in time. Of course, in the example of the sluice gate, with presumably a dedicated processor, these issues could probably be ignored. But they would be ignored at risk to life and limb if one were designing an in-flight monitor or a reactor protection system.

There should clearly be a general way to record and reason about the kind of transient issues that have been illustrated here with short-circuit or flickering sensors. In [JHJ07] we made some progress on this issue with a form of "Deontic implication" stating that (a) if errors persist for a long period of time, the system must shut down; and (b) that the system is allowed to shut down only if there was at least a (short) period of time when evidence for erroneous behaviour could be observed. In that paper we also looked at other ways of making system descriptions more robust by minimising assumptions and considering the gathering of evidence that a system is getting closer to violating its assumptions.

These topics are looked at again in Section 4 but with only indications of how we hope to achieve a perspicuous combination of idealised and exceptional behaviour.

3.3. Stochastic

Many of the fault-tolerance issues are in fact likely to be expressed in terms of probabilistic (e.g. mean time to failure) terms. For example, the overall requirement of a highly reliable sluice gate might state how often the customer is prepared to accept a failure; an implementation might need "triple modular redundancy" on the sensors to achieve the requirement. Clearly, this is more likely to be a significant issue towards the air traffic control end of the complexity spectrum. There, it is likely to be the case that one has to make stochastic assumptions about the behaviour of human players in a system. Interestingly, the role of humans also becomes important in thinking about the dependability of systems that use encryption for security (e.g. the trade-off between longer passwords being more secure and the ability of humans to remember them without recording them in ways that increase overall system vulnerability).

The only observation that is made in this paper is that it looks plausible to extend rely/guarantee thinking to stochastic statements—but there is no corresponding item in Section 4 that takes this point forward.

3.4. Making HJJ into a method

The reader might have noted that HJJ has been referred to as an "approach". There have been erudite discussions between Michael and my colleague at Newcastle, Manuel Mazzara, as to what constitutes a "method". (In fact, these discussions gave me the Latin quotation from Descartes.)

What we can say so far is that an outline of an HJJ method might include:
+ choose the system's perimeter (wider than the pure control system)
+ record (and agree with the customer) the requirements at this level
+ record (and agree with the customer) assumptions about other system components necessary for this behaviour to be realisable
+ iterate steps 2–3 with weaker assumptions to cover exceptional behaviour

+ handle the "composition issue"[5]

Here again, this point is not developed in the current paper. The reader is referred to [Maz09] for a discussion of "Layered Fault-Tolerant Systems". It is also worth remembering that Michael had the requirement that a method in the sense of [Jac75] or [Jac83] should in some reasonable sense be "normative".

3.5. Hasn't this all been done before?

When undertaking research, I prefer to have a go at a problem without reading other "possible solutions"—but there comes a point at which it is prudent to check if someone else has solved a problem that, in this case, has held up the HJJ authors for a number of years. We would in fact be delighted to find such a preemption and move on to other topics.

To make clear why we feel this is not a solved problem, it is perhaps worth reiterating some of our desiderata.[6] I have long held the view that it is possible to view the (possibly erroneous) behaviour of external components as a form of "interference". This dates back to some consulting work I did on an "Inherently Safe Automatic Trip" [SW89]: briefly, ISAT was a clever nuclear reactor protection trip system that had many internal checks (and caused reactor shut-down if these failed) but there was no proof of resilience against a stated set of exceptions. We showed that the assumptions could be captured by rely conditions. One thing that inhibited wider publication at that time was the fact that the assumptions tended to be at a different level of abstraction than the system functionality.

It is a distinctive feature of the HJJ approach that it is not intended that a model is built of the external system components; the aim is to make minimal assumptions.

It is also important to note that the HJJ approach does not construct a state in which both physical phenomena and their approximation are stored together. This feels like the same sort of confusion that dogged programming language descriptions that used "grand state" operational semantic descriptions. The HJJ approach records assumptions about the relationship between things beyond the machine and their internal representations (approximations). In so doing, it makes immediately clear that the machine cannot (directly) affect the values in the physical world. It is interesting to link this thought with the writings of another wise author: [Ken78] makes the clear distinction between "Data and Reality".

4. Where next

The frank list of open issues in Section 3 might appear off-putting. In this section, we indicate where we are looking for progress. Hayes and Jones want a

---

[5] See Section 4.
[6] For some more detailed comparisons with other approaches, see [JHJ07, Section 4.1].

way of recording the overall system specification. Furthermore, this should not consist of a massive conjunction of implications.[7] In contrast, Michael Jackson is, in cases of "normal design", prepared to leave some of the overall system properties to known engineering. (More recently, Michael has also drawn inspiration from Polanyi's writings about "operational principles".) This is not to say that Michael would reject an overall system description but he is perhaps less concerned about it than his two co-authors.

In any case, it is clear that a key to perspicuous ("layered") specifications of fault-tolerant systems is the ability to handle "phase change" conveniently. The notion of "phases" has other applications. It is for instance possible to consider the important "initialisation concern" via phases; it is also possible to consider the broader lifetime of a system including commissioning, revision and decommissioning from the point of view of phases.

These considerations have led us to look at the "Time Bands" concept described in [BH09]. In outline, like most good ideas, what underlies time bands is rather simple: it is often easier to understand (and/or describe) a system at different granularities of time. What is most easily viewed as an atomic "event" at a coarse granularity might be broken down at a finer granularity. Central to the time band model of [BH09] is the idea that there is a "precision" associated with each time band: when one says—at say the hour band—that a meeting starts at 11.00, there is no expectation this has to happen to the second. One intriguing match between time band concerns and the handling of exceptional behaviour is the way in which exceptions are often distinguished by crossing time bands.

The model developed in [BH09] is to my eyes more complicated than is needed to resolve the open issues in HJJ.[8] In fact, just the inclusion of a notion like (time) precision might resolve the phase change issue.

Another intriguing avenue is the teleo-reactive notation of Nilson [Nil94] as developed by Keith Clark. Ian Hayes [Hay08] has observed that the way in which outer guards are evaluated as the state evolves models closely the way in which exceptions cause interruption of "durative" actions. (Ian has also observed that in some sense this just shifts the semantic problem; but at least the difficulty is concentrated in one place.)

Acknowledgements

Anyone who has cooperated with Michael Jackson knows how stimulating it can be: the untiring series of challenges and the joy in discussing them (always with supreme politeness) makes him one of the most productive collaborators I know.

Since this paper is written (unusually for me) in the first person singular, I should also like to record my thanks to the other person in HJJ: Ian Hayes is ever

---

[7] Inspiration here might be taken from the **err** clauses in VDM [Jon90]. In fact, this is rather close to the otherwise operator with which we experimented in [HJJ03].

[8] We have discussed questions like "timeless time bands" and using the "fuzziness" notion on all measures not just time.

patient and thorough—also a joy as a collaborator.

My research is currently funded by the EU "Deploy" project, the (UK) EPSRC "TrAmS" project and the ARC project (that brings together Ian Hayes, Keith Clark, Alan Burns and myself) "Time Bands for Teleo-Reactive Programs".

References

[BH09]   Alan Burns and Ian Hayes. A timeband framework for modelling real-time systems. accepted for *Real-Time Systems*, 2009.

[CH04]   Zhou Chaochen and Michael R. Hansen. *Duration Calculus*. Springer, 2004.

[CHR91] Zhou Chaochen, C.A.R. Hoare, and A.P. Ravn. A calculus of durations. *Information Processing Letters*, 40:269–271, December 1991.

[CJ00]   Pierre Collette and Cliff B. Jones. Enhancing the tractability of rely/guarantee specifications in the development of interfering operations. In Gordon Plotkin, Colin Stirling, and Mads Tofte, editors, *Proof, Language and Interaction*, chapter 10, pages 277–307. MIT Press, 2000.

[CJ07]   J. W. Coleman and C. B. Jones. A structural proof of the soundness of rely/guarantee rules. *Journal of Logic and Computation*, 17(4):807–841, 2007.

[Hay08] Ian J. Hayes. Towards reasoning about teleo-reactive programs for robust real-time systems. In *SERENE '08: Proceedings of the 2008 RISE/EFTS Joint International Workshop on Software Engineering for Resilient Systems*, pages 87–94, November 2008.

[HJJ03] Ian Hayes, Michael Jackson, and Cliff Jones. Determining the specification of a control system from that of its environment. In Keijiro Araki, Stefani Gnesi, and Dino Mandrioli, editors, *FME 2003: Formal Methods*, volume 2805 of Lecture Notes in Computer Science, pages 154–169. Springer Verlag, 2003.

[Jac75] Michael Jackson. *Principles of Program Design*. Academic Press, 1975.

[Jac83] Michael Jackson. *System Design*. Prentice-Hall International, 1983.

[Jac00] Michael Jackson. *Problem Frames: Analyzing and structuring software development problems*. Addison-Wesley, 2000.

[Jac03] Michael Jackson. Aspects of system description. In Annabelle McIver and Carroll Morgan, editors, *Programming Methodology*, pages 137-160. Springer Verlag 2003. Also Chapter 9 of this volume.

[JHJ07] Cliff B. Jones, Ian J. Hayes, and Michael A. Jackson. Deriving specifications for systems that are connected to the physical world. In Cliff B. Jones, Zhiming Liu, and Jim Woodcock, editors, *Formal Methods and Hybrid Real-Time Systems: Essays in Honour of Dines Bjørner and Zhou Chaochen on the Occasion of Their 70th Birthdays*, volume 4700 of Lecture Notes in Computer Science, pages 364–390. Springer Verlag, 2007.

[Jon81] C. B. Jones. *Development Methods for Computer Programs including a Notion of Interference*. PhD thesis, Oxford University, June 1981. Printed as: Programming Research Group, Technical Monograph 25.

[Jon83a] C. B. Jones. Specification and design of (parallel) programs. In *Proceedings of IFIP'83*, pages 321–332. North-Holland, 1983.

[Jon83b] C. B. Jones. Tentative steps toward a development method for interfering programs. *Transactions on Programming Languages and System*, 5(4):596– 619, 1983.

[Jon90] C. B. Jones. *Systematic Software Development using VDM*. Prentice Hall International, second edition, 1990.

[Jon96]   C. B. Jones. Accommodating interference in the formal design of concurrent object-based programs. *Formal Methods in System Design*, 8(2):105–122, March 1996.

[JP08]   Cliff B. Jones and Ken G. Pierce. Splitting atoms with rely/guarantee conditions coupled with data reification. In *ABZ2008*, volume LNCS 5238, pages 360–377, 2008.

[Ken78]   William Kent. *Data and Reality*. North Holland, 1978.

[Maz09]   Manuel Mazzara. Deriving specifications of dependable systems: toward a method. In *Proceedings of the 12th European Workshop on Dependable Computing (EWDC 2009)*, 2009.

[MH91]   B. Mahony and I. Hayes. Using continuous real functions to model timed histories. In P. Bailes, editor, *Engineering Safe Software*, pages 257–270. Australian Computer Society, 1991.

[MH92]   B. P. Mahony and I. J. Hayes. A case-study in timed refinement: A mine pump. *IEEE Trans. on Software Engineering*, 18(9):817–826, 1992.

[Nil94]   N. Nilsson. Teleo-reactive programs for agent control. *Journal of Artificial Intelligence Research*, 1:139–158, 1994.

[SW89]   I. C. Smith and D. N. Wall. Programmable electronic systems for reactor safety. *Atom*, (395), 1989.

Part 6
The World
and the
Machine

Chapter 17

The World and the Machine
Michael Jackson

Abstract: As software developers we are engineers because we make useful machines. We are concerned both with the world, in which the machine serves a useful purpose, and with the machine itself. The competing demands and attractions of these two concerns must be appropriately balanced. Failure to balance them harms our work. Certainly it must take some of the blame for the gulf between researchers and practitioners in software development. To achieve proper balance we must sometimes fight against tendencies and inclinations that are deeply ingrained in our customary practices and attitudes in software development. In this paper some aspects of the relationship between the world and the machine are explored; some sources of distortion are identified; and some suggestions are put forward for maintaining a proper balance.

1. Introduction: Engineering and the world

Because software seems to be an intangible intellectual product we can colour it to suit our interests and prejudices. For some people the central product of software development is the computation evoked. For some it is the social consensus achieved in negotiating the specifications. For some it is a mathematical edifice of axioms and theorems. Some people have been pleased to have their programs described as logical poems. Some have advocated literate programming. Some see software as an expression of business policy.

But many people here will surely want to think of software development as a kind of engineering. The most conspicuous dissenters from this view are, presumably, absent from this conference. Yet we do not speak of engineering mathematical theorems, or poems, or works of literature, or business policies. Why, then, should we speak of engineering software?

Software development is engineering because it is concerned to make useful physical devices to serve practical purposes in the world. Software is a description of a machine. We build the machine by describing it and presenting our description to a general-purpose computer that then takes on the attributes and behaviour of the machine we have described. That is why we compare ourselves to aeronautical and electrical and automotive and chemical engineers, and aspire to emulate their enviably well-established repertoires of 'theoretical foundations and practical disciplines'. They too are concerned to make useful physical devices.

The purpose of a machine, which defines its practical value, is located in the world in which the machine is to be installed and used. The value of a word-processing system is to be judged not by examining its software structure or code but by looking at the quality of the documents it produces, and at the ease and comfort and satisfaction it affords its operators. The requirements for an Air Traffic Control system are to be sought in the aeroplanes and the airspace and the runways and the control tower. The success of a theatre reservation system depends on the ease and speed of booking, the efficiency of payment collection, the convenience of dealing with cancellations.

The requirement—that is, the problem—is in the *world*; the *machine* is the solution we construct. The point is trite and obvious. But perhaps we have yet to come to terms with it, to understand it fully, and to act on that understanding.

2. Four facets of relationship

The relationship between the world and the machine is not simple. It has several facets, and different facets are reflected with different intensity in different systems. We can recognise at least four facets:

- the modelling facet, where the machine simulates the world;
- the interface facet, where the world touches the machine physically;
- the engineering facet, where the machine acts as an engine of control over the behaviour of the world; and
- the problem facet, where the shape of the world and of the problem influences the shape of the machine and of the solution.

2.1. The modelling facet

In many systems the machine embodies a model or a simulation of some part of the world. There are data models, object models, process models. The purpose of such a model is to provide efficient and convenient access to information about the world. By capturing states and events of the world and using them to build and maintain the model we provide ourselves with a stored information asset that we can exploit later when information is needed but would be harder or more expensive to acquire directly.

The model can provide the information we need because there are certain common descriptions that are true both of the model itself inside the machine and of the aspects of the world outside that it models. Of course, the descriptions must be differently interpreted when we apply them to the world and when we apply them to the model. If a common description, written using deliberately meaningless identifiers, is:

$$\forall\, x : B(x) \cdot (\, \exists!\, y \cdot W(y) \wedge A(x,y)\,)$$

then we may interpret it in the world as asserting:

For each novel x there is a unique writer y that is the author of the novel.

And we may interpret it in the database inside the machine as asserting:

For each record of type B there is a unique record of type W to which there is a pointer from the B record.

If a mapping is provided between the database model and the world—for example, if each B record contains a character string that is the title of the novel and each A record contains a character string that is the name of the author— then information about the world can be obtained by inspecting the database.

Because the world and the machine are both physical realities and not merely abstractions, the common description captures only a part of the truth about each. For each, there are many other descriptions that might be given. Some novels have more than one author, or are anonymous; writers sometimes use pseudonyms; some novels are linked to others in a series such as Trollope's Barchester novels; some books appear in revised editions. All these aspects of the world may have been ignored in the modelling, and have no reflection in the database. In the database, similarly, records may be deleted to save space, or carefully placed in physical storage to speed access; relations may be in 3rd or 4th or 5th normal form; fields may have null values; there may be backwards pointers and indices. None of these database properties reflects any aspect of the world being modelled.

Considering the set DW of all descriptions that assert truths about the world, and the set DM of all descriptions that assert truths about the machine, the modelling relationship involves precisely those that are in their intersection:

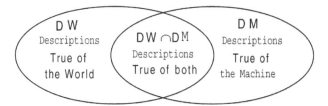

2.2. The interface facet

The problem is not in the machine; and yet the machine can provide the solution to the problem. This is possible, of course, only because there is interaction at an interface between the machine and the world. By 'interaction' I mean the sharing of phenomena. This is not interaction at a distance, by message passing or remote procedure call or writing and reading on a blackboard, but direct participation in common events. The participation is not symmetrical: one party may have the power to initiate the event, and the other may or may not have the power to inhibit it. States may be similarly shared; one party may have the power to change the value of the state, and both may have the power to sense it.

Consider, for example, a system to control a lift. There are sensor switches in the lift shaft at the floors, turned on and off by the arrivals and departures of the lift car. The states of these switches are shared with the machine. When the sensor at floor 3 in the world is on, the bit in the machine in the array element *floor_sensors[3]* is set to *1*. This is a shared state, controlled by the world.

When the upwards call button is pressed at floor 3, this is an event in the world. It is also an event in the machine, where is is observable as the occurrence of an input signal on line *U3*. This is a shared event, controlled by the world.

When the machine emits a signal on its output line *MU*, the polarity of the lift motor is set to upwards; when it emits a signal on its output line *M+*, the motor is switched on. These are shared events, controlled by the machine.

These shared events and states lock the machine and the world in a partnership, sharing the traces of events and states in which they both participate. At a certain level of abstraction, their behaviours can be described identically. But it is a very abstract level indeed, for at least two reasons.

First, because the shared phenomena are only a subset—typically, a small subset—of the phenomena of the world, and an equally small subset of the phenomena of the machine. If we call the set of phenomena of the world PW, and the set of phenomena of the machine *PM*, then the set of shared phenomena is the (relatively small) intersection of these two sets:

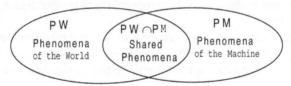

Second, because a description that describes the world and the machine identically must necessarily abstract away the control properties. An event controlled by the world has quite different significance from an event controlled by the machine. A description in which this distinction is not made is a very pallid reflection indeed of the reality with which it is concerned. As Lamport pointed out in an account of TLA [Lam89], a stack that leaves the invocation of all *new, push* and *pop* operations to the user is very different from—and infinitely preferable to—one that sometimes initiates a *push* or *pop* on its own initiative.

2.3. The engineering facet

The recognition of the two intersecting sets of phenomena suggests a systematic usage of those difficult terms: *requirements, specifications,* and *programs.*

Requirements are concerned solely with phenomena in the world: that is, with phenomena in the set *PW*. Our customers want us to engineer effects in the world, not in the machine. They want the seats profitably allocated, or the aeroplanes safely controlled, or the documents conveniently edited and neatly displayed and printed.

Programs, by contrast, are concerned solely with the machine phenomena in the set *PM*. Their purpose is to describe those properties and behaviours of the machine that will, ultimately, satisfy the customers.

The gap between the two is bridged by specifications. Specifications are concerned solely with the shared phenomena in *PW∩PM*. A specification is both a requirement and program. It is a requirement because it is concerned solely with phenomena of the world; and it is a program because it is concerned solely with phenomena of the machine. Naturally, as one might expect, it is satisfactory neither as a requirement nor as a program. It is unsatisfactory as a requirement because it is too limited. The customer's purposes are not confined to the coastline where the world meets the machine, but may range freely over any part of the world that is of interest. And it is not satisfactory as a program because it may not be executable. Programs are descriptions of desired machines, but they must be descriptions of machines that our general-purpose computers can emulate and they must be cast in terms that our computers can interpret.

The specification link is necessary because a specification is a staging post on the hazardous journey from a requirement to a program. Our engineering of the world is completely captured in our refinement of the requirement to a specification. The transition from specification to program concerns only the machine. The first part of the journey, from requirement to specification, can be illustrated by a little example. A requirement in a certain avionics system is to ensure that reverse thrust can be engaged if, and only if, the plane is landing and already on the runway. The requirement is:

REQ: *can_rev <–> on_runway*

but only the *can_rev* phenomenon is shared with the machine. It is necessary to find a way of connecting *on_runway* with the machine.

Sensors fitted to the landing wheels generate pulses when the wheels are rotating. The state *pulsing* is shared with the machine, although the state *rotating* is not. So these phenomena are available to the engineer:

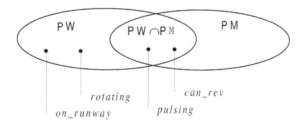

The developers decide that the following properties hold in the world:

WORLD1:   pulsing <-> rotating
WORLD2:   rotating <-> on_runway

That is, that the pulses are generated if, and only if, the wheels are rotating; and that the wheels are rotating if, and only if, the plane is landing and on the runway. Relying on these properties they derive the specification:

SPEC: can_rev <-> pulsing

That is, reverse thrust can be engaged if, and only if, wheel pulses are being generated. They prove their specification correct by showing that

WORLD1, WORLD2, SPEC ⊢ REQ

Unfortunately, property WORLD2 does not in fact hold in the world. On one occasion a plane landed in heavy rain on a runway covered with water. The wheels were aquaplaning, not turning. The pilot was prevented from engaging reverse thrust, and the plane ran off the end of the runway.

The solutions to many development problems—notably, but not only, embedded systems—involve not just engineering in the world, but also engineering of the world. In this way, software development is like building bridges. The builder must study the geology and soil mechanics of the site, and the traffic both over and under the bridge. The engineering of the bridge is also engineering of its environment. The engineer must understand the properties of the world and manipulate and exploit those properties to achieve the purposes of the system. A computer system, like a bridge, can not be designed in isolation from the world into which it fits and in which it provides the solution to a problem.

2.4. The problem facet

The problems we aim to solve by introducing and using computer systems are often complex, and demand careful structuring and decomposition. Because we hope to recognise some rationality in the problem our customer asks us to solve, we expect to be able to structure the problem convincingly and then to base the structure of the solution on the structure of the problem it solves.

But problem structures have proved elusive. It is distressingly difficult to separate discourse about problems from discourse about solutions. The distinction is somehow related to the mysterious distinction between what and how, or the distinction between the *specification* and the *implementation*.

The difficulty arises from the relationship between the machine and the world. The machine will furnish the solution, but the problem is in the world. Discourse about the problem must therefore be discourse about the world and about the requirement that our customer has in the world. Since the world is very multifarious we should expect to find that there are many different kinds of problem. Controlling an elevator is not at all like compiling source programs, which in turn is not at all like switching telephone calls; and none of them is like processing texts in a word processor.

Problems as varied as this can not be effectively structured by naïve approaches that rely on those two broken reeds: hierarchical structure and homogeneous decomposition. As a general rule, neither the world nor the problems it offers exhibit hierarchical structure. Problems usually exhibit a parallel structure, in which the key connective is the logical connective *and*. Nor do they allow homogeneous decomposition. It is certainly possible to devise effective programming environments in which homogeneity reigns: everything is a procedure, or everything is an object, or everything is a sequential process or a recursive function or a list. But the world, and its problems, are infinitely more varied and will fit no such Procrustean bed.

Effective problem decomposition means decomposing into problems that are *recognised* and *known to be soluble*. For example, the problem of constructing a simple CASE tool might be decomposed into these problems, each of a recognisable type:

- A simple *editing* problem. In an editing problem there is an inert and intangible object—such as a text—belonging to the world but realised within the machine. The operator may request the machine to perform operations on the object, rather as a piece of metal might be worked on a machine tool such as a lathe.
- A *GUI* problem. In a GUI problem there is a user who engages in an assisted dialogue with the machine. The assistance is provided by displays of options currently available and of information that the user will find helpful when choosing an option.
- A simple *information system* problem. In an information system problem there is some reality about which information is desired. For the CASE tool, this may be information about the progress of the work. Information requests are presented to the machine, which embodies a model of the reality of interest and answers them from the model.

The decomposition is parallel, not hierarchical. The different subproblems are concerned with different—but overlapping—subsets of the phenomena of the world. For example, here are some phenomena relevant to the editing problem and the information system problem:

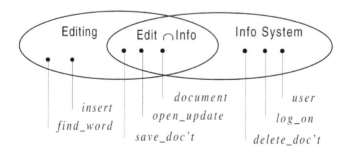

The *insert* operation is relevant only to the editing problem; information about progress is of a coarser grain. Similarly, the *log_on* operation, the individual *users*, and the *delete_doc't* operation are of interest only to the information system problem. The editing ignores any distinction between one user and another, and is not involved in *log_on* or *delete_doc't* operations. However, the *save_doc't* and *open_update* operations and the individual *documents*, are relevant to both subproblems.

3. Four kinds of denial

If indeed software development is concerned both with the machine and with the world, as I have suggested, we might still ask whether the world outside the machine is really our proper concern as software engineers. Let an aeronautical engineer study the relationship between the landing gear and the runway. Automobile engineers are not expected to be expert in route planning, or in human physiology. Electrical power distribution engineers are not expected to know about demographic shifts and the TV schedules that affect patterns of consumption. Why, then, should we as software engineers not confine our attention similarly to the machines that are our artifacts, and leave other people to analyse the world outside the machine and the problem, and to establish the customer's requirements?

Rightly or wrongly, wisely or foolishly, we answered this question long ago. We said that we would do it. With help from domain experts, perhaps; and with qualifications and disclaimers to cover ourselves in case of disaster. But as a community or as a profession we never said 'Problem analysis is not our responsibility. We are mere builders of machines to given specifications. We do not judge their fitness for any purpose. Other people must supply the specification, and we will build the machine to meet it'.

In this way we took on the responsibility of dealing with whatever part of the world furnished the context for each particular software development problem. We undertook to concern ourselves not only with the machine, but also with the purposes it is intended to serve. That is why an important department of software engineering is *requirements engineering*: the elicitation, description, and analysis of the requirements that must be satisfied by the system being built. What, exactly, does the customer demand? What, exactly, is the problem? What purposes must the system serve? What functions must it provide?

But we are not at ease with our responsibility. The relationship between the machine and the world creates a conflict. Most developers, for various reasons, are inclined to pay more attention to the machine than to the world. And they have found many ways to manifest and to justify their inclination, and to evade the responsibility that, as a community, we have implicitly undertaken.

3.1. Denial by prior knowledge

There is a legitimate kind of denial of the world. In some engineering problems a domain analysis and requirements study is essential. The bridge builder who neglected to survey the terrain and the local geology would be grossly negligent. But for some problems a detailed and careful survey of the problem context, and even of the problem itself, is less important or even quite inappropriate. A group of automobile engineers setting out to develop a five-door hatchback does not begin by asking questions about the purposes to which cars are put, or the physical constitution of the drivers and passengers, or the nature of road surfaces. They do not ask themselves whether the car should be amphibious, or capable of carrying twenty-ton loads, or of travelling at supersonic speeds.

The phrase 'five-door hatchback car' answers those questions implicitly: the requirements are already well-understood and standardised. The design of the product to satisfy those requirements is also well-understood and standardised. The designers need not consider such options as steam power, articulated legs or tracks instead of wheels, or having the driver sitting at the back facing sideways and steering by a tiller. Over a period of a hundred years the customer's needs and the automobile engineer's products have grown into a symbiotic harmony. There is no need for the machine's designers to consider the world and the problem explicitly. The world and the problem will be much as expected, and if the machine is also much as expected it will serve its purpose. For a car designer, explicit attention to the world and the requirement would be 'rethinking the motor car'.

This parallel standardisation of requirements and products is proceeding in many areas of software development too. Magazine reviews of shrink-wrapped word-processors and spreadsheets and databases and graphics packages and compilers and accounting systems read more and more like magazine reviews of cars. They apply standard criteria to measure the products against well-understood needs and against the competition. If you can drive one word-processor you expect to be able to jump into any other word-processor and drive it the same way. This is not just standardisation of user interfaces: it is standardisation of problems and solutions.

As a problem class progresses towards this standardised state, it becomes increasingly legitimate for the developers of solutions to ignore the world and concentrate on the details of their machine. The world and the problem are already well understood, and the knowledge and understanding are embodied in the standard design from which they will derive their solution by an almost imperceptibly small perturbation.

3.2. Denial by hacking

Sometimes the reasons for denying the importance of the world are more personal. The phenomenon of hacking—not in the sense of breaking into other people's systems but in the sense of obsessive devotion to interacting with computers—is well known. It is not surprising, because computers are obsessively interesting things. There are few other things in human life that put so much power into your hands, the opportunity to create a Golem and to enjoy immediately the pleasure of admiring the elaborate and intricate functioning of your creation. Who, faced with such opportunities, would want to waste time on problem statements and domain descriptions and analyses?

The fascination is not confined to computer hackers. All people who work at creating physical artifacts do so because they are in love with those artifacts. Their creations give them a huge satisfaction with which little else can compare. When Isambard Kingdom Brunel, the great builder of railways and steamships, was dying, he begged to be taken to see the new Royal Albert Bridge at Saltash, one of his most brilliant and noble creations. He did not ask to be taken into his office to see the drawings. He did not ask his assistant to remind him of the stress calculations, or to bring him his slide rule. He wanted to see the bridge.

This fascination with the machine has a long history in software development. We software developers have always offered our customers representations of the machine in place of the descriptions and analyses of their worlds and problems that they really needed. We did so when we offered flowcharts and tape record layouts; we did so when we offered structured pseudocode; and we still do it today when we offer object models and data flow diagrams and Z schemas.

3.3. Denial by abstraction

In the dimension we are considering here, formalists are closer to hackers than they may care to admit. The machine can be seen as a Protean symbol-processing device, taking as many forms as we care to invent formalisms: the Universal Turing Machine can mimic any Turing Machine, including another Universal Turing Machine. So the machine, viewed abstractly and mathematically, is an inexhaustible source of mathematical delight, and understandably so. There is no need to be concerned with the world. Our product is computations, and computations are mathematical objects.

But mathematics is no more the essence of software development than it is of bridge building. Hermann Weyl, quoted by Abelson and Sussman [Abel85], wrote:

> "We now come to the decisive step of mathematical abstraction: we forget about what the symbols stand for. ... [The mathematician] need not be idle; there are many operations he may carry out with these symbols, without ever having to look at the things they stand for."

As an expression of one important intellectual strategy this is admirable. As a rule of life for a software developer it is catastrophic. The software developer should sometimes forget what the symbols stand for, but only occasionally, and then only briefly. The world and its problems are rich and informal, and large mathematical abstractions rarely capture the important concerns.

Unfortunately, much writing and teaching on the subject of software development inculcates a disdain for the inconveniently messy real world. Courses and books need small problems that provide neatly circumscribed class exercises. If you see software development as a discipline of mathematical calculi and symbol manipulation, you will naturally seek out problems with a clean and easy formulation, purged of inconvenient informality.

So students of software development learn implicitly that typical programming problems are GCD, Eight Queens, Towers of Hanoi, and other traditional pearls. It's impossible not to be reminded of the tale of the prison visitor. The visitor, taking lunch with the prisoners, was surprised to hear one of them shout out 'Joke Number 43'. Everyone laughed. A little later another called out 'Joke Number 16' and everyone laughed again. They had reduced their jokes, by long repetition, to a standard repertoire that could be evoked by merely mentioning their numbers. GCD is simply Joke Number 1.

The implicit lesson is powerful, and harmful. It is that software development *problems* can be captured in a few words, and that all the difficulty lies in devising a *solution*. The problem itself, and therefore its context, merit no serious attention. The student learns to be impatient of the world in which the problem is found, hurrying through the tedious business of eliciting the problem from those stupid and mathematically uneducated people known as users and customers, so that the real work, the enjoyable work, of software design and programming can begin.

Martin Gardner, in one of his books of puzzles, gives an example of a kind of puzzle everyone knows well. A traveller is in a distant land where there are two kinds of people: one always lies and the other always tells the truth. The traveller meets two people, and asks one 'Are you a truthteller?' The reply is 'goom'. The other person says 'He said Yes, but he is lying'. The traveller must decide: Is the first person a truthteller?

Gardner reports that one reader produced an unusual solution. The first person clearly does not speak English, and must have said something like 'Sorry, I don't understand'. Therefore the second person is a liar. Therefore the first person is a truthteller. The reader who produced this solution had clearly not taken a course in logic. She failed to make the standard abstraction. She failed to recognise that this is Problem Number 87. But if I did go to that distant land I would feel safer with her as a companion.

3.4. Denial by vagueness

There is another subtle, and widely practised, way of avoiding the task of describing and understanding the world. Write descriptions of the machine but imply vaguely that they are actually descriptions of the world. Readers may be sufficiently confused not to notice. This technique is practised by developers of every stamp. Almost every book about a structured or object-oriented development method promises to 'analyse the problem' or to 'describe the real world', and immediately offers a description of the internal workings of the machine. Formalists do the same. Look at this extract from the preamble to a Z specification example:

> "… the Z approach is to construct a specification document which consists of a judicious mix of informal prose with precise mathematical statements. … the informal text … can be consulted to find out what aspects of the real world are being described … . The formal text on the other hand provides the precise definition of the system and hence can be used to resolve any ambiguities present in the informal text."

The book is a fine book; the example specification is a fine specification. But evidently the writer is quite unsure whether the document describes the 'real world' or the 'system'—that is, the machine.

This vagueness is possible for a number of reasons. The most cogent is the modelling facet of the relationship between the machine and the world. If the machine embodies a model of the world, then surely one description will do for both. But of course it won't, as we have already seen. There is plenty to say about the world that can not be said of the machine, and plenty to say about the machine that can not be said of the world.

(Sadly, there was a moment when an understanding of modelling was nearly captured and disseminated to the software development community, but the opportunity was missed and the butterfly escaped the net. The Codasyl committee on database systems recognised thirty years ago that the implementation details of a database did not reflect anything in the world being modelled. Two descriptions, at least, were necessary. The committee could have called them the *machine schema* and the *world schema*, and so written their names in the golden book of those who benefited the human race. Instead, alas, they called them the *physical schema* and the *conceptual schema*. What a mistake. What a shame.)

Further, modelling is a less ubiquitous facet of the relationship than many developers seem to suppose. It is only in information systems that modelling—in the sense I am using it—is a central concern. Much of what we do does not involve modelling at all. For example, the avionics system needs no *model* of the world properties that connect the wheel pulses, the wheel rotation, and the plane's position in relation to the runway. It needs a careful examination and description of those properties; and their description may play a role in the reasoning that justifies the eventual specification and implementation of the software. But there will be no part of the machine that simulates those properties. Not everything in software development is modelling in this sense.

4. Four principles for description

Traditionally, I am claiming, we pay too little attention to the world in which our problems are found. In software development, paying attention to a subject must mean describing it carefully and precisely, for description is the medium in which software developers fashion their work.

But describing the world is difficult, and our reluctance to pay it due attention is easy to understand. Four principles are suggested here that can help us to avoid some of the difficulties I have mentioned. They are:

+ von Neumann's principle;
+ the principle of reductionism;
+ the Shanley principle; and
+ Montaigne's principle.

4.1. von Neumann's principle

In *The Theory of Games* [vonN44], John von Neumann and Oskar Morgenstern wrote:

> "There is no point in using exact methods where there is no clarity in the concepts and issues to which they are to be applied."

Our very first obligation is to clarify the concepts and issues with which a system is concerned.

This means that we must begin by establishing the vocabulary of ground terms that we will use in talking about the world and the machine. We must identify the phenomena of interest, give a rule by which each kind of phenomenon can be reliably recognised, and give the formal term by which we will refer to it in our descriptions. If we want to assert that:

> For each novel *x* there is a unique writer *y* that is the author of the novel.

then we had better say, and say precisely, what we mean by 'x is a novel', what we mean by 'y is a writer', and what we mean by 'y is the author of x'. This is not an easy task, because in essence it is the task of formalising a part of the intransigently informal world. For each term we must give a—necessarily informal—*recognition rule* by which the phenomenon we are referring to can be recognised in the world. And we must also give the *formal term*—for example, a predicate symbol and formal argument list—by which we will refer to it in our descriptions. The *recognition rule* and *formal term* together constitute a *designation*.

The task is possible only because it is bounded in two ways. The first bound limits our subject area: we are not obliged to formalise the whole world, even the whole of those parts of the world in which books and writers are to be found. We are concerned, perhaps, only with English novels of the nineteenth century, and only with those that were published and offered for sale to the public.

The second bound limits the requirements of the system we are building, and so limits the aspects of our already bounded subject area that will concern us. One system will be concerned with the literary aspects; another with the commercial relationships between authors and publishers; another with the social effects of the novels and the distribution of their readers among social classes and geographic areas; another with the technology of book production. There is no bound to the number of such aspects that might be of interest, but only one or two can be of interest in a particular system. It is not possible to have a system about 'absolutely everything to do with English novels of the nineteenth century'. That is why the efforts to create enterprise models have failed. They were systems about 'absolutely everything to do with the ABC Company'.

By writing explicit *designations* and defining our ground terms precisely we give meaning to our descriptions in the most important sense. Formal semantics gives meaning only in a formal sense: the abstract formal text is explained in terms of the abstract semantic domain. We give practical meaning to our descriptions by grounding the formal text also in terms of the informal reality in the world that it describes. Explicit designations make our descriptions *refutable*, and deprive us of the evasion of saying 'Well, it all depends on what you mean by *novel* and what you mean by *writer*'. Without this grounding, formal precision has no place to stand and can not move the world.

In a crisper conversational version of his principle, von Neumann said more simply: "There is no sense in being precise when you don't know what you are talking about."

4.2. The principle of reductionism

Because we are talking about phenomena, about what appears to us to exist or to be the case, we often have considerable freedom to choose our ground terms. We should always choose those phenomena for which we can give the most exact and reliable recognition rules. Often this will involve applying a reductionist principle, choosing the simplest possible phenomena and—where appropriate—defining more elaborate constructs in terms of them.

One error to be avoided at all costs is the unthinking adoption of English language nouns as denoting entity classes or set-membership predicates. In a library administration system it seems obviously right to choose member as a ground term; in a telephone switching system to choose call; in a meeting scheduling system to choose meeting; in an airline reservation system to choose flight. But almost certainly these choices are serious errors.

In the library system, being a *member* is a state of an individual who has enrolled in the library and has not yet *resigned* or *lapsed* or been *expelled*. The events *enrol, resign, lapse,* and *expel* are probably appropriate ground terms—that is, designated phenomena. By contrast, *member* is not a ground term: it should be defined in terms of the events. The definition of *member* is not, of course, a *refutable description*. It says nothing about the world of the library, but is merely a statement about how the term will be used in descriptions. Any assertion containing the term member can be translated into an equivalent assertion about the defining events.

Telephone *calls*, scheduled *meetings*, and airline *flights* are even less appropriate as ground terms than library *members*. It is impossible to write reliable recognition rules for them. What, exactly, is a telephone call in a world where there are chat lines, conference calls, and call forwarding? Suppose that A calls B, and the call is forwarded to C. C then links in D using the conference feature, and, after a while, C drops out, leaving A talking to D. How many calls is that? Airline flights may be amalgamated, so that the person sitting in the seat next to you is on a different flight; and they may be split, so that one flight involves changing planes and sometimes even airlines. Whatever recognition rule you write will be inadequate to your purpose.

The ground terms you should be concerned with are, as often happens, events. Picking up a telephone handset, replacing it, dialling a digit, starting to receive a busy tone—all these are readily recognisable phenomena. So too are take-off and landing events in the life of an aeroplane, and boarding and disembarking events in the life of a passenger. These should be your ground terms. If you can reconstruct *calls* and *flights* by definitions using these ground terms, well and good. If not, you would only have been deceiving and confusing yourself and your customer by trying to treat them as ground terms directly.

4.3. Shanley's principle

Twenty years ago, in a famous paper on structured programming with go to statements [Knuth74], Knuth quoted Pierre Arnoul de Marneffe [deMar73]:

"... If you make a cross-section of, for instance, the German V-2 [rocket], you find external skin, structural rods, tank wall, etc. If you cut across the Saturn-B moon rocket, you find only an external skin which is at the same time a structural component and the tank wall. Rocketry engineers have used the 'Shanley Principle' thoroughly when they use the fuel pressure inside the tank to improve the rigidity of the external skin!"

De Marneffe cited the Shanley principle as a rule for efficient design. Barry Boehm has pointed out that it has disadvantages: it leads to designs with a single point of failure. And one could argue that the Shanley Principle is the direct negation of the separation of concerns. The thrust of much of the advance in programming languages and operating systems, certainly, has been towards separation of functions rather than their amalgamation. An operating system that can execute and synchronise many concurrent processes relieves the programmer of the task of composing them into a single sequential process.

But we are concerned here not with the design of our machines but with the design of the world. We must recognise that the architecture of the world has been designed with the fullest possible application of the Shanley Principle. A new book [Gam94] on patterns in object-orientation ends with a provocative quotation from the software developer's favourite architect, Christopher Alexander [Alex79]:

"It is possible to make buildings by stringing together patterns, in a rather loose way. A building made like this is an assembly of patterns. It is not dense. It is not profound. But it is also possible to put patterns together in such a way that many patterns overlap in the same physical space: the building is very dense; it has many meanings captured in a small space; and through this density it becomes profound."

The world is profound, in Alexander's sense. And the profundity reaches down to the elementary individuals. Every part of the world may play many roles, and perform many functions. Every individual may be an individual of many distinct domains; every node may be a node in many graphs; every element may be an element in many sets; every event an event in many traces.

This versatility and many-sidedness, both of larger structures and of elementary individuals, must be reflected in an appropriate approach to describing and understanding the world. At the level of domain description and problem analysis it demands parallel structuring of views and problems. The parallel decomposition of a colour picture into Cyan, Magenta, Yellow and Black colour separations is a far better metaphor for structuring than the hierarchical bill of materials assembly structures that have been the staple fare of elementary problem solving for far too long. The invention of the subroutine was not an unmixed blessing.

At the elementary level we must recognise similarly that the world is not strongly typed. It is always possible to devise a very restricted view of the world in which elementary individuals can be classified into disjoint sets and strongly typed. But such a view is always far too restricted to capture a problem of serious interest, and many such views must be adopted simultaneously. The elementary individuals in one view then appear, differently classified and differently typed, in other views. The need for multiple viewpoints is felt at the elementary level too.

4.4. Montaigne's principle

The great sixteenth-century French essayist Montaigne wrote: 'The greater part of this world's troubles are due to questions of grammar.' Perhaps there is a degree of exaggeration here, but there is at least one question of grammar that is of the greatest importance for software developers. That is the distinction between the indicative mood and the optative mood. The indicative mood expresses what we assert to be true; the optative mood expresses what we de- sire to be true.

For the developers of the system to control reverse thrust the statement:

REQ: *can_rev <-> on_runway*

is in the optative mood. It expresses what they desire to be true, the effect that their system is to bring about in the world. But the statement:

WORLD1:   pulsing <-> rotating

is in the indicative mood. It expresses what they assert to be true of the world, regardless of the behaviour of the system they are building.

The distinction is important and must be clearly made in the descriptions we write in a development. In recognition of this need, a rather confused formulation is sometimes demanded of US Government contractors:

"Absolute tense 'shall': a binding, measurable requirement ... observable when a system is delivered ... in terms of an ... output.

"Future tense 'will': a reference to the future, ... describing something ... not under control of the system being specified.

"Present tense: for all other verbs ... in all other cases."

Part of the confusion is in the grammar. Tenses are not moods. And I remember learning at school that:

"I shall drown. No-one will save me"

is a desperate cry for help, while:

"I will drown. No-one shall save me"

is the proud proclamation of a determined suicide.

Natural English usage is not easily tamed, and it is a bad idea to rely on the vagaries of English verb forms to capture crucial distinctions in technical documents.

A better approach is to avoid grammatical distinctions of mood within a single description, and to indicate the mood of a description by its place in the whole development structure. One virtue of this approach is that the mood of a description is, in fact, relative. The requirement, the properties with which we want our system to endue the world, is in the optative mood. But when the system is successfully installed and operating, the requirement becomes a reality; what we desired to be true becomes true; and the optative becomes indicative. So mood is relative to the progress of the development.

It is also relative to problem decomposition. In the editing subproblem in the CASE tool, correct performance of the requested operations on the edited texts is a requirement, in the optative mood. In the information system subproblem, we assume that the editing subproblem has been solved. Correct performance of the requested operations then becomes indicative: it is regarded as a given truth about the world.

One penalty for ignoring the distinction between indicative and optative is the confusion often felt by readers of formal specifications. Some formal specifications abstract from the distinction between the different moods. The formal specification is a homogeneous description of the behaviour of the correctly implemented machine interacting with the world. Behavioural properties attributable to indicative truths about the world are not distinguished from properties attributable to the satisfaction by the machine of the customer's optative requirements. A predicate P is given as the precondition on an operation O, but we are not told whether:

- the machine will inhibit O if P does not hold; or
- the world ought to refrain from invoking O when P does not hold; or
- the world is known never to invoke O when P does not hold.

Abstraction from the indicative/optative distinction may be useful for a number of purposes. But it is painfully confusing and frustrating to the reader who wants to draw any practical inference whatsoever from the specification.

5. Envoi

Some of what I have said may imply a hostility to formalism and to mathematical approaches. Nothing could be further from the truth. We need to make descriptions that are clear and precise, and we need to reason about them. And clarity, precision and reasoning are the business of mathematics.

Mathematics is the Queen, and the Servant, of the sciences. It has served physics and engineering well. It can serve software development well, too, if we make sure that we know what we are talking about.

References

[Abel85]   Harold Abelson and Gerald Jay Sussman with Julie Sussman; *Structure and Interpretation of Computer Programs*; MIT Press, 1985.

[Alex79]   Christopher Alexander; *The Timeless Way of Building*; Oxford University Press, 1979.

[deMar73]   Pierre-Arnoul de Marneffe; *Holon programming: A survey*; Université de Liège, Service Informatique, 1973. Quoted in [Knuth74].

[Gam94]   Erich Gamma, Richard Helm, Ralph Johnson, John Vlissides; *Design Patterns: Elements of Reusable Object-Oriented Software*; Addison-Wesley 1994.

[Knuth74]   Donald E Knuth; Structured programming with go to statements; *ACM Computing Surveys* Volume 6 Number 4, pages 261-301, December 1974.

[Lam89]   Leslie Lamport; A simple approach to specifying concurrent systems; *Comm ACM* Volume 32 Number 1, pages 32-45, January 1989.

[vonN44]   John von Neumann and Oskar Morgenstern; *Theory of Games and Economic Behaviour*; Princeton University Press, 1944.

[Weyl]   Hermann Weyl; *The Mathematical Way of Thinking*. Princeton University Press.

Chapter 18

From Worlds to Machines
Axel van Lamsweerde

Abstract: This paper provides a personal account of some of the foundational contributions made by Michael Jackson in the area of Requirements Engineering. We specifically focus on the relationship between problem worlds and machine solutions, and try to connect each contribution to related efforts while suggesting possible continuations. The anchoring of machine solutions on problem worlds is first considered together with means for delimiting, structuring, and characterizing problem worlds. The elaboration of machine specifications from world requirements is then discussed, including the use of satisfaction arguments, the questioning of requirements and assumptions, and the reuse of problem schemas. A car handbrake control system is used as a running example to illustrate the main ideas.

1. Introduction

Poor requirements were recurrently recognized to be the major cause of software problems such as cost overruns, delivery delays, failure to meet expectations, or degradations in the environment controlled by the software. The early awareness of the so-called requirements problem [2, 3, 4] raised preliminary efforts in developing modeling languages for requirements definition and analysis [1, 34, 12, 10]. With the increasing complexity of software-intensive systems, the research challenges raised by the requirements problem were so significant that an active community emerged in the nineties with dedicated conferences, workshops, working groups, networks, and journals. The term "requirements engineering" (RE) was introduced to refer to the process of eliciting, evaluating, specifying, consolidating, and changing the objectives, functionalities, qualities, and constraints to be achieved by a software-intensive system.

Michael Jackson was involved in requirements engineering research since the early days. His ICSE' 78 paper, for example, pointed out that the entities and events to be considered at RE time pertain to the real world surrounding the software to be developed [15]. In spite of this, a profound confusion persisted in software engineering research on the role and real nature of system requirements, software specifications, domain knowledge, and the relationships among them.

393

These notions were quite often considered similar. Driven by bottom-up efforts to abstract away from programming languages, a variety of diagrammatic notations and specification languages flourished. It was however generally not clear what their target was—the software objects, operations and behaviors, or their counterpart in the real world? System prescriptions or domain descriptions? The problem space or the solution space? The intrinsic intertwining of these two spaces did not help clarify such confusions and misunderstandings.

A series of papers by Michael and colleagues, written for different purposes or under different perspectives, brought the much needed clarifications. The one that hit me the most in my perceptions at that time was the first I was aware of, presented at the very first research conference dedicated to the area [19]. Fortunately enough, a marvelous essay appeared soon after [16], elaborating on the main ideas and bringing them in a form more accessible to a wider audience. I still believe that this book is among the very few ones to be included in the reading list for anyone entering the field. Some of the foundational principles introduced there were summarized in an ICSE keynote paper [17], illustrated through a detailed example [20] and made further precise for a more technical audience [38].

Central to this work is the distinction between the problem world and the machine solution. To make sure that a software solution correctly solves some problem, we must first correctly define what problem needs to be solved. The problem is generally rooted in a complex organizational, technical or physical world. The aim of a software development project is to improve this world by building some machine expected to solve the recognized problem. The RE process is concerned with the machine's effect on the surrounding world and the assumptions we make about this world.

A series of fundamental questions then arise quite naturally:

+ How should the machine be anchored on the problem world?
+ How do we characterize the problem world?
+ How do we delimit it and structure it?
+ How can we ensure a correct transition from the problem world to a machine solution so that the machine as specified will meet the requirements expressed in the problem world?
+ Can we support such transition by reuse of generic problem structures?

In his writings, Michael has provided insightful and elegant answers to these questions. The purpose of this paper is to provide a brief personal account of them, trying to situate them with respect to earlier or parallel efforts while suggesting some issues and perspectives raised by them.

This review is by no means intended to be comprehensive. It is inevitably biased by my research focus and by the ways Michael's work has influenced my own efforts.

2. Anchoring the machine on the problem world

Michael's popular visualization of the overall relationship between the world and the machine is now found in many RE courses and tutorials. Let us briefly recall it to define some important concepts and introduce the running example we will use to illustrate the main points.

The *problem world* is some problematic part of the real world that we want to improve by building some machine solution. It typically consists of components that interact according to certain rules and processes, e.g., car drivers, motors, handbrakes and rules for safe brake control (see Figure 1). In the problem world, we may apprehend certain phenomena of interest such as a car driver wishing her car to leave some place.

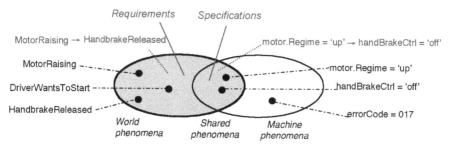

Figure 1. Phenomena and statements in the problem world and the machine solution

The machine solution is expected to solve some problem—in our example, the manual release of the car handbrake proves to be inconvenient or even unsafe in certain situations. The *machine* is an abstraction for what needs to be developed or installed in order to solve the problem. It consists of software to be developed, such as a handbrake controller in our example, possibly together with input/output devices, such as sensors and actuators, and sometimes COTS components to be purchased. In the machine solution, we may apprehend certain phenomena of interest too, such as an error code getting some specific value under certain error conditions (see Figure 1).

The problem world and the machine solution both have their own phenomena while sharing others. The *shared phenomena* define the interface through which the machine interacts with the world. They are in the intersection of the two sets in Figure 1. The machine *monitors* some of the shared phenomena while *controlling* others. For example, the machine in Figure 1 monitors the phenomenon of the shared variable "motor.Regime" getting the value "up"; it controls the phenomenon of the shared variable "handBrakeCtrl" getting the value "off". The shared phenomena yield the *boundary* beween the world and the machine; we thereby know what will be automated by the machine and what will not.

In this framework, a *requirement* is a statement about world phenomena, shared or not shared, that the machine should help satisfy (in general, jointly with other components of the problem world). A *specification* is a statement about shared phenomena that the machine must satisfy alone through the phenomena it controls. For example, the statement

the handbrake shall be released if the motor regime is physically raised

in Figure 1 is a requirement whereas the statement

handBrakeCtrl shall have the value 'off' if motor.Regime has the value 'up'

is a specification. A specification is thus a requirement while the converse is generally not true (see Figure 1). Requirements are formulated in the vocabulary of stakeholders, in terms of phenomena of the problem world, whereas specifications are formulated in the vocabulary of software developers.

Related efforts. The four-variable model developed independently by Parnas and colleagues is closely related to this framework [31]. The machine there reduces to the software-to-be; the problem world, called *environment,* includes associated input/output devices. A requirement is defined as a mathematical relation between a set of monitored variables and a corresponding set of controlled variables in the environment; a specification is a mathematical relation between a set of software input variables and a corresponding set of output variables. Value changes for the monitored/controlled variables correspond to phenomena owned by the environment whereas value changes for the software input/output variables correspond to shared phenomena. The input/output variables are "images" of the monitored/controlled ones; they define the interface between the software-to-be and its input/output devices. A specification "translates" a corresponding requirement into the vocabulary of the software input/output variables.

In our own work, the terms "system goals" and "software constraints" [5] were originally used for what Michael called "requirements" and "specifications", respectively. The former are under the responsibility of one or more system agents, including people, devices and software, whereas the latter are under the sole responsibility of the software-to-be. Michael's characterization of software specifications in terms of monitored/controlled phenomena led us to a realizability criterion for goal assignment to single agents [26], and the introduction of explicit shared interfaces among interacting agents for inductive synthesis of requirements from scenarios [25].

Earlier system development methodologies such as context analysis [34], definition study [13] or participative analysis [29] also emphasized the need for grounding software requirements into the surrounding world. The important distinction beween requirements and specifications was sometimes recognized among practitioners too, e.g., under terms such as "user requirement" *vs.* "software requirement" or "customer requirement" *vs.* "product requirement".

Issues and perspectives. Michael's introduction of the machine concept as an abstraction for what needs to be developed or installed appears very helpful through the various stages of the RE process. At the earlier stages we may consider the machine to include input/output devices (such as sensors and actuators) together with foreign software compoments; at later stages we may introduce finer-grained responsibilities among components and restrict the machine to the software-to-be only. Such machine refinement should be supported through systematic rules and patterns [22].

In the first RE phases of requirements elicitation and evaluation, we generally need to consider multiple versions of the world together with multiple alternative machines [22]. This makes the actual picture a bit more complicated than what Figure 1 may suggest.

1. *The world-as-is and the world-to-be.* In order to understand the problem to be solved and identify the requirements on a machine-based solution, we need to investigate two versions of the world:

+ The world-as-is is the problematic portion of the real world as it exists before a machine solution is built into it;
+ The world-to-be is the corresponding relevant portion of the real world as it should be when a machine solution will be built and operate into it.

In our example, the *world-as-is* is a standard car driving system with no automated support for handbrake control. We need to investigate this system in order to fully understand the concepts and components involved in it together with the rules and constraints for safe handbraking. We also need to investigate the world-*to-be* as some new concepts, components, rules and constraints emerge from automated handbrake control.

2. *Alternative machine solutions.* While investigating the world-to-be we often need to consider and evaluate alternative options for a machine solution, each generally resulting in a different set of shared phenomena. In our handbrake control example, we might consider one option where handbrake release results from a button being pressed by the driver, another where a vocal driver command is transmitted through a dedicated speech recognition component of the machine, and other options where the machine infers through different, alternative means that the driver wants to start. The world-machine boundary will in general vary from one option to the other, with more or less functionality being automated. In the preceding example, the more "intelligent" machine options will result in increased automation. The world-machine boundary is thus rarely fixed *a priori* when the RE process starts. Assessing alternative boundaries and selecting a most appropriate one is an important aspect of the RE process.

3. *World evolutions and variations.* In many software engineering projects the picture gets still more complicated.

+ For requirements prioritization and evolution, we generally need to envision future versions beyond the world-to-be, to which lower-priority requirements and likely changes will be transferred. In other words, we may need to consider worlds-to-be-next—for example, what new or modified features might be desirable once drivers will get used to automated handbrake control?
+ In product-line projects, we also need to consider multiple variants of the world-to-be and the machine solution, depending on variations among users or usage conditions—e.g., different handbrake control features for different classes of cars from the same manufacturer.

Multiple world-machine versions call for the elicitation and evaluation of multiple machine anchorings on the problem world; shared phenomena will in general vary from one version to the other.

3. Characterizing the problem world

Considering now a specific version of the problem world, how do we characterize it? Michael has introduced a fundamental distinction between three types of statements:

- *Descriptive* statements state properties about the world in the indicative mood. Such properties hold typically because of natural laws or physical constraints. For example, the statement "a car's motor regime is raising when the air conditioner starts" is a descriptive statement about the problem world in Figure 1.
- *Prescriptive* statements state desirable properties of the world in the optative mood. Such properties need to be enforced. For example, the statement "the handbrake shall be released when the car's motor regime is raising" is a prescriptive statement.
- *Definitions* are statements assigning a precise meaning to concepts or auxiliary terms used in the problem world. For example, the statement "a car's motor regime is said to be raising if it increases by X above neutral level" is a definition.

The distinction between these types of statement is essential in the context of engineering requirements. Requirements are prescriptive. Knowledge about the problem world is made explicit through descriptive statements. We may need to negotiate, weaken, or find alternatives to prescriptive statements. We cannot negotiate, weaken, or find alternatives to descriptive statements. Unlike prescriptive or descriptive statements, definitions have no truth value. It makes no sense to say that a definition is satisfied or not. We need, however, to check them for accuracy, completeness, and adequacy—the same way as prescriptive or descriptive statements.

Descriptive statements play a specific role when we reason about requirements. In particular, they are used for deriving specifications from requirements in an arguably correct way [20], see below.

In his work, Michael has also emphasized the need for complementing formalized statements with their *designation*, that is, a precise definition of what the atomic expressions and predicates in such statements mean in terms of objects and phenomena in the problem world. This often neglected aspect of formalization is essential for assertions to be fully precise and interpreted in the same way by different persons. A designation corresponds to the notion of interpretation in classical logic, where the domain of interpretation is here constrained to be the problem world.

Related efforts. The four-variable model introduced a similar distinction between the set REQ of prescriptive constraints between monitored and controlled variables, to be maintained by the machine, and the set NAT of descriptive constraints resulting from physical laws in the environment [31].

The clarification of the difference betwee these types of statements has been tremendously helpful in subsequent RE research work, including ours. In goal-oriented approaches to RE, *goals* are prescriptive statements of intent about the problem world, under the responsibility of agents structuring this world. We often need descriptive properties to prove the correctness of goal refinements into subgoals [6] or the correctness of goal operationalizations into system operations [27]. We also need descriptive statements for deriving preconditions for goal obstruction during risk analysis [24] and for deriving boundary conditions for conflict among goals during inconsistency management [23].

The role and importance of designations led modeling frameworks to enforce annotations of model items in order to make their interpretation fully precise in terms of world phenomena [22].

Issues and perspectives. Further useful distinctions can be made beyond prescriptive and descriptive statements, see Figure 2. *Assumptions* about the problem world need frequently be made; they deserve special attention during the RE process:

+ they are often involved in satisfaction arguments (see below);
+ they are especially subject to scrutiny during risk analysis and adequacy checking;
+ they may be used to discard or prefer alternative options;
+ they tend to be more volatile as the problem world evolves.

Some assumptions are prescriptive; they prescribe specific behaviors of problem world components that the machine cannot enforce. We might call these *expectations* [23, 24]. For example, "the driver shall press the acceleration pedal if he/she wants to start" is an expectation. Other assumptions are descriptive as they do not prescribe behaviors; we might call them *domain hypotheses*. The latter are not expected to hold invariably, unlike descriptive domain properties resulting from natural laws. For example, "handbrakes are never used below temperatures of –50°" is a domain hypothesis.

While both types of assumption deserve special scrutiny, expectations require a special treatment as they may call for specific actions to enforce them, e.g., the definition of dedicated procedures to be documented for people to follow them.

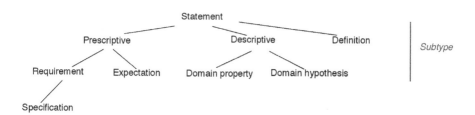

Figure 2. Further distinction among statements in the problem world

4. Delimiting and structuring the problem world

Two obvious questions arise as we elicit statements about the problem world according to those different categories:

◆ How do we organize such statements for easier evaluation, documentation, and analysis?
◆ How do we delimit the scope of investigation and determine which statements are relevant and which ones are not?

Michael suggested that the scope be limited to the *subject matter* of the problem world [38]. If the problem is about handbrake control, we should not care for control of damping devices.

He also proposed problem diagrams as a means for structuring the problem world and for defining its scope more precisely [18]. As shown in Figure 3, a *problem diagram* is a simple graph where nodes represent problem world components and edges represent connections through shared phenomena declared in the labels. In such declarations, an exclamation mark after a component name indicates that this component controls the phenomena in the declared set. A rectangle with a double vertical stripe represents the machine we need to build. A dashed oval represents a requirement. It may be connected to a component through a dashed line, to indicate that the requirement *refers* to it, or by a dashed arrow, to indicate that the requirement *constrains* it. Such connections may be labelled as well to indicate which corresponding phenomena are referenced or constrained by the requirement.

For example, Figure 3 shows a problem world structured into three components: the handbrake control machine, the car, and the car driver. The handbrake control machine *HCM* controls the changes of value of the state variable *Handbrake.Ctrl* whereas the car component *C* monitors them. The latter component controls the changes of value of the state variable *motor.Regime*. The driver component *DR* controls the events *pedalPushed* and *buttonPressed*. These events are referenced in the requirement shown in the dashed oval. The latter requirement constrains the world phenomena *BrakeActivation* and *BrakeRelease*.

Related efforts. The context diagrams in *Structured Analysis* were a rudimentary form of problem diagram showing the connections between the software-to-be and environment components through shared interfaces [8]. In KAOS, the problem world is structured along complementary views: the active elements

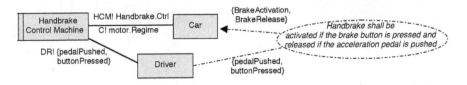

Figure 3. Problem diagram for structuring the problem world

composing it, called *agents*; the *goals* these agents must satisfy; the *operations* they need to perform in order to operationalize the goals; and the *objects* which the goals and operations refer to [5]. Each view is captured through dedicated diagrams. In particular, agent diagrams correspond to problem diagrams; they capture the various system agents together with their shared variables (monitored or controlled) and their assigned goals [22]. The problem scope is delimited by the top-level and bottom-level goals in the goal refinement graph; the former must be satisfiable through cooperation of the system's agents only whereas the latter must be satisfiable by single agents assigned to them. In *i**, the problem world is structured into agents interconnected through *dependency* links of various types; an agent may depend on another for a goal to be achieved, a task to be performed, or a resource to be made available [36].

Issues and perspectives. The scope of the problem world is not always as easy to delimit as it might appear at first sight.

◆ Feature interaction problems may call for extending the normal scope to aspects apparently unrelated to the subject matter of the problem world [23]. In our simple example, air conditioning control should be included in the scope of investigation (see below) even though it seems totally unrelated to handbrake control.

◆ The elaboration of security requirements calls for analyzing potential threats against the system in order to anticipate appropriate countermeasures [21]. The scope of the problem world should therefore be extended with malicious components. How should the normal scope be thereby extended and how far? For example, should the handbrake control world care for the possibility of handbrake release by a car robber?

◆ In open systems such as service-based systems, foreign components appear, disappear, or evolve without any control from the machine. How should the problem world be bounded accordingly?

Identifying the "right" components for structuring the problem world is not necessarily an obvious task. A variety of heuristics may be used to support this [22]. Early architectural choices can also facilitate component identification and interconnection [32].

Another interesting issue concerns the further structuring of problem diagrams. For systems of significant size and constrained by a large number of requirements, we may need to compose/decompose some components in a problem diagram as well as the requirements on them. Structuring mechanisms such as aggregation, specialization, refinement and enrichment should therefore be supported together with corresponding proof obligations.

5. Chaining satisfaction arguments

Our job as requirements engineers is to elicit, make precise, and consolidate requirements, assumptions, and domain properties. In particular, we need to ensure that the requirements will be satisfied whenever the specifications are met and provided the assumptions and domain properties hold [16, 11]. This can be achieved through entailments called *satisfaction arguments*, taking the form:

$$\{SPEC, ASM, DOM\} \mid= Req$$

which reads:

if the specifications in set *SPEC* are satisfied by the machine, the assumptions in set *ASM* are satisfied in the problem world, the domain properties in set *DOM* hold, and all those statements are consistent with each other,

then the requirements *Req* are satisfied in the problem world.

The use of such arguments was thoroughly discussed and illustrated in [16, 20]. In our simple example it might look like this:

(*Req:*) MotorRaising → HandbrakeReleased
(*Spec:*) motor.Regime = 'up' → handBrakeCtrl = 'off'
(*Asm:*) motor.Regime = 'up' ↔ MotorRaising
        handBrakeCtrl = 'off' ↔ HandbrakeReleased

To ensure that the specification *Spec* entails the requirement *Req*, we need to identify the assumptions *Asm* and make sure that the latter will be satisfied (some aren't in this example, see below). Assuming for the moment that these assumptions are adequate, we can obtain *Req* from *Spec* by the following rewriting: (a) we replace motor.Regime = 'up' in *Spec* by MotorRaising thanks to the first equivalence in the assumptions *Asm*; and (b) we replace handBrakeCtrl = 'off' in *Spec* by HandbrakeReleased thanks to the second equivalence in *Asm*.

Beyond establishing the correctness of specifications with respect to requirements, satisfaction arguments play an important role in managing the traceability among requirements, specifications and assumptions for requirements evolution [22]. If an assumption becomes no longer valid, for example, the specifications linked to it by satisfaction arguments must change accordingly.

Related efforts. Satisfaction arguments have been known for some time in programming methodology. When we build a logic program *P* in some environment *E*, the program has to satisfy its specification *S*. Therefore we need to argue that *P, E* |= *S* [14]. The use of satisfaction arguments for RE was also suggested in [37]. Such arguments were made explicit in terms of goal refinement and operationalization in [5]. The role of assumptions and domain properties in argumentation trees became however apparent only after Michael's work.

Issues and perspectives. In practice, we often need to *chain* multiple satisfaction arguments in order to establish that a set of specifications ensures some higher-level concern. The specifications are shown to entail corresponding requirements; the latter are then shown to entail higher-level requirements, and the argumentation proceeds recursively until the higher-level concern is reached [22]. Domain properties and assumptions may be used all along the argumentation chain. Figure 4 shows how such chaining of satisfaction arguments yields an *argumentation tree*. The tree shows how each parent node is satisfied by AND-satisfaction of its child nodes—the latter being specifications, requirements,

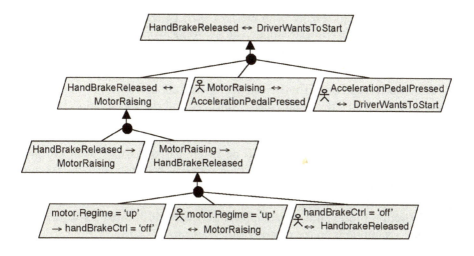

Figure 4. Chaining satisfaction arguments: an argumentation tree

domain properties, or assumptions.

Note that the bottom subtree in Figure 4, consisting of the three bottom leaf nodes and their parent node, corresponds to the satisfaction argument at the beginning of this section. This parent node and its left companion entail a new parent node in the tree, and so on. The "fellow" icon in Figure 4 is used to indicate assumptions—in this case, expectations on problem world components such as the driver, motor sensors and actuators, and the brake actuator.

6. Deriving specifications from requirements

The turnstile control example in [20] provided a convincing illustration of how requirements can be systematically refined into specifications. Such refinement consists of incrementally replacing the non-shared phenomena referenced in the requirements by shared "images". As suggested in the previous section, such replacement relies on the use of domain properties and assumptions together with corresponding satisfaction arguments.

Related efforts. At about the same time we were exploring a pattern-based approach to provide systematic guidance in the requirements refinement process [6]. Refinement patterns encode common refinement tactics as goal-subgoal AND-trees—e.g., decomposition-by-cases, decomposition-by-milestones, divide-and-conquer, guard-introduction, etc. Such patterns can be formalized and organized in a pattern catalogue for easy retrieval. They are proved formally correct and complete once for all, e.g., using some available theorem prover. The patterns are then reused in matching situations through instantiation of their meta-variables.

Michael's work led us to extend our catalogue with patterns specifically dedicated to the resolution of problems of unmonitorability or uncontrollability by the machine [26]. Figure 5 shows two such patterns together with their instantiation in our running example. The *accuracy* statements appearing as right child node in the refinement tree are often domain properties or environment assumptions.

Issues and perspectives. The derivation of specifications from requirements gets more complicated as the requirements language and the specification language are based on different paradigms. For example, the requirements language might be natural language or some temporal logic; the specification language might be an event-based language such as *SCR* or a state-based language such as *Alloy*, *Z* or *B*. Different languages often rely on different semantic frameworks and assumptions—e..g., frame conditions, concurrency model (maximal vs. lazy progress, synchrony hypothesis on environment-software interactions), etc. The derivation process must then apply additional transformations so that the semantic assumptions on the target language are met [27, 7].

As mentioned before, the derivation process may also be faced with alternative options among which to choose. Systematic support should then be available for evaluating such options [30].

7. Questioning statements

When domain properties or assumptions are used in an argumentation-based derivation, it is essential to check whether these are *adequate*. Fatal errors may originate from wrong properties or unrealistic assumptions used in correct derivations. Michael has often made this important point through convincing examples, including the A320 braking logic example [16]. The serious incident during an A320 landing on a rainy day at Warsaw airport might have resulted from the implicit use of a wrong domain property, namely, "the plane wheels are turning **iff** the plane is moving on the runway", not satisfied in case of aquaplaning. We must therefore systematically question the adequacy of critical statements used implicitly or explicitly in the RE process.

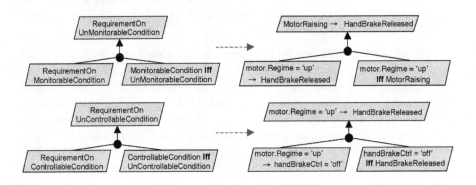

Figure 5. Unrealizability-driven refinement patterns

Related efforts. Obstacle analysis may help making such questioning more systematic [24]. For any questionable statement, we take its negation and look for alternative preconditions to make this negation true by use of domain properties. (A formal calculus is available for this.) The latter preconditions are then similarly refined until we reach fine-grained causes of obstruction of the root statement whose likelihood and criticality can be assessed by domain experts. This amounts to building a risk AND/OR tree rooted on the questioned statement. When we find fine-grained preconditions that are likely and critical, we must modify the questionable statement accordingly or add new requirements to overcome or mitigate the problem.

Figure 6 outlines such analysis in the context of the argumentation tree built in Figure 4. (The forked arrow there denotes an AND-refinement whereas multiple incoming arrows denote an OR-refinement.) The derived obstruction precondition AirConditioningRaising turns to be critical and very likely on hot summerdays. The corresponding set of requirements and assumptions should therefore be changed, leading to corrected requirements/assumptions—e.g., the weakening "HandBrakeReleased **Iff** MotorRaising **And Not** AirCo", or an alternative refinement of the root requirement that rules out brake release based on motor regime (e.g., a dedicated button to be pressed, a vocal driver command, etc.)

Issues and perspectives. The RE process may involve probabilistic requirements. They take the form "this target condition must be achieved in at least X% of the cases" or "this good condition must be maintained in at least Y% of the cases". Specification derivation, satisfaction arguments and systematic statement questioning get much more complicated then. Little support is available for handling such requirements.

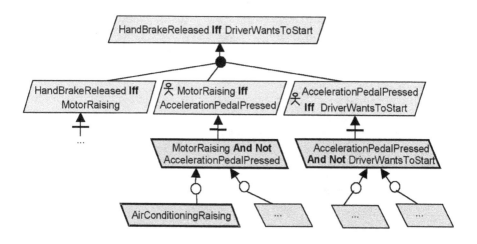

Figure 6. Systematic questioning of statements

8. Reusing problem schemas

Reusable RE processes and products may significantly help elicit and consolidate requirements. Beyond the reuse of derivation patterns discussed before, we may reuse problem structures. Instead of writing problem diagrams from scratch for every problem world we are faced with, we might predefine a number of frequent problem patterns. A specific problem diagram can then be obtained in matching situations by instantiating the corresponding pattern [18]. A *frame diagram* is a generic problem diagram capturing such problem pattern (called *frame*). The interface labels are now typed parameters; they are prefixed by "C", "E", or "Y" dependent on whether they are to be instantiated to causal, event, or symbolic phenomena, respectively. A generic component in a frame diagram can be further annotated by its type:

+ A *causal* component, marked by a "C", has some internal causality that can be enforced—e.g., it reacts predictably in response to external stimuli. The machine component is intrinsically causal.
+ A *biddable* component, marked by a "B", has no such enforceable causality— e.g., it consists of people. Constraints on them correspond to expectations (as introduced before).
+ A *lexical* component, marked by a "X", is a symbolic representation of data.

Figure 7 shows a frame diagram for the *commanded behavior* frame. It captures a class of problems where the machine must control the behavior of problem world components in accordance with commands issued by an operator [18]. The frame diagram states that the ControlMachine and the CommandedWorldComponent are causal components sharing the causal phenomena *C1* and *C2*; the former controls *C1* whereas the latter controls *C2*. On the other hand, the biddable component Operator controls command events *E4* that are monitored by the ControlMachine. The requirements constrain a set of world phenomena *C3*, connected to *C1* and *C2* through domain properties or assumptions to be provided, according to control rules refering to the commands *E4*. These rules state how the CommandedWorldComponent should behave in response to the operator's commands *E4*.

The problem diagram in Figure 3 illustrates an instantiation of the commanded behavior frame in Figure 7. This instantiation needs to be compatible with the types of the matching components and interfaces.

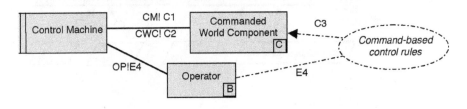

Figure 7. Problem frame diagram: commanded behavior frame

Related efforts. Various approaches were explored for the reuse of domain-specific abstractions for RE. Requirements clichés [33], analysis patterns [9], analog requirements frameworks [28] and domain theories [35] provide concept, task, and/or goal models of generic problem worlds together with their prescriptive and descriptive properties. The reuse mechanisms include specialization with single or multiple inheritance, traversal of a specialization hierarchy of domains, or structural and semantic matching based on analogical reasoning techniques.

Issues and perspectives. Many reuse approaches, including problem frames, are faced with similar challenges.

+ The description of reusable problem schemas should be sufficiently rich to favor reuse beyond structural information such as component interfaces.
+ A reusable schema should be sufficiently specific of a particular class of problems to enable transfer of useful discriminating features.
+ The catalog of reusable schemas should be comprehensive for wide applicability in diverse situations and well-organized for easy retrieval.
+ The ideal situation of perfect match is not that frequent; some support should therefore be available for validation and adaptation of the instantiated schemas.
+ Last but not least, complex problem worlds generally combine multiple types of problems. Precise mechanisms are needed for composing multiple problem schemas and their instantiations.

9. Conclusion

A reference model for RE should provide a clear, precise, general, and orthogonal set of concepts and relationships on which RE processes and techniques can rely. Michael Jackson has significantly contributed to the elaboration of such model. The complex relationships between problem worlds and machine solutions, and the important role played by domain properties, assumptions and satisfaction arguments are now much better understood. The reference model is increasingly used in RE research, education, and practice. It opens multiple windows for further understanding and investigation of interconnections between problem definition and solution exploration.

Beyond the conceptual and technical contributions outlined in this paper, the RE community owes much to Michael for the clarity and elegance of his thinking and his so enjoyable style of writing.

References

1.   Alford, M., A requirements engineering methodology for real-time processing requirements, *IEEE Transactions on Software Engineering*, Vol. 3, No. 1, January 1977, 60-69.
2.   Bell, T.E. and Thayer, T.A. Software requirements: Are they really a problem?, *Proc. 2nd International Conference on Software Engineering*, San Francisco, 1976, 61-68.
3.   Boehm, B.W. *Software Engineering Economics*. Prentice-Hall, 1981.

4. Brooks, F.P., No silver bullet: essence and accidents of software engineering, *IEEE Computer*, Vol. 20 No. 4, April 1987, pp. 10-19.

5. Dardenne, A., van Lamsweerde, A. and Fickas, S., Goal-directed requirements acquisition, *Science of Computer Programming* Vol. 20, 1993, 3-50.

6. Darimont, R. and van Lamsweerde, A., Formal refinement patterns for goal-driven requirements elaboration, *Proc Fourth ACM SIGSOFT Symp. on the Foundations of Software Engineering*, October 1996, 179-190.

7. De Landtsheer, R., Letier, E. and van Lamsweerde, A., Deriving tabular event-based specifications from goal-oriented requirements models, *Requirements Engineering Journal* Vol.9 No. 2, 2004, 104-120.

8. DeMarco, T. *Structured Analysis and System Specification*, Yourdon Press, 1978.

9. Fowler, M., *Analysis patterns: Reusable Object Models*. Addison-Wesley, 1997.

10. Greenspan, S.J., Mylopoulos, J. and Borgida, A., Capturing more world knowledge in the requirements specification, *Proc. 6th International Conference on Software Enginering*, Tokyo, 1982.

11. Hammond, J., Rawlings, R. and Hall, A., Will it work?, *Proc. 5th Intl. IEEE Symp. on Requirements Engineering (RE `01)*, Toronto, 2001, IEEE, 102-109.

12. Heninger, K.L., Specifying software requirements for complex systems: New techniques and their application, *IEEE Transactions on Software Engineering* Vol. 6 No. 1, January 1980, 2-13.

13. Hice, G.F., Turner, W.S., and Cashwell, L.F., *System Development Methodology*. North Holland, 1974.

14. C.J. Hogger, *Introduction to Logic Programming*, APIC Studies in Data Processing Nr. 21, Prentical Hall, 1984.

15. Jackson, M., Information systems: Modeling, sequencing, and transformation, *Proc. 3rd International Conference on Software Enginering*, Munich, 1978, 72-81.

16. Jackson, M., *Software Requirements & Specifications - A Lexicon of Practice, Principles and Prejudices*, ACM Press, Addison-Wesley, 1995.

17. Jackson, M., The world and the machine, *Proc. 17th International Conference on Software Engineering*, ACM-IEEE, 1995, pp. 283-292. Also Chapter 17 of this volume.

18. Jackson, M., *Problem Frames – Analyzing and Structuring Software Development Problems*, ACM Press, Addison-Wesley, 2001.

19. Jackson, M. and Zave, P., Domain descriptions, *Proc. 1st Intl. IEEE Symp. on Requirements Engineering*, January 1993, 56-64.

20. Jackson, M. and Zave, P., Deriving specifications from requirements: An example, *Proc. 17th Intl. Conf. on Software Engineering*, ACM-IEEE, May 1995, 15-24. Also Chapter 7 of this volume.

21. van Lamsweerde, A., Elaborating security requirements by construction of intentional anti-Models, *Proc. 26th International Conference on Software Engineering*, Edinburgh, May 2004, ACM-IEEE, 148-157.

22. van Lamsweerde, A., *Requirements Engineering: From System Goals to UML Models to Software Specifications*, Wiley, January 2009.

23. van Lamsweerde, A., Darimont, R. and Letier, E., Managing conflicts in goal-driven requirements engineering, *IEEE Trans. on Sofware. Engineering*, Vol. 24 No. 11, Nov. 1998, 908-926.

24. van Lamsweerde, A. and Letier, E., Handling obstacles in goal-oriented requirements

engineering, *IEEE Transactions on Software Engineering* Vol. 26 No. 10, October 2000, 978-1005.

25. van Lamsweerde, A. and Willemet, L., Inferring declarative requirements specifications from operational scenarios, *IEEE Trans. on Sofware. Engineering*, Vol. 24 No. 12, Dec. 1998, 1089-1114.

26. Letier, E. and van Lamsweerde, A., Agent-based tactics for goal-oriented requirements elaboration, *Proc. 24ᵗʰ Intl. Conf. on Software Engineering*, ACM-IEEE, May 2002.

27. Letier, E. and van Lamsweerde, A., Deriving operational software specifications from system goals, *Proc. 10ᵗʰ ACM Symp. Foundations of Software Engineering*, Charleston, Nov. 2002.

28. Massonet, P. and van Lamsweerde, A., Analogical Reuse of Requirements Frameworks, *Proc. 3rd Int. Symp. on Requirements Engineering*, 1997, 26-37.

29. Munford, E., Participative systems design: Structure and method, *Systems, Objectives, Solutions*, Vol. 1, North-Holland, 1981, 5-19.

30. Mylopoulos, J., Chung, L. and Nixon, B., Representing and using nonfunctional requirements: A process-oriented approach, *IEEE Trans. on Sofware Engineering*, Vol. 18 No. 6, June 1992, pp. 483-497.

31. Parnas, D.L. and Madey, J., Functional documents for computer systems, *Science of Computer Programming*, Vol. 25, 1995, 41-61.

32. Rapanotti, L., Hall, J.G., Jackson, M., and Nuseibeh, B., Architecture-driven problem decomposition, *Proc. 12th IEEE Joint Intl Requirements Engineering Conference*, Kyoto, September 2004.

33. Reubenstein, H.B. and Waters, R.C., The Requirements Apprentice: Automated assistance for requirements acquisition, *IEEE Transactions on Software Engineering* Vol. 17 No. 3, March 1991, 226-240.

34. Ross, D.T and Schoman, K.E., Structured analysis for requirements definition, *IEEE Transactions on Software Engineering*, Vol. 3, No. 1, January 1977, 6-15.

35. Sutcliffe, A. and Maiden, N., The domain theory for requirements engineering, *IEEE Trans. on Sofware. Engineering*, Vol. 24 No. 3, March 1998, 174-196.

36. Yu, E.S.K., Modelling organizations for information systems requirements engineering, *Proc. 1st Intl Symp. on Requirements Engineering*, 1993, 34-41.

37. Yue, K., What does it mean to say that a specification is complete?, *Proc. Fourth International Workshop on Software Specification and Design*, Monterey, IEEE Press, 1987.

38. Zave P. and Jackson, M., Four dark corners of requirements engineering, *ACM Transactions on Software Engineering and Methodology* Vol. 6 No. 1, January 1997, 1-30.

This book is set in Adobe Jenson, an old-style serif typeface drawn for Adobe Systems by type designer Robert Slimbach. Its Roman styles are based on a Venetian text face cut by Nicolas Jenson in 1470, and its italics are based on those by Ludovico Vicentino degli Arrighi. The result is an organic, somewhat idiosyncratic font, with a low x-height and inconsistencies that help differentiate letters. Adobe Jenson is a highly readable typeface appropriate for large amounts of text.